Elements of L

Sixth Course

Essentials of British and World Literature

Holt Assessment: Literature, Reading, and Vocabulary

- Entry-Level Test and End-of-Year Test
- Collection Diagnostic Tests
- Selection Tests
- Collection Summative Tests
- Answer Key

HOLT, RINEHART AND WINSTON

A Harcourt Education Company

Orlando • **Austin** • New York • San Diego • London

ISBN 0-03-078999-0

3 4 5 179 09 08 07

Contents

Collection 3   The Renaissance 1485–1660: A Flourish of Genius

Collection 4   The Restoration and the Eighteenth Century 1660–1800: The Best of All Possible Worlds

Collection 5   The Romantic Period 1798–1832: The Quest for Truth and Beauty

Selection Tests

Collection 6 The Victorian Period 1832–1901: Paradox and Progress

Collection 7 The Modern World 1900 to the Present: A Remarkable Diversity

Overview of ELEMENTS OF LITERATURE Assessment Program

Two assessment booklets have been developed for ELEMENTS OF LITERATURE.

(1) Assessment of student mastery of selections and specific literary, reading, and vocabulary skills in the **Student Edition:**

- *Holt Assessment: Literature, Reading, and Vocabulary*

(2) Assessment of student mastery of workshops and specific writing, listening, and speaking skills in the **Student Edition:**

- *Holt Assessment: Writing, Listening, and Speaking*

Diagnostic Assessment

> **NOTE:** You may wish to address the needs of students who are reading below grade level. If so, you can administer the Diagnostic Assessment for Reading Intervention, found in the front of *Holt Reading Solutions.* This assessment is designed to identify a student's reading level and to diagnose the specific reading comprehension skills that need instructional attention.

Holt Assessment: Literature, Reading, and Vocabulary contains two types of diagnostic tests:

- The Entry-Level Test is a diagnostic tool that helps you determine (1) how well students have mastered essential prerequisite skills needed for the year and (2) to what degree students understand the concepts that will be taught during the current year. This test uses multiple tasks to assess mastery of literary, reading, and vocabulary skills.

- The Collection Diagnostic Tests help you determine the extent of students' prior knowledge of literary, reading, and vocabulary skills taught in each collection. These tests provide vital information that will assist you in helping students master collection skills.

Holt Online Essay Scoring can be used as a diagnostic tool to evaluate students' writing proficiency:

- For each essay, the online scoring system delivers a holistic score and analytic feedback related to five writing traits. These two scoring methods will enable you to pinpoint the strengths of your students' writing as well as skills that need improvement.

Ongoing, Informal Assessment

The **Student Edition** offers systematic opportunities for ongoing, informal assessment and immediate instructional follow-up. Students' responses to their reading; their writing, listening, and speaking projects; and their work with vocabulary skills all serve as both instructional and ongoing assessment tasks.

Overview of ELEMENTS OF LITERATURE Assessment Program *(continued)*

- Throughout the **Student Edition,** practice and assessment are immediate and occur at the point where skills are taught.

- In order for assessment to inform instruction on an ongoing basis, related material repeats instruction and then offers new opportunities for informal assessment.

- Skills Reviews at the end of each collection offer a quick evaluation of how well students have mastered the collection skills.

Progress Assessment

Students' mastery of the content of the **Student Edition** is systematically assessed in two test booklets:

- *Holt Assessment: Literature, Reading, and Vocabulary* offers a test for every selection. Multiple-choice questions focus on comprehension, the selected skills, and vocabulary development. In addition, students write answers to constructed-response prompts that test their understanding of the skills.

- *Holt Assessment: Writing, Listening, and Speaking* provides both multiple-choice questions for writing and analytical scales and rubrics for writing, listening, and speaking. These instruments assess proficiency in all the writing applications appropriate for each grade level.

Summative Assessment

Holt Assessment: Literature, Reading, and Vocabulary contains two types of summative tests:

- The Collection Summative Tests, which appear at the end of every collection, ask students to apply their recently acquired skills to a new literary selection. These tests contain both multiple-choice questions and constructed-response prompts.

- The End-of-Year Test helps you determine how well students have mastered the skills and concepts taught during the year. This test mirrors the Entry-Level Test and uses multiple tasks to assess mastery of literary, reading, and vocabulary skills.

Holt Online Essay Scoring can be used as an end-of-year assessment tool:

- You can use *Holt Online Essay Scoring* to evaluate how well students have mastered the writing skills taught during the year. You will be able to assess student

Overview of ELEMENTS OF LITERATURE
Assessment Program *(continued)*

mastery using a holistic score as well as analytic feed-back based on five writing traits.

Monitoring Student Progress

Both *Holt Assessment: Literature, Reading, and Vocabulary* and *Holt Assessment: Writing, Listening, and Speaking* include skills profiles that record progress toward the mastery of skills. Students and teachers can use the profiles to monitor student progress.

***One-Stop Planner*® CD-ROM with ExamView® Test Generator**

All of the questions in this booklet are available on the *One-Stop Planner*® **CD-ROM with ExamView® Test Generator.** You can use the ExamView Test Generator to customize any of the tests in this booklet. You can then print a test or post it to the *Holt Online Assessment* area at my.hrw.com.

Holt Online Assessment

You can use *Holt Online Assessment* to administer and score the diagnostic and summative tests online. You can then generate and print reports to document student growth and class results. For your students, this online resource provides individual assessment of strengths and weaknesses and immediate feedback.

About This Book

Holt Assessment: Literature, Reading, and Vocabulary accompanies ELEMENTS OF LITERATURE. The booklet includes copying masters for diagnostic tests, selection tests, and summative tests to assess students' knowledge of prerequisite skills, their comprehension of the readings in the **Student Edition,** and their mastery of the skills covered in each collection.

Entry-Level Test

The **Entry-Level Test** is a diagnostic tool that enables you to evaluate your students' mastery of essential skills at the start of the year. This objective, multiple-choice test contains several reading selections followed by questions assessing students' comprehension of their reading and their knowledge of select literary skills. Other sections of the test evaluate students' command of vocabulary skills.

Collection Tests

The copying masters in *Holt Assessment: Literature, Reading, and Vocabulary* are organized by collection. There are three types of tests for each collection:

- A **Collection Diagnostic Test** is included for every collection. These multiple-choice tests cover literary terms and devices as well as reading and vocabulary skills. These tests will enable you to assess students' prior knowledge of the skills taught in each collection.

- A **Selection Test** accompanies every major selection in the **Student Edition.** Each Selection Test includes objective questions that assess students' comprehension of the selection, mastery of literary skills as they apply to the selection, and acquisition of vocabulary words. In addition, students write a brief essay in response to a constructed-response prompt that asks them to formulate answers independently using their newly acquired skills.

- A **Collection Summative Test** follows the selection tests for each collection. This test asks students to apply their new skills to a selection that does not appear in the **Student Edition.** Students are asked to read a brief selection and then respond to multiple-choice questions and constructed-response prompts that assess their comprehension of the selection and vocabulary, reading, and literary skills.

End-of-Year Test

The **End-of-Year Test** is a summative tool that assesses students' mastery of the skills and concepts taught during the year. Like the Entry-Level Test, this test uses a multiple-choice format to assess students' comprehension of several reading selections and their mastery of literary and vocabulary skills.

About This Book *(continued)*

Answer Sheets and Answer Key

Answer Sheets are provided for the Entry-Level Test and the End-of-Year Test. If you prefer, students may mark their answers on the tests themselves. For all collection tests, students should write their answers on the tests. The **Answer Key** provides answers to objective questions. It also provides model responses to constructed-response prompts.

Skills Profile

The **Skills Profile** lists the skills assessed by the tests in this booklet. You can use the Skills Profile to create a developmental record of your students' progress as they master each skill.

Administering the Tests

The format of the Entry-Level Test and the End-of-Year Test, with their accompanying answer sheets, replicates that of most standardized tests. You can use these tests to help familiarize your students with the types of standardized tests they will take in the future.

To administer these tests, prepare a copy of the appropriate test and answer sheet for each student. Some sections of the tests have sample items. Before students begin these sections, you may want to select the correct answer for the sample items with the class. Then, answer any questions students have about the samples. When students demonstrate that they understand how to do the items, have them begin these sections. Students may record their answers on the answer sheets or on the tests.

To administer the collection tests, prepare a copy of each test for your students. Students should mark their answers on the tests themselves. When administering Selection Tests that cover poetry, you may want to allow students to use the textbook, since these tests often require a response to the precise wording, rhythm, or meter of a particular poem. You also have the option of making any Selection Test an open-book test.

One-Stop Planner® CD-ROM with ExamView® Test Generator

The tests in this booklet are included on the *One-Stop Planner®* **CD-ROM with ExamView® Test Generator.** Use the ExamView Test Generator to customize and print a test tailored to the needs of your students.

Holt Online Assessment

With *Holt Online Assessment* you can administer and score the diagnostic and summative tests online. Use this online tool to generate and print reports to record student mastery and class performance.

Reading and Literary Analysis

DIRECTIONS Read the passage below, and answer the following questions.

SAMPLE

Microbes are the oldest living forms of life on earth. They are everywhere around us. In fact, a single human body is home to trillions of microbes. Microbes are so important to human life that we could not survive without them. They are instrumental in manufacturing oxygen, decomposing garbage, digesting food, and creating medicines.

Many microbes are our friends. They perform tasks that make our lives possible. One type of microbe, however, can make our lives miserable: viruses. Viruses are the smallest microbes and are also the simplest. In fact, they are so simple that some scientists do not consider them to be alive.

A All of the following statements about viruses are facts stated in the passage above *except* —

   A   they are the simplest microbes

   B   they are the smallest microbes

   C   they are not even alive

   D   they can make our lives miserable

B The phrase "They are instrumental" means that microbes —

   F   protect humans from getting diseases

   G   are helpful in bringing something about

   H   sometimes function as musical instruments

   J   enable humans to hear and appreciate music

Reading and Literary Analysis

DIRECTIONS Read the passage below, and answer the following questions.

Robert Herrick
(1591–1674)

Robert Herrick was an English poet of the late Renaissance. *Renaissance* is a French word meaning "rebirth." This period in history saw a great out-pouring of creativity in art, music, literature, science, and technology. Classical Greek and Roman literature was rediscovered and contributed to an intellectual movement called humanism, which sought answers to questions such as "What is a good life?"

Herrick attended Cambridge University and was ordained a priest. At age thirty-eight he was assigned to a parish in Dean Prior in an area far from London that Londoners generally regarded as uncivilized. According to some of Herrick's poems, this was an intolerable exile; according to others, it was heaven on earth.

Herrick's stay in Dean Prior ended when the king was overthrown, but when the crown was restored some thirteen years later, so was Herrick. He lived on at Dean Prior until he died at the age of eighty-three.

While deprived of his parish and living in London, Herrick published a book containing 1,399 poems titled *Hesperides, or the Works Both Human and Divine of Robert Herrick, Esq.* (1648). Less than a quarter of the poems fit into the "divine" category; all the rest are definitely "human." The word *Hesperides* in the title is borrowed from classical mythology; it is the collective name for the sisters who live in a garden, where they guard a tree that bears golden apples. The title implies that Herrick's book is a garden full of precious things.

Herrick borrowed more than his title from classical culture. He was so steeped in Latin poetry that he frequently wrote his poems as if he were an ancient Roman, imposing pagan customs, creeds, and rituals on the English country people and his own household. He imitated the Latin love poets, especially Catullus, when he addressed poems to beautiful women using such classical names as Julia, Corinna, Perilla, Anthea, and Electra. However, Herrick's love poems were written to imaginary ladies; no hint of scandal ever touched his bachelor life.

Her Bed

See'st thou that cloud as silver clear,
Plump, soft, and swelling everywhere?
'Tis Julia's bed, and she sleeps there.

A poem like this is clearly a pretty fantasy, an imaginative way of saying
"Julia is a goddess." But not all of Herrick's poems are pretty, for he was
also drawn to the crude and grotesque elements of Latin poetry.

Upon Blanch

Blanch swears her husband's lovely; when a scald
Has bleared his eyes; besides, his head is bald.
Next, his wild ears, like leathern wings full spread,
Flutter to fly and bear away his head.

Herrick wrote about his small house, his spaniel, his cat, his maid, the royal
family, the work and play of country people—whatever came into his
mind. Except for dividing his poems into the categories of "divine" and
"human," he did not arrange them in any order, so his book is a jumble full
of surprises. If some poems seem to be trifles, they are trifles on which their
author has lavished much care.

His Desire

Give me a man that is not dull,
When all the world with rifts[1] is full,

But unamazed dares clearly sing
When as the roof's a tottering;

And, though it falls, continues still
Tickling the cittern[2] with his quill.

Altogether, Herrick's poems give us a picture of "Merrie England," which
is not so much the England of any particular time or place but an ideal,
pastoral state where sadness is momentary and pleasure innocent.

---

1. rifts: faults.
2. cittern: guitar.

ENTRY-LEVEL TEST

1 Herrick is revealed as a Renaissance poet in his —

   A love for classical Roman poetry

   B decision to enter the clergy

   C writing poems in the English language

   D living to the age of eighty-three

2 The poem "Her Bed" shows a classical Latin influence in the —

   F image of the silvery cloud

   G subject matter of a bed

   H choice of the woman's name

   J fantastic elements of the poem

3 In the poem "Upon Blanch" the simile used to compare the husband's ears to leather wings evokes humor through —

   A realistic description

   B thoughtful analysis

   C ironic commentary

   D imaginative exaggeration

4 Herrick's most popular poem begins with these lines:

> Gather ye rosebuds while ye may,
> Old time is still a-flying.

Which of Herrick's poems presented here reflects a similar theme?

   F *Hesperides*

   G "Her Bed"

   H "Upon Blanch"

   J "His Desire"

5 In the poem "His Desire" the archetype of the artist who sings through troubles is used to reveal the —

   A need to plan ahead

   B importance of art

   C problem with singing

   D pervasiveness of disasters

6 The *carpe diem*, or "seize the day," theme in "His Desire" represents the —

   F importance of working hard

   G idea that most of life is dull

   H view that life should be enjoyed

   J need for quick action in life

7 The poems presented here suggest that Herrick's philosophical position includes which of the following ideas?

   A Life is characterized by tragedy.

   B People should emulate Catullus.

   C People should fear old age and death.

   D People should enjoy life's fleeting beauty.

8 What inference can be made about Herrick's reasons for writing the poetry in *Hesperides*?

   F He felt that writing poems about humans was blasphemous.

   G He found more human things than divine things to write about.

   H He found Latin poetry tedious and not worth mimicking.

   J He used his experiences with his wife to write about women.

GO ON ▶

9 The purpose of this passage is to —

 A   inform readers about Herrick's life and poetry

 B   question whether Herrick was really a Renaissance poet

 C   amuse readers by quoting Herrick's poetry

 D   teach readers how to write Renaissance poetry

The following questions are not about a passage. Read and answer each question.

10 The relationship between *spark* and *fire* is the same as the relationship between —

 F   joke and laughter

 G   trot and gallop

 H   night and day

 J   butterfly and caterpillar

11 The term that refers to the study of diseases of the skin is —

 A   neurology

 B   pedagogy

 C   dermatology

 D   psychology

12 The correct term for a scientist working to solve problems of the exhaustion of natural resources is —

 F   environmentalist

 G   geographer

 H   biophysicist

 J   existentialist

ENTRY-LEVEL TEST

GO ON

Reading and Literary Analysis (continued)

DIRECTIONS Read the passage below, and answer the following questions.

The Magna Carta, a document written in 1215, in which King John of England made legal concessions to his powerful barons, has been considered an early step on the path to democracy. It offered protection against arbitrary and unjust rule by the monarchy. The excerpt below lists ten of the charter's more than sixty provisions.

Magna Carta

JOHN, by the grace of God King of England, Lord of Ireland, Duke of Normandy and Aquitaine, and Count of Anjou, to his archbishops, bishops, abbots, earls, barons, justices, foresters, sheriffs, stewards, servants, and to all his officials and loyal subjects, Greeting.

KNOW THAT BEFORE GOD, for the health of our soul and those of our ancestors and heirs, to the honor of God, the exaltation of the holy Church, and the better ordering of our kingdom, at the advice of [a list of twenty-seven clergy and noblemen] and other loyal subjects:

(1) FIRST, THAT WE HAVE GRANTED TO GOD, and by this present charter have confirmed for us and our heirs in perpetuity, that the English Church shall be free, and shall have its rights undiminished, and its liberties unimpaired. . . .

TO ALL FREE MEN OF OUR KINGDOM we have also granted, for us and our heirs for ever, all the liberties written out below, to have and to keep for them and their heirs, of us and our heirs: . . .

(2) For a trivial offence, a free man shall be fined only in proportion to the degree of his offence, and for a serious offence correspondingly, but not so heavily as to deprive him of his livelihood. . . .

(3) No town or person shall be forced to build bridges over rivers except those with an ancient obligation to do so.

(4) No constable or other royal official shall take corn or other movable goods from any man without immediate payment, unless the seller voluntarily offers postponement of this.

(5) No constable may compel a knight to pay money for castle-guard if the knight is willing to undertake the guard in person, or with reasonable excuse to supply some other fit man to do it. . . .

(6) No sheriff, royal official, or other person shall take horses or carts for transport from any free man, without his consent.

(7) Neither we nor any royal official will take wood for our castle, or for any other purpose, without the consent of the owner.

(8) In future no official shall place a man on trial upon his own unsupported statement, without producing credible witnesses to the truth of it.

(9) No free man shall be seized or imprisoned, or stripped of his rights or possessions, or outlawed or exiled, or deprived of his standing in any other way, nor will we proceed with force against him, or send others to do so, except by the lawful judgment of his equals or by the law of the land.

(10) To no one will we sell, to no one deny or delay right or justice.

---

13 The Magna Carta grants liberties to —

A only the twenty-seven men listed

B the church and all free men

C all the people of the kingdom

D the Catholic Church in Rome

14 The twenty-seven advisors are listed in the second paragraph *primarily* in order to —

F establish the document's legitimacy

G prove how many friends the king has

H demonstrate who's who in England

J thank the people who helped the king

15 The meaning of the document is enhanced by the technique of —

A listing the points in order of importance

B highlighting important points in boldface type

C presenting each provision in a separate paragraph

D summarizing the main points at the beginning

16 The importance of God to the creators of the Magna Carta is shown in all the following *except* —

F John is king of England by the grace of God

G the charter is for the health of the king's soul

H all free men are granted liberties by the charter

J the church is granted undiminished rights

GO ON

READING AND LITERARY ANALYSIS

17 Which textual clues indicate the extent of the protection offered by the Magna Carta?

A   "heirs in perpetuity"

B   "all free men"

C   "ancient obligation"

D   "offers postponement"

18 Which of the following would violate provision 8?

F   Using credible witnesses at a trial

G   Allowing justice to be bought

H   Making someone stand trial

J   Accusing someone of a crime based on hearsay

19 The historical reason for the writing of the Magna Carta is that —

A   kings had unlimited power

B   barons were satisfied with the power the king had granted them

C   common people had too much power

D   the monarchy was weak and ineffectual

20 Which of the following is the *most* focused research question for a report about the Magna Carta?

F   What events occurred in England between 1066 and 1215?

G   How did King John rule his kingdom?

H   What influence did the Magna Carta have on other political documents?

J   Why do many legal terms come from Latin?

21 A philosophical and political belief revealed in this document is that —

A   all men are created equal by God

B   the king rules by divine right

C   people should decide what's right

D   free men are entitled to certain rights

22 The wording of the provisions reveals that the Magna Carta was written to address —

F   previous abuses by the king and his officials

G   the best government for the country

H   all the rights that people are entitled to have

J   twenty-seven officials of the realm

GO ON ➡

Reading and Literary Analysis (continued)

DIRECTIONS Read the poem below, and answer the following questions.

The Convergence of the Twain
Lines on the Loss of the Titanic
Thomas Hardy

1

   In a solitude of the sea
   Deep from human vanity,
And the Pride of Life that planned her, stilly couches she.

2

   Steel chambers, late° the pyres
5   Of her salamandrine fires,°
Cold currents thrid,° and turn to rhythmic tidal lyres.

3

   Over the mirrors meant
   To glass the opulent
The seaworm crawls—grotesque, slimed, dumb, indifferent.

4

10   Jewels in joy designed
   To ravish the sensuous mind
Lie lightless, all their sparkles bleared and black and blind.

5

   Dim moon-eyed fishes near
   Gaze at the gilded gear
15 And query: "What does this vaingloriousness down here?" . . .

6

   Well: while was fashioning
   This creature of cleaving wing,
The Immanent Will° that stirs and urges everything

---

4. late: not long ago.

5. salamandrine fires: fires so hot that only a salamander, a lizard said
 to be able to live in fire, could survive.

6. thrid: thread through.

18. Immanent Will: Hardy's name for the power that created and determines life and history.

GO ON ➡

7

Prepared a sinister mate
20   For her—so gaily great—
A Shape of Ice, for the time far and dissociate.

8

And as the smart ship grew
In stature, grace, and hue,
In shadowy silent distance grew the Iceberg too.

9

25   Alien they seemed to be:
No mortal eye could see
The intimate welding of their later history,

10

Or sign that they were bent
By paths coincident
30   On being anon twin halves of one august event,

11

Till the Spinner of the Years
Said "Now!" And each one hears,
And consummation comes, and jars two hemispheres.

GO ON ➤

23 The metaphor in lines 4–6 compares —

A   pyres to salamanders

B   the ship's chambers to lyres

C   fire to cold currents

D   steel to the tide

24 Seaworms crawling over mirrors intended for rich passengers (lines 7–9) is an example of —

F   satire

G   hyperbole

H   simile

J   irony

25 The tone, or attitude, that Hardy takes toward his subject is —

A   fatalistic

B   mocking

C   bitter

D   idealistic

26 Hardy uses the *Titanic* disaster as a symbol of the —

F   futility of human vanity

G   fragility of human life

H   importance of wealth and status

J   grief of losing friends and family

27 In lines 10–12, Hardy uses imagery to compare —

A   the vast sea to the singular ship

B   overwhelming joy to overwhelming sorrow

C   grandeur and strength to insignificance and weakness

D   lightness and life to darkness and death

28 "The Spinner of the Years" (line 31) refers to the Fates of Greek mythology. This reference is an example of —

F   allegory

G   allusion

H   imagery

J   alliteration

GO ON

29 Because Hardy's poem focuses more on expressing emotions and thoughts than on telling the story of the *Titanic*, it can *best* be described as a —

A   narrative

B   lyric poem

C   ballad

D   literary epic

30 Based on details from the poem, what inference can be made about the *Titanic*?

F   No one really regrets that it sank.

G   It wasn't as luxurious as people thought.

H   People were proud of its beauty and size.

J   After it sank, another ship just like it was built.

GO ON

Entry-Level Test

Vocabulary

DIRECTIONS Choose the word or group of words that means the same, or about the same, as the underlined word. Then, mark the answer you have chosen.

SAMPLE A

Something that is <u>arduous</u> is —

  A artistic
  B difficult
  C interesting
  D available

31 **Ravenous** means —

  A hungry
  B dark
  C cowardly
  D extravagant

32 Something that is <u>austere</u> is —

  F amusing
  G violent
  H loud
  J plain

33 Someone who is <u>resolute</u> is —

  A corrupt
  B talkative
  C determined
  D irresponsible

34 To <u>tarry</u> is to —

  F insult
  G delay
  H follow
  J command

35 **Sullen** means —

  A dirty
  B pale
  C useless
  D gloomy

36 To <u>expunge</u> is to —

  F erase
  G deprive
  H replace
  J extract

GO ON

Vocabulary *(continued)*

DIRECTIONS Read each sentence in the box. Then, choose the answer in which the underlined word is used in the same way. Mark the answer you have chosen.

SAMPLE B

> The social and intellectual <u>change</u> that took place had its roots in the work of three men.

A   He would <u>change</u> his mind constantly.

B   Do you have <u>change</u> for a twenty-dollar bill?

C   You'll need to <u>change</u> trains at the next stop.

D   The <u>change</u> in his attitude is commendable.

37 The environmental activists <u>spread</u> information about greenhouse gases.

A   The eagle <u>spread</u> its wings and took to the sky.

B   The villagers <u>spread</u> the news as quickly as possible.

C   May I <u>spread</u> out the payments over a period of time?

D   We watched as he <u>spread</u> butter and jam on the hot toast.

38 The social and political forces of the time produced <u>radical</u> changes.

F   I must resort to <u>radical</u> measures if I am to complete my work on time.

G   Read the mathematical expression under the <u>radical</u> sign.

H   Are you a <u>radical</u>, a moderate, or a conservative?

J   The chemical reaction produces a free <u>radical</u>.

39 His <u>claims</u> of innocence were ignored.

A   She <u>claims</u> that she was with her sister all night.

B   Fund-raising <u>claims</u> much of my time and attention.

C   We were outraged by her <u>claims</u> that we had wronged her.

D   The prospectors staked their <u>claims</u> and began searching for gold.

40 This testimony seems to contradict your <u>account</u> of what happened that evening.

F   His <u>account</u> of recent events raised questions.

G   I will take your explanation into <u>account</u>.

H   That is a matter of small <u>account</u>.

J   Did you balance your <u>account</u> book?

COLLECTION 1 DIAGNOSTIC TEST

The Anglo-Saxons 449–1066: Songs of Ancient Heroes

On the line provided, write the letter of the *best* answer to each of the following items.
(100 points; 10 points each)

_____ **1.** An **epic** is *best* described as a —

    A brief story that teaches a moral about life

    B story that focuses on a single incident

    C long narrative poem that describes the deeds of heroes

    D songlike poem that explores the speaker's feelings

_____ **2.** An **epic** usually has all of the following elements *except* —

    F a mixture of myth, legend, and history

    G gods and goddesses

    H formal, elevated language

    J a comic tone

_____ **3.** Ancient **epics** were passed down —

    A by a king to his successor

    B in written form

    C orally

    D through schools

_____ **4.** An **archetypal** character is —

    F the main character in a story who is at the center of the action

    G a character type that recurs in literature from many cultures and time periods

    H original and unconventional

    J noble and brave by nature

_____ **5.** Which of the following phrases contains **alliteration**?

    A a low noise

    B north and west

    C chirping baby birds

    D royal gems

_____ **6.** Which of the following statements about **images** is *false*?

    F Images can appeal to all five senses.

    G Images help the reader to associate one thing with another.

    H Images can affect how the reader responds to a work.

    J Images are used only in fiction.

_____ **7.** The purpose of a character **foil** is to —

    A emphasize the difference between two characters

    B highlight one character's faults

    C create conflict within the story

    D provide comic relief

_____ **8.** Which of the following sentences is an example of a **simile**?

    F The fresh snow glistened in the moonlight.

    G The branches swaying in the breeze were like long, thin arms waving farewell.

    H The wind, howling and moaning all night long, frightened the children.

    J Her mind was a well-oiled machine.

_____ **9.** What is an **epithet**?

    A A type of poem that appears in many cultures

    B The origin of a word

    C A descriptive phrase that is regularly used to describe a person or place

    D A plot element in narratives that recount a journey

_____ **10.** **Prefixes** and **suffixes** can change all of the following *except* —

    F a word's root

    G a word's tense

    H a word's meaning

    J a word's part of speech

LITERARY PERIOD INTRODUCTION TEST

The Anglo-Saxons 449–1066: Songs of Ancient Heroes

COMPREHENSION *(100 points; 10 points each)*

On the line provided, write the letter of the *best* answer to each of the following items.

_____ **1.** Great Britain has been invaded and settled by all of the following peoples *except* —

    A Romans

    B Vikings

    C Normans

    D Greeks

_____ **2.** After the Romans evacuated their troops, Britain was left with —

    F a strong army

    G a system of roads and architecture

    H Latin as its official language

    J a strong, centralized government of its own

_____ **3.** An important effect of Christianity's spread throughout Britain was that —

    A monasteries no longer had to be located in Italy and France

    B Britain became culturally linked to Europe

    C the long Roman defensive wall was demolished

    D the Anglo-Saxon religion immediately died out

_____ **4.** Celtic religion had all the following characteristics *except* —

    F priests called Druids

    G ritual dances and human sacrifice

    H worship of ancient Greek gods of wisdom

    J belief in spirits who controlled all aspects of existence

_____ **5.** Anglo-Saxon life was dominated by —

    A devotion to monastic principles and beliefs

    B industry and dedication to a strict work ethic

    C a new emphasis on education and the arts

    D close allegiances between leaders and their followers

_____ **6.** The old Anglo-Saxon religion —

    F primarily encouraged ethics and earthly virtues such as bravery

    G had much in common with the beliefs of Christianity

    H advanced an optimistic, cheerful view of life on earth

    J offered the hope of eternal reward to the good

_____ **7.** Anglo-Saxon poets held an honored position in society primarily because they —

    A preserved heroic deeds in the collective memory

    B became great warriors for their lords

    C painstakingly copied old manuscripts

    D read old books and attained great wisdom

_____ **8.** The Christian monasteries served Anglo-Saxon society by —

    F developing innovative agricultural theories and methods

    G reforming criminals and housing the homeless

    H abolishing the last remnants of Anglo-Saxon religion

    J fostering learning and preserving literary works

_____ **9.** Through the *Anglo-Saxon Chronicle,* King Alfred promoted the use of written —

    A Latin

    B Celtic

    C Old English

    D Danish

_____ **10.** The years of war between the Anglo-Saxons and the Danes came to an end with the —

    F departure of the Romans after the collapse of the Roman Empire

    G acceptance of Christianity by both groups under Alfred the Great

    H invasion by the Normans under William of Normandy

    J discovery of the Sutton Hoo treasure in Suffolk, England

from Beowulf, Part One *translated by* Burton Raffel
from Grendel John Gardner
Life in 999: A Grim Struggle Howard G. Chua-Eoan
from Beowulf, Part Two *translated by* Seamus Heaney

COMPREHENSION *(40 points; 4 points each)*

On the line provided, write the letter of the *best* answer to each of the following items.

_____ 1. Beowulf slays Grendel in order to —

     A save Hrothgar and the Danes from the monster

     B prevent Grendel from invading the land of the Geats

     C keep Herot from being destroyed

     D carry off the treasure in Grendel's lair

_____ 2. Beowulf must battle Grendel with his bare hands because —

     F the Geats traditionally did battle with their bare hands

     G Grendel had magically made all weapons useless against him

     H Beowulf wishes to prove the superiority of the Geats over the Danes

     J Beowulf wishes to prove his bravery

_____ 3. Which of the following statements about Wiglaf is *true*?

     A He believes in and speaks about the inner goodness of all people.

     B His inexperience makes him unworthy to succeed to the throne.

     C He makes an eloquent speech about the virtues of loyalty and bravery.

     D He tells Beowulf that the other warriors will desert Beowulf when he needs them most.

_____ 4. How does Beowulf die?

     F The dragon kills him as Beowulf goes out unarmed to fight the monster.

     G Surrounded by a crowd of helpful warriors, Beowulf is the last to fall.

     H Unaided by most of the warriors, Beowulf is killed as he and Wiglaf fight the dragon.

     J After killing the dragon, Beowulf and his followers fight over the treasure, and Beowulf is killed.

_____ **5.** What last thoughts does Beowulf express as he is dying?

    A A desire for respect and pride in his ability to protect his people

    B Bitterness because his soldiers did not help him fight the dragon

    C Fear that the kingdom of the Geats will fall apart after he dies

    D Affection and longing for his family

_____ **6.** The *most* important event in Beowulf's career as leader of the Geats is the —

    F attack on the dragon

    G speech for the prince

    H celebration that involved both Danes and Geats

    J tracing of the bloody footprints

_____ **7.** In Beowulf's fight to the death with Grendel's mother, the piece of his own equipment that saves his life is his —

    A woven mail shirt

    B helmet

    C sword, Hrunting

    D shield

_____ **8.** Beowulf tells Wiglaf that he wants his burned-out funeral pyre to be a —

    F reminder to his people of his greatness

    G monument to King Hrothgar

    H reminder to Wiglaf of his duties

    J sign of the new Christian faith

_____ **9.** How is the raid on Hrothgar's hall shown differently in John Gardner's *Grendel* than in *Beowulf*?

    A In *Grendel* the monster is not a man-eater.

    B The novel *Grendel* shows the action from the monster's point of view.

    C In *Beowulf* each victim is individually described.

    D *Beowulf* shows the action from Beowulf's point of view.

_____ **10.** What aspect of Anglo-Saxon life discussed in "Life in 999: A Grim Struggle" is also in full view in *Beowulf*?

    F There was no sugar and few spices.

    G Vitamin deficiencies and diseases were rampant.

    H The population was growing, but farm labor was scarce.

    J The lord's castle was viewed as a refuge from dangers.

LITERARY FOCUS: EPIC HERO, ALLITERATION, AND KENNINGS *(20 points; 5 points each)*

On the line provided, write the letter of the *best* answer to each of the following items.

_____ **11.** Which of the following quotations from *Beowulf* does not contain **alliteration**?

    A "The hoard-guard recognized / a human voice . . ."

    B "It was no easy thing / to have to give ground like that and go. . . ."

    C "Then he addressed each dear companion. . . ."

    D "'I remember that time when mead was flowing . . .'"

_____ **12.** The archetypal **epic hero** stands in relation to his or her community as the hero —

    F who, as a supreme individual, is indifferent to the fate of others

    G who saves his or her people from possible disaster

    H who gives his or her own life to protect those less worthy

    J whose individual quest has nothing to do with the community

_____ **13.** If you wanted to support the idea that Beowulf is an epic hero, you might *best* note that he —

    A displays intense pride in his country

    B becomes more humble over time

    C loves nature and abhors civilization

    D embodies the ideal of Anglo-Saxon society

_____ **14.** Which of the following quotations from *Beowulf* contains a kenning?

    F "And all at once the greedy she-wolf . . ."

    G "At last he saw the mud of the bottom."

    H "He was hunting another / Dead monster . . ."

    J "Grendel's mother / Is hidden in her terrible home . . ."

VOCABULARY DEVELOPMENT *(20 points; 4 points each)*

In the space provided, write the Vocabulary word that *best* completes the sentence.

resolute   **vehemently**   **infallible**   **furled**   **lavish**   **assail**   **extolled**

15. The hero was strong in body and _____ in his determination to win.

16. "Someone stole my treasure, and someone is going to pay!" shouted the monster

_____.

17. The fact that Beowulf is killed shows that he is an imperfect hero, not an

_____ one.

18. The warriors lift their goblets and _____ the hero with praise when he enters the hall.

19. Although the hero was confident, doubts would sometimes _____ him in the middle of the night.

CONSTRUCTED RESPONSE *(20 points)*

20. All **epic heroes** overcome powerful forces that arise from their particular ways of life. Modern heroes may conquer the unknowns of outer space or bring food or medicine to hungry people. The Anglo-Saxon hero slew monsters. Of course, monsters exist only in fantasy. But a monster may be an **archetypal symbol** for some broader problem or challenge a society faces. What challenges of Anglo-Saxon life are represented by the monsters Beowulf faces? Use your knowledge of Anglo-Saxon society and of *Beowulf*. On a separate sheet of paper, write a paragraph explaining your answer. To support your point, use specific references, including at least one example of imagery, from the poem.

SELECTION TEST   LITERARY RESPONSE AND ANALYSIS

from Gilgamesh: A Verse Narrative *retold by* Herbert Mason

COMPREHENSION *(40 points; 4 points each)*

On the line provided, write the letter of the *best* answer to each of the following items.

_____ **1.** Who is Gilgamesh?

    A A legendary Sumerian king and superhuman hero

    B Half serpent and half man

    C A king of the Hebrews

    D An ordinary Mesopotamian man who has great adventures

_____ **2.** Enkidu is Gilgamesh's —

    F king

    G slave

    H brother

    J best friend

_____ **3.** Humbaba is *not* a —

    A fearsome giant

    B guard

    C god

    D forest dweller

_____ **4.** Which of the following explanations is a reason Gilgamesh wants to destroy Humbaba?

    F Humbaba has been eating Sumerian youths and maidens.

    G Gilgamesh wants to be free of Humbaba's power over people.

    H Gilgamesh wants to defy the boundaries set by the gods.

    J The youth of Uruk have grown soft and need inspiration.

_____ **5.** What do the elders of Uruk urge Gilgamesh to do?

    A Fight Humbaba as planned

    B Give up and stay in the city

    C Take a hundred brave warriors with him

    D Use the magic potion that they offer to him

_____ **6.** Which character is most afraid of the coming battle?

    F Gilgamesh

    G Enkidu

    H Humbaba

    J The chief elder of Uruk

_____ **7.** The forest is called "Hell" by some and "Paradise" by others. What does Gilgamesh call it?

    A Death

    B The Dark

    C The Heroes' Road

    D The Place of Doom

_____ **8.** While Gilgamesh sleeps and dreams, Enkidu —

    F practices sword technique

    G makes sure the fire doesn't go out

    H prays to the gods for success

    J deals quietly with his own fear and pain

_____ **9.** When the heroes pause briefly in their attack, what does Humbaba do?

    A Pauses as well

    B Beats Enkidu to the ground

    C Kills Enkidu

    D Turns against Gilgamesh

_____ **10.** Just before he is killed, Humbaba —

    F puts a curse on Gilgamesh and Enkidu

    G breaks into a death song praising his killers' courage

    H offers to serve Gilgamesh if he will spare his life

    J calls upon the gods to help him one last time

LITERARY FOCUS: THE HERO AND HIS FOIL *(20 points; 5 points each)*

On the line provided, write the letter of the *best* answer to each of the following items.

_____ **11.** What kind of character is a **foil**?

    A A secondary character who narrates, or tells, the story

    B The main character of an epic or ballad

    C A character who opposes the hero

    D A character who helps set off another character

_____ **12.** What trait is most important in a good **foil**?

    F   Contrast with the main character

    G   Willingness to sacrifice himself or herself

    H   Swordsmanship or other fighting skills

    J   Ability to give good advice to the hero

_____ **13.** Why is it important that Enkidu, the **foil** in *Gilgamesh: A Verse Narrative*, grew up wild?

    A   It gives Enkidu and Gilgamesh something in common.

    B   Because of it, Enkidu knows secret medicinal plants.

    C   Enkidu has learned to speak the language of animals.

    D   Enkidu's childhood was the opposite of Gilgamesh's childhood.

_____ **14.** The relationship between Gilgamesh and Enkidu could be *best* described as —

    F   like father and son who can't communicate with each other

    G   like brothers who are very close

    H   very effective in battle, but not in peacetime

    J   a friendship destroyed by love for the same woman

VOCABULARY DEVELOPMENT *(20 points; 4 points each)*

On the line provided, write the letter of the *best* answer for each item.

_____ **15.** A <u>squall</u> is a kind of —

    A   boat

    B   garment

    C   storm

    D   car

_____ **16.** Someone who did a <u>contortion</u> would be —

    F   twisting his or her body

    G   lying to a jury

    H   leaping high above the ground

    J   confessing a past crime

_____ **17.** An example of an <u>austere</u> meal might be —

    A   a traditional Thanksgiving turkey and trimmings

    B   a monk's simple loaf of bread and flask of water

    C   all-you-can-eat pizza, pasta, and salad

    D   a picnic lunch where everyone eats just enough to be satisfied

_____ **18.** "The king has <u>decreed</u> silence" means the king —

    F has ordered silence

    G is going to grade the people on their amount of silence

    H has declared that silence is no longer allowed

    J has announced that he will never speak again

_____ **19.** Restrained is a synonym for —

    A decreed

    B contorted

    C squalled

    D controlled

CONSTRUCTED RESPONSE *(20 points)*

20. Evaluate Gilgamesh and Enkidu as **epic hero** and **foil**. What are their character traits? In your opinion what traits of the two characters are most effectively presented in the **epic**? How might the characters need to be changed if they were presented in a modern **epic**? On a separate sheet of paper, write a brief paragraph explaining your answer.

(**SELECTION TEST** ████████████)   **LITERARY RESPONSE AND ANALYSIS**

the Iliad, *from* Book 22, The Death of Hector
Homer   *translated by* Robert Fagles

COMPREHENSION *(40 points; 4 points each)*

On the line provided, write the letter of the *best* answer to each of the following items.

_____ **1.** Who is Hector?

    A The greatest champion of the Greeks

    B King of the Trojans

    C Prince and greatest warrior of the Trojans

    D Best friend of the hero Achilles

_____ **2.** What is occurring at the very beginning of the selection?

    F Achilles is chasing Hector around the outskirts of Troy.

    G Hector's parents are urging him to stay inside the city gates.

    H The Greeks are advancing on Troy; Hector is outside the gates.

    J The weary opposing armies are resting before facing each other again.

_____ **3.** How does the goddess Athena appear to Hector?

    A As a shining light and a thundering voice

    B As a double of Achilles

    C Dressed in the gold armor of an immortal

    D Disguised as Hector's favorite brother

_____ **4.** How does the chief god, Zeus, decide that Hector must die?

    F He has always favored Achilles.

    G He weighs Hector's and Achilles' fates on a scale.

    H He confers with the other gods and weighs their advice.

    J He leaves the question up to the warriors' own skill.

_____ **5.** What is Achilles' greatest character flaw?

    A Anger and rage

    B Fear of battle

    C Uncontrollable strength

    D Misjudgment of his enemies

_____ **6.** Hector's plea to Achilles is to —

    F let his parents have his body

    G kill him quickly, without much suffering

    H return his body to the ships of the Greeks

    J end the senseless war over Helen of Troy

_____ **7.** Hector promises that, if he defeats Achilles, —

    A Achilles' body will be hung to rot outside the gate

    B the entire Greek army will suffer defeat

    C Hector will give him an honorable funeral

    D Achilles's body will not be mutilated

_____ **8.** Achilles refuses to bury Hector because —

    F Hector betrayed him

    G Hector killed Achilles' great friend Patroclus

    H it was Hector who stole Helen and began the Trojan War

    J Achilles is simply a bad sport

_____ **9.** After Achilles kills Hector, he —

    A cuts off his head

    B drags Hector's body in the dirt behind his chariot

    C gives him back to Hector's wife

    D asks the gods to make Hector immortal

_____ **10.** When Achilles shows the Greeks the body of Hector, the Greeks —

    F step back in awe, still frightened

    G gamble for Hector's armor

    H stab the body and laugh

    J grieve for the loss of a great warrior

LITERARY FOCUS: EPIC SIMILE AND OTHER CONVENTIONS OF HOMERIC EPICS *(20 points; 5 points each)*
On the line provided, write the letter of the *best* answer to each of the following items.

_____ **11.** The difference between **epic simile** and ordinary simile is that epic simile —

    A never uses the connecting word *like* or *as*

    B is more difficult to understand

    C is longer and more complicated

    D uses strange, unearthly comparisons

Holt Assessment: Literature, Reading, and Vocabulary

_____ **12.** Which of the following phrases is *not* a **stock epithet**?

    F Hector, breaker of horses

    G Peleus's princely son

    H King Priam

    J brilliant Achilles

_____ **13.** **Invocations** in epic poems contain all of the following elements *except* a —

    A plea for the audience's attention

    B plea for help from the muse

    C statement of the poem's subject

    D statement of the poem's theme

_____ **14.** In an **epic simile**, what does Homer compare to the brightest star in the sky?

    F Hector's heroism

    G The beauty of Helen of Troy

    H The goddess Athena

    J Achilles' gleaming spear

VOCABULARY DEVELOPMENT *(20 points; 4 points each)*

groveling   **gallant**   **scourge**   **fawning**

On the lines provided, write the Vocabulary word that *best* completes the sentence. You may use a word more than once.

15. A truly _____ hero does not insult his opponents.

16. Hector, the great Trojan fighter, was the _____ of the Greeks.

17. A dog licking its owner's hand excitedly could be said to be _____.

18. A slave lying face down before a king and pleading for mercy could be said to be

_____.

19. A synonym for *fawning* that is also on this Vocabulary list is _____.

CONSTRUCTED RESPONSE *(20 points)*

20. Based on this selection, what qualities did Homer find heroic? On a separate
sheet of paper, write a paragraph explaining your answer. Cite specific passages
in the text where the qualities are shown. As evidence, include at least one
epic simile or other figure of speech.

The Anglo-Saxons 449–1066: Songs of Ancient Heroes

"The Husband's Message" is an Anglo-Saxon poem about a high-ranking husband and wife who have been kept apart by a feud. The speaker of the poem, according to many scholars, is a *rune stave*, a wood scrap on which a message has been engraved. (*Runes* were an Anglo-Saxon form of writing that could be carved easily on wood.) Read the poem carefully, and answer the questions that follow.

The Husband's Message

translated by Kevin Crossley-Holland

Now that we're alone I can explain
The secret meaning of this stave. I was once a child.
But now one of the sons of men, living far from here,
Sends me on errands over the salt-streams,
5   Commands me to carry a cunningly-carved letter.
At my master's command I have often crossed the sea,
Sailed in the ship's hold to strange destinations.
And this time I have come especially
To sow assurance in your mind
10 About my lord's great love for you.
I swear that you will find in him
Great faith to you, great loyalty.
O lady adorned with such lovely ornaments,
He who carved the words in this wood
15 Bids me ask you to remember
The oaths you swore so long ago together;
In those distant days you lived in the same country,
Lived in love together,
Sharing one estate in the beautiful city.
20 Then a feud, a cruel vendetta, forced him to leave
This land of happy people; I was told to tell you,
Joyfully, that you should undertake a journey
Just as soon as you hear the cuckoo's sad song,
That mournful sound in the mountain woods.
25 After that, let no man delay you
Or stop you from sailing over the waves.
Go down to the sea, the home of the gull;
Sail south from here over the salt-streams
To the land where your lord waits in high expectations.
30 He nurses no greater wish in the world
(With his own words he told me),

"The Husband's Message" by Kevin Crossley-Holland from *The Battle of Maldon and Other Old English Poems* by Bruce Mitchell and Kevin Crossley-Holland. Copyright © 1982 by Kevin Crossley-Holland. Reproduced by permission of **Kevin Crossley-Holland, c/o Rogers, Coleridge & White Ltd., 20 Powis Mews, London W11 1JN.**

Than that both of you together, by the grace of God,
May give rings once again to men in the mead-hall;
Bestow gifts as before on companions
35   And warriors. He has won
Wealth enough, though he lives
Far away amongst a foreign people
In a beautiful land.
Forced by the feud to launch his boat from here,
40   He went over the waves alone in his youth,
Set forth on the way of the flood, eager to
Depart and divide the quiet waters. Now at last your lord
Leaves his sorrows behind him. He will lack nothing,
Neither horses, nor treasure, nor joy in the mead-hall,
45   O daughter of the prince,
He will want nothing else in the world
If only he may have *you* for his own,
Fulfilling the former vow between you.
I hear the runes S. and R.,
50   EA., W. and M. join in an oath
That he will wait for you in that country,
And will always love you for as long as he lives,
Faithful and true to your vows to each other,
The oaths you swore so long ago together.

VOCABULARY SKILLS (15 points; 3 points each)

On the line provided, write the letter of the *best* answer to each of the following items.

_____ **1.** *Cunningly* (line 5) means that the message was carved with —

    A trickery

    B confusion

    C expertise

    D no straight lines

_____ **2.** *Sow*, as used in line 9, means —

    F farmer

    G piglet

    H field

    J plant

_____ **3.** *Vendetta* (line 20) refers to a(n) —

    A bitter quarrel

    B vendor of rune staves

    C offensive joke

    D nasty satire

_____ **4.** When the husband *nurses*, in line 30, he is —

     F questioning the purpose of his life

     G holding a thought in his mind

     H discovering that he loves his wife

     J patching together the broken rune stave

_____ **5.** *Bestow* (line 34) means that the husband wants to —

     A open gifts

     B ask for gifts

     C give gifts

     D return gifts

COMPREHENSION *(15 points; 3 points each)*

On the line provided, write the letter of the *best* answer to each of the following items.

_____ **6.** The message on the rune stave was written by —

     F the husband to the wife

     G the wife to the husband

     H the child to its parents

     J a priest to the married couple

_____ **7.** "The Husband's Message" is primarily about —

     A a broken oath of loyalty

     B a difficult sea voyage

     C the loss of an important letter

     D the desire to be reunited with a loved one

_____ **8.** Judging from what the speaker says about his master, the husband has —

     F prospered in a foreign land

     G experienced many misfortunes after the feud

     H become the captain of a large ship

     J taken his wife's rings and other ornaments

_____ **9.** The husband wants his wife to —

     A travel around the world

     B send their children to him

     C forget him

     D join him

_____ **10.** The **tone** of the poem can *best* be described as —

    F fearful

    G harshly combative

    H lovingly sincere

    J apologetic

LITERARY FOCUS: CONSTRUCTED RESPONSE *(20 points)*

11. Is "The Husband's Message" an epic or not? Complete the following chart, listing ways in which the poem both does and does not meet the pattern of an epic in three important categories. Then, state your overall conclusions on the lines provided.

	"The Husband's Message"	
	▶ **Is Like an Epic**	▶ **Is Unlike an Epic**
the hero		
the events		
the setting		

All in all, "The Husband's Message" (is / is not) an epic because —

_____

_____

_____

_____

_____

_____

_____

READING SKILLS AND STRATEGIES *(50 points)*

Recognizing Archetypes *(4 points)*

_____ **12.** Which **archetypal** pair do the husband and wife in the poem *most* closely resemble?

   F Achilles and Hector, deadly enemies alike in spirit

   G King Arthur and Queen Guinevere, royal couple facing problems

   H Romeo and Juliet, young lovers doomed to die tragically

   J Gilgamesh and Enkidu, best friends who have been through it all together

Identifying Literary Conventions *(6 points; 2 points each)*

13. Analyze the **sounds, imagery,** and **figurative language** of "The Husband's Message" as follows.

(1) List two examples of alliteration in the poem.

_____

(2) Find a **kenning** that is used twice in the poem to describe the sea.

_____

(3) What **image** does the husband use to describe how soon the wife should begin her journey?

_____

_____

Analyzing Literary Conventions *(10 points)*

14. How do the poet's choices of imagery, figurative language, and alliterative sounds work together to create a **mood** or feeling in the poem? On a separate sheet of paper, describe that mood or feeling.

Using the Philosophical and Historical Approaches *(30 points; 15 points each)*

15. What view of Anglo-Saxon life does "The Husband's Message" provide? Compare and contrast it with the view of life found in *Beowulf*. On a separate sheet of paper, explain your answer. Use details to support your position.

16. In pleading with his wife, the husband emphasizes the oaths they have taken. What are those oaths? How does the emphasis on oaths show "The Husband's Message" to be a work of its own historical period, different from the present day? On a separate sheet of paper, write a short paragraph explaining your answer.

COLLECTION 2 DIAGNOSTIC TEST

The Middle Ages 1066–1485: The Tales They Told

On the line provided, write the letter of the *best* answer to each of the following items.
(100 points; 10 points each)

_____ 1. Which of the following elements is usually found in **ballads**?

  A Refrain

  B Asides

  C Free verse

  D Complicated language

_____ 2. To aid in **characterization,** an author might do all of the following *except* —

  F describe the character's appearance

  G depict how others respond to the character

  H use details to heighten suspense

  J show how the character speaks and acts

_____ 3. To **satirize** something is to —

  A write a flattering tribute

  B provide a faithful historical account

  C ridicule with the intention of reforming

  D compose a story in verse

_____ 4. **Situational irony** occurs when —

  F a character says one thing but means another

  G a writer uses a symbol with multiple meanings

  H what actually happens is the opposite of what is expected

  J a writer hints at what is going to happen next in a story

_____ 5. The **narrator** of a story —

  A is always the same as the author

  B never plays a role in the story's plot

  C can reveal his or her character through the story's subject and tone

  D must be an objective observer who does not express personal opinions

_____ **6.** A **couplet** is composed of —

    F two words that share an initial consonant sound

    G a stanza containing internal rhyme

    H two consecutive lines of poetry that rhyme

    J a line of poetry that contains a pause

_____ **7.** **Half rhymes**, also called **approximate rhymes**, are words that —

    A sound nothing alike

    B share similar but not identical sounds

    C end with the same consonant

    D end with the same vowel sound

_____ **8.** What is a **fable**?

    F A brief story that teaches a moral or practical lesson about life

    G A story that explains a culture's beliefs and customs

    H A story that imitates another literary work for comic purposes

    J A medieval story with a simple plot

_____ **9.** Which of the following statements about the **etymology** of words is *true*?

    A Two definitions of a word cannot derive from a single word origin.

    B Prefixes and suffixes do not help to explain word origins.

    C All words have accumulated more than one meaning over time.

    D Different meanings of a word can have different origins.

_____ **10.** A **word analogy** is —

    F a word part that is added to a root

    G two pairs of words with the same relationship

    H a clue to the meaning of an unfamiliar word

    J two words that have the same meaning

LITERARY PERIOD INTRODUCTION TEST

The Middle Ages 1066–1485: The Tales They Told

COMPREHENSION *(100 points; 10 points each)*

On the line provided, write the letter of the *best* answer to each of the following items.

_____ **1.** After William the Conqueror triumphed at the Battle of Hastings, England changed because of its —

    A defeat of the Germanic tribes

    B adoption of the Norman feudal system

    C acceptance of Anglo-Saxon culture

    D emergence as the leading European political power

_____ **2.** Feudalism's religious concept of hierarchy featured —

    F a caste system of lords, vassals, and serfs

    G classes in Latin for young knights

    H endless international warfare

    J romantic attitudes toward women

_____ **3.** In the Middle Ages, women of rank —

    A had political rights concerning domestic affairs

    B were never allowed to manage their husbands' estates

    C held social positions determined by the status of their husbands or fathers

    D improved their social positions through peaceful protest

_____ **4.** The growth of cities in the Middle Ages led to all of the following events *except* the —

    F rise of courtly love and a system of chivalry

    G development of lower, middle, and upper-middle classes

    H rise of "people's art" such as the ballad and the mystery play

    J eventual collapse of the European feudal system

_____ **5.** The Crusades influenced everyday life in England by —

    A causing writers to publish in many different languages

    B exposing the English to other civilizations

    C recapturing Jerusalem for Christianity

    D inspiring the authors of the Magna Carta

_____ **6.** The 1170 martyrdom of Thomas à Becket, the Archbishop of Canterbury, led to —

    F hardships for the common people of England

    G the establishment of a new religion

    H changes within the Church of England

    J greater power in England for the Church of Rome

_____ **7.** The *most* positive effect of the medieval church was —

    A the creation of a refuge for landless serfs

    B a rebellion against the monarchy

    C the use of Latin for everyday business

    D the fostering of common beliefs and symbols

_____ **8.** The signing of the Magna Carta by King John at Runnymede signaled the —

    F alliance of the English barons with the Pope

    G king's heightened power over the people

    H aristocrats' interest in the rights of commoners

    J renewal of older, democratic ideals

_____ **9.** As a result of the Hundred Years' War between England and France, —

    A England lost most of its population to disease and warfare

    B the English aristocracy disappeared as a political force

    C the yeoman class became the backbone of England

    D France gave part of Normandy to England

_____ **10.** The Black Death ultimately resulted in —

    F increased awareness of proper sanitation

    G freedom for the serfs and greater power for the lower classes

    H victory for the Lancasters over the Tudors

    J the reemergence of Anglo-Saxon religion

SELECTION TEST

Lord Randall
Get Up and Bar the Door

COMPREHENSION (40 points; 4 points each)

On the line provided, write the letter of the *best* answer to each of the following items.

_____ 1. "Lord Randall" contains all the following elements *except* —

    A domestic tragedy

    B murder

    C return of the hero from seafaring

    D dialogue between mother and son

_____ 2. If you were to describe the mother in "Lord Randall," your *best* description might be that she —

    F is too meek to take action against a killer

    G is strong-willed and independent

    H is inquisitive and is afraid for her son

    J has never liked her son's girlfriend

_____ 3. Where has Lord Randall been?

    A At war against the Normans

    B Across the ocean, chasing the Norse

    C On a crusade with his brothers

    D Hunting and having dinner with his love

_____ 4. Who killed Lord Randall?

    F His girlfriend

    G A rival for his girlfriend's love

    H His girlfriend's father

    J The killer's identity is not known

_____ 5. What was the motive, or reason, for the murder?

    A Lord Randall's girlfriend had been betrayed by him.

    B A jealous rival wanted the young lady for himself.

    C The young lady's father wanted her to marry a richer nobleman.

    D No motive is given in the ballad.

_____ **6.** "Get Up and Bar the Door" —

    F illustrates the rituals of courtly love

    G shows the importance of holiday puddings in the Middle Ages

    H pokes fun at the absurd bickering of a husband and wife

    J condemns bandits who prey on simple folk

_____ **7.** The intruders into the couple's house are two —

    A kings

    B members of the gentry, or landowning class

    C escaped convicts

    D serfs from the neighboring manor

_____ **8.** The two intruders have come because —

    F they have a long-standing feud with the couple

    G the couple are known far and wide for their hospitality

    H they are traveling and need a place to stay for the night

    J they are at war and need to take over the house

_____ **9.** What word *best* describes the two intruders' behavior toward the couple?

    A friendly

    B loyal

    C honest

    D threatening

_____ **10.** The final stanza of "Get Up and Bar the Door" —

    F reveals the narrator's relation to the couple

    G provides a comic twist to the story

    H serves the intruders their comeuppance

    J describes the husband's tragic downfall

LITERARY FOCUS: BALLAD *(40 points; 10 points each)*
On the line provided, write the letter of the *best* answer to each of the following items.

_____ **11.** All of the following elements are typical characteristics of **ballads** *except* —

    A sensational or supernatural events

    B tragic subject matter

    C omission of details

    D mixed metaphors

_____ **12.** What is a **refrain**?

    F Another word for a ballad

    G A repeated word, line, or group of lines

    H A character's action or lack of action

    J The standard meter for English ballads

_____ **13.** "Lord Randall" is an example of a ballad whose structure is —

    A a question-and-answer conversation

    B a description of a murder

    C a series of events narrated in chronological order

    D built of large numbers of small details

_____ **14.** How is "Get Up and Bar the Door" *not* a typical ballad?

    F It is comic.

    G The characters are not superhuman.

    H It is set in England.

    J Characters' motives are not spelled out.

CONSTRUCTED RESPONSE *(20 points)*

15. What characteristics of the two ballads, "Lord Randall" and "Get Up and Bar the Door," show that they were intended to appeal mainly to a general audience rather than an elite audience? Consider the ballads' story lines and styles and the characteristics that are associated with ballads (such as refrains or sensational, sordid, or tragic subject matter). On a separate sheet of paper, write a brief paragraph explaining your answer.

SELECTION TEST ▮▮▮▮

The Prologue *from* The Canterbury Tales
Geoffrey Chaucer *translated by* Nevill Coghill

COMPREHENSION *(40 points; 4 points each)*

On the line provided, write the letter of the *best* answer to each of the following items.

_____ **1.** In "The Prologue," Chaucer's main objective is to —

    A analyze religious customs

    B reveal the narrator's thoughts

    C introduce his cast of characters

    D describe a London inn

_____ **2.** The pilgrims are traveling to Canterbury because —

    F the shrine of St. Thomas à Becket is there

    G they want to escape the plague that is attacking London

    H the innkeeper has dared them to make the journey

    J it is part of a longer tour of England

_____ **3.** The pilgrims agree to tell tales during the journey to —

    A preserve their stories for the future

    B win a free meal and entertain one another

    C reduce fighting and bickering

    D teach the innkeeper a lesson about pride

_____ **4.** You know the Cook's dishes may not be quite as appetizing as might be hoped when Chaucer mentions that the Cook —

    F refuses to consult recipe books

    G has a large, festering sore

    H adds too much salt to his cake

    J burns everything he makes

_____ **5.** The Wife of Bath is a —

    A pious churchgoer and religious teacher

    B well-traveled vendor of fine silk clothing

    C veteran of several pilgrimages and marriages

    D widow of a prosperous doctor in Bath

_____ **6.** The character in *The Canterbury Tales* who most closely resembles Chaucer himself is the —

    F innkeeper

    G narrator

    H Knight

    J Merchant

_____ **7.** In describing the individual pilgrims, Chaucer begins with the —

    A Knight

    B Wife of Bath

    C Pardoner

    D innkeeper

_____ **8.** The unworldly student who prefers philosophy to riches is the —

    F Merchant

    G Franklin

    H Oxford Cleric

    J Reeve

_____ **9.** The Haberdasher, the Dyer, the Carpenter, the Weaver, and the Carpet-maker are all —

    A members of the clergy

    B landowners

    C skilled members of crafts guilds

    D too poor to join the pilgrimage

_____ **10.** Which profession found among Chaucer's pilgrims can still be found today?

    F Reeve

    G Manciple

    H Pardoncr

    J Parson

LITERARY FOCUS: CHARACTERIZATION *(15 points; 5 points each)*

On the line provided, write the letter of the *best* answer to each of the following items.

_____ **11.** Chaucer's **characterization** —

    A uses the same basic techniques that writers use today

    B is based on dialogue rather than action

    C never shows the reader what the character is feeling

    D shows the characters as basic types rather than as believable individuals

_____ **12.** The member of the clergy given the most admiring, flattering description is the —

    F Parson

    G Friar

    H Nun

    J Monk

_____ **13.** Which of the following quotations from "The Prologue" is the *best* example of imagery?

    A "Thinly they fell, like rat-tails, one by one."

    B "In fifteen mortal battles he had been."

    C "Just home from service, he had joined our ranks."

    D "He'd seen some service with the cavalry."

READING SKILLS: ANALYZING STYLE: DETAILS *(5 points)*

_____ **14.** Which **detail** is *least* directly connected to characterization?

    F Dress

    G Behavior

    H Chronology

    J Appearance

VOCABULARY DEVELOPMENT *(20 points; 4 points each)*

Match the definition on the left with the Vocabulary word on the right. On the line provided, write the letter of the Vocabulary word.

_____ **15.** thrifty; careful with money   **a.** benign

_____ **16.** ability to move quickly and easily   **b.** obstinate

_____ **17.** kind; gracious   **c.** frugal

_____ **18.** sly dealings; skill in deceiving   **d.** agility

_____ **19.** unreasonably stubborn   **e.** guile

CONSTRUCTED RESPONSE (*20 points*)

20. Choose your favorite character from "The Prologue," and describe the character's traits in your own words. Then, analyze how Chaucer's description—his choice of words and details—brings out the traits you described. Finally, discuss how your chosen character represents English life in the Middle Ages. You may refer to your knowledge of the Middle Ages from the Literary Period Introduction as well as from this selection. Write your answers on a separate sheet of paper.

SELECTION TEST ████████   **LITERARY RESPONSE AND ANALYSIS**

from The Pardoner's Tale
Geoffrey Chaucer *translated by* Nevill Coghill

COMPREHENSION *(40 points; 4 points each)*
On the line provided, write the letter of the *best* answer to each of the following items.

_____ **1.** A Pardoner is an official of the —

    A king

    B church

    C local government

    D feudal manor

_____ **2.** The Pardoner earns money from all of the following activities *except* —

    F preaching against greed

    G begging from church to church

    H selling relics and papal pardons

    J making and selling baskets

_____ **3.** The stories about Death that the servant boy and the tavern-knave tell suggest that —

    A death from violence and plague is rampant

    B Death will be hard to find

    C people are dying of plague

    D people looked forward to death

_____ **4.** The rioters go looking for Death because they —

    F want to repent of their sins and find salvation

    G plan to avenge the deaths of their friends

    H know he has great treasure

    J want to banish him from England

_____ **5.** In "The Pardoner's Tale," Death is portrayed as —

    A both the price of wickedness and an actual person

    B both a skeletal figure and an evil angel

    C an old man selling wares by the side of the road

    D an archangel who kills people through natural disaster and war

_____ **6.** Which of the following statements *best* describes the end of the tale?

    F The rioters become rich.

    G The rioters meet death.

    H Death takes the gold florins.

    J Death takes a holiday.

7. The character who prevents a fight between the Pardoner and the Host is the —

   A Squire

   B Knight

   C Monk

   D Oxford Clerk

8. The Pardoner's pious story reveals his —

   F honesty

   G ignorance

   H sensitivity

   J immorality

9. Which of the following words *best* describes the Pardoner's treatment of the Host?

   A angry

   B generous

   C uneducated

   D mocking

10. After telling his tale, what does the Pardoner offer to do for his fellow pilgrims?

   F Buy them a round of drinks

   G Explain the moral of the tale

   H Sell them relics and pardons

   J Pray for their souls

LITERARY FOCUS: IRONY *(20 points; 5 points each)*

On the line provided, write the letter of the *best* answer to each of the following items.

11. The old man's comment to the three rioters that Death "isn't one to hide for all your prating" is an example of —

   A imagery

   B a moral

   C verbal irony

   D situational irony

_____ **12.** It is ironic that the Pardoner preaches against avarice, because he is —

    F especially greedy

    G a pious man

    H a friend of the Summoner's

    J rude to the Host

_____ **13.** What is ironic about the attitude that the old man has toward Death?

    A Most people seek to avoid death, but the old man looks for it.

    B He has seen death more than once.

    C He refers to his grave as his "mother."

    D Most people refer to death as an event not a person.

_____ **14.** After the rioters abandon their search for Death, they murder one another. This act is an example of —

    F dramatic irony

    G situational irony

    H poetic irony

    J verbal irony

VOCABULARY DEVELOPMENT *(20 points; 4 points each)*

On the line provided, write the Vocabulary word that *best* completes the sentence.

avarice	abominable	superfluity	grisly	adversary
pallor	prudent	transcend	credentials	absolve

15. It is not considered _____ to go out looking for Death.

16. _____ , or greed, is one of the seven deadly sins.

17. Once in a while a great writer like Chaucer can _____ even his own talent.

18. Death is the _____ of all living things.

19. The Pardoner is a sinner whose job is to _____ others of their sins.

CONSTRUCTED RESPONSE *(20 points)*

20. What is the most valid moral that you find in "The Pardoner's Tale"—in other words, what message or idea in it still applies *best* to life today? On a separate sheet of paper, discuss how this message is delivered in the tale. Analyze any way in which the message is **ironic,** such as a discrepancy between the tale and the teller; between what is expected and what happens; or between what is said and what is meant.

SELECTION TEST ▓▓▓▓▓▓▓

from The Wife of Bath's Tale

Geoffrey Chaucer *translated by* Nevill Coghill

COMPREHENSION *(40 points; 4 points each)*

On the line provided, write the letter of the *best* answer to each of the following items.

_____ **1.** The knight undertakes a quest to —

    A discover the most beautiful noblewoman in England

    B find a perfect wife for himself

    C learn what it is that women want most

    D protect women from evil upon the road to Canterbury

_____ **2.** The knight's quest is a(n) —

    F task given to him by the queen

    G test of courage set by the king

    H ambitious mission he sets himself

    J duty imposed on him by the church

_____ **3.** Before he sees the old woman in the woods, the knight sees —

    A the figure of Death

    B more than twenty-four ladies dancing

    C his own face reflected in a pool of water

    D his own future in a dream

_____ **4.** According to the old woman, what women really want is —

    F money, jewels, and treasure

    G to be flattered and attended to

    H freedom and entertainment

    J mastery over their husbands

_____ **5.** As a reward for giving him the answer that will save his life, the old woman demands —

    A a large sum of money

    B to learn the secret of youth

    C to marry the knight

    D to be pardoned by the queen

_____ **6.** The knight shows that he has learned what women want most when he —

    F keeps his promise to return after a year and a day

    G agrees to marry the old woman

    H pays the old woman as much as she asks

    J asks his wife to decide which form she will take

_____ **7.** The old woman makes an eloquent philosophical argument about —

   A the harmfulness of greed

   B true and false gentility and virtue

   C the differences between men and women

   D the magical beauty of nature

_____ **8.** The Wife of Bath's philosophy of marriage shows that she —

   F is a strong person with a keen sense of her own rights

   G tends to say one thing and do the opposite

   H cares only for pleasure, not for right and wrong

   J   trusts too much to thought instead of feeling

_____ **9.** Chaucer's characterizations of the Prioress, the Monk, and others connected with the church are *mainly* —

   A idealized

   B realistic

   C flattering

   D satirical

_____ **10.** Who narrates the tale about the knight and the old woman?

   F The knight

   G The old woman

   H The Wife of Bath

   J   Chaucer

LITERARY FOCUS: NARRATOR AND COUPLETS *(15 points; 5 points each)*
On the line provided, write the letter of the *best* answer to each of the following items.

_____ **11.** The **narrator** of a story should *not* be confused with —

   A the author

   B the main character

   C one of the minor characters

   D the storytelling voice

_____ **12.** Which adjective does *not* describe the Wife of Bath's narrative voice?

   F mournful

   G witty

   H lively

   J   earthy

The Wife of Bath's Tale

_____ **13.** Which of the following quotations from "The Wife of Bath's Tale" is a **couplet**?

    A "In honor to us both, I don't care which; / Whatever pleases you suffices me."

    B "The knight thought long, and with a piteous groan / At last he said, with all the care in life . . ."

    C "His heart went bathing in a bath of blisses / And melted in a hundred thousand kisses . . ."

    D "May I go howling mad and take my life / Unless I prove to be as good and true . . ."

READING SKILLS: INTERPRETING CHARACTER *(5 points)*

_____ **14.** The Wife of Bath's opinions suggest that she may be described by all the following words *except* —

    F well-read

    G humorous

    H modest

    J bossy

VOCABULARY DEVELOPMENT *(20 points; 4 points each)*

On the line provided, write the letter of the choice that is the *best* synonym for the Vocabulary word.

_____ **15.** pestilence

    A insect

    B termite

    C poison

    D plague

_____ **16.** contemptuous

    F scornful

    G respectful

    H admiring

    J indifferent

_____ **17.** prowess

    A lack

    B ability

    C foresight

    D judgment

NAME _____ CLASS _____ DATE _____ SCORE _____

_____ **18.** reprove

      F approve

      G decide

      H disapprove

      J doubt

_____ **19.** concede

      A grant

      B dispute

      C contest

      D overcome

CONSTRUCTED RESPONSE *(20 points)*

20. Based on "The Wife of Bath's Tale," what is Chaucer's view of life? Compare and contrast Chaucer's view with the Wife of Bath's view of life. Give evidence from the text for the presence of each view of life. Write your answer on a separate sheet of paper.

SELECTION TEST   LITERARY RESPONSE AND ANALYSIS

Right-Mind and Wrong-Mind
from the Panchatantra   *translated by* Arthur William Ryder

COMPREHENSION *(40 points; 4 points each)*

On the line provided, write the letter of the *best* answer to each of the following items.

_____ **1.** Right-Mind and Wrong-Mind are *not* —

    A friends

    B princes

    C sons of merchants

    D symbolic figures

_____ **2.** Wrong-Mind commits a crime against Right-Mind when Wrong-Mind —

    F tricks Right-Mind into stealing the money

    G forces Right-Mind to violate a sacred duty

    H steals the money and blames Right-Mind

    J kills a heron and blames Right-Mind

_____ **3.** When Wrong-Mind accuses Right-Mind of stealing, Right-Mind —

    A quotes verse to proclaim his innocence

    B retires to his tent to sulk

    C appeals to Wrong-Mind's father for help

    D willingly takes on Wrong-Mind's guilt

_____ **4.** When the court threatens Wrong-Mind with a trial by ordeal, he —

    F confesses his guilt and asks for mercy

    G claims he has a forest goddess as a witness

    H bribes the judges

    J turns into a heron and flies away

_____ **5.** To persuade his son not to carry out the deception, Wrong-Mind's father —

    A tells a story

    B whips Wrong-Mind

    C prays for Wrong-Mind

    D delivers a stern lecture to Wrong-Mind

_____ **6.** Right-Mind exposes Wrong-Mind's treachery by —

    F bringing in several gods and goddesses for his defense

    G reciting holy chants

    H winning the trial by ordeal

    J smoking out the fake forest goddess

_____ **7.** When the court discovers the truth, Right-Mind is —

    A hanged from a branch of the mimosa tree

    B serenaded with poetry

    C rewarded with the king's favor

    D jailed for stealing the money

_____ **8.** The story of Right-Mind and Wrong-Mind is used as a frame story for —

    F the *Panchatantra*

    G a second story about the same characters

    H "A Remedy Worse Than the Disease"

    J the punishment of Wrong-Mind

_____ **9.** The heron in the inner story is like Wrong-Mind because both —

    A are thieves

    B are named after human qualities

    C try to solve their problems in ways that only bring more suffering

    D care more for money than for their loved ones

_____ **10.** The crab in the inner story is like Wrong-Mind because both —

    F are deceitful

    G lie about hidden treasure

    H are punished in the end

    J wish ill to their fathers

LITERARY FOCUS: FABLE *(20 points; 5 points each)*
On the line provided, write the letter of the *best* answer to each of the following items.

_____ **11. Fables** always —

    A are short

    B come from ancient times

    C teach lessons

    D are about animals

_____ **12.** A **beast fable** is a fable in which —

    F humans act like animals

    G animals speak or act like humans

    H humans use beasts for transportation, work, or food

    J animals make war against one another

_____ **13.** An **epigram** is a(n) —

    A signature in fancy handwriting

    B sealed letter sent by one noble to another

    C brief, clever verse with a moral

    D fable

_____ **14.** The **moral** of "Right-Mind and Wrong-Mind" might be stated as —

    F "Be honest."

    G "Do not kill."

    H "Do not try to be what you are not."

    J "Make sure you are right, and then act."

VOCABULARY DEVELOPMENT *(20 points; 4 points each)*

Match the definition on the left with the Vocabulary word on the right. On the line provided, write the letter of the Vocabulary word.

_____ **15.** cunning; treachery

_____ **16.** leftover portion; remainder

_____ **17.** preparing for the main event; introductory

_____ **18.** the action of making the first move

_____ **19.** recognize; make out clearly

    a. initiative

    b. discern

    c. duplicity

    d. residue

    e. preliminary

CONSTRUCTED RESPONSE *(20 points)*

20. How do you think "Right-Mind and Wrong-Mind" would have been different if it had been written by Chaucer? How do you think it would have remained the same? Write your answer on a separate sheet of paper.

from The Third Voyage of Sindbad the Sailor
from The Thousand and One Nights   *translated by* N. J. Dawood

COMPREHENSION *(40 points; 4 points each)*

On the line provided, write the letter of the *best* answer to each of the following items.

_____ **1.** Sindbad decides to go to sea again because he —

    A is bored and wants profit and adventure

    B is being hunted by the authorities and must escape

    C wants to learn more about foreign customs

    D wants to find a bride across the sea

_____ **2.** Why does the captain of the ship get upset when the wind blows the ship off course?

    F He doesn't know how to navigate.

    G He isn't sure where they are.

    H They are dangerously close to the island of the dwarves.

    J They are running out of supplies.

_____ **3.** What do the dwarves *not* do when they see Sindbad's ship?

    A Board the ship

    B Kill the crew

    C Take over the ship

    D Sail the ship away

_____ **4.** When Sindbad and his companions enter the palace courtyard, there is a hint of danger when they see a —

    F lion in a cage

    G knife that can cut holes in the universe

    H table laid with fattening foods

    J large heap of bones

_____ **5.** The giant passes over Sindbad and chooses another victim because Sindbad —

    A tearfully pleads for his life

    B successfully hides from the giant

    C is too thin

    D is too strong

_____ **6.** What does the giant do to his victims?

    F Makes them wrestle him

    G Roasts and eats them

    H Asks them a riddle that can't be solved

    J Feeds them until they cannot walk

_____ **7.** Why don't Sindbad and the others hide from the giant?

    A They can find nowhere on the island to hide.

    B They are under the giant's spell and cannot leave.

    C The giant locks them inside the palace.

    D The giant ties them all together.

_____ **8.** Sindbad and his companions try to stop the giant by —

    F tying him up as he sleeps

    G putting a spell on him

    H thrusting hot iron spits into his eyes, blinding him

    J poisoning him

_____ **9.** Sindbad's good planning allows him to escape the island when he thinks of building —

    A a signal fire, and it alerts a passing ship

    B a canoe, and in it he escapes alone

    C the house, and he then swims off the island

    D a raft, and on it he and others row away

_____ **10.** What *final* surprise does the giant have for Sindbad?

    F The giant has a hidden third eye.

    G He and a hag chase Sindbad and his crew and throw boulders at the raft.

    H He leaps on the lion's back and follows Sindbad.

    J He cries out to the dwarves and gets their help in attacking the sailors.

LITERARY FOCUS: ARCHETYPES *(20 points; 5 points each)*

On the line provided, write the letter of the *best* answer to each of the following items.

_____ **11.** An **archetype** is a(n) —

    A exaggerated example

    B important church official

    C memory device used in storytelling

    D very old pattern used in storytelling

_____ **12.** **Archetypes** can appear as all of the following elements *except* a —

    F plot

    G character

    H new idea

    J familiar setting

_____ **13.** All of the following elements in "The Third Voyage of Sindbad the Sailor" are **archetypes** *except* a(n) —

    A voyage of profit and adventure

    B race of dwarfs with monkey features

    C island with unknown inhabitants

    D monster who eats men

_____ **14.** Sindbad and Scheherazade have one thing in common: They both —

    F are sailors

    G are threatened by the sultan

    H live in the same time and place

    J narrate stories

VOCABULARY DEVELOPMENT *(20 points; 4 points each)*

On the line provided, write a short answer to each of the following questions.

15. If you eat a meal **disconsolately,** how do you eat it?

_____

16. What does a **corpulent** person look like?

_____

17. Do you want people's **approbation**? Why or why not?

_____

18. If a softball fielder makes an error, does he or she field the ball **nimbly** or not?

_____

19. "We **contrived** to escape," says a sailor. Did he succeed or fail at escaping?

_____

CONSTRUCTED RESPONSE *(20 points)*

20. On a separate sheet of paper, describe the characteristics of an **archetype** that you think Sindbad belongs to. Then, analyze how Sindbad represents his era rather than just being a universal archetype.

SELECTION TEST

Federigo's Falcon *from the* Decameron
Giovanni Boccaccio *translated by* Mark Musa *and* Peter Bondanella

COMPREHENSION *(40 points; 4 points each)*

On the line provided, write the letter of the *best* answer to each of the following items.

_____ **1.** Federigo uses up his family fortune by —

    A spending it on hunting with his falcon

    B spending it on foreign travel

    C putting it into bad investments

    D wasting it trying to impress Monna Giovanna

_____ **2.** Leaving Florence for Campi, Federigo lives —

    F simply on his one remaining farm

    G outdoors, walking from village to village

    H with relatives who still have wealth

    J on loans that he cannot repay

_____ **3.** Why does Monna Giovanna move closer to Federigo after the death of her husband?

    A It is the custom among Italian widows of her time to grieve in the country.

    B She is planning to return Federigo's love.

    C She hopes the country air will cure her son.

    D She wants Federigo's protection.

_____ **4.** What does Monna Giovanna's son think will cure him?

    F A richer diet

    G A simpler diet such as the one peasants are used to

    H Federigo's falcon

    J A friendly visit from Federigo

_____ **5.** When she first presents herself to Federigo at his farm, Monna Giovanna —

    A begs his forgiveness for her past coldness

    B implores him to move to the city, away from her

    C declares that she really has loved him all along

    D invites herself to dinner

_____ **6.** In honor of Monna Giovanna, Federigo —

    F invites her to stay for the weekend

    G asks for her hand in marriage

    H sings a song he has written for her

    J serves her a dish of roast falcon

_____ **7.** According to Monna Giovanna, what allows her to defy good manners and impose upon Federigo?

    A The fact that they know they love each other.

    B The fact that she is the mother of a sick child.

    C She is so wealthy and beautiful that the rules do not apply to her.

    D They are neighbors and thus must help each other.

_____ **8.** When Federigo realizes he has made a terrible mistake, he —

    F weeps over his bad luck

    G shrugs it off and tries again

    H laughs at the irony of fate

    J coldly reproaches Monna Giovanna

_____ **9.** Monna Giovanna's son eventually —

    A becomes an expert falconer

    B dies

    C becomes like a son to Federigo

    D grows up to become the author of "Federigo's Falcon"

_____ **10.** Monna Giovanna finally —

    F rejects Federigo because of his poverty

    G marries Federigo because of his merit and noble birth

    H marries Federigo for his money and social position

    J rejects Federigo to enter a convent

LITERARY FOCUS: SITUATIONAL IRONY *(15 points; 5 points each)*

On the line provided, write the letter of the *best* answer to each of the following items.

_____ **11.** In **situational irony** —

    A what is said is the opposite of what is meant

    B someone behaves deceptively toward people who trust him or her

    C what is expected is the opposite of what happens

    D the actors know something that the characters they play don't know

_____ **12.** The *main* situational irony in the story is that —

    F Federigo and Monna Giovanna love each other but can never marry

    G shortly after their marriage, Federigo and Monna Giovanna realize they no longer love each other

    H although Federigo gives the boy the falcon, the boy dies anyway

    J Federigo kills the thing which Monna Giovanna is about to ask him for

_____ **13.** Which of the following aspects of the story's ending shows situational irony?

    A Monna Giovanna's brothers urge her to marry but oppose her choice of man.

    B Federigo is "a man without money" rather than "money without a man."

    C The reader expects a happy ending, but the son's death prevents a truly happy ending.

    D Federigo and Monna Giovanna return to Florence.

READING SKILLS: EVALUATING HISTORICAL CONTEXT *(5 points)*

_____ **14.** What is *most* remarkable about the enduring fame of Boccaccio's *Decameron*?

    F It graphically depicts the horrors of the Black Death of 1348.

    G It describes human relationships that are limited to its own time.

    H Boccaccio didn't think much of it, but it is the best record of life in Italy at the time.

    J Chaucer read it when he was in Italy, and it influenced his *The Canterbury Tales*.

VOCABULARY DEVELOPMENT *(20 points; 4 points each)*
On the line provided, write the letter of the *best* answer to each of the following items.

_____ **15. Dire** poverty is —

    A extreme poverty

    B poverty in money but not in spirit

    C temporary poverty

    D unexpected poverty

_____ **16.** To **compensate** someone is to —

    F pay the person back

    G leave the person alone

    H take the person's trust

    J take the person's goods

_____ **17.** Which of the following situations shows **presumption**?

    A A dog who plays with a cat

    B A falcon that kills a mouse

    C A person who asks a stranger for money

    D A crow that is scared by a scarecrow

_____ **18.** "I shall never be able to **console** myself again" means —

    F "I will never go hungry again."

    G "I will never be full again."

    H "I shall always be in sorrow."

    J "I will never get away with it again."

_____ **19.** To be **reproached** is to be —

    A doubted

    B disapproved of

    C rewarded

    D summoned

CONSTRUCTED RESPONSE (20 points)

20. In what ways did Federigo and Monna act as they did because they were fourteenth-century Florentines, and in what ways did they act as they did because they were a man and a woman, regardless of historical era? Which of the two kinds of influences do you think was greater? Write your answer on a separate sheet of paper.

SELECTION TEST   LITERARY RESPONSE AND ANALYSIS

from The Day of Destiny *from* Le Morte d'Arthur
Sir Thomas Malory   *retold by* Keith Baines

COMPREHENSION *(40 points; 4 points each)*

On the line provided, write the letter of the *best* answer to each of the following items.

_____ **1.** In a dream that foretells his own death, King Arthur —

    A is stabbed by his own son, Modred

    B is taken on a barge to Avalon

    C is flung into water where monstrous beasts await him

    D finds a magical sword stuck into a stone

_____ **2.** What does Sir Gawain advise King Arthur to do?

    F Surrender to Modred

    G Attack Modred by night

    H Talk peace with Modred, then wait for Launcelot

    J Challenge Modred to single combat in front of both armies

_____ **3.** The two leaders meet between their massed armies in order to —

    A fight single-handedly

    B call their armies to attack

    C pray for a sign from heaven

    D sign a treaty

_____ **4.** How does the battle start?

    F King Arthur orders his men forward.

    G Modred cries out, "Kill my father and his evil knights!"

    H A bugle call sets things in motion automatically.

    J A soldier unthinkingly flashes his sword, and the armies react.

_____ **5.** As night falls, how many men are left standing on the battlefield?

    A Modred, Arthur, and two of Arthur's followers

    B Arthur alone, Modred, and one of Modred's best knights

    C Only Arthur and Modred

    D Only Modred

_____ **6.** Who is the only survivor of the battle?

    F Sir Bedivere

    G Sir Lucas

    H Modred

    J Arthur

_____ **7.** Sir Bedivere disappoints King Arthur by —

     A going over to Modred's side

     B failing to throw Arthur's sword into the lake

     C running away with Arthur's sword

     D running away from the battle

_____ **8.** What happens to King Arthur's sword in the end?

     F A hand rising from the lake pulls the sword underwater.

     G It remains lodged in the body of Modred.

     H Sir Bedivere takes it for his own.

     J King Arthur falls upon it, with Sir Bedivere's help.

_____ **9.** How does King Arthur get to Avalon?

     A Arthur, severely wounded, hobbles there himself.

     B A boat full of beautiful ladies wearing black hoods take him there.

     C Arthur's few remaining knights carry him there on his shield.

     D Arthur's chief magical advisor, Merlin, arranges a magical trip.

_____ **10.** "HIC IACET ARTHURUS, REX QUONDAM REXQUE FUTURUS" means —

     F "Jacketed by night and mist, here the great Arthur lies."

     G "He pulled the sword out of the stone, and now he is stone himself."

     H "Here lies Arthur, the once and future king."

     J "Arthur was once king here, but every man must be a king."

LITERARY FOCUS: ROMANCE HERO (20 points; 5 points each)

On the line provided, write the letter of the *best* answer to each of the following items.

_____ **11.** Which of the following **archetypes** has the *most* in common with the **romance hero**?

     A Epic hero

     B Wise old man

     C Fatal temptress

     D Best friend

_____ **12.** The **romance hero's** childhood usually does *not* include —

     F mysterious origins

     G obscure upbringing

     H wealthy surroundings

     J magical initiation

_____ **13.** The **romance hero** is *usually* aided by —

  A faithful wives and children

  B hard work and determination

  C magical weapons, loyal followers, and wise mentors

  D a Round Table of more than a hundred knights

_____ **14.** Which of King Arthur's final actions most clearly shows him to be a **romance hero**?

  F Suffering a disaster on the battlefield

  G Being troubled by a bad dream

  H Killing his illegitimate son

  J Hinting that he will return in the distant future

VOCABULARY DEVELOPMENT *(20 points; 4 points each)*

Match the definition on the left with the Vocabulary word on the right. On the line provided, write the letter of the Vocabulary word.

_____ **15.** gained the desired effect   **a.** righteous

_____ **16.** shaking in a threatening way   **b.** prevailed

_____ **17.** morally right   **c.** piteous

_____ **18.** deserving of pity   **d.** dissuade

_____ **19.** advise against   **e.** brandishing

CONSTRUCTED RESPONSE *(20 points)*

20. Imagine that you are one of the first citizens of England to read *Le Morte d'Arthur* when it is first published in 1485. How accurate do you find the book as a portrait of life in your time? To answer this question, use your knowledge of the Middle Ages as well as your reading of this selection. Write your answer on a separate sheet of paper.

COLLECTION 2 SUMMATIVE TEST

The Middle Ages 1066–1485: The Tales They Told

This Norman-French ballad tells a sad tale about a forester's son who is in love with a woman, although he has little chance of winning her hand in marriage. Immersed in thoughts of being with her, he does not realize that she is dead. Read the poem carefully, and then answer the questions that follow.

Ballade de Marguerite

translated by Oscar Wilde

> I am weary of lying within the chase
> When the knights are meeting in the market-place.
>
> Nay, go not thou to the red-roofed town
> Lest the hoofs of the war-horse tread thee down.
>
> 5   But I would not go where the Squires ride,
> I would only walk by my Lady's side.
>
> Alack, and alack, thou art overbold,
> A Forester's son may not eat of gold.
>
> Will she love me the less that my Father is seen
> 10   Each Martinmas day in a doublet green?
>
> Perchance she is sewing at tapestries;
> Spindle and loom are not meet for thee.
>
> Ah, if she is working the arras bright
> I might ravel the threads by the fire-light.
>
> 15   Perchance she is hunting of the deer,
> How could you follow o'er hill and mere?
>
> Ah, if she is riding with the court,
> I might run beside her and wind the morte.
>
> Perchance she is kneeling in St. Denis,
> 20   (On her soul may our Lady have gramercy).
>
> Ah, if she is praying in lone chapelle,
> I might swing the censer and ring the bell.
>
> Come in, my son, for you look sae pale,
> The father shall fill thee a stoop of ale.
>
> 25   But who are these knights in bright array?
> Is it a pageant the rich folks play?
>
> 'Tis the king of England from over the sea,
> Who has come unto visit our fair countrie.
>
> But why does the curfew toll sae low?
> 30   And why do the mourners walk a-row?
>
> A 'tis Hugh of Amiens, my sister's son,
> Who is lying stark, for his day is done.

Nay, nay, for I see white lilies clear;
It is no strong man who lies on the <u>bier</u>.

35 O 'tis old Dame Jeannette that kept the hall,
I knew she would die at the autumn fall.

Dame Jeannette has not that gold-brown hair,
Old Jeannette was not a maiden fair.

O 'tis none of our kith and none of our kin,
40 (Her soul may our Lady assoil from sin).

But I hear the boy's voice chaunting sweet,
"Elle est morte, la Marguerite."

Come in, my son, and lie on the bed,
And let the dead folk bury their dead.

45 O mother, you know I loved her true:
O mother, hath one grave room for two?

VOCABULARY SKILLS *(15 points; 3 points each)*

On the line provided, write the letter of the word or phrase that *best* completes each sentence.

_____ **1.** The spindle and the loom are not **meet** (line 12) for the lady because they are —

   A too difficult to learn to use

   B broken

   C too elegant for someone of her rank

   D not suitable for someone of her social status

_____ **2.** If the lady is sewing **tapestries** (line 11), she is probably making —

   F sweaters to keep out winter's cold

   G pictures on cloth

   H armor for her love

   J her own dresses

_____ **3.** "Knights in bright **array**" (line 25) means that the knights are —

   A soldiers

   B actively engaged in combat

   C splendidly outfitted

   D riding on prancing horses

_____ **4.** A **bier** (line 34) is a —

   F platform for a coffin

   G bed

   H hot, reviving drink

   J fancy carriage

_____ **5.** If the forester's son follows the lady "o'er hill and **mere**" (line 16), he follows her —

    A over hills and underground

    B past the stream and the mill

    C over hills and by lakes

    D past the hill, but no further

COMPREHENSION (15 points; 3 points each)

On the line provided, write the letter of the *best* answer to each of the following items.

_____ **6.** The two speakers in the ballad can be identified as —

    F a young couple in love

    G a knight and a forester's son

    H two neighbor women

    J a mother and her son

_____ **7.** The young man is eager to —

    A joust with the other knights

    B court Lady Marguerite

    C attend an important funeral

    D learn how to be a squire

_____ **8.** The young man's desires are unrealistic because of difference between his and the young lady's —

    F classes

    G ages

    H religions

    J nationalities

_____ **9.** As they speak, the woman and the young man are observing —

    A a great hunt in the fields

    B Marguerite on her way to church

    C Marguerite riding with members of the court

    D a funeral procession

_____ **10.** The woman's responses to the young man's questions indicate that she is —

    F ignorant of his feelings

    G unaware of what is going on in town

    H trying to shield him from the truth

    J deceitful and jealous

READING SKILLS AND STRATEGIES *(15 points; 5 points each)*
Analyzing Style: Details

_____ **11.** The young forester's son in "Ballade de Marguerite" imagines that Marguerite may be involved in various activities, such as sewing, hunting, and praying. For each of these activities he imagines himself as her —

    A husband

    B employer

    C servant

    D priest

Interpreting Character

_____ **12.** Based on his comments on life and death, you could assume that the forester's son is inclined to be —

    F shy

    G pessimistic

    H jovial

    J demonstrative

Evaluating Historical Context

_____ **13.** Based on the period in which this ballad was popular and the places mentioned in it, you might assume it originated in —

    A France

    B England

    C Italy

    D Canterbury or Florence

LITERARY FOCUS: CONSTRUCTED RESPONSE *(55 points)*
Identifying the Characteristics of a Ballad *(10 points)*

14. What makes this poem a **ballad**? Discuss the elements of ballad form that the poem does (or does not) contain. Discuss both the form of the ballad and its contents. How is "Ballade de Marguerite" similar to, and different from, the other ballads you have read in this chapter, "Lord Randall" and "Get Up and Bar the Door"? (For example, how is its tone different from the tones of those ballads?)

Identifying and Evaluating Historical Content *(15 points)*

15. If no one had told you the time frame of this selection, how could you tell from reading the poem that it is set in the Middle Ages? On a separate sheet of paper, present as many clues as you can find, analyzing all three of the following elements:

(1) the **story** the poem tells (its setting, characters, events, etc.)

(2) the poem's **meaning** (the themes, issues, social relations, and views of life depicted or implied in the poem)

(3) the poem's **language and style**

Analyzing Irony *(15 points)*

16. Where in the poem can you find **situational irony**? In your answer, include a definition of **situational irony**, and show that it applies to this case. Write your answer on a separate sheet of paper.

Analyzing an Archetype *(15 points)*

17. How does the young man in the poem match the ideal, or **archetype**, of the courtly lover? How does he not match it? Write your answer on a separate sheet of paper.

LITERATURE
INFORMATIONAL TEXT
VOCABULARY

The Renaissance 1485–1660:
A Flourish of Genius

On the line provided, write the letter of the *best* answer to each of the following items.
(100 points; 10 points each)

_____ **1.** A fourteen-line poem that traditionally conforms to strict patterns of rhythm and rhyme is known as a(n) —

    A couplet

    B sestet

    C ode

    D sonnet

_____ **2.** A speech that an actor delivers to the audience when no one else is onstage is called a(n) —

    F dialogue

    G soliloquy

    H aside

    J monologue

_____ **3. Tone** can *best* be described as the writer's —

    A choice of words

    B philosophical beliefs

    C attitude toward the reader, a subject, or a character

    D central idea about human experience

_____ **4.** What is a **paradox**?

    F An apparent contradiction that is actually true

    G An illogical comparison

    H A false statement

    J An idea that is implied, not stated

_____ **5.** Which of the following quotations contains an example of **parallelism, or parallel structure**?

    A "Let tyrants fear."

    B "Farewell, thou child of my right hand, and joy"

    C "Read not to contradict and confute; nor to believe and take for granted; nor to find talk and discourse; but to weigh and consider."

    D "No man prospers so suddenly as by others' errors."

_____ **6.** The unique manner in which writers use language to express their ideas is known as —

    F mood

    G point of view

    H style

    J cadence

_____ **7.** Which of the following quotations contains **personification**?

    A "Shall I compare thee to a summer's day?"

    B "My mistress, when she walks, treads on the ground."

    C "Revenge is a kind of wild justice"

    D "There will the river whispering run"

_____ **8.** When comparing authors' **points of view** about a subject, you should —

    F dismiss ideas that an author implies but does not state

    G consider the time period in which each author wrote the work

    H look only for similarities between the arguments

    J disregard the authors' choice of words

_____ **9.** A knowledge of **Greek and Latin roots** can help you do all of the following *except* —

    A recognize that particular mathematical terms have related meanings

    B define certain unfamiliar scientific terms

    C understand the origin of some medical terms

    D appreciate the complexity of a biological process

_____ **10.** Which of the following statements about **synonyms** is *false*?

    F Synonyms must derive from the same root.

    G Synonyms can have nearly the same meaning.

    H Synonyms may have different connotations.

    J The contexts in which two synonyms are used may differ.

LITERARY PERIOD INTRODUCTION TEST

The Renaissance 1485–1660:
A Flourish of Genius

COMPREHENSION *(100 points; 10 points each)*

On the line provided, write the letter of the *best* answer to each of the following items.

_____ 1. Why are historical periods inexact and generally unknown to the people who live during them?

    A They are too complex to be understood by most people.

    B They are named later by historians to describe general trends rather than precise beginnings and endings.

    C They come and go with such suddenness that people usually cannot distinguish what historical period they live in.

    D They are completely artificial constructs and have no basis in documented reality.

_____ 2. Which of the following statements *best* characterizes the intellectual environment of the Renaissance?

    F Most people could not read, in part because they could not gain access to books.

    G Most Europeans were highly sensitive to the achievements of people from other cultures, particularly people of the Middle East.

    H As people became interested in the writings of ancient Greece and Rome, they became more inquisitive and creative.

    J Through their superior knowledge, scholars established power over the masses.

_____ 3. The intellectual movement known as **humanism** —

    A joined the wisdom of the classics with that of the Bible, emphasizing ideals of wisdom and virtue

    B taught that people should use knowledge to accumulate wealth and achieve fame

    C accepted the teachings of the classics but rejected those of the Bible

    D could not tolerate contradictory texts and thus could not refer to many ancient books

_____ 4. Why did the invention of printing with movable type have a great impact?

    F Printed documents were more beautiful than handwritten ones.

    G The wide availability of reading material allowed ideas to spread quickly.

    H Books became more expensive and therefore were more valued.

    J The ability to print with movable type gave Germany an edge over other countries.

_____ **5.** How did the monk Martin Luther contribute to the beginning of the Reformation?

    A By renewing people's devotion to studying and following the words of the pope

    B By teaching that other religions were as valid as Christianity

    C By developing a personal form of Christianity not based on papal decrees

    D By ridiculing ancient habits and traditions, such as superstition

_____ **6.** In the mid-1500s, many people in England were dissatisfied with the Church of England because they —

    F felt that the church was insufficiently reformed, merely a copy of Catholicism

    G felt that the pope was too remote, and they wanted him to have more of a presence in England

    H were beginning to reject the idea of leading a religious life

    J disagreed with the idea that religion was a private matter between the individual and God

_____ **7.** King Henry VIII of England could be considered a "Renaissance man" because he —

    A went to extremes to ensure that he had a male heir

    B ended foreign invasions of England by creating the royal navy

    C was arrogant, ruthless, and an unfaithful husband

    D was literary, musical, athletic, and scholarly

_____ **8.** England's independence from the Catholic countries of the Mediterranean was ensured by —

    F Gutenberg's invention of the printing press

    G the English navy's defeat of the Spanish Armada in 1588

    H the readmission of Jews to England

    J Queen Elizabeth I's execution of Mary Stuart, Queen of Scots

_____ **9.** What caused an eleven-year gap in the line of English monarchs between 1649 and 1660?

    A England was ruled by a woman, Queen Elizabeth I.

    B That was the period described in the Book of Judges, where each person did what was right in his or her own eyes.

    C England was ruled by Parliament and by the Puritan dictator Oliver Cromwell.

    D A change in the calendar system resulted in a gap in the records of leadership for those years.

_____ **10.** The end of the English Renaissance was characterized by —

    F increased growth of moral and religious values

    G the pillaging of resources from the Americas

    H the rise of humanism as a way of thought and study

    J increasing interest in secular, rather than religious, values

Holt Assessment: Literature, Reading, and Vocabulary

SELECTION TEST   LITERARY RESPONSE AND ANALYSIS

The Passionate Shepherd to His Love
Christopher Marlowe

The Nymph's Reply to the Shepherd Sir Walter Raleigh

To the Virgins, to Make Much of Time Robert Herrick

To His Coy Mistress Andrew Marvell

Give Us This Day Our Daily Bread
Joseph Papp *and* Elizabeth Kirkland

COMPREHENSION *(40 points; 4 points each)*

On the line provided, write the letter of the *best* answer to each of the following items.

_____ **1.** In "The Passionate Shepherd to His Love," the shepherd offers the charms of —

   A monetary wealth

   B lifelong love

   C rustic pleasures

   D a long life

_____ **2.** The speaker in "The Nymph's Reply to the Shepherd" regards the shepherd's promised pleasures as being —

   F realistic

   G temporary

   H too few

   J perfect

_____ **3.** The speakers in the two poems —

   A strongly agree

   B strongly disagree

   C are uncertain

   D form a meeting of the minds

_____ **4.** The shepherd's plea might have been accepted by a woman who —

   F had lived in the country before

   G did not want luxury

   H did not believe she would grow old

   J had a pessimistic view of life

_____ **5.** The two poems are similar in —

    A fundamental views of life

    B emotions expressed

    C no way

    D form, length, and rhythm

_____ **6.** The speaker in "To the Virgins, to Make Much of Time" uses the setting of the sun to emphasize —

    F his love

    G a religious faith

    H respect for the elderly

    J the shortness of life

_____ **7.** In "To the Virgins, to Make Much of Time," the line "That age is best which is the first" means —

    A this is the best century to live in

    B the older you are, the wiser you become

    C youth is the best time of life

    D life is what you make it

_____ **8.** Both Herrick and Marvell urge young women to —

    F wait for the right man before marrying

    G travel to distant parts of the world

    H love passionately without waiting any longer

    J value their old age as much as their youth

_____ **9.** In "To His Coy Mistress" the speaker says that he would wait patiently for the woman he addresses if —

    A there were no limit to our time on earth

    B she were not so reluctant

    C she would assure him of her eventual consent

    D he had more wealth to offer her

_____ **10.** Which of the following images from "To His Coy Mistress" *best* emphasizes the speaker's sense of urgency?

    F "by the Indian Ganges' side . . ."

    G "To walk, and pass our long love's day . . ."

    H "My vegetable love should grow / Vaster than empires and more slow; . . ."

    J "But at my back I always hear / Time's wingèd chariot hurrying near; . . ."

LITERARY FOCUS: PASTORAL AND CARPE DIEM (40 points; 10 points each)

On the line provided, write the letter of the *best* answer to each of the following items.

_____ **11.** The word *pastoral*, describing a kind of poem about country life, comes from the Latin word meaning —

    A country, or rural

    B shepherd

    C priest or minister

    D farmer

_____ **12.** How is the depiction of rural life in pastoral poems different from its depiction in "Give Us This Day Our Daily Bread"?

    F The article emphasizes peasants' religious faith, while pastoral poems downplay it.

    G Peasants in real life were not as rough and uneducated as in pastoral poems.

    H There are few significant differences between the two depictions.

    J The article depicts rural life realistically; pastoral poems depict rural life idealistically.

_____ **13.** Which of the following phrases *best* summarizes the idea of *carpe diem*?

    A Live life to the fullest.

    B Hope for the unattainable.

    C Love from afar.

    D Take what does not belong to you.

_____ **14.** Which quotation from the poems *best* relates to the concept of *carpe diem*?

    F "The glorious lamp of heaven . . ."

    G "Sits on thy skin like morning dew, . . ."

    H "Old Time is still a-flying; . . ."

    J "My vegetable love should grow . . ."

CONSTRUCTED RESPONSE (20 points)

15. Based on the four poems and the Connection article, "Give Us This Day Our Daily Bread," what is your impression of what life was like in Renaissance England? On a separate sheet of paper, cite specific images from the poems and the article to support your view.

SELECTION TEST ▮▮▮▮▮▮ **LITERARY RESPONSE AND ANALYSIS**

Sonnet 29, Sonnet 30 William Shakespeare

COMPREHENSION (40 points; 4 points each)

On the line provided, write the letter of the *best* answer to each of the following items.

_____ 1. The first four lines of Sonnet 29 could be paraphrased as —

    A when I think about how much I miss my beloved . . .

    B when I sit alone and feel sorry for myself and my bad luck . . .

    C when I get into a fight with my friends and we curse one another . . .

    D when I make a fortune and don't know what to do with it . . .

_____ 2. In lines 5–7 of Sonnet 29 the speaker wishes for some of the things other people have. Which of the following things does he *not* mention?

    F Money

    G Artistic ability

    H Power

    J Popularity

_____ 3. The speaker rouses himself out of his sadness by —

    A remembering that he is able to write fine poetry

    B recalling good times he has had with his friends

    C summoning his family around the fire

    D thinking of the person he loves

_____ 4. In lines 10–12, the speaker compares a bird at daybreak to his —

    F beloved

    G body

    H mood

    J poetry

_____ 5. Sonnet 29 concludes with a feeling of —

    A jealousy

    B doom

    C doubt

    D happiness

_____ 6. "When to the sessions of sweet silent thought / I summon up remembrance of things past" means —

    F When I think about the past . . .

    G When I try to forget the past . . .

    H When I have to go to court . . .

    J When I behave more sweetly than I feel inside . . .

_____ **7.** What kind of sorrow does the speaker think about in line 3 of Sonnet 30 when he says, "I sigh the lack of many a thing I sought"?

    A Sorrow over things he wanted but never got

    B Sorrow over things he got but let slip through his fingers

    C Sorrow over how few opportunities he has had in life

    D Sorrow over riches that have lost their appeal

_____ **8.** In Sonnet 30, the speaker laments departed friends. However, he is cheered when thinking —

    F that they really weren't such great friends after all

    G that they will return someday

    H of the friend the poem is addressed to

    J all the friends he has now

_____ **9.** The metaphors in Sonnet 30 come *mostly* from the fields of —

    A war and shipping

    B poetry and journalism

    C law and finance

    D religion and science

_____ **10.** The message of Sonnets 29 and 30 could be summarized as —

    F there is no cure for sorrow

    G love is the remedy for sorrow

    H life is short, but art lasts forever

    J it is better to keep busy than to lose oneself in thoughts and memories

LITERARY FOCUS: SHAKESPEAREAN SONNET *(40 points; 10 points each)*

On the line provided, write the letter of the *best* answer to each of the following items.

_____ **11.** The main subject of Shakespeare's 154 sonnets is —

    A love

    B art

    C tragedy

    D the self

_____ **12.** The form of a **Shakespearean sonnet** is —

    F fourteen lines of unrhymed iambic pentameter

    G three quatrains followed by a couplet

    H an octave followed by a sestet

    J seven rhymed couplets

_____ **13.** The **turn** after the first two quatrains of a Shakespearean sonnet usually signifies a —

    A summation of the poem's theme

    B sudden change in the speaker's tone

    C shift from one figure of speech to another

    D shift in the poem's focus or thought

_____ **14.** The turn in Sonnet 29 begins with the word —

    F like

    G with

    H haply

    J yet

CONSTRUCTED RESPONSE (20 points)

15. On a separate sheet of paper, list two emotions that are present throughout both Sonnet 29 and Sonnet 30. Explain how these emotions are expressed in figures of speech, sound devices, and tone.

SELECTION TEST

Sonnet 71, Sonnet 73 William Shakespeare

COMPREHENSION *(40 points; 4 points each)*

On the line provided, write the letter of the *best* answer to each of the following items.

_____ **1.** The common subject of both Sonnets 71 and 73 is the —

    A beloved's physical beauty

    B beloved's inner beauty

    C speaker's mortality

    D poet's ambition

_____ **2.** The essential message of the first twelve lines of Sonnet 71 could be paraphrased as —

    F preserve my poetry when I am gone

    G forget me as soon as I'm gone

    H please don't replace me with a newer love

    J life is awful and I won't miss it

_____ **3.** In lines 6–8 of Sonnet 71, the speaker explains that he —

    A doesn't want to cause his beloved the pain of remembering him

    B feels that all of life is an illusion, including love

    C believes that there is room in one life for only one love, not two

    D despises the vanity of life so much that he is unable to feel genuine love

_____ **4.** In the final couplet of Sonnet 71, the speaker further explains that he —

    F doesn't want his memory to keep his beloved from attaining happiness

    G doesn't want the world to make fun of his beloved for being attached to him

    H feels that although love can be preserved in art, it cannot survive long in real life

    J feels that his beloved's beauty is too great to be spoiled by tears and grief

_____ **5.** What poetic device is *not* found in Sonnet 71?

    A Simile

    B Alliteration

    C Rhyme

    D Iambic pentameter

_____ **6.** What season of the year is the speaker describing in lines 1–4 of Sonnet 73?

    F Winter

    G Spring

    H Summer

    J Autumn

_____ **7.** In line 4 of Sonnet 73, what does Shakespeare compare to the choir lofts of churches?

    A Singing birds

    B Tree branches

    C Yellow leaves

    D Sunset

_____ **8.** What season of life does Sonnet 73 describe?

    F Childhood

    G Adolescence

    H The prime of life

    J Old age

_____ **9.** According to the speaker of Sonnet 73, what effect does his condition have on his beloved?

    A His joy is contagious and makes her joyous, too.

    B His depression makes her want to stay away from him.

    C It causes her to value the little time they have left together.

    D His illness causes her to treat him as a patient, not a lover.

_____ **10.** In line 10 of Sonnet 73, what poetic device is used in the description of a fire: "That on the ashes of his youth doth lie"?

    F Alliteration

    G Simile

    H Personification

    J Metaphor

LITERARY FOCUS: SHAKESPEAREAN SONNET AND TONE *(40 points; 10 points each)*

On the line provided, write the letter of the *best* answer to each of the following items.

_____ **11.** What is a **quatrain**?

    A The first section of a sonnet, which states a problem

    B The concluding section, which resolves the problem

    C A repeated line or group of lines in a poem

    D A group or stanza of four lines

_____ **12.** In a Shakespearean sonnet, how many different sounds do the ends of lines contain?

    F Four

    G Five

    H Six

    J Seven

_____ **13.** What is a poem's **tone**?

    A The attitude an author or speaker takes toward the material in a poem

    B A word or phrase that sums up the general atmosphere or feeling of the poem

    C The central idea that the poet or speaker is trying to get across

    D The way the poem would sound if it were read aloud

_____ **14.** How can the sounds of a poem affect its tone?

    F They cannot because sound and meaning are two separate things.

    G The sounds of a poem can change the meaning of its tone.

    H By imagining the poem spoken by a human voice, the reader can get a sense of the poem's tone.

    J Hearing a poem read aloud enables the audience to better understand the author's philosophy of life.

CONSTRUCTED RESPONSE (20 points)

15. Which sonnet do you prefer, 71 or 73? Explain why, discussing both poems' sounds and devices as well as their meanings. Write your answer on a separate sheet of paper.

SELECTION TEST █████████   LITERARY RESPONSE AND ANALYSIS

Sonnet 116, Sonnet 130 William Shakespeare

COMPREHENSION (40 points; 4 points each)

On the line provided, write the letter of the *best* answer to each of the following items.

_____ 1. From reading Sonnets 116 and 130, one can conclude that Shakespeare's idea of love involves the premise that —

    A true love ends when circumstances turn for the worse

    B people must be close in age to be truly in love

    C real love brings a person money, fame, and respect

    D true love is indifferent to wealth, beauty, age, and circumstance

_____ 2. In Sonnet 116, "Let me not to the marriage of true minds / Admit impediments" could be paraphrased as —

    F these two people should not get married

    G obstacles cannot change true love

    H love of the mind is more important than love of the body

    J marriage is the necessary fulfillment of true love

_____ 3. "Love is not love / Which alters when it alteration finds" means that —

    A love is a fake, a romantic illusion

    B what people usually call love is not really love

    C true love does not change with circumstance

    D as life progresses, love must be prepared to change

_____ 4. In Sonnet 116, lines 9–12, beginning "Love's not Time's fool," suggest that love —

    F is not deceived by material wealth

    G cannot last forever

    H outlives the end of youth

    J is strongest when people are young

_____ 5. Which of the following conclusions is *not* suggested in the final couplet of Sonnet 116?

    A The poet's view of love may be wrong.

    B It would take a lot to convince the poet he is wrong.

    C If the poet is wrong, then love itself is false.

    D It is impossible for the poet to be wrong about love.

_____ 6. Before the final couplet of Sonnet 130, the speaker seems to be —

    F blinded by his mistress's beauty

    G criticizing his mistress

    H criticizing society

    J praising his mistress's modesty

_____ **7.** By the end of Sonnet 130, the reader knows that the speaker's feelings toward his mistress are —

A ambivalent

B affectionate

C uninterested

D contemptuous

_____ **8.** Which of the following senses is appealed to by the imagery in lines 7–8 of Sonnet 130?

F Sight

G Hearing

H Touch

J Smell

_____ **9.** What aspect of literature does Sonnet 130 mock?

A Shakespearean tragedy

B The theater

C Sentimental love poems

D The idea of lasting love

_____ **10.** How does the poet feel about his mistress's voice?

F Its grating sound makes him cringe.

G He loves to hear it.

H He thinks she needs singing lessons.

J He thrills at its commanding power.

LITERARY FOCUS: SHAKESPEARE'S SONNETS AND FIGURES OF SPEECH *(40 points; 10 points each)*
On the line provided, write the letter of the *best* answer to each of the following items.

_____ **11.** Which of the following questions about Shakespeare's sonnets is *not* a mystery?

A Who is the "dark lady"?

B Who is the beloved male friend?

C Who really wrote the sonnets?

D Could the sonnets be rearranged to tell a story?

_____ **12.** All the couplets at the ends of the sonnets —

    F add a statement of impact and importance

    G confirm what was said at the beginning

    H reverse what was said at the beginning

    J express the speaker's sorrow

_____ **13.** According to the speaker in Sonnet 130, music, roses, and perfume —

    A are not as lovely as his mistress's voice, skin, and breath

    B are false comparisons to make with the charms of true love

    C are divine gifts that should not be compared with anything else

    D have nothing to do with love

_____ **14.** Lines 5–8 of Sonnet 116 compare love to —

    F waves and currents that are ever-shifting

    G the changing of the weather from calm to stormy

    H a mark that every athlete tries to surpass

    J a landmark or star that guides ships in rough seas

CONSTRUCTED RESPONSE *(20 points)*

15. Choose either Sonnet 116 or Sonnet 130, and describe its mood. Show how Shakespeare uses figures of speech to help create that mood. Write your answer on a separate sheet of paper.

SELECTION TEST   LITERARY RESPONSE AND ANALYSIS

Blow, Blow, Thou Winter Wind William Shakespeare
Fear No More the Heat o' the Sun William Shakespeare
Full Fathom Five William Shakespeare

COMPREHENSION *(40 points; 4 points each)*
On the line provided, write the letter of the *best* answer to each of the following items.

_____ **1.** The first three lines of "Blow, Blow, Thou Winter Wind" could be paraphrased as —

   A   people are such ingrates, their coldness is worse than a cold winter wind

   B   winter, with its suffering, comes every year whether we're ready for it or not

   C   you don't have to pretend to like winter or pretend to be grateful

   D   wind or calm, cold or hot, rain or sun—it doesn't matter, we must all die someday

_____ **2.** The message of line 8 of "Blow, Blow, Thou Winter Wind" is that —

   F   in an uncertain world, friendship and love are the only things we can count on

   G   love and friendship are illusions, not realities

   H   love endures even after death

   J   human evil is worse than nature's destructiveness

_____ **3.** Line 10 of "Blow, Blow, Thou Winter Wind," "This life is most jolly," accomplishes all of the following purposes *except* —

   A   sarcastically express Amiens's disgust with life

   B   express Amiens's continued zest for life despite its harshness

   C   imply a desire for cheer and warmth in the face of bitter cold

   D   plead for love as the only remedy for Amiens's sadness

_____ **4.** Which aspect of the winter wind in "Blow, Blow, Thou Winter Wind" is *not* personification?

   F   It is unkind in line 2.

   G   It has teeth in line 4.

   H   It is invisible in line 5.

   J   It breathes in line 6.

_____ **5.** In "Fear No More the Heat o' the Sun," line 4, "Home art gone, and ta'en thy wages" means that the person addressed is —

   A   home

   B   poor

   C   satisfied

   D   dead

6. Line 4 of "Fear No More the Heat o' the Sun" uses the kind of figure of speech called —

    F personification

    G onomatopoeia

    H simile

    J metaphor

7. In the last two lines of "Fear No More the Heat o' the Sun," what does the singer wish for the person addressed?

    A A haunted, restless afterlife

    B To leave him, the singer, alone

    C Rest and a good reputation after death

    D A lavish funeral with many mourners

8. Lines 1–6 of "Full Fathom Five" could be paraphrased as —

    F no one knows what will happen to us after we die

    G lying beneath the sea, your father's body will be changed into something beautiful

    H don't grieve for your father's death, for the same thing is about to happen to you

    J your father's manner of death shows that he was actually a water spirit, not a human being

9. Line 7, "Sea nymphs hourly ring his knell," means that —

    A every hour, sea nymphs return to the body to hammer its bones

    B water spirits play music in grief for the dead man

    C sea nymphs adorn the body with jewels such as rings

    D water goddesses kneel by the dead man's body and weep

10. Which of the three songs are dirges, or elegies?

    F "Full Fathom Five" and "Blow, Blow, Thou Winter Wind"

    G Only "Blow, Blow, Thou Winter Wind"

    H "Blow, Blow, Thou Winter Wind" and "Fear No More the Heat o' the Sun"

    J "Fear No More the Heat o' the Sun" and "Full Fathom Five"

LITERARY FOCUS: DRAMATIC SONG *(40 points; 10 points each)*

On the line provided, write the letter of the *best* answer to each of the following items.

_____ **11.** In Shakespeare's time dramatic songs were —

    A sung in plays

    B recorded on wax

    C accompanied by orchestras

    D spoken rather than sung

_____ **12.** The purposes of Shakespeare's dramatic songs included all of the following goals *except* to —

    F sell copies

    G please the audience

    H advance the dramatic action

    J enhance mood or characterization

_____ **13.** How is a Shakespearean song different from a Shakespearean sonnet?

    A The song is shorter.

    B The song does not deal with serious themes.

    C The sonnet has a more rigid, less varied form.

    D The song uses rhyme.

_____ **14.** One thing that dramatic songs and ballads have in common is that both —

    F are often about violent, sensational, or supernatural events

    G commonly use a question-and-answer format

    H are often traditional works handed down orally for generations

    J are intended to be sung by the human voice

CONSTRUCTED RESPONSE *(20 points)*

15. Agree or disagree with the following statement: "In spite of the melancholy mood of these three songs, they show that Shakespeare loved life." Use imagery, word choices, and figures of speech from the songs to help justify your view. Write your answer on a separate sheet of paper.

To be, or not to be William Shakespeare
Tomorrow, and tomorrow, and tomorrow
William Shakespeare
St. Crispin's Day Speech William Shakespeare
Our revels now are ended William Shakespeare

COMPREHENSION *(40 points; 4 points each)*
On the line provided, write the letter of the *best* answer to each of the following items.

_____ **1.** What is Hamlet's feeling about death?

  A He has no fear of it; he welcomes it.

  B He feels that the most odious life is better than death.

  C He wants to escape life, but fears what might come after death.

  D He is indifferent to whether he lives or dies.

_____ **2.** According to Hamlet, people desperately want to stay alive because they —

  F wish to achieve something before they go

  G are afraid of suffering after they die

  H are terrified of vanishing into nothingness

  J live for the sheer joy of life, though it is illogical

_____ **3.** In lines 15–19 of his soliloquy, Hamlet lists —

  A reasons for wanting to die

  B honors that come to heroes

  C the burdens of the living

  D lies told about people after their deaths

_____ **4.** In a metaphor, Macbeth compares each day of life to —

  F an actor on the stage

  G a king or queen who has been killed

  H a candle lighting the path toward death

  J a song with melody but no words

_____ **5.** In the phrases "petty pace," "dusty death," "poor player," "Tale / Told by an idiot," and "sound and fury, / Signifying," Shakespeare hammers home the speaker's feelings through the rhetorical device of —

  A rhyme

  B alliteration

  C persuasion

  D parallelism

_____ **6.** The message of Henry V's monologue is similar to the modern military slogan —

    F "The Few, the Proud"

    G "Join the Navy and See the World"

    H "Uncle Sam Wants You"

    J "Be All that You Can Be"

_____ **7.** What does Henry V claim to value above all other things in life?

    A Victory

    B Money

    C Love

    D Honor

_____ **8.** What does Henry V promise to do for his soldiers?

    F Protect them from harm

    G Make sure they are properly fed, equipped, and rested

    H Use all of his persuasive powers to keep them from leaving

    J Let them leave in safety, but reward them for staying

_____ **9.** Prospero uses a figure of speech to compare each of the following items to life *except* —

    A clowns

    B buildings

    C clouds

    D dreams

_____ **10.** Prospero views life as —

    F basically unreal

    G a battle to be fought, win or lose

    H a series of dull, unpleasant burdens

    J a nightmare from which to awaken

LITERARY FOCUS: MONOLOGUE AND SOLILOQUY *(40 points; 10 points each)*

On the line provided, write the letter of the *best* answer to each of the following items.

_____ **11.** What is the difference between monologues and soliloquies?

    A Soliloquies are spoken onstage; monologues are not.

    B Soliloquies are more dramatic than monologues.

    C Soliloquies reveal character; monologues advance the action.

    D Soliloquy is spoken alone; other actors can be onstage for a monologue.

_____ **12.** What line in Hamlet's soliloquy is *not* spoken to either the audience or himself?

    F "To be, or not to be—that is the question."

    G "To sleep—perchance to dream. Aye, there's the rub . . ."

    H "Thus conscience does make cowards of us all, . . ."

    J "Nymph, in thy orisons / Be all my sins remembered."

_____ **13.** Which of the four speeches in this selection is spoken to the largest group of characters?

    A Hamlet's "To be, or not to be"

    B Macbeth's "Tomorrow, and tomorrow, and tomorrow"

    C Henry V's "St. Crispin's Day Speech"

    D Prospero's "Our revels now are ended"

_____ **14.** Which of the four speeches *most* clearly presents life as a heroic adventure?

    F Hamlet's "To be, or not to be"

    G Macbeth's "Tomorrow, and tomorrow, and tomorrow"

    H Henry V's "St. Crispin's Day Speech"

    J Prospero's "Our revels now are ended"

CONSTRUCTED RESPONSE *(20 points)*

15. On a separate sheet of paper, write an answer to any one of the four Shakespearean heroes, either agreeing or disagreeing with the view of life shown in his speech. Give your reasons. As part of your argument, analyze two figures of speech used in the character's speech, showing how they either do or do not adequately describe life.

SELECTION TEST ████████████   LITERARY RESPONSE AND ANALYSIS

Song John Donne

COMPREHENSION (40 points; 4 points each)

On the line provided, write the letter of the *best* answer to each of the following items.

_____ **1.** The speaker in "Song" seems to think that finding a sincere woman is —

    A not difficult

    B a matter of chance

    C moderately difficult

    D impossible

_____ **2.** The statement that one could "get with child a mandrake root" before satisfying the search for a true woman is an example of —

    F allusion

    G literary conceit

    H hyperbole

    J simile

_____ **3.** In the second stanza, how long does the speaker ask the listener to ride in search of a true woman?

    A Nine months

    B About thirty years

    C Forever

    D Longer than the human life span

_____ **4.** How far does the speaker say he would travel to meet an honest woman?

    F No distance

    G A thousand miles

    H A mile or two

    J As long as it takes

_____ **5.** Why is the speaker wary of meeting an honest woman?

    A He is afraid of her power.

    B He believes that, in the time it took to reach her, she would become untrue.

    C He does not really trust the judgment of the person he is sending on the search.

    D As a clergyman, he has sworn not to be tempted by women's attractions.

_____ **6.** What is the rhyme scheme of "Song"?

    F *aabbcddee*

    G *abba abba*

    H *abab cdcd*

    J *ababccddd*

_____ **7.** Which emotion is *not* displayed by the speaker of this poem?

    A Envy

    B Suspicion

    C Trust

    D Jealousy

_____ **8.** "Song" differs from the songs of Shakespeare because it —

    F shows a harsher view of life

    G shows a sunnier view of life

    H was not written for the stage

    J was not written to be set to music

_____ **9.** Which fact about Donne's life seems to fit *best* with the fact that he wrote "Song"?

    A As a young man he was "a great visitor of ladies."

    B He attended Oxford University at age twelve.

    C He secretly married his true love when she was only seventeen.

    D He became a respected member of the clergy.

_____ **10.** The tone of "Song" could be described as —

    F merry

    G carefree

    H harsh

    J sweet

LITERARY FOCUS: METAPHYSICAL POETRY *(40 points; 10 points each)*

On the line provided, write the letter of the *best* answer to each of the following items.

_____ **11. Metaphysical poetry** is a label for a style of —

    A Elizabethan poetry

    B Middle English poetry

    C poetry of the 1600s

    D poetry of the present day

_____ **12. Metaphysical poetry** does *not* usually include —

    F   abstract ideas

    G clear, simple, flowing lines

    H witty word play

    J   complicated figures of speech

_____ **13.** The sounds and rhythms of metaphysical poetry tend to be —

    A harshly or irregularly metered

    B musical, with soothing vowel and consonant sounds

    C smooth, with predictable line lengths

    D unmetered, like free verse

_____ **14.** The imagery in Donne's metaphysical poetry is rarely —

    F   far-fetched and surprising

    G taken from everyday activities

    H taken from the science and philosophy of Donne's time

    J   reliant on traditional love imagery such as roses or Cupid's arrows

CONSTRUCTED RESPONSE *(20 points)*

15. Do you think the speaker's extreme position on women's honesty helps or hurts the poem? On a separate sheet of paper, explain why, supporting your ideas with at least two details from the poem and at least one fact about Donne's time.

SELECTION TEST

LITERARY RESPONSE AND ANALYSIS

A Valediction: Forbidding Mourning John Donne

COMPREHENSION (40 points; 4 points each)

On the line provided, write the letter of the *best* answer to each of the following items.

_____ **1.** In plain English the title "A Valediction: Forbidding Mourning" means —

     A a graduation speech commending the senior class

     B a greeting to a person who had been thought missing

     C a vow never to fall in love again

     D a farewell urging the listener not to be sad

_____ **2.** The scene described in the first stanza is —

     F a childbirth

     G a wedding

     H lovemaking

     J a deathbed

_____ **3.** Lines 7–8, "'Twere profanation of our joys / To tell the laity our love," mean —

     A our love is profane but confessing it would absolve us

     B we are the only happy people in a society of miserable souls

     C our love is so sacred that we should not speak of it to others

     D mere physical love is very different from true spiritual love

_____ **4.** What phrase does the speaker use to describe the *opposite* of his and his wife's love?

     F "Dull sublunary lovers' love . . ."

     G "a love, so much refined . . ."

     H "Our two souls therefore, which are one . . ."

     J "Care less eyes, lips, and hands to miss."

_____ **5.** In a simile in line 24, the lovers' souls are said to resemble gold in that they —

     A are rare and precious

     B are the envy of the world

     C are beautiful

     D can be drawn thin without being broken

_____ **6.** According to the speaker, absence from a lover is easiest to bear when the —

     F couple have not known each other very long

     G attraction is only on the surface

     H two people are extremely close

     J pair have been separated for a long time

_____ **7.** The device that the speaker compares his and his wife's love to is for —

    A finding true north

    B drawing circles

    C measuring angles

    D measuring distances

_____ **8.** In line 27, "Thy soul, the fixed foot" means that the —

    F speaker is the moving needle on the compass

    G speaker's wife has had successful surgery on her foot

    H speaker's wife likes to make puns about the words *soul* and *sole*

    J speaker's wife is the prong of the compass that remains still in the center

_____ **9.** The poem is made of four-line stanzas (quatrains) in which the rhyme scheme is —

    A *abab*, and there are four iambic feet

    B *aabb*, and there are five iambic feet

    C *abab*, and there is no formal meter

    D *aabb*, and there is no formal meter

_____ **10.** What fact about Donne's life fits *best* with the message of "A Valediction: Forbidding Mourning"?

    F As a young man, he was ambitious to become a courtier.

    G He faced legal discrimination because of his Roman Catholic faith.

    H He gave up many advantages to marry his wife, and they had twelve children together.

    J He converted to the Church of England and wrote passionately against Catholicism.

LITERARY FOCUS: METAPHYSICAL CONCEITS *(40 points; 10 points each)*

On the line provided, write the letter of the *best* answer to each of the following items.

_____ **11.** A **metaphysical conceit** is a type of —

    A figure of speech

    B rhyme

    C metrical pattern

    D tone or voice

_____ **12.** The term **metaphysical conceit** does *not* imply —

    F keen analysis

    G feelings of superiority

    H powerful intelligence

    J unusual comparisons

_____ **13.** The compass conceit in "A Valediction: Forbidding Mourning" can be seen in lines —

    A 1–8

    B 13–16

    C 21–24

    D 25–36

_____ **14.** Both the admirers and the critics of metaphysical conceits would probably agree that such conceits —

    F are not deserved by the poet

    G are the best way to analyze human relations deeply

    H show off the poet's skill and cleverness

    J make pleasing comparisons between unlike things

CONSTRUCTED RESPONSE *(20 points)*

15. On a separate sheet of paper, evaluate the compass conceit in "A Valediction: Forbidding Mourning." What do you think are its strong and weak features? How effective do you think this conceit is? How does it affect the impact of the poem?

SELECTION TEST   LITERARY RESPONSE AND ANALYSIS

Meditation 17 John Donne

COMPREHENSION *(40 points; 4 points each)*

On the line provided, write the letter of the *best* answer to each of the following items.

_____ 1. The saying "never send to know for whom the bell tolls; it tolls for thee" means that —

   A you are so ill that you don't even notice your illness

   B church bells ring for each member of the congregation

   C the church is there for all its members, not just a few

   D you will die one day, whether or not you are dying now

_____ 2. "If a clod be washed away by the sea, Europe is the less, as well as if a promontory were" means that —

   F Europe is such a small continent, every inch of land is valuable

   G even the smallest is important in life's plan, no less than the biggest

   H it's important to watch for early signs of disaster, to avoid later, larger disasters

   J no one realizes how unimportant he or she really is

_____ 3. The saying "No man is an island" means that —

   A a stranger's death does not matter

   B all humankind is interconnected

   C people cannot live together harmoniously

   D people with different religious ideas can work out their differences

_____ 4. In a metaphor, Donne says that humanity is a book and God is its author. In that metaphor, death is the book —

   F going out of print

   G selling unexpectedly well

   H falling apart through excessive wear

   J being translated into another language

_____ 5. In the metaphor of the book, what is the Library?

   A The afterlife

   B The Church

   C The physical universe

   D Human consciousness

_____ **6.** Which of the following factors is *not* used in "Meditation 17" as the basis for a philosophical metaphor?

    F Marriage

    G The human body

    H Money

    J Natural disaster

_____ **7.** According to Donne, why should we be glad to hear church bells toll for us?

    A Death brings us closer to union with God.

    B The inspiring sound of bells promotes healing.

    C If the church rings bells for you, you must be important.

    D It is good to rise early in the morning.

_____ **8.** What does "no man hath affliction enough that is not matured, and ripened by it" mean?

    F Everyone has room for more suffering.

    G As people grow older and wiser, they usually suffer more.

    H Suffering is worthwhile if it prepares us to meet God.

    J God never gives us more suffering than we can bear.

_____ **9.** Which of the following passages uses parallel structure to enhance clarity and meaning?

    A "Truly it were an excusable covetousness if we did; for affliction is a treasure. . . ."

    B "Tribulation is treasure in the nature of it, but it is not current money. . . ."

    C "Both piety and dignity, religion and estimation, were mingled. . . ."

    D "Who casts not up his eye to the sun when it rises?"

_____ **10.** When church bells ring, they ring over and over again in the same way for a long time. This practice is one reason why Donne used the rhetorical device of —

    F parallel structure

    G metaphor

    H repetition

    J rhetorical question

LITERARY FOCUS: TONE *(40 points; 10 points each)*

On the line provided, write the letter of the *best* answer to each of the following items.

_____ **11.** A synonym for tone in literature is —

    A noise

    B attitude

    C pitch

    D note

_____ **12.** What is the relationship between tone and subject?

    F Writers can approach the same subject in different tones.

    G There is no clear relationship between tone and subject.

    H For each writer, there is only one good choice of tone for any one subject.

    J The subject of a piece of writing determines its tone.

_____ **13.** The tone of "Meditation 17" could *not* be called —

    A inspired

    B solemn

    C lighthearted

    D intellectual

_____ **14.** In "Meditation 17," Donne's tone helps him achieve the purpose of —

    F entertaining the reader

    G informing the reader

    H explaining how to pray more effectively

    J making the reader think about serious issues

CONSTRUCTED RESPONSE *(20 points)*

15. What meaning did you gather from "Meditation 17"? In your response, be sure to point to specific passages in the text whose language, rhetoric, or organization helped clarify the meaning for you. Write your answer on a separate sheet of paper.

SELECTION TEST ███████████████ LITERARY RESPONSE AND ANALYSIS

Death be not proud John Donne
from W;t Margaret Edson

COMPREHENSION (40 points; 4 points each)

On the line provided, write the letter of the *best* answer to each of the following items.

_____ **1.** According to the speaker, how will Death die?

    A Kings will take over all power.

    B People will develop medicines to prevent death.

    C War and sickness will kill people first.

    D Eternal life will triumph over Death.

_____ **2.** The image, "One short sleep," in line 13 stands for —

    F a nap

    G dying

    H sickness

    J immortality

_____ **3.** "Thou art slave to fate, chance, kings, and desperate men, / And dost with poison, war, and sickness dwell" (lines 9–10) implies that —

    A death depends upon human action

    B no matter what we do or where we go, we must still die

    C fate, chance, kings, desperation, poison, war, and sickness are not always fatal—only sometimes

    D to avoid death, people need to avoid risks

_____ **4.** Which aspect of Death in the poem is *not* a personification?

    F Death is a slave.

    G Death kills people.

    H Death thinks.

    J Death is proud of himself.

_____ **5.** What tone does the speaker take toward the subject of death?

    A Friendly

    B Neutral

    C Fearful

    D Defiant

_____ **6.** Lines 7–8 could be paraphrased as —

    F It's fortunate that the good die young.

    G Wisdom is found in learning to conquer death.

    H The best people are those who try to find ways of delaying death.

    J The best people are those who have the deepest religious faith.

_____ **7.** In line 5, what kind of figure of speech is used in calling rest and sleep the "pictures" of death?

    A Personification

    B Simile

    C Metaphor

    D Hyperbole

_____ **8.** In the scene from the play *W;t*, a —

    F dying woman is reassured by the message of "Death be not proud"

    G professor ridicules the idea that Death can be overthrown

    H professor claims that Donne was a greater poet than Shakespeare

    J professor shows a subtle way of interpreting Donne's poem

_____ **9.** In the scene from *W;t*, the disagreement between Vivian Bearing and the professor centers on a question of —

    A medical diagnosis

    B teaching style

    C punctuation

    D liking Donne

_____ **10.** John Donne and Margaret Edson would probably agree that —

    F the sonnet is a more sublime form than the drama

    G death is to be greatly feared

    H words cannot do justice to the importance of life

    J death is not necessarily an evil

LITERARY FOCUS: PARADOX *(40 points; 10 points each)*
On the line provided, write the letter of the *best* answer to each of the following items.

_____ **11.** A **paradox** is a —

    A contradiction that proves true

    B contradiction that cannot be solved

    C statement that is seemingly simple but really contradictory

    D statement that is truer at first sight than when you look at it deeply

_____ **12.** Which of the following common sayings is a paradox?

    F Less is more.

    G There's more here than meets the eye.

    H I see it in my mind's eye.

    J What goes in one ear goes out the other.

_____ **13.** In "Death be not proud" a paradox can be found in the saying —

    A "Death be not proud . . ."

    B "poor Death . . ."

    C "Death, thou shalt die."

    D "We wake eternally. . . ."

_____ **14.** The explanation for the central paradox in "Death be not proud" is that —

    F death does not really exist

    G death is not really inevitable

    H death can be overcome spiritually

    J thinking about death too often makes life a living death

CONSTRUCTED RESPONSE *(20 points)*
15. How convincing do you find the argument in "Death be not proud"? Give specific reasons, including both the content and the rhetoric of the poem. Write your answer on a separate sheet of paper.

LITERARY RESPONSE AND ANALYSIS

On My First Son Ben Jonson
Song: To Celia Ben Jonson

COMPREHENSION *(40 points; 4 points each)*
On the line provided, write the letter of the *best* answer to each of the following items.

_____ **1.** The speaker in "On My First Son" compares the years of his son's short life to —

    A the fingers of his right hand

    B the world's harshness

    C the length of a loan

    D his own bad deeds

_____ **2.** The line "My sin was too much hope of thee, loved boy" suggests that the speaker —

    F thinks the boy's death is punishment for loving him too much

    G thinks he sinned too much to deserve to keep his son

    H expected his son to be too much like him

    J thinks he can still make up for the boy's sins

_____ **3.** The lines "for why / Will man lament the state he should envy" mean that —

    A people don't appreciate life while they have it

    B although people grieve, death is not really sad

    C parenthood is a state that many people envy, but they shouldn't

    D the speaker does not understand basic human emotions such as love and grief

_____ **4.** "Here doth lie / Ben Jonson his best piece of poetry" means —

    F Ben Jonson was his own best poem, for his life was a work of art

    G Ben Jonson made a practice of burying the manuscripts of his poems

    H here lies Ben Jonson, who wrote a lot of good poetry

    J Jonson's son, not his poetry, was his greatest creation

_____ **5.** The last two lines of "On My First Son" suggest that Jonson was —

    A so upset by the loss of his son, he could never be his old likable, lovable self

    B not upset enough by his son's death to give up writing poetry

    C too upset to write more than twelve lines about his son's death

    D so upset by his son's death, he resolved not to get close to anyone again

_____ **6.** In "Song: To Celia," Jonson compares the smallest of Celia's attentions to —

    F a drink worthy of the gods

    G a wreath of flowers

    H the beginning of a romance

    J an ocean

_____ 7. In the lines "The thirst that from the soul doth rise / Doth ask a drink divine," the phrase "drink divine" represents —

  A religious faith

  B children

  C immortality

  D love

_____ 8. In lines 9–14, we learn that —

  F the speaker has actually never met Celia

  G Celia and the speaker are husband and wife

  H Celia is married to the speaker's rival

  J Celia has rejected the speaker's gift

_____ 9. The last two lines of "Song: To Celia" mask the speaker's —

  A disappointment

  B joy

  C impatience

  D admiration

_____ 10. In both poems the speaker is responding to —

  F the creation of a bond of love

  G the breaking of a bond of love

  H the death of a loved one

  J rejection by someone he loves

LITERARY FOCUS: EPIGRAM *(40 points; 10 points each)*

On the line provided, write the letter of the *best* answer to each of the following items.

_____ 11. One characteristic of an **epigram** is —

  A metaphysical complexity

  B romanticism

  C the theme of love

  D a pithy point

_____ 12. A good **epigram** should be written in words that are —

  F alliterative

  G elaborate

  H memorable

  J conversational

_____ **13.** Which of the following statements *best* summarizes the epigram of "On My First Son"?

    A Children are like right hands because they help parents.

    B Children are often our best accomplishments.

    C Those who die young should rest in peace.

    D The plague kills children as well as adults.

_____ **14.** For Ben Jonson and for the ancients, the purpose of an epigram was to —

    F defeat a rival epigrammatist in a contest of wit

    G give permanence to an event or observation

    H create a saying that would be on everyone's lips

    J write something that could be carved on a tombstone

CONSTRUCTED RESPONSE *(20 points)*

15. Words that can describe the epigram subgenre include *brief, clever, pointed, polished,* and *striking*. With that in mind, how successful are these two Ben Jonson epigrams? Support your opinion with specific reasons based on the texts. Write your answer on a separate sheet of paper.

SELECTION TEST

Of Studies Francis Bacon
Axioms *from the* Essays Francis Bacon

COMPREHENSION *(40 points; 4 points each)*

On the line provided, write the letter of the *best* answer to each of the following items.

_____ **1.** When Bacon suggests that reading poetry makes people "witty," he implies that it makes them —

    A thoughtful

    B brave

    C imaginative

    D sad

_____ **2.** What does Bacon recommend for someone whose "wit be wandering"?

    F Reading poetry

    G Studying mathematics

    H Joining a debating society

    J Reading philosophy

_____ **3.** Bacon's warning that using studies "too much for ornament is affectation" means that —

    A those who don't study should be scorned

    B there are limits to what one can learn

    C teachers should be respected because they are studious

    D learning should not be used mainly to impress others

_____ **4.** According to Bacon, people should read for —

    F laughter and excitement

    G pleasure and education

    H enlightenment and spiritual knowledge

    J wealth and power

_____ **5.** Bacon would probably say that the *most* important reason you were assigned "Of Studies" at school is —

    A that "histories make men wise . . . "

    B because "logic and rhetoric [make people] able to contend . . ."

    C that "bowling is good for the stone and reins . . ."

    D "the mathematics [make people] subtle . . ."

_____ **6.** According to Bacon, people who are learned are better than unlearned people at —

    F paying attention to details

    G carrying out complicated plans

    H giving general advice

    J remembering their instructions

_____ **7.** In Bacon's remark "They perfect nature and are perfected by experience," what is, or who are, *they*?

    A Studies

    B Learned people

    C Poets

    D Essays

_____ **8.** Bacon wrote, "Some books are to be tasted, others to be swallowed, and some few to be chewed and digested." What reading tip, often taught in today's schools, restates that point?

    F Monitor your comprehension as you read.

    G Take notes and outline to check your understanding.

    H Pause to ask yourself questions about what you read.

    J Vary your reading rate to suit the material.

_____ **9.** The "Axioms" in the Primary Source feature *most* clearly show Bacon's understanding of —

    A study

    B power

    C human nature

    D science

_____ **10.** The overall message of Bacon's axioms could be summarized as —

    F live luxuriously and relish pleasure

    G abandon material things and embrace a spiritual path

    H strive for a reasonable, balanced approach to life

    J focus every waking minute on improving one's mind

LITERARY FOCUS: PARALLEL STRUCTURE *(15 points; 5 points each)*

On the line provided, write the letter of the *best* answer to each of the following items.

_____ **11. Parallel structure** is the repetition of —

    A words, phrases, or sentences that have the same grammatical structure

    B a theme in several different selections by one author

    C words, phrases, or sentences that have different grammatical structure

    D vowel and consonant sounds in words that are close together

_____ **12.** Which of the following sentences is *not* an example of Bacon's parallel structure?

    F "If his wit be not apt to distinguish or find differences, let him study the Schoolmen. . . ."

    G "Studies serve for delight, for ornament, and for ability."

    H "The virtue of prosperity is temperance; the virtue of adversity is fortitude."

    J "Reading maketh a full man; conference a ready man; and writing an exact man."

_____ **13.** What is the *best* summary of Bacon's overall message in "Of Studies"?

    A One must read as much as one can because book learning is the most important kind of learning.

    B Studying and reading are recommended for scholars only; they are lost on most people.

    C A carefully balanced approach to study is best. Allow plenty of time for learning that does not come from books.

    D Every person should study a special field rather than general subjects.

READING SKILLS: ANALYZING ARGUMENTS *(5 points)*

On the line provided, write the letter of the *best* answer to the following item.

_____ **14.** Which of the following statements is *not* a belief or assumption that Bacon asserts to support his main idea in "Of Studies"?

    F Studies can serve several purposes.

    G People have different purposes for reading and studying.

    H Reading should be a privilege reserved only for the elite.

    J Reading can expand a person's knowledge.

VOCABULARY DEVELOPMENT *(20 points; 4 points each)*

Match the definition on the left with the Vocabulary word on the right. On the line provided, write the letter of the Vocabulary word.

_____ **15.** artificial behavior designed to impress others   **a.** impediment

_____ **16.** laziness   **b.** diligence

_____ **17.** care; carefulness   **c.** discourse

_____ **18.** speech   **d.** affectation

_____ **19.** obstacle; stumbling block   **e.** sloth

CONSTRUCTED RESPONSE (20 points)

20. On a separate sheet of paper, identify an assumption or belief about the world that you feel underlies Bacon's message in "Of Studies." It may be something either stated or unstated in the essay. Using references to the text, show how this belief or assumption plays a part in Bacon's argument.

SELECTION TEST

LITERARY RESPONSE AND ANALYSIS

Tilbury Speech Queen Elizabeth I
from Female Orations Margaret Cavendish, duchess of Newcastle

COMPREHENSION *(40 points; 4 points each)*

On the line provided, write the letter of the *best* answer to each of the following items.

_____ 1. According to Queen Elizabeth I in "Tilbury Speech," she does not fear treachery among her people because —

    A she is not a tyrant

    B being female, she will be well treated

    C she does not allow them to bear arms

    D she is naturally a trusting person

_____ 2. Which does Queen Elizabeth I *not* offer to do for the English people in "Tilbury Speech"?

    F Die for them

    G Command them on the battlefield

    H Give them freedom of religion

    J Grant them material rewards

_____ 3. Counselors have advised Queen Elizabeth to —

    A resort to tough policing measures to prove her strength

    B avoid crowds for fear of assassination

    C reduce taxes to quell dissent

    D reassure the people that they will be protected

_____ 4. When Queen Elizabeth I says that she has "the heart and stomach of a king," she means that —

    F she has the courage and ruthlessness of a man to be worthy of her people's trust

    G women are not capable of prosecuting a war

    H she loves England as much as any king would

    J she is physically strong enough to fulfill her office

_____ 5. What does the speaker in Oration I plead for?

    A Freedom for women to associate

    B Permission to write for publication

    C More time to speak about women's rights

    D Education for all girls in England

Holt Assessment: Literature, Reading, and Vocabulary

_____ **6.** In the phrase, "Ladies, gentlewomen, and other inferior women, but not less worthy," what does *inferior* mean?

    F Of lower social class

    G Weaker in physical strength

    H Female as opposed to male

    J Less keen in intelligence

_____ **7.** What remedy does the speaker of Oration II propose for the problems of women?

    A Vocal and written protest

    B Refusal to comply with husbands' wishes

    C Education as the first step toward progress

    D She does not believe there is any remedy

_____ **8.** Regarding men, the speaker of Oration III —

    F feels they are the source of women's sufferings

    G feels that although they have often mistreated women, men's point of view needs to be understood

    H feels that men are superior to women and women are almost nothing without them

    J feels that if men had to bear children, and women didn't, power would be reversed

_____ **9.** The speaker of Oration VII desires to —

    A be like a man in power and prestige

    B exert power over men through beauty and grace

    C live peacefully on her manor with her husband and sons

    D resolve the question of women's rights through intellectual discourse

_____ **10.** What do Queen Elizabeth I and Margaret Cavendish, duchess of Newcastle, *not* have in common?

    F Eloquence

    G Education

    H Power over a nation

    J Rank and privilege

ANALYZING: POLITICAL POINTS OF VIEW *(40 points; 10 points each)*

On the line provided, write the letter of the *best* answer to each of the following items.

_____ **11.** In "Tilbury Speech," which of the following lines is meant to quiet a possible objection from the crowd?

     A "My loving people . . ."

     B "I have placed my chiefest strength and safeguard in the loyal hearts and goodwill of my subjects."

     C "I myself will be your general, judge, and rewarder of every one of your virtues in the field."

     D "I am come amongst you . . . not for my recreation and disport . . ."

_____ **12.** In a critique of an author's views, you should *not* consider the —

     F author's choice of words, or diction

     G tone of the text

     H reader's dislike of the author's reputation

     J reader's knowledge and experience

_____ **13.** At the beginning of Oration VII, the speaker says, "The former oratoress's speech was to persuade us out of ourselves and to be that which Nature never intended us to be, to wit, masculine." From this statement, you can logically infer that the speaker of Oration —

     A I was correct in urging women to educate themselves

     B VI encouraged women to try to be more like men

     C VII's description of the former speech is wrong

     D VIII will bring together the opposing views of previous speakers

_____ **14.** The speaker of Oration VII goes on to ask, "But why should we desire to be masculine, since our own sex and condition is far the better?" What inference could you *not* logically draw from this or the previous quotation from the same speech?

     F Speaker VII has never experienced suffering.

     G Speaker VII would rather be queen of England than be a male commoner.

     H Speaker VII is female.

     J Speakers VI and VII disagree on a major issue.

CONSTRUCTED RESPONSE *(20 points)*

15. You have read four Orations in which Margaret Cavendish, duchess of Newcastle, puts various views into the mouths of four different fictitious women. What do you think were Cavendish's own beliefs and assumptions about women? On what do you base your inference? Finally, how clearly and effectively do you think Cavendish's own views come through in the Orations? Write your answer on a separate sheet of paper.

SELECTION TEST | LITERARY RESPONSE AND ANALYSIS

Psalm 23, Psalm 137 King James Bible

COMPREHENSION *(40 points; 4 points each)*
On the line provided, write the letter of the *best* answer to each of the following items.

_____ 1. Which of the following descriptions of God's gifts to humankind is *not* stated in Psalm 23?

    A Protection from evil

    B Goodness and mercy

    C Ecstasy and joy

    D Righteousness

_____ 2. According to the author of Psalm 23, the speaker's interactions with God resemble the relationship of a flock to its shepherd because both the psalmist and a flock —

    F follow and trust

    G live in a large group

    H wander and wonder

    J fear and flee

_____ 3. The banquet in Psalm 23 is a(n) —

    A ritual meal celebrated by God's most devout followers

    B metaphor representing the wealth one will receive in exchange for trusting God

    C example of how followers of God will not need shepherds

    D metaphor for the comfort and protection God provides his followers

_____ 4. Psalm 23 suggests that in exchange for following God, people can expect —

    F material gain

    G prestige and power

    H peace and serenity

    J a long, healthy life

_____ 5. In Psalm 137, what does "Let my tongue cleave to the roof of my mouth" mean?

    A Let me be burned by scalding hot food.

    B Let me be unable to speak.

    C Let me be able to stick out my tongue as far as possible.

    D Leave me alone while I am making faces.

_____ 6. What do the children of Edom want to do to the city of Jerusalem?

    F Rebuild it

    G Destroy it

    H Settle in it

    J Write about it

Holt Assessment: Literature, Reading, and Vocabulary

_____ **7.** The Hebrews weep by the waters of Babylon because they —

 A regret going to war

 B miss their children

 C are wounded

 D are homesick

_____ **8.** In Psalm 137, when the Hebrews remember and praise Zion, they are also recalling and hoping to regain a —

 F chance to sing psalms

 G chance to make peace with the Babylonians

 H lost belief in their own God

 J safe place of their own to live

_____ **9.** In Psalm 137, Mount Zion can be said to represent —

 A all of Israel

 B a national park in the Sinai desert

 C the countries of the Middle East

 D peace and prosperity

_____ **10.** At the end of Psalm 137, the psalmist expresses hope for —

 F the destruction of Israel's enemies

 G reunion with the people of Edom

 H many descendants

 J a return of the barren desert into fertile farmland

LITERARY FOCUS: PARALLELISM *(40 points; 10 points each)*
On the line provided, write the letter of the *best* answer to each of the following items.

_____ **11. Parallelism** is the repetition of words, phrases, or sentences that have the same grammatical structure or that —

 A sound good together

 B have different grammatical structure

 C state the same basic idea

 D name the same human or divine persons

_____ **12.** The psalmists did *not* use parallelism to —

    F show relationships among ideas

    G increase the emotional impact of an idea or statement

    H create rhythm and balance

    J use sounds that closely resemble one another

_____ **13.** Parallelism was especially appropriate to the Psalms because —

    A there were 150 of them, so length was required

    B they were created to be sung or recited

    C they were originally written in Hebrew

    D they were translated by a committee named by King James I

_____ **14.** Which quotation from the Psalms shows parallelism?

    F "Remember, O Lord, the children of Edom in the day of Jerusalem . . ."

    G "If I forget thee, O Jerusalem, / Let my right hand forget her cunning. / If I do not remember thee, / Let my tongue cleave to the roof of my mouth . . ."

    H "The Lord is my shepherd; I shall not want."

    J "How shall we sing the Lord's song / In a strange land?"

CONSTRUCTED RESPONSE *(20 points)*

15. On a separate sheet of paper, discuss how metaphor and parallelism help the psalmist achieve his goals and evoke the readers' emotions. Identify at least two specific examples of each.

The Parable of the Prodigal Son King James Bible

COMPREHENSION (40 points; 4 points each)

On the line provided, write the letter of the *best* answer to each of the following items.

_____ **1.** This parable is set in —

    A a heavenly kingdom

    B ancient Rome

    C Jesus' time and culture

    D Egypt when the Hebrews were enslaved

_____ **2.** The lesson Jesus provides in the parable is to —

    F welcome sinners who return to the fold

    G try to avoid feeling morally superior

    H stay home and avoid risky travel

    J abandon material pleasures and seek holiness

_____ **3.** The action of the parable is set in motion when the —

    A younger son kicks out the older son

    B father kicks out the younger son

    C older son leaves to find his fortune

    D younger son leaves to find a new life

_____ **4.** Which of the following descriptions *most* closely follows the scenario of "The Parable of the Prodigal Son"?

    F When a young runaway returns home, his parents rejoice.

    G A young man finds money in the street and turns it in to the police.

    H A young man offers to mow a neighbor's lawn but refuses any payment.

    J A child goes riding with a stranger and is killed.

_____ **5.** What prompts the prodigal son to return to his father's house?

    A Homesickness

    B Hunger

    C The need to help with the harvest

    D Desire to claim his inheritance

_____ **6.** What does the father *not* do to the prodigal son?

    F Clothe him

    G Feed him

    H Punish him

    J Embrace him

_____ **7.** While the prodigal son was away from home, what was his brother doing?

    A Eating his parents out of house and home

    B Slacking off on his parents' property

    C Dutifully serving his parents

    D Studying the Bible

_____ **8.** In the parable the character who "was lost, and is found" is the —

    F father

    G man who raised swine

    H prodigal son

    J prodigal son's brother

_____ **9.** The character who seems to feel resentful at the end of the parable is the —

    A father

    B mother

    C elder son

    D younger son

_____ **10.** What moral question does the parable answer?

    F What is written in the law?

    G How shall repentant sinners be treated?

    H Is it acceptable to raise unclean animals that are then eaten?

    J What is necessary to achieve eternal life?

LITERARY FOCUS: PARABLE *(40 points; 10 points each)*
On the line provided, write the letter of the *best* answer to each of the following items.

_____ **11.** A **parable** can be defined as a —

    A brief tale that teaches a moral lesson about life

    B law that proscribes moral behavior

    C comparison between religious and nonreligious teachings

    D biblical form of poetry that pleads for God's mercy

_____ **12.** **Parables** are concerned with —

    F the secret to religious rituals

    G awareness of all sentient beings

    H the answers to obscure riddles

    J profound truths and moral laws

_____ **13.** Jesus uses parables *mainly* to —

    A entertain his followers

    B avoid giving definite advice

    C make his messages clear

    D demystify his relationship with God

_____ **14. Parables** use the literary devices of —

    F rhythm and metrical balance

    G varied line length and startling imagery

    H symbolism and allegory

    J figures of speech and ornate diction

CONSTRUCTED RESPONSE *(20 points)*

15. Looking at the aspects of "The Parable of the Prodigal Son" that belong specifically to the parable genre, how do they contribute to the story's moral ideas? How might the story of the prodigal son be different if it were a realistic short story with the same characters and setting, instead of a parable?

SELECTION TEST ▮▮▮▮▮

Night *from the* Koran *translated by* N. J. Dawood
from Philosophy and Spiritual Discipline
from the Bhagavad-Gita *translated by* Barbara Stoler Miller
Zen Parables *compiled by* Paul Reps
from The Analects of Confucius
translated and annotated by Arthur Waley
from the Tao Te Ching Laotzu *translated by* Stephen Mitchell
Taoist Anecdotes *translated and edited by* Moss Roberts
Sayings of Saadi *translated by* Idries Shah
African Proverbs *compiled by* Charlotte *and* Wolf Leslau

COMPREHENSION *(40 points; 4 points each)*

On the line provided, write the letter of the *best* answer to each of the following items.

_____ **1.** "Night," from the *Koran*, teaches that —

     A day is superior to night as good is superior to evil

     B charity and good works are the way to blessedness

     C he who seeks a godly life must withdraw from society

     D a blazing fire awaits all but a select few holy men

_____ **2.** Which of the following statements *best* describes the overall message of the selection from "Philosophy and Spiritual Discipline" from the *Bhagavad-Gita*?

     F Do what you have to do without second-guessing yourself.

     G To achieve inner strength, cut your attachments to sensory things.

     H It is by suffering that we learn and grow.

     J It is just as bad to imagine a sin as to commit it.

_____ **3.** According to the *Bhagavad-Gita*, what is the source of anger, confusion, and ultimate ruin?

     A War

     B Desire

     C Poverty

     D Satan

_____ **4.** In the first three Zen parables, "The Moon Cannot Be Stolen," "Temper," and "The Gates of Paradise," what do all the Zen masters have in common?

    F Self-control and patience

    G Impatience with fools and thieves

    H Single-minded devotion to finding truth

    J No sin in their personal lives

_____ **5.** The message of the Zen parable "The First Principle" might be stated as —

    A even the newest student can sometimes be wiser than the oldest teacher

    B sometimes, just when you're about to give up, success comes

    C students should not presume to criticize their teachers

    D people are at their best when they act spontaneously

_____ **6.** The message of the passage from the *Tao Te Ching* might be stated as —

    F sin is inescapable, so don't try to avoid it

    G don't show weakness or people will take advantage of you

    H be yourself and go with the flow

    J nothing is really the way it seems

_____ **7.** Confucius's sayings about knowledge indicate that he —

    A knew he was very wise

    B modestly resisted being called "Master"

    C humbly admitted the possibility of his own ignorance

    D preferred to speak of good and evil rather than of knowledge or its lack

_____ **8.** The two Taoist anecdotes in this selection offer wisdom about —

    F human frailties

    G the ultimate nature of reality

    H how to become enlightened

    J proper punishment for sin

_____ **9.** Saadi's "The Fox and the Camels" is an example of a(n) —

    A aphorism

    B maxim

    C fable

    D sermon

_____ **10.** Which of the African proverbs in this selection could be paraphrased, "Don't get too big for your britches"?

    F When the heart overflows, it comes out through the mouth.

    G He who cannot dance will say: 'The drum is bad.'

    H Evil enters like a needle and spreads like an oak tree.

    J The frog wanted to be as big as the elephant, and burst.

LITERARY FOCUS: DIDACTIC LITERATURE *(40 points; 10 points each)*
On the line provided, write the letter of the *best* answer to each of the following items.

_____ **11. Didactic** literature —

  A is not much fun to read

  B gives instruction

  C discusses the difference between good and evil

  D comes from an ancient or distant culture

_____ **12.** Most wisdom literature, such as the sayings of Taoist and Buddhist masters and *The Analects of Confucius*, began in the form of —

  F oral discourse

  G music

  H ceremonial law

  J epic poetry

_____ **13.** What do proverbs, fables, anecdotes, folk tales, and maxims have in common?

  A All these writings ultimately share one basic universal message.

  B These forms are not found in present-day European literature.

  C They are forms of sacred text used in a variety of the world's religions.

  D They are secular forms that can serve as didactic literature.

_____ **14.** What kinds of questions does didactic literature try to answer?

  F Questions of history, such as, "What was Laotzu really like?"

  G Questions of prophecy, such as, "When will the world end?"

  H Questions of etiquette, such as, "How should I seat guests at a formal dinner?"

  J Questions of life's essential meaning and purpose, such as, "How should I live?"

CONSTRUCTED RESPONSE *(20 points)*

15. From two different sources in this Connecting to World Literature selection, choose the two passages that you like *best*. (Do not choose two Zen parables or two of Confucius's sayings, for example.) On a separate sheet of paper, compare and contrast them by discussing what you like about them, and how the passages are similar and different in both form and meaning.

SELECTION TEST

LITERARY RESPONSE AND ANALYSIS

The Fall of Satan *from* Paradise Lost   John Milton

COMPREHENSION *(40 points; 4 points each)*

On the line provided, write the letter of the *best* answer to each of the following items.

_____ 1. The reason given by the poet for concentrating on Satan is that Satan —

   A seduced Adam and Eve, the ancestors of all humankind

   B helped create Heaven and Hell

   C had more to do with human nature than God

   D was the most extraordinary actor in the epic drama of human life

_____ 2. Which of the following quotations from "The Fall of Satan" refers to the atmosphere of Hell?

   F "No light, but rather darkness visible . . ."

   G "round he throws his baleful eyes . . ."

   H "as far as angels ken . . ."

   J "Heaven hides nothing from thy view."

_____ 3. In "The Fall of Satan," Hell contains —

   A answers

   B lies

   C worries

   D sorrow

_____ 4. Satan is described as —

   F having burning hands and a mouth like a volcano

   G rolling on a huge fiery lake

   H being wrapped, screaming, in flaming chains

   J having several servants who feed him hot coals

_____ 5. Who is Beelzebub?

   A Satan's chief assistant

   B One of the souls of the damned

   C Another name for Satan himself

   D An upstart demon whom Satan destroys

_____ 6. What theme is explored in "The Fall of Satan"?

   F Good and evil are related; good has no meaning without evil.

   G Adam and Eve are not responsible for their actions.

   H God only occasionally protects humans from Satan.

   J Man does not have free will in the presence of God and Satan.

_____ **7.** The tone of "The Fall of Satan" is —

    A frivolous

    B serious

    C hopeless

    D humorous

_____ **8.** Milton's original source for *Paradise Lost* was —

    F one of the legends of King Arthur

    G a famous parable of Jesus

    H a folk tale about the Devil tempting a woman

    J the book of Genesis in the Bible

_____ **9.** Which of the following phrases from "The Fall of Satan" does *not* demonstrate regular iambic pentameter?

    A "And courage never to submit or yield . . ."

    B "Who now triumphs, and in the excess of joy . . ."

    C "And put to proof his high supremacy . . ."

    D "The mind is its own place, and in itself . . ."

_____ **10.** According to line 26, the author's purpose for writing *Paradise Lost* is to —

    F forgive sin in the descendants of Adam and Eve

    G understand what made Satan rebel against God

    H explain God's ways to a human audience

    J plumb the greatest depths and heights of poetry

LITERARY FOCUS: STYLE *(20 points; 5 points each)*

On the line provided, write the letter of the *best* answer to each of the following items.

_____ **11.** All of the following elements are part of Milton's style *except* —

    A footnotes

    B omitted words

    C inverted sentences

    D ornate language

_____ **12.** In "The Fall of Satan," Milton includes allusions to all of the following sources *except* —

    F the Old Testament

    G the New Testament

    H Greek mythology

    J Celtic legend

Holt Assessment: Literature, Reading, and Vocabulary

_____ **13.** Milton uses epic simile so that —

    A readers will not confuse his epic with the Bible

    B readers will have to work hard to decipher hidden meanings

    C he can show off his prodigious learning

    D his poem will match the scope and gravity of ancient traditions

_____ **14.** Which of the following quotations is an example of inverted word order?

    F "So spake the apostate Angel. . . ."

    G "The mind is its own place. . . ."

    H "And rest can never dwell, hope never comes. . . ."

    J "He trusted to have equaled the Most High. . . ."

VOCABULARY DEVELOPMENT (*20 points; 4 points each*)

On the line provided, write the Vocabulary word below that *best* completes the sentence.

infernal   guile   contention   impetuous   malice

15. Satan does not love or fear God, but instead feels angry _____.

16. A decision to rebel against God must be rash, _____, and foolish.

17. Milton's descriptions give a vivid mental picture of the _____ region.

18. Milton's characterization of Satan shows him to be a figure of _____ and cunning.

19. Two armies, one of Good and one of Evil, met in a scene of fierce _____.

CONSTRUCTED RESPONSE *(20 points)*

20. In *Paradise Lost*, Milton uses a style grand enough to suit its subject matter. On a separate sheet of paper, identify two specific elements of Milton's style and, using examples from the text, analyze how they succeed in this purpose.

Holt Assessment: Literature, Reading, and Vocabulary

SELECTION TEST   ·LITERARY RESPONSE AND ANALYSIS

When I consider how my light is spent John Milton

COMPREHENSION (*40 points; 8 points each*)
On the line provided, write the letter of the *best* answer to each of the following items.

_____ **1.** In "When I consider how my light is spent," *light* stands for —

   A blindness

   B sight

   C poetic talent

   D life

_____ **2.** The rhyme scheme of the octave in "When I consider how my light is spent" is *abba abba*. What is the rhyme scheme of the sestet?

   F *cdc dcd*

   G *ccddee*

   H *cdcd ee*

   J *cde cde*

_____ **3.** Which abstract quality is personified in "When I consider how my light is spent"?

   A Talent

   B Patience

   C Faith

   D Labor

_____ **4.** What great frustration does the speaker of "When I consider how my light is spent" feel?

   F He finds it hard to spend his time doing the things he likes best.

   G He longs for a way to serve God and fears he won't be able to.

   H Sighted people go on voyages and journeys, while he remains at home.

   J God has sent him more troubles than he can bear.

_____ **5.** The last line, "They also serve who only stand and wait," suggests that —

   A many are called, but few are chosen

   B the early bird catches the worm

   C there is nothing new under the sun

   D God has a plan for everybody

LITERARY FOCUS: ALLUSION *(40 points; 10 points each)*

On the line provided, write the letter of the *best* answer to each of the following items.

_____ **6.** If you make an **allusion** to popular culture, you —

    F make a contribution to popular culture

    G criticize popular culture

    H refer to something in popular culture

    J declare your love for popular culture

_____ **7.** An **allusion** works *best* if —

    A it is about sports or current events

    B it is about a work no one has ever heard of

    C it is about a sacred text

    D at least some readers recognize it

_____ **8.** Which line from the sonnet contains an allusion to one of Jesus' parables?

    F "And that one talent which is death to hide . . ."

    G "To serve therewith my Maker . . ."

    H "Doth God exact day-labor . . . ?"

    J "Thousands at His bidding speed . . ."

_____ **9.** Which of the following quotations alludes to one of Jesus' sayings?

    A "dark world and wide . . ."

    B "My true account . . ."

    C "Bear His mild yoke . . ."

    D "ocean without rest . . ."

CONSTRUCTED RESPONSE *(20 points)*

10. In this sonnet, Milton repeatedly personifies abstract qualities, such as patience and time. What effect do you think Milton intended this rhetorical strategy to have? Write your answer on a separate sheet of paper.

from The Pilgrim's Progress John Bunyan

COMPREHENSION *(40 points; 4 points each)*

On the line provided, write the letter of the *best* answer to each of the following items.

_____ **1.** The title *The Pilgrim's Progress* reflects the fact that the book narrates —

    A the imagination of John Bunyan

    B a dream of the narrator's

    C a description of the Celestial City

    D a religious journey

_____ **2.** Christian sets out on his "progress" because he —

    F is trying to learn enough to become a preacher

    G and his wife have decided to break up

    H needs to get medicine for his sick child

    J wants to get rid of a burden

_____ **3.** Christian's first companion on the road is named —

    A Apollyon

    B John

    C Faithful

    D Legion

_____ **4.** Vanity-Fair symbolizes the —

    F Europe of Bunyan's time

    G Holy Land

    H afterlife

    J New World

_____ **5.** What would Christian like to buy at Vanity-Fair?

    A A horse

    B A kingdom without sin

    C His child's health and life

    D Truth

_____ **6.** In addition to items for sale, what can be seen free of charge at Vanity-Fair?

    F A security force consisting of Satan's rebellious angels

    G A museum of history's greatest villains

    H One pure and innocent soul, caged and on display

    J Thefts, murders, adulteries, and other sins

_____ **7.** Who is the chief of the fair?

    A Beelzebub

    B The Mayor

    C The dreaming narrator

    D King Charles II

_____ **8.** Mr. Blind-man, Mr. No-good, Mr. Malice, Mr. Love-lust, Mr. Live-loose, Mr. Heady, Mr. High-mind, Mr. Enmity, Mr. Liar, Mr. Cruelty, Mr. Hate-light, and Mr. Implacable —

    F are standing in the tavern when Christian walks in

    G are the jury who try Christian and Faithful

    H defend Christian against attack by the townspeople

    J are slain by Christian as he escapes Vanity-Fair

_____ **9.** According to the foreman, what are the pilgrims on trial for?

    A Wickedness

    B Lewdness

    C Heresy

    D Christianity

_____ **10.** "[A]s poor as poor might be, with not so much household stuff as a dish or spoon" is John Bunyan's description of —

    F himself and his wife

    G the Celestial City

    H Christian's household

    J Vanity-Fair

LITERARY FOCUS: ALLEGORY *(20 points; 5 points each)*

On the line provided, write the letter of the *best* answer to each of the following items.

_____ **11.** The narrative in an allegory is intended to —

    A be interesting only for its symbolic meaning

    B operate on both the literal and the symbolic levels at once

    C be immediately understood without deeper examination

    D raise doubts about the author's philosophical positions

_____ **12.** On an **allegorical journey,** —

    F places and landmarks do not stand for themselves

    G there are more ideas near the end of the journey than near the beginning

    H the traveler's adventures usually affect his mental and moral development

    J the landscape should be familiar to the reader

_____ **13.** In Vanity-Fair, allegory can be seen *most* clearly in the —

    A presence of good and evil forces

    B characters' names

    C landscape of the journey

    D narrator's opinions

_____ **14.** The *main* purpose of most **allegories** is to —

    F persuade

    G teach

    H provoke debate

    J entertain

VOCABULARY DEVELOPMENT *(20 points; 4 points each)*

On the line provided, write the letter of the *best* synonym for each of the following Vocabulary words.

_____ **15.** allure

    A attract

    B capture

    C repel

    D defend

_____ **16.** reproachfully

    F mistakenly

    G viciously

    H accusingly

    J pleadingly

_____ **17.** confounded

    A confused

    B misused

    C abused

    D refused

_____ **18.** implacable

      F   destructive

      G changeable

      H unchangeable

      J   constructive

_____ **19.** respite

      A hurry

      B hunger

      C spite

      D postponement

CONSTRUCTED RESPONSE (20 points)

20. What is the central philosophical idea that John Bunyan wants to argue for in
The Pilgrim's Progress? Do you think Bunyan's sincerity makes this a stronger,
more appealing allegory, or a less interesting, more obvious one? On a separate
sheet of paper, defend your opinions with references to the text.

COLLECTION 3 SUMMATIVE TEST

The Renaissance 1485–1660: A Flourish of Genius

Read the following poem carefully, and then answer the questions that follow.

Sonnet 57

by William Shakespeare

Being your slave, what should I do but tend
Upon the hours and times of your desire?
I have no precious time at all to spend,
Nor services to do, till you require.
Nor dare I chide the world-without-end hour
Whilst I, my sovereign, watch the clock for you,
Nor think the bitterness of absence sour
When you have bid your servant once adieu;
Nor dare I question with my jealous thought
Where you may be, or your affairs suppose,
But like a sad slave, stay and think of nought
Save where you are how happy you make those!
       So true a fool is love, that in your will
       (Though you do any thing) he thinks no ill.

VOCABULARY SKILLS *(20 points; 4 points each)*

Each of the underlined words below has also been underlined in the selection. Re-read those passages, and use context clues to help select an answer. On the line to the left of each sentence, write the letter of the word or phrase that *best* completes each sentence.

_____ **1.** To chide something is to —

    A delight in it

    B find fault with it

    C miss it

    D praise it

_____ **2.** When the speaker calls his love "my sovereign," he is comparing her to a —

    F trusty dog

    G valuable coin

    H supreme ruler

    J favorite sister

_____ **3.** To bid adieu is to —

    A say goodbye

    B threaten with death

    C declare one's love

    D bet on a card

_____ **4.** The word *affairs* refers to —

    F any activities

    G international conflict

    H business deals

    J romantic entanglements

_____ **5.** *Nought* is another word for —

    A heaven

    B nothing

    C a day's work

    D love's knot

COMPREHENSION *(20 points; 4 points each)*

On the line provided, write the letter of the *best* answer to each of the following items.

_____ **6.** The explicit statement made in this sonnet could be paraphrased as —

    F sometimes you really make me mad

    G I'm so in love with you, I don't care what do you

    H if you continue to keep me waiting, you won't find me waiting much longer

    J I'm thinking of leaving you, but I'm giving you one more chance

_____ **7.** The speaker probably wishes that —

    A his beloved were more beautiful

    B he loved his beloved more helplessly

    C his beloved spent more time with him

    D his beloved would leave him alone

_____ **8.** The person addressed in the poem is —

    F the speaker's official employer

    G inseparable from the speaker

    H too clinging and dependent

    J not very attentive to the speaker

_____ **9.** "Your servant" is the —

    A speaker

    B person addressed in the poem

    C husband of the speaker's beloved

    D beloved's serving-woman

_____ **10.** This poem is like many other Renaissance poems in its —

    F irrational purpose

    G emphasis on love

    H rough humor

    J mood of mourning

READING SKILLS AND STRATEGIES: CONSTRUCTED RESPONSE *(30 points; 15 points each)*

Analyzing Tone

11. On a separate sheet of paper, identify two different tones or attitudes that the speaker in Sonnet 57 takes toward his beloved. Supply evidence for each. Which tone or attitude do you think he feels more deeply, and why?

Critiquing Summations

12. Which of the following statements is the *best* summation of the main idea, or theme, of Sonnet 57? On a separate sheet of paper, write the letter of the answer you choose, and briefly defend your choice.

    a. The speaker is lamenting that he loves someone who does not love him in return.

    b. The speaker is expressing his passionate devotion to his beloved.

    c. Other: _____

LITERARY FOCUS: CONSTRUCTED RESPONSE *(30 points; 10 points each)*

13. In the left-hand side of the following chart, identify an image in the sonnet
that helps express the speaker's attitudes and feelings. In the right-hand
side, describe the emotional effect the image evokes in the reader.

▸ Image	▸ Emotional Impact on Reader

14. On a separate sheet of paper, identify two instances of **irony** in the sonnet, and
explain how they are ironic.

15. Based on this sonnet, what do you think is Shakespeare's view of love?
Explain, offering evidence from the text. Write your answer on a separate
sheet of paper.

The Restoration and the Eighteenth Century 1660–1800: The Best of All Possible Worlds

On the line provided, write the letter of the *best* answer to each of the following items.
(100 points; 10 points each)

_____ 1. A writer who chooses words that express the opposite of what he or she means is using —

    A verbal irony

    B situational irony

    C paradox

    D allegory

_____ 2. Writers use words with strong **connotations,** either positive or negative, for all of the following reasons *except* —

    F to influence the reader

    G to convey the writer's viewpoint

    H to create regular rhythm

    J to evoke associations in the mind of the reader

_____ 3. **Satire** is used for all of the following purposes *except* —

    A to expose errors and absurdities

    B to bring about change

    C to show both sides of an issue

    D to make people laugh

_____ 4. The imitation of a literary work for amusement or instruction is called a(n) —

    F farce

    G cliché

    H allusion

    J parody

_____ 5. What is the purpose of **tone**?

    A To express the author's attitude toward the reader or a subject

    B To quicken the pace of the plot

    C To elaborate on ideas or situations in a literary work

    D To use exaggeration to make a point

_____ **6.** Which of the following words is an **iamb**?

    F borrow

    G late

    H return

    J prettier

_____ **7.** A **theme** is *best* described as —

    A a moral lesson presented in a work of literature

    B the central idea or insight about life revealed in a literary work

    C the subject of a work of literature

    D a series of related events in a literary work

_____ **8.** When analyzing **persuasive writing,** the reader should consider all of the following *except* —

    F logical appeals

    G emotional appeals

    H the author's bias

    J atmosphere

_____ **9.** In a **public document** a writer might use a **counterargument** to —

    A point out a parallel between two subjects

    B anticipate the audience's objections and openly address them

    C ask a question for which an answer is not expected

    D illustrate a point with a brief story

_____ **10.** A **word analogy** compares two pairs of words to —

    F create a metaphor

    G show how the pairs are alike

    H help define the words

    J determine the origin of the words

LITERARY PERIOD INTRODUCTION TEST

The Restoration and the Eighteenth Century 1660–1800: The Best of All Possible Worlds

COMPREHENSION *(100 points; 10 points each)*

On the line provided, write the letter of the *best* answer to each of the following items.

_____ **1.** Which of the following statements *best* describes how England from 1660 to 1800 resembled the Roman empire?

    A People fled from England to North America; similarly, many people in ancient Rome fled to Latin America.

    B England's colonies struggled for and achieved independence from England just as the colonies of ancient Rome successfully rebelled against Roman rule.

    C Just as the Emperor Augustus restored order to ancient Rome, the Stuart monarchs restored order to England.

    D James II fled from political persecution in England while Emperor Augustus retained a secure hold on his rule.

_____ **2.** British writing of the Augustan era is often called **neoclassical** because it —

    F imitates the Latin classics

    G aims to create a uniquely English style

    H was written by the Emperor Octavian, who was called "Augustus"

    J was translated from the Roman and Greek languages

_____ **3.** Modern English prose emerged in an age in which the Royal Society of London for the Promotion of Natural Knowledge called for writing that was —

    A humorous and lighthearted

    B epic and poetic

    C scholarly and ornate

    D precise and exact

_____ **4.** During the eighteenth century, natural phenomena were increasingly explained by —

    F poets and statesmen

    G scientific observation

    H religious doctrine

    J superstition

_____ **5.** King Charles II reestablished the —

    A Anglican Church as the official church of England and tried to outlaw dozens of religious sects

    B Puritan Church as the official church of England and tried to incorporate the doctrines of dissenting sects into law

    C Roman Catholic church as the official church of England and recognized the Pope as supreme authority over the land

    D Deist Church as the official church of England and named Sir Isaac Newton as Archbishop of Canterbury

_____ **6.** The Glorious Revolution of 1688 —

    F was marked by bitter gun battles in the streets of London

    G resulted in the beheading of King Charles II and a government by commoners

    H forced the Roman Catholic king, James II, to flee England and his Protestant daughter, Mary, to take the throne

    J marked the first loss of overseas colonies for the British Empire

_____ **7.** Alexander Pope and Jonathan Swift could both be described as —

    A hopeful and optimistic

    B smug and indifferent

    C respectful and humble

    D critical and unsatisfied

_____ **8.** The first English novels were —

    F written by former poets such as William Wordsworth

    G complicated mixtures of poetry, drama, and prose

    H read only by scholars and scientists

    J long and often comical narratives

_____ **9.** Samuel Johnson was skeptical, or doubtful, about the value of —

    A progress

    B literature

    C learning

    D religion

_____ **10.** At the end of the eighteenth century, writers began to choose topics such as natural landscapes and humble life. This choice reflected their —

    F dismay at changes brought about by the Industrial Revolution

    G lack of knowledge about urban life or poverty

    H desire to imitate Augustan literature

    J optimism about industrial progress

SELECTION TEST   LITERARY RESPONSE AND ANALYSIS

A Modest Proposal Jonathan Swift
Top of the Food Chain T. Coraghessan Boyle

COMPREHENSION *(40 points; 4 points each)*

On the line provided, write the letter of the *best* answer to each of the following items.

_____ **1.** *A Modest Proposal* satirizes —

    A English policy in Ireland

    B Irish bankers

    C people who do not pay rent

    D problems caused by overpopulation

_____ **2.** The narrator of *A Modest Proposal* assumes the character of a(n) —

    F American giving advice to politicians in England

    G Irish Catholic who criticizes the inefficiency of the British

    H political planner devising strategies to conquer Ireland

    J economic planner acting for the benefit of England and Ireland

_____ **3.** The narrator claims that landlords will benefit from his proposal because they will be able to —

    A lower their rents

    B sell excess children

    C stop domestic violence

    D easily evict poor tenants

_____ **4.** Which of the following outcomes is *not* an advantage anticipated by the narrator of *A Modest Proposal*?

    F A decrease in the number of papists

    G A decrease in the number of beggars

    H A decrease in the number of marriages

    J A decrease in the number of poor people

_____ **5.** The narrator claims to have no personal motive behind his proposal because he —

    A does not have any children to sell

    B does not own a tavern

    C does not have a wife

    D has all the money he could want

6. What does Swift offer as a serious solution to Ireland's problems?

    F   Mass emigration to America

    G The overthrow of the king

    H The establishment of a revolutionary government

    J   Prudent living and the buying of Irish products

7. What do Swift's *A Modest Proposal* and "Top of the Food Chain" have in common? Both —

    A recommend eating babies as a way to end overpopulation

    B poke fun at the poor for being responsible for their own condition

    C satirize misguided efforts to solve social problems

    D support the government's efforts to end poverty

8. What public health issue starts the escalation of misery in "Top of the Food Chain"?

    F   Too much bureaucracy

    G Insects in Borneo

    H Cats eating geckoes

    J   The government's refusal to ban DDT

9. Swift's attitude in *A Modest Proposal* can be best described as —

    A frivolous

    B carefree

    C harsh

    D joyous

10. In "Top of the Food Chain" the speaker addresses his remarks to the —

    F   government of Borneo

    G United States Senate

    H World Health Organization

    J   Sultan of Brunei

LITERARY FOCUS: VERBAL IRONY *(15 points; 5 points each)*
On the line provided, write the letter of the *best* answer to each of the following items.

_____ **11.** In **verbal irony** —

    A what happens is the opposite of what is expected

    B there is almost always a tone of hostility or sarcasm

    C what is meant is the opposite of what is said

    D the characters do not know what is coming, but the reader does

_____ **12.** Which of the narrator's comments about the poor does Swift *not* intend ironically?

    F "I am not in the least pain upon that matter. . . ."

    G "They are every day dying, and rotting, by cold, and famine, and filth, and vermin. . . ."

    H "Infant's flesh will be in season throughout the year, but more plentiful in March. . . ."

    J "The remaining hundred thousand [babies] may at a year old be offered in sale to the persons of quality. . . ."

_____ **13.** Swift uses irony to satirize people who —

    A dislike children

    B have a cold-blooded attitude toward human suffering

    C offer proposals that are not likely to be accepted

    D believe that the problem of poverty in Ireland can be solved

READING SKILLS: RECOGNIZING PERSUASIVE TECHNIQUES *(5 points)*
On the line provided, write the letter of the *best* answer to the following item.

_____ **14.** Swift's main persuasive strategy in *A Modest Proposal* is —

    F the use of logical appeals to demonstrate the fairness of his proposal

    G satire of logical appeals to awaken the reader's conscience

    H use of ethical appeals to ward off the reader's concern about the subject matter

    J use of emotional appeals to insult the Irish and the Americans

VOCABULARY DEVELOPMENT *(20 points; 4 points each)*
Match the definition on the left with the Vocabulary word on the right. On the line provided, write the letter of the Vocabulary word.

_____ **15.** shortness

_____ **16.** food or money to support life

_____ **17.** obtain; get

_____ **18.** hostilities; violent hatreds or resentments

_____ **19.** wandered off the subject

a. sustenance

b. digressed

c. brevity

d. animosities

e. procure

CONSTRUCTED RESPONSE *(20 points)*

20. Using *A Modest Proposal*, analyze how Swift uses irony and satire to achieve rhetorical purposes. Support your answer with specifics from the text. Write your answer on a separate sheet of paper.

| SELECTION TEST ████████████ | LITERARY RESPONSE AND ANALYSIS |

Heroic Couplets Alexander Pope
from An Essay on Man Alexander Pope

COMPREHENSION *(60 points; 6 points each)*

On the line provided, write the letter of the *best* answer to each of the following items.

_____ **1.** What does Pope say about learning?

    A Specialized learning is impossible.

    B A small amount of knowledge can be dangerous.

    C It is possible to learn everything.

    D In order to play an instrument one must practice.

_____ **2.** Pope recommends forgiveness because it —

    F is good for business

    G is a religious commandment

    H helps one rise above being merely human

    J makes one happy about being human

_____ **3.** "Be thou the first true merit to befriend; / His praise is lost, who stays till all commend" advises the reader to —

    A praise oneself rather than waiting to be praised by others

    B avoid waiting to hear what others say before you praise something

    C avoid commending false merit because people might believe you

    D avoid commending false merit because people might not believe you

_____ **4.** According to couplet 10, which of the following statements *best* describes Pope's attitude toward satire?

    F He disapproves of satire because he thinks it is too harsh.

    G He uses satire but is careful not to be overly aggressive.

    H He refrains from satire, preferring a more subtle approach.

    J He uses satire and relishes the power it gives him to wound others.

_____ **5.** Based on couplets 1 and 4, Pope believes the arts —

    A can be learned through practice but cannot be taught

    B can be taught by a teacher who is committed to reaching students on their own level

    C can never be thoroughly learned; every artist is a lifelong apprentice

    D are best left only to those who show early and rare talent

Holt Assessment: Literature, Reading, and Vocabulary

_____ **6.** According to Pope, what emotion can never be quenched in the human heart?

    F Fear

    G Love

    H Anger

    J Hope

_____ **7.** In *An Essay on Man,* Pope recommends that people —

    A forget about themselves

    B study religion

    C eliminate passion from their lives

    D examine themselves

_____ **8.** *An Essay on Man* is written in the form of —

    F heroic couplets

    G iambic tetrameter with the rhyme scheme *abab cdcd*

    H a Shakespearean sonnet

    J blank verse

_____ **9.** Which of the following statements *best* describes what Pope is trying to accomplish in his heroic couplets?

    A He wants the reader to respect human individuality.

    B He wants the reader to recognize the genius of common people.

    C He wants to give useful advice in a manner that is pleasing.

    D He wants to use his poetry to criticize the policies of his country.

_____ **10.** The beliefs and values Pope expresses in *An Essay on Man* and "Heroic Couplets" —

    F reflect only the opinions of Pope

    G should not be taken as sincere expressions

    H contradict one another

    J show that Pope was representative of his age

LITERARY FOCUS: ANTITHESIS (15 points; 5 points each)
On the line provided, write the letter of the *best* answer to each of the following items.

_____ 11. **Antithesis** in rhetoric is —

    A a brief expression of an essay's theme

    B the point of greatest emotional intensity in a plot

    C a contrast of ideas presented in a grammatically balanced statement

    D the character who opposes the protagonist

_____ 12. Which of the following statements contains an antithesis?

    F The couple pledged to remain committed to each other for better or worse.

    G The one who succeeds most is the one who fails best.

    H People who are forewarned are "forearmed."

    J Do not cut off your nose to spite your face.

_____ 13. Of the following statements, the one that is *most* grammatically balanced is —

    A Ask not what your country can do for you, ask what you can do.

    B Ask not what your country can do for you, ask what you can do for your country.

    C Ask not what your country can do for you, ask what you can do for your town.

    D Ask not what your country can do for you, ask not what you can do for your country.

READING SKILLS: IDENTIFYING THE WRITER'S STANCE (5 points)
On the line provided, write the letter of the *best* answer to the following item.

_____ 14. Which of the following is *not* a subject on which Pope expresses his views in these couplets?

    F Proper education

    G Religion

    H Human nature

    J Good writing

CONSTRUCTED RESPONSE (20 points)
15. The early eighteenth century was an age of reason and moderation, in which classical virtues such as balance and order were the ideals. On a separate sheet of paper, discuss how Pope's poetry supports this view. How did he use his poetry to convey his views on life?

SELECTION TEST   LITERARY RESPONSE AND ANALYSIS

from The Rape of the Lock   Alexander Pope

COMPREHENSION *(40 points; 4 points each)*

On the line provided, write the letter of the *best* answer to each of the following items.

_____ **1.** The title *The Rape of the Lock* refers to the —

    A breaking of the lock on Belinda's door

    B Baron's attempt to break into Belinda's room

    C dyeing of Belinda's hair

    D theft of a lock of Belinda's hair

_____ **2.** What does Umbriel bring from the Cave of Spleen?

    F Magical powers to replace the lock

    G Belinda and her grieving mother

    H Sighs, sobs, and passions

    J A knife for Belinda to use

_____ **3.** The sylphs try to prevent —

    A the theft of the lock

    B Umbriel from going to the Cave of Spleen

    C a fight between Umbriel and the Baron

    D Belinda from hurting the Baron

_____ **4.** During the fight between Belinda and the Baron, —

    F the Baron attacks Belinda with a sword

    G Belinda attacks the Baron with a sword

    H the Baron throws snuff at Belinda

    J Belinda throws snuff at the Baron

_____ **5.** What happens to the lock?

    A It rises into the stars.

    B It is kept hidden in a box.

    C It is picked and opened, then closed.

    D It is reattached.

_____ **6.** The line "Where Thames with pride surveys his rising towers" is an example of the figure of speech called —

    F personification

    G onomatopoeia

    H simile

    J metaphor

_____ **7.** The meaning of the couplet "But when to mischief mortals bend their will, / How soon they find fit instruments of ill!" is that —

    A once you decide to be bad, the rest is easy

    B the instruments of evil are themselves evil

    C humans will is weak

    D good workers need the right tools

_____ **8.** Pope's point in the poem is summarized in the line —

    F "And chiefs contend till all the prize is lost!"

    G "What mighty contests rise from trivial things . . ."

    H "All that I dread is leaving you behind!"

    J "With such a prize no mortal must be blessed . . ."

_____ **9.** The line "At every word a reputation dies" is a description of —

    A Pope's verbal wit

    B the argument between Belinda and the Baron

    C gossip at Hampton Court

    D the courtroom of the "hungry judges"

_____ **10.** In Pope's time "The Cave of Spleen" meant —

    F Cave of the Winds

    G Entrance to the Castle

    H Corridor of Power

    J Cave of Depression

LITERARY FOCUS: MOCK EPIC (20 points; 5 points each)

On the line provided, write the letter of the *best* answer to each of the following items.

_____ **11.** A **mock epic** parodies a serious epic by treating a —

    A minor subject in a trivial manner

    B trivial subject in a heroic manner

    C major subject in a trivial manner

    D heroic subject in a lofty manner

_____ **12.** The tone of Pope's mock epic could *best* be described as —

    F solemn and portentous

    G cold and impersonal

    H lofty yet gently satirical

    J humbly apologetic

_____ **13.** Pope's epic includes all the following elements of most serious epics *except* —

    A formal language

    B a national hero

    C extended comparison

    D battles

_____ **14.** Pope seems to believe that humans are essentially —

    F angry

    G weak

    H vile

    J jealous

VOCABULARY DEVELOPMENT *(20 points; 4 points each)*

On the lines provided, write the Vocabulary word that *best* completes the sentences below.

exulting   **repast**   **desist**   **recesses**   **titillating**   **dejects**

15. "At last, I've clipped a lock of her beautiful hair!" the Baron said, _____ over his good fortune.

16. "Now that I've achieved my goal," said the Baron, "let us withdraw to enjoy a glorious

_____."

17. "Oh woe, how the loss of this lock of hair _____ me!" moaned Belinda.

18. "I wish people would _____ from trying to clip off locks of my hair," Belinda complained.

19. "In the deepest _____ of my heart," Alexander Pope wondered, "do I really care about the Baron and Belinda and her lock of silly hair?"

The Rape of the Lock   **157**

CONSTRUCTED RESPONSE *(20 points)*

20. How do you think Alexander Pope viewed the people who were the real-life
subjects of his poem? On a separate sheet of paper, use evidence from the text
to support your answer.

SELECTION TEST   LITERARY RESPONSE AND ANALYSIS

from Candide Voltaire *translated by* Richard Aldington

COMPREHENSION (*40 points; 4 points each*)

On the line provided, write the letter of the *best* answer to each of the following items.

_____ **1.** Candide got his name because —

  A he was as sweet as candy

  B it was a name that had long been used in his family

  C of his honest, simple nature

  D a nurse suggested it when no one knew what to call him

_____ **2.** Which of the following situations is *not* among the benefits of Candide's life at the Baron's castle?

  F A good education

  G A luxurious setting

  H A secure status as the Baron's rightful heir

  J Freedom from manual labor

_____ **3.** Apparently, Candide is —

  A the Baron's son

  B the Baron's illegitimate nephew

  C an orphan whom the Baron and Baroness had adopted

  D a village boy who had befriended the Baron's family

_____ **4.** Who is Pangloss?

  F The Baron's best friend

  G The Baron's spiritual advisor

  H Candide's scheming relative

  J The Baron's family tutor

_____ **5.** Pangloss believes that this world —

  A came into being for no reason

  B does not really exist

  C is the best of all possible worlds

  D is filled with evil, despair, and confusion

_____ **6.** The Baron banishes Candide for —

  F kissing the Baron's daughter Cunegonde

  G having a disrespectful attitude

  H stealing money from the castle treasury

  J arguing with Pangloss and pulling his beard

_____ **7.** Candide ends up in the Bulgarian army when he —

    A   joins because Cunegonde is serving as an army nurse

    B   joins as a way of escaping the Baron

    C   joins after losing all his money on a foolish bet

    D   is taken away in chains and forcibly enlisted

_____ **8.** The two men in the inn ask Candide whether he tenderly loves —

    F   Cunegonde

    G   the King of the Bulgarians

    H   the Baron and his castle

    J   France

_____ **9.** Why do his fellow soldiers look upon Candide as a prodigy?

    A   Candide is the best shot in the regiment.

    B   Cunegonde is prettier than any of the other soldiers' girlfriends.

    C   Candide's soldiering improves so swiftly that he only receives ten strokes' punishment.

    D   Candide receives packages of sweetmeats that the others have never seen before.

_____ **10.** Rather than be shot in the head, what does Candide choose to do?

    F   Run the gantlet of the regiment thirty-six times

    G   Be banished for life

    H   Run two leagues with his legs bound in chains

    J   Marry the Colonel's daughter

LITERARY FOCUS: SATIRE *(20 points; 5 points each)*

On the line provided, write the letter of the *best* answer to each of the following items.

_____ **11. Satire** —

    A   is too broad a genre to be defined concisely

    B   ridicules human weakness, vice, or folly

    C   is another word for humor

    D   is comedy that relies on verbal wit

_____ **12.** The ultimate purpose of **satire** is to —

    F   change society for the better

    G   use rhetorical tools on fictional material

    H   provide readers with instructions for social revolt

    J   help inspire the French Revolution

_____ **13.** Which of the following elements is *not* one of the major techniques of satire?

    A   Slapstick, or physical humor

    B   Deadpan understatement

    C   Outrageous exaggeration

    D   Warped logic

_____ **14.** In *Candide*, what is satirized, and for what purpose?

    F   Voltaire satirizes himself to make fun of the French nobility.

    G   Religious institutions are satirized in order to promote spirituality.

    H   Ignorance, weakness, and folly are satirized in order to improve humanity.

    J   Human suffering is satirized in order for Voltaire to obtain political office.

VOCABULARY DEVELOPMENT *(20 points; 4 points each)*

On the lines provided, write the letter of the *best* choice to answer each question.

_____ **15.** If you are <u>endowed</u> with sense, you probably —

    A   are able to use good judgment in many situations

    B   need to be rescued by your friends time and again

    C   keep making the same mistakes over and over

    D   don't know what you're doing most of the time

_____ **16.** If you speak to a friend with <u>candor</u>, you are —

    F   tactfully concealing the full truth

    G   telling the truth even if it hurts

    H   making up an excuse for something you did

    J   making up an excuse for something your friend did

_____ **17.** "You're looking <u>pensive</u> today," your friend says, meaning that you are looking —

    A   mean

    B   friendly

    C   thoughtful

    D   lost

_____ **18.** Which action shows the greatest vivacity?

    F Leading the cheers at a pep rally

    G Assigning the class extra homework

    H Complaining that there is too much homework

    J Knuckling down and doing the homework

_____ **19.** If the principal treats a student with clemency, the principal is *most* likely to —

    A give the student detention

    B take the student out of class

    C shorten the student's assigned detention

    D ask the student's opinion of the punishment

CONSTRUCTED RESPONSE *(20 points)*

20. In terms of the tone of their satire, how would you compare the passages you read from *Candide* with those from *A Modest Proposal* and *The Rape of the Lock*? Support your comparisons (and contrasts) by supplying evidence from *Candide*. Include details from *A Modest Proposal* and *The Rape of the Lock*. Write your answer on a separate sheet of paper.

SELECTION TEST
LITERARY RESPONSE AND ANALYSIS

from Don Quixote   Miguel de Cervantes   *translated by* Samuel Putnam

COMPREHENSION *(40 points; 4 points each)*

On the line provided, write the letter of the *best* answer to each of the following items.

_____ **1.** Which is *not* a fact about the life of Miguel de Cervantes, author of *Don Quixote*?

    A He spent five years as a slave in Africa.

    B He was deluded into thinking he was a knight.

    C He supposedly got the idea for *Don Quixote* while serving time in prison.

    D He did not become famous until he was fifty-eight, and even then he still remained poor.

_____ **2.** There is no evidence to show that Miguel de Cervantes —

    F was jailed for nonpayment of debts

    G wanted to be an army captain

    H once met with Shakespeare

    J lost the use of his left hand in war

_____ **3.** Chapter eight of *Don Quixote* contains the famous scene in which Don Quixote —

    A first declares his love for Dulcinea

    B hires Sancho Panza as his squire

    C spends four days thinking of a name for his horse

    D fights against a group of windmills

_____ **4.** Before engaging in battle, Don Quixote takes a moment to —

    F have his squire make sure all his straps and buckles are secure

    G kneel in prayer that no harm shall befall any righteous man

    H go to a nearby church for confession, in case he is killed

    J commend himself to his lady love and ask for her aid

_____ **5.** Before the battle, Sancho Panza warns Don Quixote that —

    A he will not help the Don, because he is a coward

    B what Don Quixote thinks are giants are not really giants

    C Dulcinea does not really love him—in fact she scorns him

    D the horse Rocinante is not likely to remain standing through such an ordeal

_____ **6.** To what does Don Quixote attribute his loss of the skirmish?

    F He thinks a magician has turned giants into windmills.

    G He imagines that his enemy is the mythical hundred-armed giant Briareus.

    H He thinks the skirmish was lost because of Sancho Panza's laziness.

    J He blames Dulcinea's lack of attentiveness.

_____ **7.** After his spear is broken, what does Don Quixote use as a replacement?

    A Sancho Panza's spear

    B Sancho Panza's cane

    C A flask of wine

    D A branch of a tree

_____ **8.** Refusing Sancho Panza's food, Don Quixote nourishes himself on —

    F nuts and berries

    G flour from the windmills

    H chicory water boiled in a hat

    J memories

_____ **9.** Which of the following actions is permitted under the laws of chivalry?

    A Sancho Panza can join Don Quixote in his battles against other knights.

    B Sancho Panza can take up arms in self-defense against commoners.

    C Don Quixote is allowed to complain about his injuries.

    D Don Quixote can admit he doesn't have the heart for battle.

_____ **10.** What does Sancho Panza promise to respect "as I would the Sabbath day"?

    F The papal ban against fighting on Sundays

    G Don Quixote's warning about not fighting with gentlemen

    H Don Quixote's search for Dulcinea

    J Don Quixote's plea that Sancho Panza fight by his side against the giants

LITERARY FOCUS: PARODY *(20 points; 5 points each)*
On the line provided, write the letter of the *best* answer to each of the following items.

_____ **11.** One difference between a **parody** and a **satire** is that —

    A parody imitates works of literature

    B satire usually imitates politicians

    C satire requires more knowledge to understand

    D parody is usually funnier than satire

_____ **12.** One of the major techniques of parody is incongruity, or —

    F extreme imitation

    G pairings that don't belong together

    H insults and name-calling

    J objective observation

_____ **13.** *Don Quixote* is mainly a parody of —

    A tales of chivalry

    B war veterans

    C servants and their masters

    D romantic poetry

_____ **14.** According to the definition, parody's main purposes are —

    F persuasion and information

    G explanation and self-expression

    H amusement and instruction

    J entertainment and diversion

VOCABULARY DEVELOPMENT *(20 points; 4 points each)*

Match the definition on the left with the Vocabulary word on the right. On the line provided, write the letter of the Vocabulary word.

_____ **15.** act of staying watchfully awake   **a.** enmity

_____ **16.** limp; flabby   **b.** vigil

_____ **17.** provisions; pieces of food   **c.** flaccid

_____ **18.** natural qualities of personality   **d.** disposition

_____ **19.** hostility   **e.** victuals

CONSTRUCTED RESPONSE *(20 points)*

20. On a separate sheet of paper, write a paragraph explaining why you agree or disagree with the following assertion: "*Don Quixote, Candide, The Rape of the Lock,* and *A Modest Proposal* are all parodies, and they are all satires, too." Use evidence from the texts to support your views.

SELECTION TEST   LITERARY RESPONSE AND ANALYSIS

from A Vindication of the Rights of Woman
Mary Wollstonecraft

COMPREHENSION *(40 points; 4 points each)*

On the line provided, write the letter of the *best* answer to each of the following items.

_____ **1.** Wollstonecraft devotes the beginning of her introduction to the claim that women have been harmed by —

    A insufficient attention

    B lack of independent spending power

    C lack of choice in their careers

    D a neglected education

_____ **2.** What trait does Wollstonecraft hope to develop in women?

    F Athletic ability

    G Willingness to dominate others

    H Love of the outdoors

    J Strength of character

_____ **3.** What "law of nature" does Wollstonecraft accept?

    A Men should decide money matters.

    B Males are physically stronger than females.

    C Logic is male; emotion is female.

    D Females are nurturers while males are aggressors.

_____ **4.** Which group of people does Wollstonecraft characterize in her statement "as a class of mankind they have the strongest claim to pity"?

    F Rich women

    G The rural poor

    H Factory workers

    J The middle class

_____ **5.** According to Wollstonecraft, people who are only the objects of pity and condescending love will eventually become objects of —

    A truer love

    B contempt

    C indifference

    D longing

_____ **6.** For Wollstonecraft the *first* task of any human being, male or female, is to —

    F   find a mate

    G   earn a living

    H   refrain from hurting others

    J   build his or her own character

_____ **7.** In the long sentence beginning "Animated by this important object, I shall disdain to cull my phrases," Wollstonecraft tells her audience that she —

    A   refuses to be swayed by the prejudices of her time

    B   has broken her resolution never to marry

    C   will speak her mind and her heart without restraint or artifice

    D   has no desire to overturn social institutions

_____ **8.** According to Wollstonecraft, the training of women as objects of desire causes —

    F   men to be unfaithful

    G   women to squander their inheritances

    H   women to lack the necessary mothering skills

    J   men to take over the duties of running a household

_____ **9.** According to Wollstonecraft, which of the following is *not* a result of the "artificial weakness" that is bred into women?

    A   A "propensity to tyrannize"

    B   The development of "cunning, the natural opponent of strength"

    C   A "contemptible, infantine" way of acting and speaking

    D   A "chaste and modest" deportment

_____ **10.** Wollstonecraft concludes her introduction by pointing out that in the struggle for social power, the governing force will always be —

    F   the emotions

    G   thoughts that are pure and just

    H   the greater physical strength of men

    J   the intellect

LITERARY FOCUS: TONE (15 points; 5 points each)
On the line provided, write the letter of the *best* answer to each of the following items.

_____ **11.** Writers establish **tone** by all of the following means except —

    A the use of comparisons

    B the use of connotative words

    C choice of details

    D careful diction

_____ **12.** An ironic tone can be heard in the line —

    F "They only live to amuse themselves. . . ."

    G "My own sex, I hope, will excuse me, if I treat them like rational creatures. . . ."

    H "I wish also to steer clear of an error which many respectable writers have fallen into. . . ."

    J "Many individuals have more sense than their male relatives. . . ."

_____ **13.** In the first paragraph, Wollstonecraft declares that many women are "wretched." If she had wanted to choose a synonym with milder connotations, she might have used the word —

    A wicked

    B discontented

    C happy

    D neutral

READING SKILLS: PATTERNS OF ORGANIZATION (5 points)
On the line provided, write the letter of the *best* answer to the following item.

_____ **14.** In the introduction to *A Vindication of the Rights of Woman,* the author prepares the reader for the rest of the essay by —

    F presenting her arguments in brief form

    G satirizing the arguments she will go on to make

    H acknowledging the people who supported her work

    J listing her professional credentials

Holt Assessment: Literature, Reading, and Vocabulary

VOCABULARY DEVELOPMENT *(20 points; 4 points each)*

On the lines provided, write the Vocabulary word that *best* completes each sentence below.

solicitude	**fastidious**	**specious**	**abrogated**	**cursory**
partial	**vitiate**	**deplore**	**propensity**	**insipid**

15. The opposite of *genuine* is _____.

16. An experience that is not exciting or lively, but boring and stale, is _____.

17. Most of the best writers are _____ in their choice of words.

18. An inclination or tendency to do something is a _____ to do it.

19. You cannot fully understand a difficult nonfiction text if you read it in a

_____ way.

CONSTRUCTED RESPONSE *(20 points)*

20. How does the tone of Wollstonecraft's essay help to convey her views on women's rights? Choose an argument she makes in her essay, and show how she argues her case. Use references from the text in your answer. Write your answer on a separate sheet of paper.

SELECTION TEST ████████████ LITERARY RESPONSE AND ANALYSIS

To the Ladies   Mary, Lady Chudleigh
from The Education of Women   Daniel Defoe

COMPREHENSION *(80 points; 8 points each)*

On the line provided, write the letter of the *best* answer to each of the following items.

_____ 1. According to Lady Chudleigh, what is the difference between a wife and a servant?

   A   Servants are not expected to produce heirs for their husbands.

   B   A servant can be either female or male, a wife only female.

   C   Servants get days off; wives do not.

   D   They differ from each other only in name.

_____ 2. According to Lady Chudleigh, what is the immediate and lasting effect of the marriage contract?

   F   The wife's money belongs to the husband.

   G   All kindness on the husband's part is put aside.

   H   The wife can no longer sign legal papers in her own name.

   J   The wife can no longer visit her own family.

_____ 3. Lines 11–12, "Then but to look, to laugh, or speak, / Will the Nuptial Contract break," imply that the husband feels —

   A   proud in possessing his wife

   B   that he has married beneath him

   C   jealous of his wife's communications with others

   D   uncertain whether he should go through with the wedding

_____ 4. Chudleigh's advice to women can be summed up in these words of advice: —

   F   Don't get married

   G   Sign a prenuptial agreement before marriage

   H   Be careful whom you select for a husband

   J   Get a college degree, and prepare to earn your own living

_____ 5. Daniel Defoe agrees with Mary Wollstonecraft when he says that the *main* obstacle preventing women from higher achievement is —

   A   the view that women are inferior

   B   women's own lack of self-esteem

   C   a lack of a sound education

   D   a class system that values wealth above ability

_____ **6.** What logical contradiction does Defoe point out?

    F Men view women as objects, but women objectify men, too.

    G Men complain of women's foolishness yet prevent their education.

    H Men seek companionship from women without trying to understand them.

    J Men claim they want to get along with women, but they don't act that way.

_____ **7.** For Defoe, what fact is "too evident to need any demonstration"?

    A Women are treated as second-class human beings.

    B Women are naturally the equals of men.

    C The rich have greater opportunities than poor people.

    D Education is what separates humans from animals.

_____ **8.** According to Defoe, the *real* reason men have denied women the advantages of an education is that men —

    F fear the competition from women

    G think women are incapable of learning

    H don't see the point of a woman's education

    J don't want men to have to do household chores

_____ **9.** What does Defoe think women should be taught?

    A Anything their wit allows

    B Mainly dancing and music

    C Art and foreign languages

    D Just enough to make them good conversationalists

_____ **10.** Chudleigh and Defoe definitely agree that —

    F Mary Wollstonecraft has dealt with the issue of women's rights best of all

    G women should be allowed to receive the attentions of courtly swains

    H continued education is preferable to a too-early or unwise marriage

    J journalism is better than poetry for addressing serious social issues

CONSTRUCTED RESPONSE *(20 points)*

11. Identify a point upon which you think Chudleigh and Defoe would disagree. Why do you think so? In supporting your assertions, use references to the two texts as well as your own understanding. Write your answer on a separate sheet of paper.

COLLECTION 4 SUMMATIVE TEST

The Restoration and the Eighteenth Century 1660–1800: The Best of All Possible Worlds

Joseph Addison, with his partner Sir Richard Steele, wrote and published a daily magazine in London called *The Spectator*, whose writings have been held up as models of the English prose style. Addison found a perfect subject for a *Spectator* article when he observed upper-class women applying "patches," or artificial beauty spots, to their faces. The patches were not just cosmetic— they had a political purpose. When applied to one side of the face, a patch signaled that its wearer favored the Tory party; when affixed to the other side, it meant that the wearer supported the Whigs.

This test asks you to use the skills and strategies you have learned in this collection. Read carefully the following excerpt from Addison's essay. Then, answer the questions that follow it.

FROM **"Party Patches"**

by Joseph Addison

About the middle of last winter I went to see an opera at the theater in the Haymarket, where I could not but take notice of two parties of very fine women that had placed themselves in the opposite side boxes and seemed drawn up in a kind of battle array one against another.

After a short survey of them, I found they were patched differently, the faces on one hand being spotted on the right side of the forehead and those upon the other on the left. I quickly perceived that they cast hostile glances upon one another and that their patches were placed in those different situations as party signals to distinguish friends from foes. In the middle boxes between these two opposite bodies were several ladies who patched indifferently on both sides of their faces and seemed to sit there with no other intention but to see the opera.

Upon inquiry I found that the body of Amazons on my right hand were Whigs, and those on my left, Tories; and that those who had placed themselves in the middle boxes were a neutral party, whose faces had not yet declared themselves. These last, however, as I afterwards found, diminished daily, and took their party with one side or the other; insomuch as I observed in several of them the patches which were before dispersed equally are now all gone over to the Whig or Tory side of the face.

The censorious say that the men whose hearts are aimed at are very often the occasions that one part of the face is thus dishonored and lies under a kind of disgrace, while the other is so much set off and adorned by the owner; and that the patches turn to the right or to the left according to the principles of the man who is most in favor. But whatever may be the motives of a few fantastical coquettes, who do not patch for the public good so much as for their own private advantage, it is certain that there are several women of honor who patch out of principle and with an eye to the interest of their country. Nay, I am informed that some of them adhere so steadfastly to their party and are so far from sacrificing their zeal for the public to their passion for any particular person that in a late draft of marriage articles a lady has stipulated with her husband that, whatever his opinions are, she shall be at liberty to patch on which side she pleases.

I must here take notice that Rosalinda, a famous Whig partisan, has most unfortunately a very beautiful mole on the Tory part of her forehead; which, being very conspicuous, has occasioned many mistakes and given a handle to her enemies to misrepresent her face, as though it had revolted from the Whig interest. But, whatever this natural patch may seem to intimate, it is well known that her notions of government are still the same. This unlucky mole, however, has misled several coxcombs and, like the hanging out of false colors, made some of them converse with Rosalinda in what they thought the spirit of her party, when on a sudden she has given them an unexpected fire that has sunk them all at once.

If Rosalinda is unfortunate in her mole, Nigranilla is as unhappy in a pimple, which forces her, against her inclinations, to patch on the Whig side.

I am told that many virtuous matrons, who formerly have been taught to believe that this artificial spotting of the face was unlawful, are now reconciled by a zeal for their cause to what they could not be prompted by a concern for their beauty. This way of declaring war upon one another puts me in mind of what is reported of the tigress, that several spots rise in her skin when she is angry; or, as Mr. Cowley has imitated the verses that stand as the motto of this paper,

> *She swells with angry pride,*
> *And calls forth all her spots on ev'ry side.*

VOCABULARY SKILLS (25 points; 5 points each)

Each of the following underlined words has also been underlined in the selection. Re-read the passages containing these words, and use context clues to select an answer. On the line provided, write the letter of the choice that *best* completes each sentence.

_____ **1.** To be reconciled to something you have disapproved of is to —

    A accept it

    B reject it

    C have trouble making up your mind about it

    D try it

_____ **2.** Censorious people —

    F find fault with others

    G borrow money from others

    H rescue others from danger

    J have highly developed senses, such as smell

_____ **3.** A wife who stipulated something with her husband —

    A shared it

    B specified it as part of an agreement

    C took care of it as part of her duty

    D disagreed with him about its importance

_____ **4.** If a mole is <u>conspicuous</u> on someone's forehead, it is —

    F noticeable

    G tiny

    H easy to overlook

    J infected

_____ **5.** To <u>intimate</u> a fact is to —

    A hide it

    B question it

    C suggest it

    D state it

COMPREHENSION (25 points; 5 points each)

On the line provided, write the letter of the *best* answer to each of the following items.

_____ **6.** If a woman sits in the middle boxes of the theater and patches both sides of her face, she —

    F is a supporter of the Labour Party

    G is married

    H is unmarried

    J has not yet taken sides politically

_____ **7.** Some observers say that a woman decides which side of her face to patch according to —

    A which side of her face is prettier

    B which side friends' faces are patched

    C the political views of the man whose attention she seeks

    D the instructions of her husband

_____ **8.** According to Addison, if a woman had a natural beauty spot on one side of her face, she would *probably* —

    F have it surgically removed

    G cover it with makeup

    H not be able to attend the theater for fear of offending people

    J be subject to misinterpretation of her political views

_____ **9.** What is Addison's attitude toward "patching"?

    A He is outraged.

    B He lightheartedly mocks it.

    C He strongly approves of it.

    D He sees it as a symbol of Britain's decline.

_____ **10.** Addison states that many women who disapprove of applying beauty spots for the sake of appearance —

    F also refuse to apply them for political reasons

    G agree, however, to apply them for political reasons

    H persuade their friends to remove their political beauty spots

    J wear ribbons as substitutes for spots

READING SKILLS AND STRATEGIES *(5 points)*
Recognizing Persuasive Techniques

On the line provided, write the letter of the *best* answer to the following item.

_____ **11.** In his article, Addison uses the persuasive technique of —

    A logical appeals

    B ethical appeals

    C emotional appeals

    D medical appeals

LITERARY FOCUS: CONSTRUCTED RESPONSE *(45 points; 15 points each)*
Evaluating a Comment on Life

12. How do you think Addison's view of the world connects to the views of Wollstonecraft, Chudleigh, and Defoe? On a separate sheet of paper, write one paragraph in which you discuss similarities and differences between Addison's view of women (or of English society in general) in "Party Patches" and the stance of at least one of the three authors.

Comparing and Contrasting Tone

13. The tone of "Party Patches" is clearly satiric. Compare and contrast Addison's satire with those of Swift and Pope. Include comments on both style and substance. Write your answer on a separate sheet of paper.

Analyzing Satire

14. In each row of the left-hand column of the following chart, describe an example of irony from the excerpt of "Party Patches." In the middle column, identify each example of irony according to type (verbal, situational, dramatic). In the third column briefly explain the point Addison is making through each example.

Example of Irony	Type of Irony	Implied Meaning

COLLECTION 5 DIAGNOSTIC TEST

The Romantic Period 1798–1832: The Quest for Truth and Beauty

On the line provided, write the letter of the *best* answer to each of the following items.
(100 points; 10 points each)

_____ **1.** Which of the following statements about **symbols** is *false*?

    A People, places, animals, and objects can be symbols.

    B Symbols can have only one meaning.

    C Symbols have both a literal and a figurative meaning.

    D Some symbols have widely recognized meanings.

_____ **2.** What is **blank verse**?

    F Poetry that has no regular meter

    G Poetry that rhymes

    H Poetry written in unrhymed iambic pentameter

    J Poetry containing stanzas that are three lines long

_____ **3.** What is an **allusion**?

    A A sound device used in poetry

    B A moment of revelation in a story

    C An example from an author's own experiences

    D A reference to something from literature, history, or religion

_____ **4.** In a traditional **ode** —

    F there are only fourteen lines

    G the speaker expresses his feelings for his lover

    H an object, creature, or force is addressed

    J a general truth is expressed in a brief, clever manner

_____ **5.** Which of the following features characterizes **haiku**?

    A The use of complex figures of speech to express the poet's attitude

    B The use of narrative to tell a story in verse

    C A series of short stanzas

    D A reliance on imagery to suggest emotions and themes

_____ **6.** The pattern of rhymed lines in a poem is called its —

    F consonance

    G internal rhyme

    H rhyme scheme

    J conceit

_____ **7.** What is the **mood** of a poem?

    A The overall feeling or atmosphere in the poem

    B The speaker's distinct personality

    C The structure of the poem

    D The poet's attitude toward a subject

_____ **8.** Which of the following quotations contains a **metaphor**?

    F "She walks in beauty, like the night"

    G "The lone and level sands stretch far away."

    H "And here were forests ancient as the hills"

    J "O wild West Wind, thou breath of Autumn's being"

_____ **9.** Which of the following terms is a useful type of **context clue**?

    A Clichés

    B Archaic words

    C Restatements

    D Alliterative words

_____ **10.** Examples, which serve as **context clues,** can be introduced by all of the following words and phrases *except* —

    F namely

    G however

    H such as

    J for instance

LITERARY PERIOD INTRODUCTION TEST

The Romantic Period 1798–1832:
The Quest for Truth and Beauty

COMPREHENSION *(100 points; 10 points each)*

On the line provided, write the letter of the *best* answer to each of the following items.

_____ **1.** Which of the following statements does *not* describe the **Romantic** period in England?

   A It was partly inspired by the French Revolution of 1789 and the works of French and German writers.

   B It is generally associated with the publication of *Lyrical Ballads* in 1798.

   C The Parliamentary Reforms of 1832 mark the end of this period.

   D During this time England was a placid, agrarian nation.

_____ **2.** Which of the following writers are second-generation Romantic poets?

   F John Milton, John Donne, and Thomas Gray

   G William Wordsworth, Samuel Taylor Coleridge, and Alexander Pope

   H John Keats; Percy Bysshe Shelley; and George Gordon, Lord Byron

   J William Blake, Sir Walter Raleigh, and Edmund Spenser

_____ **3.** Which of the following events did *not* take place during the Romantic period?

   A Napoleon Bonaparte became emperor of France.

   B England was at war with France.

   C England lost its American colonies.

   D Population increased in urban areas.

_____ **4.** In response to the political climate, the British government —

   F became less conservative than before

   G introduced repressive measures

   H increased the political rights of agitators

   J expanded collective bargaining practices

_____ **5.** During the Industrial Revolution —

   A a greater percentage of goods were made by hand

   B populations in the cities decreased

   C private owners took over communal farming areas

   D most factory owners provided housing for their workers

_____ **6.** Under the policy of laissez faire —

    F there is very little government interference in economic policy

    G the rich give a percentage of their profits to charitable organizations

    H the government takes control of the means of production

    J children cannot work in factories

_____ **7.** Which of the following statements does *not* apply to the term *romantic* as it is used to describe the literary period?

    A The term *romantic* suggests a fascination with youthful innocence.

    B The term *romantic* refers to sentimental novels with great popular appeal.

    C The term *romantic* refers to a period of idealism in which people questioned authority.

    D The term *romantic* implies an awareness of social change.

_____ **8.** Through their **lyric poetry,** Romantic poets —

    F related traditional stories

    G found an outlet for rebellion

    H revealed passionate and heartfelt beliefs

    J created best-selling romances

_____ **9.** For the Romantic poets, nature is a —

    A force that acts on the human mind

    B constant source of pleasure

    C menacing and hostile presence in our lives

    D force that humans can control

_____ **10.** The Romantic poet can be described by all of the following phrases *except* —

    F "a man speaking to men"

    G one who "reasons in verse"

    H one of the world's "unacknowledged legislators"

    J a "physician" to all humanity

SELECTION TEST   LITERARY RESPONSE AND ANALYSIS

The Tyger William Blake
"Blake Is a Real Name …" Charles Lamb
The Lamb William Blake

COMPREHENSION (40 points; 4 points each)

On the line provided, write the letter of the *best* answer to each of the following items.

_____ **1.** The speaker's attitude toward the tiger can *best* be described as —

    A affectionate

    B awed

    C indifferent

    D contemptuous

_____ **2.** The speaker in "The Tyger" imagines the creature as having been made in a —

    F coal mine

    G blacksmith's forge

    H laboratory

    J factory

_____ **3.** In the poem the tiger is compared to —

    A other creatures

    B fire, heat, and brightness

    C human mortality

    D heroes of Greek mythology

_____ **4.** The speaker wonders if the tiger's creator —

    F feels unfulfilled

    G will create other tigers

    H is good or evil

    J feels pride in creation

_____ **5.** The symmetry of "The Tyger" is enhanced by the —

    A appearance of the lamb

    B speaker's confusion

    C repetition of the first stanza

    D image of the furnace

_____ **6.** In "The Lamb" the speaker's questions refer to the lamb's —

    F meekness

    G purpose

    H creator

    J descendants

_____ **7.** The speaker in "The Lamb" describes Christ as a —

    A meadow

    B river

    C voice

    D child

_____ **8.** According to the speaker, the lamb is endowed with the qualities of —

    F joy and mildness

    G energy and enthusiasm

    H wisdom and intelligence

    J innocence and humor

_____ **9.** In "Blake Is a Real Name ..." we learn that the author, Charles Lamb, first encountered Blake's poem "The Tyger" when —

    A he heard the poem recited aloud

    B he found Blake's original manuscript

    C he chanced upon the poem in an old book shop

    D Blake asked him to evaluate the poem

_____ **10.** According to Charles Lamb, Blake in his own lifetime was —

    F ignored

    G unknown

    H appreciated by a few

    J disliked

LITERARY FOCUS: SYMBOL *(40 points; 10 points each)*

On the line provided, write the letter of the *best* answer to each of the following items.

_____ **11.** To be effective, a **literary symbol** should be —

    A something everyone recognizes

    B both itself and something more

    C a poetic image from nature

    D an object that represents the main character

_____ **12.** A **symbol** that is widely recognized as standing for peace is a —

      F fist

      G circle

      H dove

      J heart

_____ **13.** In "The Tyger" the stars probably symbolize —

      A the tiger

      B angels

      C fellow poets

      D humankind

_____ **14.** For Blake the symbolic opposite of the tiger is —

      F the lamb

      G the furnace

      H God

      J humanity

CONSTRUCTED RESPONSE *(20 points)*

15. On a separate sheet of paper, explain what you think the tiger and the lamb symbolize in the two Blake poems. Point to specific images and figures of speech in "The Tyger" and "The Lamb" that make the symbolism clear.

SELECTION TEST ███████████

The Chimney Sweeper *from* Songs of Innocence
William Blake
The Chimney Sweeper *from* Songs of Experience
William Blake
from Evidence Given Before the Sadler Committee

COMPREHENSION *(40 points; 4 points each)*
On the line provided, write the letter of the *best* answer to each of the following items.

_____ 1. In "The Chimney Sweeper" from *Songs of Innocence*, the speaker has spent most of his life —

  A   recruiting young chimney sweepers

  B   caring for his parents

  C   sweeping chimneys

  D   promoting his religious beliefs

_____ 2. Ultimately Tom Dacre believes that everything will be fine as long as he —

  F   does his duty

  G   does not give in to his boss

  H   lives in London

  J   gets plenty of sleep

_____ 3. How are the last lines of "The Chimney Sweeper" from *Songs of Innocence* ironic?

  A   The speaker wants readers to feel sorry for Tom, but they don't.

  B   In describing the boys' hopefulness, the speaker reveals their suffering.

  C   The speaker tells us that even though the morning was warm, Tom was cold.

  D   The speaker reveals that he is really Tom.

_____ 4. The comparison of Tom with a lamb suggests his —

  F   confusion

  G   sorrow

  H   silence

  J   innocence

Holt Assessment: Literature, Reading, and Vocabulary

_____ **5.** Tom Dacre would probably *not* be described as —

    A rebellious

    B sensitive

    C imaginative

    D spiritual

_____ **6.** In "The Chimney Sweeper" from *Songs of Experience,* the speaker describes his situation as being full of —

    F hard work and good pay

    G new friendships

    H adventure in the city

    J misery and woe

_____ **7.** In "The Chimney Sweeper" from *Songs of Experience,* the speaker —

    A accepts his condition

    B resents his parents

    C is too miserable to sing or dance

    D seeks comfort in religion

_____ **8.** Which statement *best* summarizes the difference between the sweepers in the two poems?

    F In the first he is accepting of his poverty; in the second he is angry.

    G In the first he is sorrowful; in the second he is full of hope.

    H In the first he is grounded in reality; in the second he lives in a dream world.

    J In the first he is lighthearted; in the second he is gloomy.

_____ **9.** Peter Smart, the young man interviewed in the excerpt from "Evidence Given Before the Sadler Committee," worked as a —

    A textile mill hand

    B police informant

    C pickpocket

    D chimney sweeper

_____ **10.** Which statement *best* describes the relationship between Peter Smart's testimony and the experiences of the children in the "Chimney Sweeper" poems?

    F The poems exaggerate how hard English children really had to work.

    G Judging from the testimony, Blake's poems falsely reassure the reader about child labor.

    H Neither source can be trusted because they are all the products of authors' imaginations.

    J Although Peter Smart was a real person and Tom Dacre a character in a poem, both boys' experiences ring true.

LITERARY FOCUS: PARALLELISM *(40 points; 10 points each)*

On the line provided, write the letter of the *best* answer to each of the following items.

_____ **11. Parallelism** is *not* a repetition of —

    A consonants that sound similar

    B similarly structured sentences

    C similarly structured words

    D similar ideas

_____ **12.** Poets use parallelism for all the following reasons *except* to —

    F make their poems easier to remember

    G reinforce ideas

    H connect to the world of nature

    J create dramatic effects

_____ **13.** Aside from poetry, parallelism is often found in —

    A realistic novels

    B political speeches

    C letters to the editor

    D newspaper articles

_____ **14.** An example of parallelism from one of the "Chimney Sweeper" poems is —

    F "So if all do their duty they need not fear harm."

    G "And wash in a river, and shine in the Sun."

    H "When my mother died I was very young . . ."

    J "A little black thing among the snow . . ."

CONSTRUCTED RESPONSE *(20 points)*

15. Choose one of the three statements below to write about on a separate sheet of paper. Support the statement with details from the poems.

    a. Blake's purpose in writing his "Chimney Sweeper" poems was primarily political.

    b. Blake's purpose in writing his "Chimney Sweeper" poems was primarily religious.

    c. For Blake, in these poems, political and religious purposes were one and the same.

SELECTION TEST ████████████

LITERARY RESPONSE AND ANALYSIS

A Poison Tree William Blake

COMPREHENSION (*40 points; 4 points each*)
On the line provided, write the letter of the *best* answer to each of the following items.

_____ **1.** As a result of the speaker's anger toward his friend, the speaker —

    A confesses his anger and ends the friendship

    B hides his feelings and the anger disappears

    C hides his anger at his friend but suffers silently

    D confesses his anger and the friendship is repaired

_____ **2.** As a result of the speaker's anger toward his enemy, the —

    F two discuss it and end up making peace

    G two discuss it but cannot come to an agreement

    H speaker nurses his grudge in private

    J speaker seeks advice from a friend, who helps him get over it

_____ **3.** In this poem the speaker's anger is represented by —

    A an apple

    B his garden

    C his tears

    D a tree

_____ **4.** The speaker's anger feeds on —

    F negative emotions

    G water and sun

    H kind words and soft music

    J prayer and forgiveness

_____ **5.** The foe steals the apple because —

    A he wants to defy God's prohibition

    B he wants to prove it is not really poisoned

    C it belongs to the speaker

    D he wants it for his sweetheart

_____ **6.** When his foe is harmed, the speaker feels —

    F glad

    G sad

    H unmoved

    J unlucky

_____ **7.** The poem conveys a feeling of —

  A innocence

  B contentment

  C intensity

  D curiosity

_____ **8.** The rhyme scheme of each stanza in the poem is —

  F *aabb*

  G *abab*

  H *abba*

  J *baab*

_____ **9.** How many beats, or stressed syllables, does each line of the poem have?

  A Three

  B Four

  C Five

  D Between three and five

_____ **10.** Which of the following word patterns is *not* repeated in this poem?

  F "I was angry with . . ."

  G "I told . . ."

  H ". . . an apple bright . . ."

  J ". . . my wrath did . . ."

LITERARY FOCUS: THEME *(40 points; 10 points each)*

On the line provided, write the letter of the *best* answer to each of the following items.

_____ **11.** Which of the following words is *not* a synonym for **theme** in literature?

  A subject

  B meaning

  C idea

  D insight

_____ **12.** What is the *best* way to figure out a poem's theme?

  F Look for a line in which the poet states the theme directly.

  G Infer the theme from details, images, and symbols.

  H Analyze the rhyme scheme and meter of the poem.

  J Use the poet's biography as a clue.

_____ **13.** Which of the following statements does *not* reflect a theme of "A Poison Tree"?

    A Anger is one of the most difficult human emotions to resolve.

    B Emotions are a part of nature; they can grow like plants.

    C The consequences of wrath are determined by individual responses.

    D Happiness is contagious; it spreads from one person to another.

_____ **14.** Which of the following comparisons does Blake use to help develop his theme?

    F Evil is compared to a snake.

    G The results of anger are compared to a poisoned apple.

    H London is compared to the biblical Eden.

    J Rage is compared to a howling wind.

CONSTRUCTED RESPONSE *(20 points)*

15. What ideas about anger does the poem express? On a separate sheet of paper, refer to specific images or figures of speech in analyzing the poem's theme of anger.

SELECTION TEST   LITERARY RESPONSE AND ANALYSIS

Lines Composed a Few Miles Above Tintern Abbey William Wordsworth

COMPREHENSION *(30 points; 5 points each)*

On the line provided, write the letter of the *best* answer to each of the following items.

_____ 1. The speaker has lived away from a country setting for a long time and has found solace in nature by —

     A   returning in his memory to the country

     B   taking weekend trips to his farm

     C   reading nature books in the British Museum

     D   enjoying London parks

_____ 2. According to the speaker, the influence of nature —

     F   can be felt only in the wild

     G   cannot be felt without thoughtful effort

     H   does not affect those who do not believe in it

     J   flows through everyone and everything

_____ 3. The speaker makes the observation that when he was a boy, —

     A   he understood the countryside better than he does now

     B   his feelings about nature were more spontaneous but less deep

     C   he did not have as much physical energy as others his age

     D   his love of nature was squelched by his city existence

_____ 4. In this poem the speaker expresses a feeling of —

     F   bitterness

     G   celebration

     H   forgetfulness

     J   indifference

_____ 5. Which of the following effects does the speaker *not* give nature credit for?

     A   Inspiring his kindest moments

     B   Putting him in touch with a sense of eternal mystery

     C   Providing the setting in which he met his true love

     D   Acting as a moral guide throughout his life

_____ **6.** The statement in lines 75–76, "I cannot paint / What then I was . . . ," implies that the speaker —

    F is much better with words than with other artistic media

    G finds the core of his younger self to be indescribable

    H is too heartbroken to think about the past

    J feels little sympathy for the kind of boy he was

LITERARY FOCUS: BLANK VERSE *(30 points; 10 points each)*

On the line provided, write the letter of the *best* answer to each of the following items.

_____ **7.** Which of the following statements is *true* of **blank verse**?

    A It is written in rhymed iambic pentameter.

    B It is written in unrhymed iambic pentameter.

    C It was invented by Shakespeare.

    D It was adapted by English poets who were inspired by the Hebrew psalms.

_____ **8.** In "Lines Composed a Few Miles Above Tintern Abbey," Wordsworth uses —

    F a rigidly metrical style of blank verse

    G passages of blank verse alternating with passages of free verse

    H a rhythmically relaxed, conversational style of blank verse

    J full lines of verse alternating with half lines at brief intervals

_____ **9.** Which of the following lines from the poem is *not* strict blank verse?

    A "And passing even into my purer mind"

    B "The landscape with the quiet of the sky."

    C "Five years have past; five summers, with the length"

    D "The day is come when I again repose"

READING SKILLS: RECOGNIZING PATTERNS OF ORGANIZATION *(20 points; 10 points each)*
On the line provided, write the letter of the *best* answer to each of the following items.

_____ **10.** Wordsworth organizes his thoughts in this poem by —

    F grouping lines that develop main ideas

    G chronological order

    H order of importance

    J dividing stanzas into problems and solutions

_____ **11.** One way Wordsworth unifies his ideas in this selection is —

    A by posing questions and then answering them

    B through repetition of key words and phrases

    C through dialogue between the speaker and his sister

    D through numbering each new section

CONSTRUCTED RESPONSE *(20 points)*
12. How well suited is Wordsworth's style to his subject and ideas in this poem?
    On a separate sheet of paper, answer the question using examples from the text.

SELECTION TEST   LITERARY RESPONSE AND ANALYSIS

Composed Upon Westminster Bridge William Wordsworth

COMPREHENSION *(40 points; 5 points each)*

On the line provided, write the letter of the *best* answer to each of the following items.

_____ **1.** The speaker's attitude toward London is mainly one of —

    A disgust

    B admiration

    C reluctant tolerance

    D melancholy

_____ **2.** Wordsworth describes London as —

    F gloomy

    G dangerous

    H dirty

    J splendid

_____ **3.** The speaker imagines that London is —

    A praying

    B thinking

    C meditating

    D sleeping

_____ **4.** Which adjectives does the speaker apply to London?

    F silent, bare, smokeless

    G dark, pitted, awesome

    H tall, busy, shabby

    J neon-lit, hivelike, hardworking

_____ **5.** According to the speaker, who ought to be able to appreciate his view of London?

    A Everyone except dull people

    B Romantic poets

    C City dwellers, but perhaps not rural dwellers

    D Those who have been away from the city a long time

_____ **6.** One feature that makes this poem characteristic of the Romantic period is its —

    F vivid landscape description

    G rigid metrical form

    H function as a teaching tool

    J emphasis on the speaker's emotions

_____ **7.** What is unusual about the poet's approach to his subject in this poem?

    A Wordsworth describes London without ever having actually seen it.

    B Wordsworth describes a huge city as if it were a peaceful part of nature.

    C The entire poem is ironic, meaning exactly the opposite of what it seems to say.

    D The poem has an "I" speaker who is obviously not Wordsworth.

_____ **8.** The poem's title suggests that it —

    F is a criticism of urban life

    G is set in a vague, undefined place and time

    H was written while Wordsworth was standing on the bridge

    J contains Wordsworth's inner thoughts

LITERARY FOCUS: PERSONIFICATION *(40 points; 10 points each)*
On the line provided, write the letter of the *best* answer to each of the following items.

_____ **9.** When a writer uses **personification,** —

    A people are described as if they had animal or plant traits

    B nonhuman things are described as if they were human

    C nonliving things are described as if they could move and speak

    D characters are described through their settings

_____ **10.** The quotation that is an example of personification is —

    F "Ships, towers, domes, theaters . . ."

    G "glittering in the smokeless air."

    H "Ne'er saw I, never felt, a calm so deep!"

    J "The river glideth at his own sweet will . . ."

_____ **11.** Wordsworth's imagery personifies the city as someone who is —

    A not yet awake

    B lying ill in bed

    C unaware of beauty

    D lying in wait for victims

_____ **12.** In lines 4–5, the beauty of the morning is compared to the city's —

    F clothes

    G clock

    H eyes

    J ears

CONSTRUCTED RESPONSE *(20 points)*

13. What emotions does Wordsworth evoke in "Composed upon Westminster Bridge"? On a separate sheet of paper, discuss how he uses personification to breathe life into his sonnet.

SELECTION TEST   LITERARY RESPONSE AND ANALYSIS

The World Is Too Much with Us William Wordsworth

COMPREHENSION *(60 points; 10 points each)*

On the line provided, write the letter of the *best* answer to each of the following items.

_____ 1. "The world is too much with us" means that —

     A the world is getting too large because of growing population

     B everyone needs a break from work now and then

     C there are too many things to buy and to choose from in this world

     D material concerns get in the way of people's appreciation of deeper things

_____ 2. Which of the following sentences might be a paraphrase of the statement "Little we see in Nature that is ours"?

     F People no longer feel that they are part of nature.

     G Even the smallest piece of natural beauty is important.

     H Although humans are masters of nature, they do not control nature.

     J Nature is not the place to find what we're looking for.

_____ 3. In line 4, the speaker says, "We have given our hearts away." What is he referring to?

     A The speaker's love for his beloved

     B A parent's love for a child

     C People who have chosen unwisely in love

     D The lack of true emotional richness in our lives

_____ 4. The speaker believes that —

     F worldly striving wastes people's talents and energy

     G the world is still ruled by the ancient Greek deities

     H the love of nature stops people from examining their own lives

     J nature was created to serve human needs

_____ 5. Instead of losing his connection to nature, the speaker would "rather be / A Pagan." A pagan is someone who —

     A believes in one god and is chaste

     B creates poems and myths for our time

     C worships nature

     D gives up poetry for a life of prayer

_____ 6. The speaker compares the winds to —

     F the sea and the moon

     G ghostly beasts

     H sleeping flowers

     J a musical tune

LITERARY FOCUS: ALLUSION AND ROMANTIC LYRICS *(20 points; 4 points each)*
On the line provided, write the letter of the *best* answer to each of the following items.

_____ **7.** Poets generally use **allusion** to —

    A disguise their political views

    B make readers think about how much progress humankind has made

    C deepen a poem's meaning

    D display their knowledge of various fields

_____ **8.** The allusions in "The World Is Too Much with Us" refer to —

    F Roman buildings

    G Greek gods

    H Roman epics

    J Greek tragedies

_____ **9.** Wordsworth uses allusions to emphasize the speaker's connection to —

    A the sea

    B ancient civilizations

    C Christianity

    D the material world

_____ **10.** Instead of merely taking over poetic forms from previous eras, the Romantic poets developed the form known as the —

    F ode

    G elegy

    H conversation poem

    J sonnet

_____ **11.** An **ode** usually —

    A compresses its message into fewer than twelve lines

    B uses heightened language to address an object, creature, or powerful idea

    C responds to a death

    D describes the rural countryside in an idealized way

CONSTRUCTED RESPONSE *(20 points)*

12. On a separate sheet of paper, identify two figures of speech from the poem, and analyze how they contribute to the poem's tone, emotion, and meaning.

Holt Assessment: Literature, Reading, and Vocabulary

SELECTION TEST

Tanka Poetry *translated by* Geoffrey Bownas *and* Anthony Thwaite
Haiku Poetry *translated by* Harold G. Henderson, Peter Beilenson, *and* Harry Behn

COMPREHENSION *(40 points; 4 points each)*
On the line provided, write the letter of the *best* answer to each of the following items.

_____ **1.** In Princess Nukada's "I Waited and I," what is the significance of the stirring of the blind?

   A The speaker cannot see, so she can only hear what is happening.

   B Her lover is sneaking in through the window.

   C The sound of the breeze makes her imagine her lover coming to her.

   D Impatient, she pushes through the frail paper window covering, breaking it.

_____ **2.** What are the tone and mood of Princess Nukada's poem?

   F The tone is one of longing or grief, and the mood is one of loneliness.

   G The tone is one of rejoicing, and the mood is one of happiness.

   H The tone is one of accusation, and the mood is one of murkiness.

   J The tone is one of indifference, and the mood is one of chilly menace.

_____ **3.** What is the traveler doing in Oshikochi Mitsune's "The End of My Journey"?

   A Arriving at his destination, tired but happy

   B Taking a rest in the middle of his journey

   C Setting off with expectations, hopes, and doubts

   D Pausing to record his impressions in a notebook

_____ **4.** The images in "The End of My Journey" suggest a feeling of —

   F the sweltering heat of summer

   G an arid desert, dry and barren

   H floating in the midst of warmth and ease

   J seeking warmth while shivering in the cold

_____ **5.** In Ki Tsurayuki's "Now, I Cannot Tell," the speaker compares his friend to a —

   A plum tree

   B dying fire

   C winding stream

   D charred pot

_____ **6.** Figuratively speaking, in Onitsura's poem the stones in the streams —

    F laugh as the water showers them

    G set up barricades against the onrushing water

    H compose songs to the surrounding woods

    J wear fallen leaves as hats

_____ **7.** The scene in Buson's poem consists of —

    A a woman eating fruit at an outdoor table

    B ladies and their serving maids laughing as they pick spring flowers

    C moonlight, a flowering tree, and a woman reading a letter

    D a poet imagining his far-off love reading his poetry

_____ **8.** Buson's poem is about —

    F good times with friends

    G despair over a bad harvest

    H longing and loneliness

    J illness and mortality

_____ **9.** In Issa's poem the image of a morning-glory vine thatching a hut implies —

    A irresponsible neighbors who let their home be overrun by vegetation

    B finding joy in the simple beauty of nature in the midst of poverty

    C the potential use of many plant species as medicines

    D the speaker's indifference to his physical surroundings

_____ **10.** In the third Bashō poem a flower —

    F decorates a room

    G is used as a substitute for rice

    H is given to the speaker as a souvenir on his travels

    J simply grows in the ground, its loveliness a gift to all

LITERARY FOCUS: IMAGERY *(40 points; 10 points each)*
On the line provided, write the letter of the *best* answer to each of the following items.

_____ **11. Tanka** —

    A had its origins in the oral tradition

    B always rhyme

    C is a lengthy and complicated poetic form

    D means "short songs"

_____ **12.** Traditional tanka contain —

    F seventeen syllables and three lines

    G thirty-seven syllables and ten lines

    H ten lines of fifteen syllables each

    J thirty-one syllables and five lines

_____ **13. Haiku** are usually about —

    A the beauty of seemingly insignificant things

    B the glory of Japanese culture

    C the life of the Emperor and his court

    D love, war, and death

_____ **14.** Haiku are difficult to translate because —

    F the Japanese language uses ideographs instead of an alphabet

    G many have been lost over the centuries

    H they leave a great deal unsaid and often have many interpretations

    J they were composed orally rather than written down

CONSTRUCTED RESPONSE *(20 points)*

15. How do these tanka and haiku make you feel? What view of life do you find reflected in these poetic forms? On a separate sheet of paper, discuss how imagery, tone, mood, and language in the individual poems or either group of poems help evoke the reader's emotions.

SELECTION TEST ████████████████   **LITERARY RESPONSE AND ANALYSIS**

Kubla Khan Samuel Taylor Coleridge

COMPREHENSION *(40 points; 4 points each)*

On the line provided, write the letter of the *best* answer to each of the following items.

_____ 1. The speaker in "Kubla Khan" describes a —

    A moment in history

    B recent event in his life

    C vision he has had

    D vacation he has taken

_____ 2. What is unusual about the sacred river Alph?

    F It is lifeless.

    G It goes underground.

    H It is frozen even in summer.

    J Its waters can cure diseases.

_____ 3. According to lines 6–7, what is the size of Kubla Khan's pleasure-dome?

    A Several acres

    B Ten square miles

    C The size of Solomon's temple

    D Too big to calculate

_____ 4. The pleasure-dome is situated —

    F near the towers of Kubla's capital city

    G in an underground cave

    H on the seashore

    J amid forests, hills, gardens, and chasms

_____ 5. Who was Kubla Khan?

    A A real person in history

    B A fictional character popular in Coleridge's day

    C A figure that appeared to Coleridge in a dream

    D Another name for Coleridge himself

_____ 6. In the stanza beginning on line 12, the speaker describes the pleasure-dome as —

    F haunted and wild

    G cozy and safe

    H ruined over time

    J impossible to imagine

_____ **7.** The dominant image used in the middle of the poem is the image of —

    A women's voices calling to the speaker

    B a river bursting from underground

    C maidens playing instruments

    D the poet waking from his dream

_____ **8.** The overall mood of the poem could *not* be described as —

    F mystical

    G ecstatic

    H apathetic

    J fantastic

_____ **9.** The speaker's vision suddenly changes with the image of the —

    A pleasure-dome

    B romantic chasm

    C "miracle of rare device"

    D damsel with the dulcimer

_____ **10.** The speaker believes that as a result of his vision, ordinary people should —

    F avoid him

    G accept his religious beliefs

    H visit the pleasure-dome

    J have their own visions

LITERARY FOCUS: ALLITERATION *(40 points; 10 points each)*

On the line provided, write the letter of the *best* answer to each of the following items.

_____ **11. Alliteration** is the repetition of —

    A ending sounds of words

    B vowel sounds

    C ending sounds of lines

    D consonant sounds

_____ **12.** In lines 15–16, "As e'er beneath a waning moon was haunted / By woman wailing for her demon-lover!," alliteration is found in the words —

    F as, a, was

    G demon, lover, woman

    H her, e'er, haunted

    J waning, woman, wailing

Kubla Khan

_____ **13.** In "Kubla Khan," Coleridge uses alliteration to create —

    A   a feeling of doubt and dismay

    B   realistic details

    C   an enchanted mood

    D   a tone of disgust with modern life

_____ **14.** Alliteration is generally used for all of the following purposes except to —

    F   establish a rhythm

    G   emphasize an idea

    H   clarify an argument

    J   impart a musical quality

CONSTRUCTED RESPONSE *(20 points)*

15. Choose one of the statements below, and on a separate sheet of paper, analyze how the poem's words, sounds, and images helped evoke that response in you.

    a.   I wish I could be in Coleridge's Xanadu.

    b.   I'm glad I'm not in Coleridge's Xanadu.

    c.   I had another emotional response to Coleridge's Xanadu.

SELECTION TEST   **LITERARY RESPONSE AND ANALYSIS**

The Rime of the Ancient Mariner Samuel Taylor Coleridge
Coleridge Describes His Addiction Samuel Taylor Coleridge
from In Patagonia Bruce Chatwin

COMPREHENSION *(40 points; 5 points each)*

On the line provided, write the letter of the *best* answer to each of the following items.

_____ **1.** After killing the albatross, the Mariner realizes that the bird —

    A had evil intentions

    B had been guiding the ship

    C would be forgotten

    D would bring happiness

_____ **2.** The crew first views the bird's death as the cause of a —

    F storm

    G drought

    H calm

    J mist

_____ **3.** The men's gazes, which rest upon the Mariner even after they die, symbolize —

    A their devotion to the Mariner

    B the Mariner's continuing hope

    C the men's obedience to the Mariner

    D the Mariner's guilty conscience

_____ **4.** What happens to the Mariner whenever he tells his tale?

    F His soul is thrown into agony.

    G His anguished soul at last finds relief.

    H Listeners gather 'round, and his self-esteem is boosted.

    J He feels more alone than ever in this wide, wide world.

_____ **5.** How does the Mariner select his audience?

    A When he feels he can no longer bear the pain, he stops the next person he meets.

    B He knows the right person as soon as he looks into that person's eyes.

    C He travels from wedding to wedding and inn to inn, telling his tale in return for a seat at the feast and a night's lodging.

    D His popularity makes it possible for him to choose from among many offers.

_____ **6.** Whom does the Mariner tell his tale to in "The Rime of the Ancient Mariner," and where is he when he tells it?

    F To the assembled guests at a welcome-home party in his honor

    G To his grandson, years afterward, sitting by the fireplace

    H To one of the wedding guests passing in the street

    J To a minister beside the Mariner's deathbed at home in England

_____ **7.** According to "Coleridge Describes His Addiction," what treatment did Coleridge feel would work *best* for him?

    A Imprisonment after detoxification

    B Treatment in a private medical facility under a doctor's care

    C Freedom to continue taking laudanum at a dose he thought reasonable

    D Going "cold turkey" without any medical supervision

_____ **8.** The excerpt from Bruce Chatwin's *In Patagonia* helps to —

    F persuade the reader that in real life albatrosses are not "bad luck" birds

    G persuade the reader that in real life penguins are "bad luck" birds

    H inform the reader about real-life inspirations for "The Rime of the Ancient Mariner"

    J explain the natural history of albatrosses

LITERARY FOCUS: THE LITERARY BALLAD *(15 points; 5 points each)*
On the line provided, write the letter of the *best* answer to each of the following items.

_____ **9.** **Ballads** began as an oral tradition, meaning that —

    A they were passed down by being told aloud

    B only certain bards could tell them

    C they were initially written down

    D they were meant to be enjoyed in solitude

_____ **10.** In Coleridge's day, much of the language of his literary ballad was considered —

    F antique

    G up-to-date

    H too ornate

    J incomprehensible

_____ **11.** Which of the following excerpts is an example of internal rhyme, a literary device Coleridge uses in his ballad?

   A "Instead of the cross, the Albatross / About my neck was hung."

   B "A weary time! a weary time! / How glazed each weary eye."

   C "Water, water, everywhere, . . . / Nor any drop to drink."

   D "The western wave was all aflame. / The day was well nigh done! / Almost upon the western wave / Rested the broad bright Sun."

READING SKILLS: READING ARCHAIC WORDS *(5 points)*

On the line provided, write the letter of the *best* answer to the following item.

_____ **12.** Which meaning for the archaic word below is *incorrect*?

   F *trow* means "believe"

   G *uprist* is a mild oath

   H *welladay* is an exclamation of sorrow

   J *wist* means "knew"

VOCABULARY DEVELOPMENT *(20 points; 4 points each)*

Match the definition on the left with the Vocabulary word on the right. On the line provided, write the letter of the Vocabulary word.

_____ **13.** gloomy   **a.** tyrannous

_____ **14.** harsh; oppressive   **b.** dismal

_____ **15.** anguished; grief-stricken   **c.** ghastly

_____ **16.** dreadful; ghostly   **d.** abated

_____ **17.** lessened   **e.** wrenched

CONSTRUCTED RESPONSE *(20 points)*

18. Suppose you are the Wedding Guest. You have just finished listening to the Mariner tell his tale. What emotional effect did it have on you? On a separate sheet of paper, analyze the causes of this effect, including references to the imagery, figurative language, sound, and style of this ballad.

The Rime of the Ancient Mariner . . . In Patagonia   **207**

SELECTION TEST ▮▮▮▮▮▮▮   LITERARY RESPONSE AND ANALYSIS

She Walks in Beauty George Gordon, Lord Byron

COMPREHENSION *(40 points; 4 points each)*

On the line provided, write the letter of the *best* answer to each of the following items.

_____ 1. Byron compares the woman's beauty to the beauty of —

  A heaven

  B light

  C day

  D night

_____ 2. Which of the following words in the poem means the woman's appearance?

  F gaze

  G style

  H aspect

  J mien

_____ 3. What does the speaker find so beautiful about the woman?

  A Her dark hair

  B Her voice

  C Her mind

  D Her laugh

_____ 4. What is the interaction between the speaker and the woman?

  F He watches her as she passes.

  G He introduces himself but is rebuffed.

  H He briefly flirts with her.

  J He begins a love affair with her.

_____ 5. The speaker thinks that the woman's beauty reflects her —

  A wisdom

  B inner beauty

  C need for attention

  D wit and intelligence

_____ 6. In lines 5–6, "Thus mellowed to that tender light / Which heaven to gaudy day denies," the speaker asserts that the —

  F woman's eyes are not as beautiful as the sun

  G woman is most beautiful in moonlight

  H woman is even more beautiful in daylight than she is in moonlight

  J woman's darkness is more beautiful than the brightness of day

_____ **7.** Lines 7–9, "One shade the more, one ray the less, / Had half impaired the nameless grace / Which waves in every raven tress," mean that the —

    A woman's hair is as black as a raven's feathers

    B woman's hair would be better a shade darker

    C woman's hair has the right combination of dark and light

    D speaker feels incapable of describing the beauty of the woman's hair

_____ **8.** To confirm his high opinion of the woman, the speaker supplies —

    F knowledge of her past actions

    G information from her friends

    H understanding based on his acquaintance with her

    J no evidence at all

_____ **9.** The poem's rhyme scheme is —

    A *ababab ababab ababab*

    B *abbabb cddcdd abbcdd*

    C *ababab cdcdcd efefef*

    D *abcd efgh abcgh*

_____ **10.** The poem's structure consists of —

    F three five-line stanzas

    G four four-line stanzas

    H two eight-line stanzas

    J three six-line stanzas

LITERARY FOCUS: SIMILE (*40 points; 10 points each*)

On the line provided, write the letter of the *best* answer to each of the following items.

_____ **11.** The defining characteristic of **simile** is —

    A a comparison of nonhuman to human things

    B the use of linking words such as *like* or *as*

    C the use of words that sound like what they mean

    D an object that stands for something greater than itself

_____ **12.** Which line of "She Walks in Beauty" consists of a **simile**?

    F Line 1

    G Line 6

    H Line 9

    J Line 18

_____ **13.** The speaker compares the woman to a —

    A clear, starry night

    B hot, tropical night

    C misty, cloudy night

    D still, cold night

_____ **14.** Because "She Walks in Beauty" contains one simile that is carried through the entire poem, the simile is referred to as —

    F universal

    G extended

    H epic

    J romantic

CONSTRUCTED RESPONSE (*20 points*)

15. Aside from her physical beauty, what qualities does the speaker imagine that the woman possesses? In your opinion, is Byron's use of simile effective in describing these qualities? On a separate sheet of paper, evaluate the simile based on how well it evokes the woman's character and the emotional impact it had on you.

SELECTION TEST ██████████ LITERARY RESPONSE AND ANALYSIS

from Childe Harold's Pilgrimage, Canto IV
George Gordon, Lord Byron

COMPREHENSION *(40 points; 5 points each)*

On the line provided, write the letter of the *best* answer to each of the following items.

_____ **1.** The phrase "society, where none intrudes . . ." (line 3) expresses the speaker's feeling that —

  A he wants to be alone with only his mind for companionship

  B nature is good company

  C he enjoys nature in the company of others

  D on the seashore, he feels immortal

_____ **2.** According to the speaker, people have no control over —

  F the land

  G the sea

  H themselves

  J one another

_____ **3.** In the second stanza, to what does the speaker compare a drop of rain?

  A A single day

  B A person drowning

  C The sea of humanity

  D The world in miniature

_____ **4.** The third stanza describes the pleasures and terrors of —

  F swimming

  G flying

  H writing

  J love

_____ **5.** The "mane" in line 27 describes —

  A a lion's head

  B the water line under a street

  C a length of a woman's hair

  D the froth of a breaking wave

_____ **6.** Byron seems to comment directly on his own work in the lines —

    F "From these our interviews, in which I steal / From all I may be, or have been before . . ."

    G "Ten thousand fleets sweep over thee in vain . . ."

    H "Without a grave, unknelled, uncoffined, and unknown."

    J " —and what is writ, is writ; / Would it were worthier!"

_____ **7.** In the fourth stanza, what does the speaker claim about his spirit and imagination?

    A Although in his twenties, he still feels like a teenager.

    B Although middle-aged, he still feels like a young man.

    C He feels that his powers are greater than ever.

    D He feels that his powers are feebler than before.

_____ **8.** The essential message of the fifth stanza is that the —

    F poet hopes the reader has found something memorable in the poem

    G speaker wishes Childe Harold glory in his future life as a knight

    H poet dwells obsessively on how his poem could have been improved

    J speaker announces his intention to give up poetry

LITERARY FOCUS: APOSTROPHE *(30 points; 10 points each)*

On the line provided, write the letter of the *best* answer to each of the following items.

_____ **9.** The literary term **apostrophe** refers to —

    A the return of the poem to ideas expressed previously

    B conversation between the speaker and another character

    C direct address by the speaker to an absent person or abstract quality

    D a punctuation mark that signals the beginning of a dialogue

_____ **10.** In the fifth stanza, beginning "Farewell!," the speaker apostrophizes the —

    F ocean

    G shore

    H reader

    J poem

_____ **11.** Apostrophe was a popular literary device among —

    A writers of the eighteenth century

    B Romantic poets

    C English poets

    D Elizabethan playwrights

READING SKILLS: READING RHYME AND RHYTHM *(10 points)*

On the line provided, write the letter of the *best* answer to the following item.

_____ **12.** The final line of a Spenserian stanza is intended to —

    F sum up the previous eight lines

    G introduce the first line of the next stanza

    H stand on its own as a pithy, witty saying

    J confuse the reader by reversing expectations

CONSTRUCTED RESPONSE *(20 points)*

13. "There is a pleasure in the pathless woods" is the first line of this selection. In addition to pleasure identify one other emotion from the selection. Then, for *each* of the two emotions, identify at least three specific passages in which figures of speech or the sound of language help evoke the emotion. Write your answer on a separate sheet of paper.

SELECTION TEST　　　　　　　　　　　　　　**LITERARY RESPONSE AND ANALYSIS**

Ozymandias Percy Bysshe Shelley

COMPREHENSION *(40 points; 4 points each)*

On the line provided, write the letter of the *best* answer to each of the following items.

_____ **1.** In the poem the monument to Ozymandias is —

    A　grand and stunning

    B　a ruin

    C　buried underground

    D　part of a museum exhibit

_____ **2.** The face of Ozymandias —

    F　looks down threateningly

    G　speaks mysteriously

    H　is unforgettable for its ferocity

    J　lies broken in the desert

_____ **3.** Which of the following is *not* a speaker in the poem?

    A　The poet himself

    B　The traveler

    C　The pedestal

    D　Ozymandias

_____ **4.** The words conveyed in lines 10–11 are those of the —

    F　sculptor

    G　narrator

    H　king

    J　traveler

_____ **5.** The traveler seems to believe that —

    A　monuments are eternal

    B　the passage of time is necessary and inevitable

    C　we must preserve relics of past civilizations

    D　even the greatest works are destroyed by time

_____ **6.** This poem is written in the form of a(n) —

    F　parody

    G　epic

    H　sonnet

    J　ode

_____ **7.** The traveler describes the statue of Ozymandias as a(n) —

    A figure without legs or a head

    B armless figure without a head

    C figure without legs or arms

    D figure with two legs and pieces of the head

_____ **8.** The traveler thinks that the sculptor —

    F cunningly showed the king's arrogance

    G flattered the king, who had paid him

    H was not very competent at doing faces

    J had spirit but not much technical skill

_____ **9.** The complicated passage "those passions read / Which yet survive, stamped on these lifeless things, / The hand that mocked them, and the heart that fed . . ." could be interpreted as meaning that —

    A human passion outlives memory and cannot be mocked

    B time does not destroy passion—in fact it feeds passion

    C we have only lifeless objects to remind us of human passions

    D the legend of Ozymandias will remain despite the ravages of time

_____ **10.** The *central* idea of the poem might be that —

    F people's attempts to make things of lasting value are futile

    G poetry has a longer life span than sculpture

    H Ozymandias was an arrogant ruler who has been forgotten by time

    J it can be just as valuable to hear about someone else's travels as to travel oneself

LITERARY FOCUS: IRONY *(40 points; 10 points each)*

On the line provided, write the letter of the *best* answer to each of the following items.

_____ **11.** There are several types of **irony,** but the thing they all have in common is —

    A witty use of language

    B character's ignorance of a situation

    C discrepancy between expectation and reality

    D nasty, sarcastic intent

_____ **12.** The type of irony used in this poem is **situational irony,** in which —

    F the reader is kept in the dark

    G the outcome of a situation is the opposite of what was expected

    H the last line comes as a big surprise

    J characters say the opposite of what they mean, for effect

_____ **13.** Ironically Ozymandias had expected —

    A his monument to fall into ruins, and it did

    B his name to be remembered forever, but it has been forgotten

    C his works to endure, but they have fallen into ruin

    D to be forgotten, but he has left a historic ruin behind

_____ **14.** What makes line 11, "'Look on my works, ye Mighty, and despair!'," ironic?

    F Ozymandias meant it as a boast, but the contemporary reader interprets it as an admission of futility.

    G The words were carved in a language that can no longer be read.

    H There is no such thing as the "Mighty" anymore.

    J Ozymandias had no idea his words would be quoted thousands of years later.

CONSTRUCTED RESPONSE *(20 points)*

15. On a separate sheet of paper, write down what you think is the central message in "Ozymandias." Discuss how specific passages reflect this message. How does Shelley use irony to reinforce his ideas?

NAME _____ CLASS _____ DATE _____ SCORE _____

SELECTION TEST   **LITERARY RESPONSE AND ANALYSIS**

Ode to the West Wind Percy Bysshe Shelley

COMPREHENSION (32 points; 4 points each)

On the line provided, write the letter of the *best* answer to each of the following items.

_____ **1.** "Thou," used throughout the poem, refers to —

    A the speaker himself

    B God

    C the wind

    D Byron, Shelley's friend and rival

_____ **2.** With which season does the speaker associate the west wind?

    F Spring

    G Summer

    H Fall

    J Winter

_____ **3.** In order to be lifted by the west wind, the speaker wishes to be any of the following items *except* a —

    A boat

    B leaf

    C wave

    D cloud

_____ **4.** The speaker wishes to become a lyre —

    F so that the wind blowing through his strings can make beautiful sounds

    G because he despairs of finding words and wants only to make music

    H because he thinks of the lyre as the happiest of instruments

    J in order to challenge the gods, as did Orpheus in Greek mythology

_____ **5.** In a striking simile the poet compares his words to —

    A thunderclaps that will wake the world

    B ashes and sparks from a fading fire

    C a torrential rainfall

    D the beauty of the natural world

_____ **6.** Lines 55–56, "A heavy weight of hours has chained and bowed / One too like thee: tameless, and swift, and proud," mean that the speaker —

    F has lost hope of ever capturing the wind's qualities

    G feels he is even mightier than the wind

    H thinks of every human soul as the wind's brother or sister

    J feels that his spirit resembles the wind

Ode to the West Wind   **217**

_____ 7. The phrase "the incantation of this verse" in line 65 shows that Shelley thinks of poetry as akin to —

    A love or hate

    B magic, prophecy, or religion

    C a declaration of war on injustice

    D a defense against boredom and sorrow

_____ 8. Shelley expresses such extreme empathy with his subject that he —

    F imagines the world entirely surrendering to the wind

    G wants to become the wind and wants the wind to become him

    H wants to resist the wind as if it were a great temptation

    J refuses to grant the wind an identity of its own

LITERARY FOCUS: ODE, TERZA RIMA AND THE SONNET, AND APOSTROPHE *(48 points; 8 points each)*

On the line provided, write the letter of the *best* answer to each of the following items.

_____ 9. Which of the following descriptions would *not* apply to the **ode** form as practiced by the English Romantics?

    A Meditative

    B Complex

    C Introspective

    D Singsong

_____ 10. In general what do **English Romantic odes** have as their subjects?

    F Aspects of nature

    G The poet's youth

    H The folly or vanity of human life

    J Topics of serious reflection

_____ 11. Because it directly addresses the wind—an invisible, powerful presence—Shelley's ode is also a(n) —

    A apostrophe

    B elegy

    C ballad

    D pastoral

_____ **12.** Each of the five sections of "Ode to the West Wind" —

    F   deals with the wind at a different time of year

    G   shows a different natural disaster caused by the wind

    H   has the form of a sonnet

    J   has a different speaker

_____ **13.** Each section of Shelley's "Ode to the West Wind" contains twelve lines in terza rima; in other words, —

    A   a twelve-line stanza of blank verse

    B   three quatrains of rhymed verse

    C   three-line stanzas with interlocking rhyme

    D   conversational free verse

_____ **14.** Each section of Shelley's "Ode to the West Wind" ends with a(n) —

    F   musical coda

    G   rhymed couplet

    H   direct plea to the west wind

    J   answer to the question raised in the previous lines

CONSTRUCTED RESPONSE *(20 points)*

15. On a separate sheet of paper, write down what emotions you think Shelley wishes to convey to his readers through the image of the west wind. Using specific examples from the poem, analyze how Shelley uses figures of speech to evoke readers' emotions.

SELECTION TEST | **LITERARY RESPONSE AND ANALYSIS**

Jade Flower Palace Tu Fu *translated by* Kenneth Rexroth
Night Thoughts Afloat Tu Fu *translated by* Arthur Cooper

COMPREHENSION *(40 points; 4 points each)*

On the line provided, write the letter of the *best* answer to each of the following items.

_____ **1.** The scene described in "Jade Flower Palace" is —

    A the aftermath of a wild party at the palace

    B a poet sitting on the grass outside a ruined old palace

    C a prince, in solitude, contemplating the future of his reign

    D ghosts patrolling indoors and outdoors

_____ **2.** The image in lines 8–9, "Ten thousand organ / Pipes whistle and roar," describes —

    F a musical concert for the prince

    G the ecstasy of an imagined pleasure palace

    H the wailing of ghosts and the howling of werewolves

    J the wind swirling in and around a ruined building

_____ **3.** Where does the Jade Flower Palace stand?

    A In the heart of a more modern, bustling city

    B In the midst of a ruined city studied by archaeologists

    C At the side of a cliff, by a stream, near pine woods

    D Only a few feet from the howling, stormy ocean

_____ **4.** The speaker visits the Jade Flower Palace during —

    F an autumn storm

    G the Jade Flower Festival

    H the depths of winter, snowbound and still

    J a heat wave when he flees the crowded city

_____ **5.** In "Night Thoughts Afloat" the setting is made clear through images of —

    A bent grasses, straight mast, stars, and moon

    B the speaker's thoughts about his career

    C a single bird drifting in the sky

    D ill health and solitude

_____ **6.** Amid his troubles the speaker of "Night Thoughts Alone" seems to find comfort in —

    F thoughts of family and home

    G fantastic visions of paradise

    H the beauty of nature

    J the idea of his impending death

_____ **7.** The speaker imagines himself to be —

    A a raft bumping against the rocks of the river

    B a lone gull drifting, drifting

    C an officially successful court poet

    D clumsy with words; a stumbling, drunken serenader

_____ **8.** The poet Tu Fu is known for all of the following characteristics *except* —

    F use of shifting moods

    G mastery of classical forms

    H compassion for suffering humankind

    J unfailing optimism

_____ **9.** Which statement best sums up the major themes of both "Jade Flower Palace" and "Night Thoughts Afloat"?

    A Nothing lasts forever.

    B Palaces are temples of illusion.

    C Man is in an eternal battle with himself.

    D Love, like nature, is cruel.

_____ **10.** Tu Fu's poetry often conveys a sense of —

    F mockery

    G disillusionment

    H celebration

    J hilarity

LITERARY FOCUS: MOOD *(40 points; 10 points each)*

On the line provided, write the letter of the *best* answer to each of the following items.

_____ **11.** Lyric poets usually establish a **mood,** or atmosphere, by —

    A choosing expressive details and words

    B letting their speakers speak for them

    C creating realistic dialogue

    D stating their feelings

_____ **12.** In both classical Chinese poetry and English Romantic poetry, one subject that evokes a mood of meditative solitude is the —

    F adoration of a woman

    G observation of nature

    H struggle against injustice

    J importance of poetry

_____ **13.** In "Night Thoughts Afloat" the speaker does *not* feel —

    A lonely

    B furious

    C melancholy

    D insignificant

_____ **14.** Which pairing of an English Romantic poem and a Tu Fu poem offers the closest unity of subject and mood?

    F Blake's "The Tyger" and "Jade Flower Palace"

    G Byron's "She Walks in Beauty" and "Night Thoughts Afloat"

    H Shelley's "Ozymandias" and "Jade Flower Palace"

    J Coleridge's "Kubla Khan" and "Night Thoughts Afloat"

CONSTRUCTED RESPONSE *(20 points)*

15. There is a mood of sadness in both Tu Fu poems in this selection. On a separate sheet of paper, state which poem has a sadder view of life. Analyze the themes and imagery of both poems when composing your response.

SELECTION TEST   **LITERARY RESPONSE AND ANALYSIS**

Quiet Night Thoughts Li Po *translated by* Arthur Cooper
Question and Answer Among the Mountains Li Po
translated by Robert Kotewall *and* Norman L. Smith
Letter to His Two Small Children Li Po
translated by Arthur Cooper

COMPREHENSION *(40 points; 4 points each)*

On the line provided, write the letter of the *best* answer to each of the following items.

_____ **1.** The central image in "Quiet Night Thoughts" is of a man —

     A floating on a quiet river

     B contemplating moonlight

     C writing to his family

     D crying

_____ **2.** In the example of parallelism in lines 5–8, the speaker expresses his —

     F constant longing for home

     G wish to go out into the moonlight

     H repeated refusal to live conventionally

     J desire for adventure

_____ **3.** In the first stanza of "Letter to His Two Small Children," the images of green mulberries and of silkworms having "three sleeps" convey —

     A the speaker's joy

     B Li Po's restlessness to resume traveling

     C the season of the year

     D the suffering of the people of Wu

_____ **4.** Where does the speaker of "Letter to His Two Small Children" say he wants to be?

     F Exactly where he is

     G Home in Eastern Lu

     H Back at court with the other poets

     J Sailing the Yangtze once again

_____ **5.** Like the speaker in Shelley's "Ode to the West Wind," the speaker of "Letter to His Two Small Children" —

     A wishes the wind would carry him away

     B has left his family far away

     C waits for spring

     D compares himself to a musical instrument

_____ **6.** Like the speaker in Coleridge's "Kubla Khan," the speaker of "Letter to His Two Small Children" describes —

    F his love for his children

    G an intoxicating imaginary paradise

    H the sadness of being alone

    J a dream that prompted him to write the poem

_____ **7.** The peach tree in "Letter to His Two Small Children" does *not* represent the —

    A speaker's roots in his family

    B speaker's children, growing up in his absence

    C speaker's heart, broken like a blossom

    D tears of the speaker's wife

_____ **8.** The original Chinese poems and the translated versions might differ in the —

    F creation of a mood

    G use of nature imagery

    H attention to the way the words sound

    J number of lines in the poems

_____ **9.** The speaker of "Question and Answer Among the Mountains" dwells in the green mountain because he —

    A is content in a world far away from other people

    B is a devoted climber

    C is hiding from the Emperor's palace guard

    D feels that the country is the best place to raise children

_____ **10.** In "Question and Answer Among the Mountains" a peach blossom represents the —

    F arrival of spring

    G speaker's sorrow

    H inevitable decay of all life

    J speaker separating himself from the world

LITERARY FOCUS: IMAGERY *(40 points; 10 points each)*

On the line provided, write the letter of the *best* answer to each of the following items.

_____ **11. Imagery** is found —

    A only in poetry

    B only in Chinese poetry

    C only in English literature

    D in literature in general

_____ **12.** Li Po uses imagery to help readers —

    F remember what they read

    G understand the theme

    H respond emotionally to a scene

    J identify with him

_____ **13.** Li Po relies on imagery to evoke emotional responses because his poems —

    A are hard to translate accurately

    B rarely state an emotion directly

    C are stiff and formal

    D are chaotic and confused

_____ **14.** The poem "Quiet Night Thoughts" appeals *mainly* to the sense of —

    F sight

    G smell

    H touch

    J hearing

CONSTRUCTED RESPONSE *(20 points)*

15. The poems of Li Po are filled with emotional images and, in these translations as well as in the original Chinese, the sounds of the words enhance the emotions. Select the image in any of the Li Po poems that has the greatest emotional effect on you. On a separate sheet of paper, describe that effect, and discuss how the image achieves it. Show how the image helps establish the poem's tone or mood.

SELECTION TEST   LITERARY RESPONSE AND ANALYSIS

On First Looking into Chapman's Homer John Keats
When I Have Fears John Keats

COMPREHENSION *(60 points; 6 points each)*

On the line provided, write the letter of the *best* answer to each of the following items.

_____ **1.** The speaker of "On First Looking into Chapman's Homer" believes that reading Chapman's translation of Homer —

   A cannot compare with a real journey

   B is a dull but important exercise

   C is fascinating and transcendent

   D was a mistake but an enjoyable one

_____ **2.** Before reading Homer, the speaker had —

   F read a great deal

   G not read any poetry

   H already formed an opinion of Homer's works

   J never heard of him

_____ **3.** In a simile meant to express his awe of Homer's poetry, the speaker compares himself to —

   A the Greek god Apollo

   B the king of a vast realm

   C an explorer

   D the ocean

_____ **4.** According to the poem, Chapman's translation of the *Iliad* has —

   F a lack of focus

   G great clarity and confidence

   H too many footnotes

   J great power but no authenticity

_____ **5.** The metaphorical "realms of gold" stands for —

   A fields of poetry

   B riches of the speaker's individual mind

   C the Americas

   D the British empire

_____ **6.** "When I Have Fears" describes the speaker's reaction to —

    F the transience of life

    G the unexpected appearance of love

    H his first experience of literature

    J the innocence of childhood

_____ **7.** The speaker compares the content of great books to —

    A fleeting time

    B lurking shadows

    C fleecy clouds

    D a rich harvest

_____ **8.** The speaker's fear causes him to —

    F give up literature

    G make many friends and avoid his enemies

    H attempt to forget love and fame

    J lash out at others

_____ **9.** Who is the "fair creature of an hour" in line 9?

    A The speaker

    B The reader

    C The speaker's beloved

    D All humanity

_____ **10.** "When I Have Fears" ends with an expression of the speaker's —

    F fear of death

    G tremendous anger and rage

    H attempt to detach himself from desire

    J devotion to his mentor

On First Looking into Chapman's Homer / When I Have Fears   **227**

LITERARY FOCUS: SONNET *(15 points; 5 points each)*
On the line provided, write the letter of the *best* answer to each of the following items.

_____ **11.** All **sonnets** have fourteen lines, and *most* have —

    A fame as their subject

    B Shakespearean diction

    C an irregular rhyme scheme

    D two parts

_____ **12.** To understand that "On First Looking into Chapman's Homer" is a Petrarchan sonnet and that "When I Have Fears" is a Shakespearean sonnet, you should know that they —

    F have different rhyme schemes

    G were written in different historical periods

    H deal with different themes

    J have different moods

_____ **13.** Which two lines from one of the sonnets constitute a couplet?

    A "When I have fears that I may cease to be / Before my pen has gleaned my teeming brain . . ."

    B "Much have I traveled in the realms of gold, / And many goodly states and kingdoms seen . . ."

    C "Looked at each other with a wild surmise— / Silent, upon a peak in Darien."

    D "Of the wide world I stand alone, and think / Till Love and Fame to nothingness do sink."

READING SKILLS: READING INVERTED SYNTAX *(5 points)*
On the line provided, write the letter of the *best* answer to the following item.

_____ **14.** Which of the following excerpts from Keats uses **inverted syntax**?

    F "I may never live to trace / Their shadows . . ."

    G "I have fears that I may cease to be . . ."

    H "Till Love and Fame to nothingness do sink."

    J "I shall never look upon thee more . . ."

CONSTRUCTED RESPONSE *(20 points)*

15. The speaker of "When I Have Fears" sometimes feels that love and fame are "nothingness." Based on *both* sonnets, what values do you think Keats holds to be the highest in life? On a separate sheet of paper, support your claim with evidence from the poems' contents, tone, and style, and include imagery and figures of speech.

SELECTION TEST

LITERARY RESPONSE AND ANALYSIS

Ode to a Nightingale John Keats

COMPREHENSION *(40 points; 4 points each)*
On the line provided, write the letter of the *best* answer to each of the following items.

_____ **1.** The speaker is overwhelmed by the nightingale's —

    A beauty

    B neutrality

    C grief

    D joy

_____ **2.** The nightingale inspires the speaker to —

    F find faith

    G write poetry

    H fall in love

    J study ecology

_____ **3.** The speaker is impressed by the fact that the nightingale's song —

    A has changed so much over the years

    B has not changed in centuries

    C shares exactly his own mood

    D is not understandable

_____ **4.** "Where but to think is to be full of sorrow" (line 27) expresses Keats's —

    F insistence on thinking positive thoughts

    G belief that the only way to avoid suffering is through philosophy

    H pleasure that he has avoided the pitfalls of excessive thinking

    J sense that life is sad for anyone who thinks about it

_____ **5.** In the third stanza the speaker says that the nightingale has never known the —

    A troubles of human life

    B cruel life-and-death struggle of nature

    C joys of art and beauty

    D desire to be something other than what it is

_____ **6.** The speaker is obsessed with thoughts and images of —

    F death

    G artistic failure

    H romantic love

    J forgetfulness

Holt Assessment: Literature, Reading, and Vocabulary

_____ **7.** Which of the following images from the poem expresses a sense of sadness?

    A A light-winged tree spirit

    B Moss-covered paths

    C A homesick woman

    D Wild fruit trees

_____ **8.** At the conclusion of the poem, the speaker wonders whether the nightingale —

    F has lost its voice

    G was a dream or vision

    H will survive as long as the speaker's poems

    J has flown to a warmer climate.

_____ **9.** In this poem the speaker's mood —

    A never changes

    B changes slightly

    C is unimportant

    D becomes progressively gloomier

_____ **10.** Which line from the poem echoes an important biographical fact about Keats?

    F "That I might drink, and leave the world unseen . . ."

    G "Where Beauty cannot keep her lustrous eyes . . ."

    H "Where youth grows pale, and specter-thin, and dies . . ."

    J "She stood in tears amid the alien corn . . ."

LITERARY FOCUS: SYNESTHESIA *(40 points; 10 points each)*

On the line provided, write the letter of the *best* answer to each of the following items.

_____ **11.** A concise definition of **synesthesia** is that it —

    A confuses truth and falsity

    B intermingles fantasy and reality

    C describes one sense in terms of another

    D mixes past, present, and future

_____ **12.** Which of the following phrases from "Ode to a Nightingale" uses synesthesia?

    F "Cooled a long age in the deep-delvèd earth . . ."

    G "Of beechen green, and shadows numberless . . ."

    H "Here, where men sit and hear each other groan . . ."

    J "And leaden-eyed despairs . . ."

_____ **13.** Suppose Keats were describing a flower and wanted to use synesthesia in the image. Which of the following descriptions would he probably use?

    A Sweet-voiced flower

    B Star-white flower

    C Clove-scented flower

    D Soft-petaled flower

_____ **14.** Synesthesia is often used for the purpose of —

    F creating a somber mood

    G creating a joyful mood

    H describing things in original ways

    J persuading the reader that the five senses are illusory

CONSTRUCTED RESPONSE *(20 points)*

15. On a separate sheet of paper, describe how Keats uses figurative language to create a mood in "Ode to a Nightingale." What mood would you say he creates? Support your ideas with details from the poem.

SELECTION TEST

LITERARY RESPONSE AND ANALYSIS

Ode on a Grecian Urn John Keats

COMPREHENSION (40 points; 5 points each)

On the line provided, write the letter of the *best* answer to each of the following items.

_____ **1.** In the first stanza the speaker wants to know —

    A how old the urn is

    B how much money the urn is worth

    C the particulars of the scene depicted on the urn

    D what civilization created the urn

_____ **2.** The painting of the couple on the urn reminds the speaker of —

    F a couple he knows

    G the artist's calling

    H the fleeting nature of existence

    J the woman he loves

_____ **3.** The couple is frozen —

    A with their lips pressed in a kiss

    B at the moment of pursuit

    C by fear of death

    D at the end of their relationship

_____ **4.** The priest is portrayed —

    F leading a cow to be sacrificed

    G praying to God

    H pursuing the woman

    J helping the poor and sick

_____ **5.** The speaker claims that melodies that are never heard are —

    A the only real kind of music

    B a waste of musical talent

    C lovelier than heard melodies

    D like the air around us

_____ **6.** The speaker feels that the urn —

    F is inferior to poetry as a work of art

    G will change society

    H is beautiful but false

    J will outlast him

_____ **7.** What does "All breathing human passion far above" mean in line 28?

    A Human love is far above the kind of artificial love portrayed on the urn.

    B The frozen passions shown on the urn are far above the turmoil of living human passion.

    C The ancient Grecian figures on the urn would probably think they were superior to modern Europeans.

    D Modern European civilization has advanced far past ancient Greek civilization.

_____ **8.** In the poem's last five lines the speaker imagines the urn —

    F serving as a centerpiece at his wedding to his beloved

    G comforting future generations as it does his own

    H learning more about human life as it survives through the centuries

    J shattering one day, inevitably, as an example of tragic waste

LITERARY FOCUS: METAPHOR *(30 points; 10 points each)*
On the line provided, write the letter of the *best* answer to each of the following items.

_____ **9.** A **metaphor** is a type of —

    A personification

    B mood

    C style

    D figure of speech

_____ **10.** Metaphor compares two things that are essentially —

    F unlike

    G related

    II beautiful

    J puzzling

_____ **11.** In the first two lines of the poem, what kinds of images does Keats use as metaphors for the urn?

    A Metaphors of war

    B Metaphors of marriage and family

    C Metaphors of music and art

    D Metaphors of travel and pleasure

READING SKILLS: VISUALIZING IMAGERY *(5 points)*

On the line provided, write the letter of the *best* answer to the following item.

_____ **12.** Which of the following passages provides the best example of imagery?

    F "To what green altar, O mysterious priest, / Lead'st thou that heifer lowing at the skies, / And all her silken flanks with garlands dressed?"

    G "What men or gods are these? What maidens loath?"

    H "Thou, silent form, dost tease us out of thought / As doth eternity: Cold Pastoral!"

    J "'Beauty is truth, truth beauty,'—that is all / Ye know on earth, and all ye need to know."

CONSTRUCTED RESPONSE *(25 points)*

13. On a separate sheet of paper, write about how Keats uses metaphors to express a major theme of Romanticism: the lasting power of art. Use details from the poem to support your analysis.

The Romantic Period 1798–1832:
The Quest for Truth and Beauty

Read the following poem carefully, and then answer the questions that follow.

To a Highland Girl
At Inversnyede, Upon Loch Lomond
by William Wordsworth

Sweet Highland Girl, a very shower
of beauty is thy earthly <u>dower</u>!
Twice seven consenting years have shed
Their utmost bounty on thy head:
5   And these gray rocks; that household lawn;
Those trees, a veil just half withdrawn;
This fall of water that doth make
A murmur near the silent lake;
This little bay; a quiet road
10   That holds in shelter thy Abode —
In truth together do ye seem
Like something fashioned in a dream;
Such forms as from their <u>covert</u> peep
When earthly cares are laid asleep!
15   But, O fair creature! in the light
Of common day, so heavenly bright,
I bless Thee, vision as thou art,
I bless thee with a human heart;
God shield thee to thy latest years!
20   Thee, neither know I, nor thy peers;
And yet my eyes are filled with tears.

With earnest feeling I shall pray
For thee when I am far away:
For never saw I <u>mien</u>, or face,
25   In which more plainly I could trace
Benignity and home-bred sense
Ripening in perfect innocence.
Here scattered like a random seed,
Remote from men, Thou dost not need
30   The embarrassed look of shy distress,
And maidenly shamefacedness:
Thou wear'st upon thy forehead clear
The freedom of a Mountaineer:

A face with gladness overspread!
35   Soft smiles, by human kindness bred!
And seemliness complete, that sways
Thy courtesies, about thee plays;
With no restraint, but such as springs
From quick and eager visitings
40   Of thoughts that lie beyond the reach
Of thy few words of English speech:
A bondage sweetly brooked, a strife
That gives thy gestures grace and life!
So have I, not unmoved in mind,
45   Seen birds of tempest-loving kind —
Thus beating up against the wind.

What hand but would a garland cull
For thee who art so beautiful?
O happy pleasure! here to dwell
50   Beside thee in some healthy dell;
Adopt your homely ways and dress,
A shepherd, thou a shepherdess!
But I could frame a wish for thee
More like a grave reality:
55   Thou art to me but as a wave
Of the wild sea; and I would have
Some claim upon thee, if I could,
Though but of common neighborhood.
What joy to hear thee, and to see!
60   Thy elder Brother I would be,
Thy Father—anything to thee!

Now thanks to Heaven! that of its grace
Hath led me to this lonely place,
Joys have I had; and going hence
65   I bear away my recompense.
In spots like these it is we prize
Our Memory, feel that she hath eyes:
Then, why should I be loth to stir?
I feel this place was made for her;
70   To give new pleasure like the past,
Continued long as life shall last.
Nor am I loth, though pleased at heart,
Sweet Highland Girl! from thee to part;
For I, methinks, till I grow old,
As fair before me shall behold,
75   As I do now, the cabin small,
The lake, the bay, the waterfall;
And Thee, the spirit of them all!

VOCABULARY SKILLS (20 points; 4 points each)

Each of the underlined words below has also been underlined in the selection.
Re-read those passages, and use context clues to help you select an answer.
On the line provided, write the letter of the word or phrase that *best* completes
each sentence.

_____ 1. The girl's beauty is her "earthly dower" because she —

    A is lucky to be intelligent as well as beautiful

    B would bring her beauty, as if it were a valuable dowry, to her marriage

    C is sure to have an easy life because of her beauty and charm

    D is so beautiful that she astonishes everyone she meets

_____ 2. When the forms "peep" from their covert, they are in a —

    F stream

    G sunny spot

    H hidden place

    J cloud

_____ 3. When the speaker praises the girl's mien, he is referring to her —

    A appearance

    B cruelty

    C personality

    D Highland dress

_____ 4. In this poem, recompense is another word for —

    F punishment

    G rest

    H regret

    J reward

_____ 5. If the speaker were loth to leave the Highland Girl, he would —

    A regret his departure

    B want to leave promptly

    C have no qualms about departing

    D want to leave the next day

COMPREHENSION (20 points; 4 points each)

On the line provided, write the letter of the *best* answer to each of the following items.

_____ 6. The speaker is impressed by the Highland Girl's —

    F graciousness

    G strength

    H intellect

    J determination

_____ **7.** Why does the Highland Girl have "only a few words of English speech"?

    A She is an ancient Greek mountain spirit.

    B She is hearing-impaired.

    C Her native language is Scots Gaelic.

    D She lives during the Anglo-Saxon period.

_____ **8.** Each stanza of the poem ends —

    F after the traditional fourteen lines of a sonnet

    G at the conclusion of an idea on the topic

    H with a declaration of the speaker's love

    J with an irony

_____ **9.** The poem's form is *least* like the form of the —

    A pastoral

    B meditative or conversation poem

    C apostrophic ode

    D sonnet

_____ **10.** As in Byron's "She Walks in Beauty," Keats's "When I Have Fears," and Li Po's "Letter to His Two Small Children," the speaker of "To a Highland Girl" addresses a female character who —

    F is plain but charming

    G speaks her mind

    H says nothing in reply

    J has angered the speaker

READING SKILLS AND STRATEGIES: CONSTRUCTED RESPONSE *(20 points)*
Reading Rhyme and Rhythm

11. Complete the following chart by defining the terms listed and providing examples of those literary elements from the poem. Then, on a separate sheet of paper, write a paragraph explaining how these elements add to the musical sound of the poem.

▶ Literary Element	▶ Definition	▶ Example
rhythm		
rhyme		

LITERARY FOCUS: CONSTRUCTED RESPONSE (40 points)
Identifying Theme (5 points)

On the line provided, write the letter of the *best* answer to the following item.

_____ **12.** All of the following subjects are major themes of the Romantic poets *except* —

    F transience of beauty

    G power of nature

    H longing for the past

    J the quest for progress

Understanding Symbolism (10 points)

13. On a separate sheet of paper, write what you think the Highland Girl symbolizes for the speaker. Use at least two examples from the poem to support your ideas.

Evaluating Imagery (10 points)

14. On a separate sheet of paper, write a paragraph in which you describe the images used to depict the Highland Girl. State which of these images you believe is the strongest, and explain why. Support your ideas with examples from the poem.

Analyzing Alliteration and Simile (15 points)

15. In lines 55–56, the poet uses a simile to describe his feelings for the young woman. On a separate sheet of paper, write down what you think this simile is. What purpose does it serve?

COLLECTION 6 DIAGNOSTIC TEST

The Victorian Period 1832–1901: Paradox and Progress

On the line provided, write the letter of the *best* answer to each of the following items.
(100 points; 10 points each)

_____ **1.** All of the following elements contribute to the musical effect of a poem *except* —

    A rhyme

    B personification

    C meter

    D alliteration

_____ **2.** Which of the following statements about **theme** is *false*?

    F Writers rarely state their themes directly.

    G Readers may have different interpretations of the theme of a work.

    H The theme of a work is the same as the subject.

    J Sometimes the theme of a work is related to the time period in which the work was written.

_____ **3.** A **dramatic monologue** is a poem in which —

    A the speaker is the voice of the poet

    B the poet uses heightened language to tell a story

    C two characters address each other in turn

    D a speaker who is not the poet addresses a silent listener

_____ **4.** A traditional **Petrarchan,** or **Italian, sonnet** —

    F is divided into an octave and a sestet

    G does not rhyme

    H contains three quatrains

    J has more than one speaker

_____ **5.** The **mood** in a literary work —

    A never changes in the course of the work

    B is defined by the subject of the work

    C is always established in the opening of the work

    D can shift at various points in the work

_____ **6.** Which of the following word pairs is **assonant**?

    F sun and shade

    G hill and dale

    H erase and fade

    J daily and dull

_____ **7.** Which of the following statements about **couplets** is *true*?

    A Couplets are elements that repeat throughout a poem.

    B A couplet consists of two consecutive lines of poetry that rhyme.

    C A pair of rhyming words forms a couplet.

    D Couplets always appear at the end of poems.

_____ **8.** What is the difference between an **internal conflict** and an **external conflict**?

    F An internal conflict takes place between two characters, while an external conflict takes place between a character and society.

    G An internal conflict takes place within a character, but an external conflict takes place between a character and a group, a force of nature, or another character.

    H An external conflict is the major conflict in a work, and an internal conflict is a struggle that takes place between subordinate characters.

    J Whereas an external conflict relates to the historical context of a literary work, an internal conflict relates to the particular lives of the characters.

_____ **9.** Which of the following statements about **allegories** is *true*?

    A They can be understood on both a literal and symbolic level.

    B They do not use traditional plot devices.

    C They are meant to be read literally.

    D They are not open to multiple interpretations.

_____ **10.** Which of the following statements about **antonyms** is *true*?

    F The definition of *antonym* is "a word with a prefix meaning 'not' added to it."

    G Every word has only one antonym.

    H Antonyms differ from synonyms only in their connotations.

    J An antonym has the opposite or nearly the opposite meaning as another word.

The Victorian Period 1832–1901: Paradox and Progress

COMPREHENSION *(100 points; 10 points each)*

On the line provided, write the letter of the *best* answer to each of the following items.

_____ **1.** On the whole the Victorian era was characterized by —

    A prolonged wars

    B economic recession

    C peace and prosperity

    D revolution

_____ **2.** An immediate influence on the Victorian era was the —

    F Industrial Revolution

    G Age of Reason

    H Restoration of the Monarchy

    J High Renaissance

_____ **3.** For writers such as Thomas Babington Macaulay, progress was measured in —

    A spiritual contentment

    B the size of the Empire

    C material improvements

    D population growth

_____ **4.** The social problems in Queen Victoria's reign led to many different types of —

    F wars

    G elections

    H political parties

    J reforms

_____ **5.** The word that best describes the ideal behavior of literary Victorians is —

    A immoral

    B genteel

    C defiant

    D slothful

_____ **6.** The scientific and technological advances of the period gave early Victorians a sense of —

    F confidence

    G inferiority

    H pessimism

    J uncertainty

_____ **7.** Many Victorian writers hoped that their work would —

    A create new styles of comedy

    B reestablish Romantic ideals

    C eliminate poverty

    D raise doubts about materialism

_____ **8.** John Ruskin used the term *plague wind* to describe what we now refer to as —

    F hurricane

    G smog

    H epidemic

    J economic depression

_____ **9.** By the end of the nineteenth century, many writers, finding it difficult to believe in an infinite power, became —

    A optimistic

    B patriotic

    C skeptical

    D trusting

_____ **10.** Late Victorian literature, such as the work of Thomas Hardy and A. E. Housman, focused on —

    F emigration and fantasy as escapes from misery

    G the experience of transcendent joy in nature

    H admiration for literary devices and classical allusions

    J human troubles in an indifferent world

SELECTION TEST

The Lady of Shalott Alfred, Lord Tennyson

COMPREHENSION (40 points; 4 points each)

On the line provided, write the letter of the *best* answer to each of the following items.

_____ 1. The mirror shows the Lady of Shalott her —

    A tapestry and shadowy images of the world outside

    B tapestry and the approach of King Arthur

    C tapestry and visions of the cruel life she left behind in Camelot

    D future, including her death

_____ 2. Which of the following statements *best* describes Camelot?

    F It is a dream.

    G It is the real, outside world.

    H It is a perfect place where no one ever dies.

    J It is a castle of incredible beauty surrounded by dirty huts.

_____ 3. The Lady of Shalott finally leaves the island because of —

    A her desire to sell her tapestries in Camelot

    B the lure of exotic places

    C her hatred of Shalott

    D the sight of Sir Lancelot

_____ 4. The Lady of Shalott dies while —

    F destroying her tapestry

    G singing angry love songs about betrayal

    H attempting to tell Sir Lancelot that she loves him

    J floating down the river in a boat

_____ 5. The image that *best* foreshadows, or hints at, the ending of the poem is the —

    A "long-haired page in crimson clad"

    B "mighty silver bugle"

    C mirror cracking "from side to side"

    D "slow horses"

_____ 6. The reapers are aware of the Lady of Shalott's presence on the island because —

    F they have seen her through a window

    G they have seen her wandering the island

    H they hear her singing

    J Lancelot tells them about her

_____ **7.** The crisis, or turning point, in the poem is the Lady of Shalott's realization that she no longer wishes to —

    A live with shadows

    B help other people when she is unhappy

    C devote her life to study

    D live in society

_____ **8.** The Lady of Shalott believes a curse will fall upon her if she —

    F spends too much time weaving

    G looks out toward Camelot

    H falls in love

    J leaves Shalott

_____ **9.** What do the following lines from the poem suggest?

"And down the river's dim expanse / Like some bold seër in a trance, / Seeing all his own mischance— / With a glassy countenance / Did she look to Camelot."

    A She regrets not having left her loom earlier.

    B She always thought she'd hate Camelot, and now she knows it.

    C She expected Sir Lancelot to meet her in his own boat.

    D She knows she won't make it to Camelot.

_____ **10.** Sir Lancelot's reaction to the death of the Lady of Shalott could *best* be described as —

    F cruel but perceptive

    G chivalrous and stricken

    H uninvolved but sympathetic

    J agitated and sad

LITERARY FOCUS: WORD MUSIC *(30 points; 10 points each)*

On the line provided, write the letter of the *best* answer to each of the following items.

_____ **11.** The term **word music** includes all the following devices *except* —

    A rhythm and meter

    B rhyme and repetition

    C simile and metaphor

    D alliteration and assonance

_____ **12.** The line "willows whiten, aspens quiver" demonstrates Tennyson's use of —

    F alliteration and assonance

    G assonance and rhyme

    H rhyme and dissonance

    J dissonance and alliteration

_____ **13.** One notable characteristic of "The Lady of Shalott" that contributes to its verbal music is the —

    A lack of alliteration

    B lack of rhyme

    C regular rhyme scheme

    D irregular meter

READING SKILLS: IDENTIFYING CONTRASTING IMAGES *(10 points)*

_____ **14.** The Lady of Shalott's "snowy white clothing" and "dead-pale" demeanor are in opposition to —

    F the ghostly figures she sees in her mirror

    G the storm that occurs as she sets off for Camelot

    H Lancelot's brilliant appearance as he travels to Camelot

    J the shepherd traveling to Camelot

CONSTRUCTED RESPONSE *(20 points)*

15. This poem can be interpreted as a comment on artists—their need for seclusion so they can create—and their relationship with the world. Based on your reading of the poem, do you think Tennyson believes that artists need isolation? Or do you think he believes that artists should interact with the world? On a separate sheet of paper, answer these questions in a brief essay. Make at least two references to the poem to support your ideas.

SELECTION TEST LITERARY RESPONSE AND ANALYSIS

Ulysses Alfred, Lord Tennyson

COMPREHENSION *(60 points; 6 points each)*

On the line provided, write the letter of the *best* answer to each of the following items.

_____ 1. The first four lines of the poem express Ulysses' —

    A frustration at being back home in peacetime

    B gratitude to the gods for bringing him home safely

    C respect and affection for his people

    D unconditional love for his wife and son

_____ 2. "I will drink / Life to the lees" (lines 6–7) can be paraphrased as —

    F "I will drink more."

    G "I will drink less."

    H "I will live life to its fullest."

    J "I will become as rich as possible."

_____ 3. Ulysses plans to spend the rest of his life —

    A writing down his adventures

    B enjoying the company of old friends

    C on a journey

    D teaching his son how to rule Ithaca

_____ 4. Ulysses believes that old age is —

    F to be feared

    G another adventure

    H to be spent in retirement

    J a time for reflection

_____ 5. Ulysses expects that Telemachus will —

    A have a wild youth

    B never amount to very much

    C rule Ithaca fairly and with honor

    D be driven crazy by wives and children

_____ 6. Ulysses regards his subjects as —

    F admiring

    G savage

    H courageous

    J generous

_____ **7.** When Ulysses says, "As though to breathe were life!" (line 24), he is saying —

    A every breath is a blessing

    B old age makes it hard to enjoy life

    C experience can be "breathed in" even at home beside a quiet hearth

    D mere existence is not enough

_____ **8.** Ulysses hopes that Telemachus will follow —

    F in his father's footsteps

    G his own path

    H his mother's wishes

    J the instructions of the oracle

_____ **9.** Ulysses feels that at this point in life he is —

    A stronger in body and will than he ever was

    B as strong in will as he ever was, but not in body

    C as strong in body as he ever was, but not in will

    D not as strong in body or will as he used to be

_____ **10.** In the last line of the poem, Ulysses refuses to "yield"; however, the poem shows that he *is* yielding to —

    F the temptation to flee his home

    G the pleas of his wife and son

    H the approach of old age and death

    J the needs of his people

LITERARY FOCUS: THEME AND PERSONIFICATION (20 points; 5 points each)

On the line provided, write the letter of the *best* answer to each of the following items.

_____ **11.** The **theme** of a work of literature has to do mostly with its —

    A words

    B details

    C images

    D ideas

Ulysses

_____ **12.** Which of the following lines from "Ulysses" shows Tennyson's use of personification?

    F "Life piled on life / Were all too little, and of one to me / Little remains . . ."

    G "This is my son . . . Telemachus, / To whom I leave the scepter and the isle . . ."

    H "The deep / Moans round with many voices."

    J "Come, my friends, / 'Tis not too late to seek a newer world."

_____ **13.** Which of the following lines from "Ulysses" does *not* contain personification?

    A "There lies the port; the vessel puffs her sail . . ."

    B "Old age hath yet his honor and his toil."

    C "Death closes all; but something ere the end, / Some work of noble note, may yet be done . . ."

    D "It may be that we shall touch the Happy Isles, / And see the great Achilles, whom we knew."

_____ **14.** Which quotation from the poem is *not* a thematic statement?

    F "I am a part of all that I have met . . ."

    G "Far on the ringing plains of windy Troy."

    H "Old age hath yet his honor and his toil."

    J "Though much is taken, much abides . . ."

CONSTRUCTED RESPONSE (20 points)

15. On a separate sheet of paper, write down what you think Tennyson's view of aging is. How does he think a person ought to behave in old age? (To answer, you may want to ask yourself whether Tennyson agrees with his character Ulysses.) Use textual evidence to support your interpretation.

SELECTION TEST

LITERARY RESPONSE AND ANALYSIS

My Last Duchess Robert Browning
Scenes from a Modern Marriage
Julia Markus

COMPREHENSION *(40 points; 4 points each)*

On the line provided, write the letter of the *best* answer to each of the following items.

_____ **1.** "My Last Duchess" shows what formal occasion?

    A A nobleman's employee is making dowry arrangements with a widower.

    B A relative has called to express regret at the Duchess's death.

    C An elderly duke is negotiating the marriage of his only daughter.

    D An art connoisseur is inspecting the art collection of a rich man.

_____ **2.** The Duke was angered by the fact that the Duchess —

    F had too many parties

    G smiled freely at others

    H did not have a dowry

    J spent his money foolishly

_____ **3.** The Duke did not discuss his feelings with the Duchess because he —

    A felt that to do so would be beneath him

    B was shy in the presence of women, even his own wife

    C was so busy with affairs of state that he had no time for personal discussions

    D was unaware of his own feelings at the time

_____ **4.** Frà Pandolf is the —

    F listener

    G Count's emissary

    H painter of the portrait

    J Duke's brother

_____ **5.** The question "Will 't please you sit and look at her?" (line 5) is addressed to the —

    A Duke

    B Duke and Duchess's family physician

    C painter

    D Count's emissary

_____ **6.** Which adjective *best* describes the Duchess's character at the beginning of her marriage?

    F scheming

    G bored

    H depressed

    J congenial

_____ **7.** Which adjective does *not* describe the Duke's character?

    A modest

    B controlling

    C jealous

    D arrogant

_____ **8.** The speaker in "My Last Duchess" is —

    F the Duke of Ferrara

    G the Duke's first wife

    H Robert Browning

    J the Count

_____ **9.** The listener in the poem is the —

    A Duke

    B Count

    C Count's emissary

    D painter

_____ **10.** The Brownings's marriage was quite different from that of the Duke and Duchess. According to "Scenes from a Modern Marriage," which of the following statements is *not* true about the marriage of Robert and Elizabeth Barrett Browning?

    F In the Brownings' marriage, husband and wife were equals.

    G Robert Browning did not mistreat Elizabeth Barrett Browning.

    H In the Brownings' marriage the wife was a powerful public figure in her own right.

    J Elizabeth Barrett Browning's dowry was a sticking point.

LITERARY FOCUS: DRAMATIC MONOLOGUE *(20 points; 10 points each)*

On the line provided, write the letter of the *best* answer to each of the following items.

_____ **11.** A **dramatic monologue** is a poem in which a speaker other than the poet addresses —

    A an imagined theater audience

    B the poet

    C a listener who speaks in reply

    D a listener who does not speak

_____ **12.** Because "My Last Duchess" is a dramatic monologue, the reader —

    F can read the speaker's unvoiced thoughts

    G can read the poet's comments about the speaker

    H must infer all meanings from what the speaker says

    J can "overhear" the conversation between the speaker and the listener

READING SKILLS: DRAWING INFERENCES FROM TEXTUAL CLUES *(20 points; 10 points each)*

On the line provided, write the letter of the *best* answer to each of the following items.

_____ **13.** From the Duke's statement that no one pulls back the curtain from the portrait except him, the reader can infer that the Duke —

    A can't endure sharing the image of his late wife

    B is jealous of the listener

    C is knowledgeable about preservation of art

    D likes to control his artworks

_____ **14.** When the Duke says of the portrait, "There she stands / As if alive," we can infer that —

    F he is happier with the portrait than with the real person

    G when he sees the portrait, he remembers their happy marriage

    H he is experiencing a hallucination in which the portrait seems to breathe

    J he is upset to the point of delusional fantasy

CONSTRUCTED RESPONSE *(20 points)*

15. On a separate sheet of paper, briefly describe the Duke's character as you have inferred it from his monologue. Then, discuss how tone helps shape Browning's characterization of the Duke in this monologue.

SELECTION TEST ██████████ **LITERARY RESPONSE AND ANALYSIS**

Sonnet 43 Elizabeth Barrett Browning

COMPREHENSION *(40 points; 5 points each)*
On the line provided, write the letter of the *best* answer to each of the following items.

_____ 1. Barrett Browning's sonnets were titled *Sonnets from the Portuguese* because —

    A they are based on Portuguese folk tales and ballads about love and honor

    B Robert Browning suggested the title as a joke

    C Barrett Browning was reluctant to admit that the sonnets were autobiographical

    D Barrett Browning translated the poems from Portuguese into English

_____ 2. The speaker claims that she will love her beloved —

    F with excessive devotion

    G steadily and conservatively

    H even better after she dies

    J madly and wildly

_____ 3. The love expressed in the poem can *best* be described as —

    A violent and dangerous

    B temporary and insignificant

    C spontaneous and fleeting

    D lasting and profound

_____ 4. The speaker's statement that she loves with "childhood's faith" means that her love is —

    F small and noisy

    G pure and trusting

    H immature

    J selfish

_____ 5. Although the speaker alludes to her lost childhood faith, the concluding lines indicate that —

    A love has replaced religious belief

    B she has retained a Christian belief in God's will

    C her lover will appreciate her love after her death

    D the poem is really about faith and not love

_____ 6. What does the phrase "as they turn from Praise" in line 8 mean?

    F As people are embarrassed by praise

    G As people do things without needing praise

    H As people usually do in spite of themselves

    J As people rarely do

254   Holt Assessment: Literature, Reading, and Vocabulary

_____ **7.** As a respectable Victorian, Barrett Browning does *not* describe her love as —

    A a replacement for her lost religious belief

    B the equivalent of a search for justice and truth

    C a powerful physical passion

    D a quiet, everyday domestic companionship

_____ **8.** As the poem progresses, both its sentiments and its expressions become more —

    F serious

    G emotional

    H humorous

    J ironic

LITERARY FOCUS: PETRARCHAN SONNET *(30 points; 5 points each)*

On the line provided, write the letter of the *best* answer to each of the following items.

_____ **9.** The **Petrarchan sonnet** form is characterized by —

    A an octave and a sestet

    B four terza rima stanzas and a couplet

    C three quatrains and a couplet

    D seven couplets

_____ **10.** What typical feature of the Petrarchan sonnet does Barrett Browning's Sonnet 43 *lack*?

    F The quatrain

    G The turn

    H The couplet

    J The coda

_____ **11.** What is the rhyme scheme of Sonnet 43?

    A *abab abab cdc dcd*

    B *abab cdcd efef gg*

    C *abba cddc efgefg*

    D *abbaabba cdcdcd*

_____ **12.** In this poem the word *grace* rhymes with —

    F face

    G ways

    H saints

    J place

_____ **13.** Which line from the poem is *not* in strict iambic pentameter?

    A "How do I love thee? Let me count the ways."

    B "For the ends of Being and ideal Grace."

    C "With my lost saints—I love thee with the breath . . ."

    D "I shall but love thee better after death."

_____ **14.** Which sound device is *not* used in lines 8–9?

    F Onomatopoeia

    G Alliteration

    H Repetition

    J Meter

CONSTRUCTED RESPONSE (*30 points*)

15. Assuming that the poet wishes her readers to share her emotions, how does she use the **sounds** of words to help get those emotions across? Write your answer on a separate sheet of paper.

SELECTION TEST ████████████   LITERARY RESPONSE AND ANALYSIS

Pied Beauty Gerard Manley Hopkins

COMPREHENSION *(40 points; 5 points each)*

On the line provided, write the letter of the *best* answer to each of the following items.

_____ **1.** Which word is a synonym for *pied*?

    A secret

    B perfect

    C spotted

    D tried

_____ **2.** According to the speaker, beauty is —

    F brief

    G found only in art and nature

    H unreal and should be ignored

    J found in imperfection

_____ **3.** Items praised by the speaker include —

    A mushrooms, flowers, and trees

    B paintings, sculptures, and tapestries

    C trout, farmers' fields, and freckles

    D churches, chapels, and cherubs

_____ **4.** The items described in the poem support its meaning in that they —

    F are beautiful and belong in a museum

    G are flawed but praiseworthy

    H are depressing reminders of the fall of Adam and Eve

    J reflect the perfection of humankind

_____ **5.** Which of the following quotations expresses the essential message of the poem?

    A "Praise him."

    B "Landscape plotted and pieced . . ."

    C "Fresh-firecoal chestnut-falls . . ."

    D ". . . sweet, sour . . ."

_____ **6.** What is Hopkins's description for the act of divine creation?

    F "past change"

    G "who knows how?"

    H "fathers-forth"

    J "dappled things"

_____ **7.** Which of the following words originated with Hopkins?

    A dappled

    B brinded

    C stipple

    D couple-color

_____ **8.** Which of the following four words is *not* synonymous with the others?

    F dappled

    G beauty

    H stippled

    J freckled

LITERARY FOCUS: ALLITERATION AND ASSONANCE *(30 points; 5 points each)*

On the line provided, write the letter of the *best* answer to each of the following items.

_____ **9.** In its form and purpose, "Pied Beauty" *most* closely resembles a —

    A dirge or elegy

    B psalm

    C tanka

    D Romantic ode

_____ **10.** In order to strengthen the connections among his words and ideas, Hopkins uses —

    F rhythm

    G alliteration and assonance

    H related images

    J all of the above

_____ **11. Assonance** is repetition of —

    A similar vowel sounds

    B vowel sounds at the ends of words

    C consonant sounds

    D grammatical structures

_____ **12.** What is repeated in **alliteration**?

    F Consonant sounds

    G Vowel sounds

    H Invented compound words

    J Grammatical structures

_____ **13.** An example of alliteration from "Pied Beauty" is —

    A   "As a brinded cow . . ."

    B   "Fresh-firecoal chestnut-falls . . ."

    C   "For dappled things . . ."

    D   "Whose beauty is past change . . ."

_____ **14.** An example of assonance from "Pied Beauty" is —

    F   Glory/God/dappled

    G   skies/brinded/cow

    H   rose-moles/firecoal/fold

    J   swift/slow/sweet/sour

CONSTRUCTED RESPONSE (30 points)

15. What do you think Hopkins wants you to feel when reading this poem? On a separate sheet of paper, analyze how he uses style and sound to attain this purpose. How successful do you think Hopkins is in this purpose, and why?

Pied Beauty

SELECTION TEST

LITERARY RESPONSE AND ANALYSIS

Dover Beach Matthew Arnold

COMPREHENSION (40 points; 4 points each)

On the line provided, write the letter of the *best* answer to each of the following items.

_____ **1.** Dover Beach faces the channel of water that separates England and —

    A France

    B Ireland

    C Scotland

    D Spain

_____ **2.** The speaker remarks that the sounds of the waves bring in a note of —

    F peace

    G sadness

    H joy

    J love

_____ **3.** The speaker wants to find comfort in —

    A nature

    B learning

    C his family

    D love

_____ **4.** The speaker believes that the world beyond individual relationships has neither —

    F riches nor rewards

    G light nor love

    H peace nor prosperity

    J glory nor glamour

_____ **5.** The universal condition that Arnold addresses in this poem is —

    A despair

    B physical suffering

    C beauty

    D greed

_____ **6.** The rhythm of the poem is —

    F strictly iambic

    G loosely iambic

    H nursery-rhyme-like

    J meterless, free

_____ **7.** According to the speaker, what did the sound of the sea bring to mind for Sophocles long ago?

    A Human misery

    B Hope for a better world

    C Faith in the gods

    D Desire for immortality

_____ **8.** What does the speaker compare to a sea whose waters are retreating?

    F His love

    G His faith

    H Material progress in the Victorian era

    J The shrinking British Empire

_____ **9.** In the last stanza the speaker claims that the world really resembles a —

    A dreamland

    B decaying city

    C barren moonscape

    D battlefield at night

_____ **10.** What is the speaker doing as he makes the observations in this poem?

    F Standing at the edge of the shore, watching the waves approach his feet

    G Sitting in his study far away from Dover Beach

    H Landing on a very different beach during wartime

    J Standing at his window facing the sea at night

LITERARY FOCUS: MOOD *(40 points; 10 points each)*

On the line provided, write the letter of the *best* answer to each of the following items.

_____ **11.** Two other words for **mood** are *feeling* and —

    A meaning

    B tone

    C gloom

    D atmosphere

_____ **12.** The mood of "Dover Beach" is generally —

    F happy

    G carefree

    H melancholy

    J angry

_____ **13.** In the third stanza the image "vast edges drear / And naked shingles of the world" means —

    A beaches on waters where no fish can live

    B human misery and suffering

    C areas with no belief or faith

    D beaches with no place to swim or sail

_____ **14.** In the final stanza, what additional **mood** appears in the poem?

    F tenderness

    G jealousy

    H vengefulness

    J indifference

CONSTRUCTED RESPONSE (*20 points*)

15. In your opinion, does "Dover Beach" present a pessimistic view of life focusing on loss of faith or an optimistic view focusing on the power of love? Both answers are supportable. On a separate sheet of paper, defend your point of view, using at least two references to the poem.

SELECTION TEST ████████████   **LITERARY RESPONSE AND ANALYSIS**

To an Athlete Dying Young   A. E. Housman
Death and Other Grave Matters
from **What Jane Austen Ate and Charles Dickens Knew**   Daniel Pool

COMPREHENSION *(40 points; 4 points each)*

On the line provided, write the letter of the *best* answer to each of the following items.

_____ **1.** Housman uses the image of quickly withering laurels to communicate the —

     A rapid passing of the victories of youth

     B temporary nature of the boy's illness

     C bitter attitude of an athlete whose glory has faded

     D withering stares of jealous competitors

_____ **2.** When the speaker mentions carrying the young man "shoulder-high," he is referring to —

     F carrying the athlete off the track and holding him up for the gold medal

     G lifting the athlete after a victory and holding a coffin aloft

     H taking the athlete to the hospital

     J transporting the athlete through the weeping spectators to the winner's circle

_____ **3.** According to the speaker, the only people who admire the athlete now are —

     A other athletes

     B coaches and sportswriters

     C the dead

     D other young men

_____ **4.** In lines 9–20, the speaker claims that the athlete is fortunate because —

     F at least he lived to experience a great victory

     G he won through luck instead of through natural speed

     H by dying young, he has avoided seeing his records broken and his fame fade

     J his family has given him a lavish funeral that will keep his memory alive

_____ **5.** In the final stanza what point does the speaker make about the victory garland?

     A It is hard to see in a girl's long, curly hair.

     B Girls usually make garlands of flowers, not of laurel leaves.

     C The athlete, having died young, will not live to see his victory garland wither.

     D The victories of boys are often briefer than those of girls.

_____ **6.** Which of the following statements *best* expresses an important meaning of this poem?

 F Strong, young, healthy athletes are the most fortunate people in the world.

 G Glory lasts only while an athlete wins, and no athlete continues to win forever.

 H Glory is fulfilling only to very innocent young people.

 J Athletes' memories of their own athletic accomplishments eventually fade.

_____ **7.** What is "the road all runners come" (line 5)?

 A Death

 B Victory

 C Old age

 D Defeat

_____ **8.** To be "townsman of a stiller town" (line 8) means to —

 F be an athlete on the day after a victory, when the cheering has stopped

 G move to a smaller, more remote place, away from the public eye

 H be seated in church, praying silently among townspeople

 J be dead, lying in the graveyard

_____ **9.** Which word below *best* describes the Victorian attitude toward death shown in "To an Athlete Dying Young" and "Death and Other Grave Matters"?

 A terror

 B fascination

 C nonchalance

 D disbelief

_____ **10.** Both the poem and "Death and Other Grave Matters" reflect the fact that for the Victorians, death was —

 F all too familiar

 G "out of sight, out of mind"

 H not dwelled on after the deceased's passing

 J an opportunity for greedy disputes about wills

LITERARY FOCUS: COUPLET *(40 points; 10 points each)*
On the line provided, write the letter of the *best* answer to each of the following items.

_____ **11.** Which of the following statements is *not* true of **couplets**?

    A The couplet is a subgenre of poetry.

    B A couplet consists of two lines.

    C A couplet's lines rhyme.

    D A couplet's lines are usually in the same meter.

_____ **12.** In "To an Athlete Dying Young," how are the couplets arranged?

    F Each couplet is a complete stanza.

    G The couplets are bunched into sonnets.

    H The couplets are linked by interlocking rhymes.

    J Pairs of couplets are joined into four-line stanzas.

_____ **13.** Which statement *best* describes the effect of the couplets on the rhythm of this poem?

    A They create a flexible, conversational flow.

    B They have a neutral effect since couplets are often used in English poetry.

    C Their sprightly tone is intended to lift the spirits of the reader.

    D They mimic the slow march of a funeral parade.

_____ **14.** Housman probably chose to write this poem in couplets because —

    F they are relatively easy to understand, and he wanted his poem to appeal to everyone

    G he mastered the couplet form before mastering more demanding verse techniques

    H his couplets' strong rhythm matches his serious subject: death

    J the use of couplets marks him as a distinct, typically late-Victorian poet

CONSTRUCTED RESPONSE *(20 points)*

15. Choose an eight-line passage (two stanzas) in "To an Athlete Dying Young" that you consider especially effective and meaningful. On a separate sheet of paper, analyze how Housman's **style** and the **sound** of his words help make the poem meaningful and moving.

SELECTION TEST

LITERARY RESPONSE AND ANALYSIS

The Mark of the Beast Rudyard Kipling

COMPREHENSION *(40 points; 4 points each)*

On the line provided, write the letter of the *best* answer to each of the following items.

_____ 1. What theory does the narrator propose in the first paragraph of the story?

    A In Asia, Asian gods rather than the Christian God control most events.

    B The British Empire is doomed because it disregards the values and traditions of native peoples.

    C Western religion is true, and Eastern religion is false.

    D All religions are really saying the same thing despite differences of detail.

_____ 2. What occasion brings the English characters together in the first scene?

    F An outbreak of disease has scared them into returning to the British station.

    G A native uprising has caused them all to gather in the British fort for protection.

    H The annual cricket championships are about to take place, and the British consider it more important than their professional duties.

    J The characters are attending a New Year's Eve bash at a colonial station.

_____ 3. Who is the Silver Man?

    A The high priest of the Hindu temple

    B The British paymaster

    C An Indian suffering from leprosy

    D A British police officer who abuses the Indians

_____ 4. What incident infuriates the Indian populace?

    F Fleete refuses to enter the temple and starts a fight.

    G Fleete grinds a cigar butt into the stone image of Hanuman, the monkey god.

    H Strickland tries to bribe the temple priest.

    J Strickland is overheard making insulting comments about the Silver Man's religion.

_____ 5. After Fleete is marked by the Silver Man, he —

    A craves meat, howls, and becomes increasingly animal-like

    B turns into a well-behaved but frightening werewolf

    C develops the first symptoms of leprosy

    D denounces British colonialism and begins to "go native"

_____ 6. The point of view used in this story is —

    F omniscient

    G first person

    H second person

    J limited third person

_____ **7.** Some aspects of this story allude to —

    A Greek and Roman myths about wolves

    B a New Testament revelation about a great beast that marks its followers

    C a Bible story in which a woman is transformed into a pillar of salt

    D an Indian parable about a child who mocks the gods

_____ **8.** The Englishmen make a cultural allusion when they mention that —

    F the leper must be taken alive and unhurt

    G a horse could probably tell them something important

    H the gun barrel is singeing the carpet

    J in *H.M.S. Pinafore* an unknown noise is attributed to a cat

_____ **9.** The proverb quoted at the beginning of the story suggests the —

    A opposition of Eastern and Western systems of belief

    B struggle between right and wrong, justice and injustice

    C friction between science and faith

    D disagreement over who is to rule India—the British, or the Indians themselves

_____ **10.** *Outrage* is the name of a —

    F monkey

    G servant

    H horse

    J leper

LITERARY FOCUS: CONFLICT *(10 points; 5 points each)*

On the line provided, write the letter of the *best* answer to each of the following items.

_____ **11.** In general, conflict is either **external** or **internal**. In other words, it is —

    A between people and nature or between one person and another person

    B between the main character, or protagonist, and the opposing character, or antagonist

    C between a character and an outside force or within the character

    D a conflict that can be resolved or one that cannot be resolved

_____ **12.** Dr. Dumoise is conflicted about whether —

    F   to worship as a Christian or as a Hindu

    G   to believe in the science he has learned or in the evidence before his own eyes

    H   or not to tell Fleete's tale when he, Dumoise, returns to England

    J   or not his oath as a physician allows him to remain at the drunken party

READING SKILLS: IDENTIFYING CONFLICTS AND RESOLUTIONS *(10 points; 5 points each)*

On the line provided, write the letter of the *best* answer to each of the following items.

_____ **13.** The **conflict** between the temple priests and Fleete is **resolved** when —

    A   Fleete apologizes

    B   the Silver Man touches Fleete and leaves the mark

    C   Strickland offers to give money to the temple

    D   the priests realize that Fleete is drunk

_____ **14.** The **conflict** between the English culture and the native culture of India is—

    F   explored in the story but left unresolved

    G   resolved when the priests deny that any white man ever touched the idol

    H   resolved through the defeat of the Silver Man

    J   revealed in the story to be only an imagined conflict

VOCABULARY DEVELOPMENT *(20 points; 4 points each)*

Match the definition on the left with the Vocabulary word on the right. On the line provided, write the letter of the Vocabulary word.

_____ **15.** extremely agitated   **a.** genial

_____ **16.** mild-mannered; friendly   **b.** divinity

_____ **17.** god; sacred being   **c.** distraught

_____ **18.** false belief   **d.** delusion

_____ **19.** without emotion; impartially   **e.** dispassionately

CONSTRUCTED RESPONSE *(20 points)*

20. What lesson or meaning do you think this story held for the British audience of the Victorian era? On a separate sheet of paper, analyze how the story relates to specific issues of that time. Be sure to cite details from the story.

SELECTION TEST

LITERARY RESPONSE AND ANALYSIS

How Much Land Does a Man Need?

Leo Tolstoy   *translated by* Louise *and* Aylmer Maude

COMPREHENSION *(40 points; 4 points each)*

On the line provided, write the letter of the *best* answer to each of the following items.

_____ **1.** An elder sister comes from town to visit her younger sister in the country. As a result of their conversation, Pahom decides that he —

    A works very hard and hates it

    B wants to move to town and enjoy himself

    C is perfectly secure in his present life

    D needs to own land to feel secure

_____ **2.** Which of the following features is *not* one of the values of country life, according to Pahom's wife?

    F Fine clothes

    G Enough to eat

    H Self-sufficiency

    J No temptations

_____ **3.** When Pahom *first* becomes a landowner, he —

    A is very happy and tries to be patient with peasant trespassers

    B yells at everyone who attempts to trespass on his land

    C fences off his land so that no one can trespass

    D patrols his land with a shotgun to keep away trespassers

_____ **4.** Later, when trespassers appear on his land, Pahom —

    F fines them

    G shoots them

    H reasons with them

    J forgives them

_____ **5.** Every time Pahom gets more land, he —

    A is happier than before

    B makes more friends than before

    C gets along better with his wife

    D becomes dissatisfied and wants more land

_____ **6.** In order to buy land from the Bashkirs, Pahom must —

    F outdo the Bashkir chief at drinking kumiss, a drink made from fermented mare's milk

    G walk the boundary of his purchase and return to his starting point before sunset

    H beat the Bashkir champion in a horse race

    J pay more money than he can really afford

_____ **7.** How much land does Pahom end up with?

    A Thirty-five square miles

    B A vast tract

    C Three square miles

    D Six feet

_____ **8.** The sunset is delayed a bit for Pahom because the Bashkirs are —

    F not sticklers for the details of the deal

    G situated on a hillock

    H not serious about the terms of the deal

    J in league with the Devil

_____ **9.** Pahom believes the Bashkirs are _____ but asks for _____.

    A laughing at him; their respect

    B thieves; only their word

    C ignorant and childlike; a deed, or legal document of ownership

    D fair; a lower price

_____ **10.** How is it true that Pahom both gains the Bashkirs' land and loses it?

    F He awakens to find it was all a dream.

    G After selling him the land, the Bashkirs kill him.

    H He reaches the starting point but then dies.

    J Although he gets the land, he has sold his soul to the Devil.

LITERARY FOCUS: ALLEGORY *(10 points; 5 points each)*

On the line provided, write the letter of the *best* answer to each of the following items.

_____ **11.** "How Much Land Does a Man Need?" is an allegory because —

    A the devil appears at least once

    B it presents and answers a question

    C it deals with simple people

    D its characters and events are symbolic

_____ **12.** One reason you might suspect that the story is an allegory is that the —

    F title poses a moral question

    G devil appears as a character in the story

    H story takes place among serfs

    J main character is punished in the end

READING SKILLS: SUMMARIZING THEME _(10 points; 5 points each)_

_____ **13.** Which is the _best_ statement of the theme of this story?

    A Ownership can produce destructive greed.

    B Deal firmly with the people who work for you.

    C Do not believe that Bashkirs are ignorant.

    D Do not own anything.

_____ **14.** The themes of the story probably reflect Tolstoy's —

    F wealthy, aristocratic upbringing

    G writing of _War and Peace_ and _Anna Karenina_

    H concern for the fate of the Russian peasants

    J experiences as a young officer during the Crimean War

VOCABULARY DEVELOPMENT _(20 points; 4 points each)_

On the line provided, write the letter of the _best_ antonym (a word or phrase with opposite meaning) for each of the following Vocabulary words.

_____ **15. aggrieved**

    A offended

    B resentful

    C contented

    D injured

_____ **16. disparaged**

    F praised

    G belittled

    H insulted

    J scorned

_____ **17. arable**

    A fertile

    B planted

    C infertile

    D harvested

_____ **18. haggled**

    F agreed

    G bargained

    H argued

    J wrangled

_____ **19. prostrate**

    A bowing low

    B lying down

    C showing humility

    D standing upright

CONSTRUCTED RESPONSE *(20 points)*

20. On a separate sheet of paper, write about how **allegory** and **realism** help Tolstoy comment on life in "How Much Land Does a Man Need?" Cite specific examples from the story.

SELECTION TEST   LITERARY RESPONSE AND ANALYSIS

The Bet   Anton Chekhov   *translated by* Constance Garnett

COMPREHENSION *(40 points; 4 points each)*

On the line provided, write the letter of the *best* answer to each of the following items.

_____ **1.** The bet is made when a group of friends at a party disagree about whether —

    A capital punishment is preferable to life imprisonment

    B a human being will always go mad after a few years apart from society

    C people raised in isolation can ever develop mature personalities

    D wisdom was achievable by the average educated person in Russia in 1870

_____ **2.** Why does the lawyer extend the term of the bet from five years to fifteen years?

    F The banker offers him more money to do so.

    G The lawyer suffers from a mental disorder which causes him to act in extreme ways.

    H The lawyer wishes to impress his future wife.

    J The story gives no explanation of this action.

_____ **3.** The lawyer is confined to —

    A a lodge in the banker's garden

    B his own attic room

    C the local jail

    D a hospital run by one of the guests

_____ **4.** During his confinement the lawyer is allowed to do anything —

    F that does not require electricity

    G of a serious nature—nothing fun

    H that can be done within the bounds of solitude

    J except drinking and smoking

_____ **5.** For fifteen years the lawyer's relations with the outside world consist of —

    A supervised walks every other day

    B a monthly visit from family or friends

    C communication through a small window

    D annual physical examinations by his doctor

_____ **6.** During the solitary confinement the lawyer reads everything from philosophy and history to —

    F Russian novels

    G technical treatises

    H theology

    J nothing

The Bet   **273**

_____ **7.** The lawyer's fifteen-year solitude leaves him —

    A fat and messy

    B thin and feeble

    C grateful for learning

    D eager for vengeance

_____ **8.** At the end of the fifteen years, when the time comes to pay the lawyer, the banker —

    F is glad to be able to perform such a generous act

    G doesn't want to pay because he is no longer as rich as he used to be

    H doesn't want to pay because he is a dishonest person by nature

    J is willing to pay the money as a dowry if the lawyer agrees to marry his daughter

_____ **9.** The banker enters the lawyer's room on the day before the end of the bet because the banker —

    A hopes to tempt the lawyer to make an early escape

    B wants to negotiate with the lawyer for a lower payment

    C imagines killing the lawyer

    D wishes to have a private, profound discussion with the lawyer before anyone else intrudes

_____ **10.** After the lawyer renounces the money, the banker is sleepless with "tears and emotion." According to the text, which of the following emotions is the banker probably *not* feeling?

    F hatred

    G relief

    H greed

    J self-contempt

LITERARY FOCUS: THEME *(15 points; 5 points each)*
On the line provided, write the letter of the *best* answer to each of the following items.

_____ **11.** The theme of "The Bet" is —

    A obvious from the title

    B open to interpretation

    C about banking verses litigation

    D about capital punishment

_____ **12.** Which line from "The Bet" makes an *explicit* thematic statement?

    F "Fifteen years' imprisonment had taught him to sit still."

    G "His reading suggested a man swimming in the sea among the wreckage of his ship and trying to save his life by greedily clutching first at one spar and then at another."

    H "The one means of being saved from bankruptcy and disgrace is the death of that man!"

    J "'You have lost your reason and taken the wrong path. You have taken lies for truth and hideousness for beauty.'"

_____ **13.** "The Bet" is a story that raises questions. Which of the following questions is *most* thematically important to the story?

    A Will the lawyer be able to survive intact for all that time?

    B What would the lawyer have done with his life if he hadn't taken the bet?

    C What is the best way for human beings to spend their time on earth?

    D Is capital punishment right or wrong?

READING SKILLS: MAKING PREDICTIONS *(5 points)*

On the line provided, write the letter of the *best* answer to the following item.

_____ **14.** When the banker realizes that the lawyer has almost fulfilled his side of the bet, you might confidently predict that the —

    F lawyer will not get the money from the bet

    G lawyer will break out of his cottage just before the time is up

    H banker will kill the lawyer, perhaps by poisoning him

    J banker will claim that there was no bet, and that the lawyer is insane

VOCABULARY DEVELOPMENT *(20 points; 4 points each)*

On the lines provided, write the Vocabulary word that *best* completes each sentence. Not every word will be used.

frivolous   compulsory   caprice   zealously   indiscriminately

ethereal   illusory   posterity   renounce

15. In prison he read books _____, going from one subject to another without a plan.

16. The lawyer had to _____ most of the ordinary pleasures of life, such as walking in the sunshine or going to a restaurant.

17. The bet sounded _____ at first, but it soon became clear that the bettors were very serious.

18. The banker _____ watched the clock, not willing to release the lawyer a moment too early.

19. After years away from society, he concluded that all of society's values were

_____ rather than real.

CONSTRUCTED RESPONSE *(20 points)*

20. On a separate sheet of paper, write about what Chekhov is saying about life in this story. Support your claim with evidence from the text.

SELECTION TEST

LITERARY RESPONSE AND ANALYSIS

The Jewels Guy de Maupassant *translated by* Roger Colet

COMPREHENSION *(40 points; 4 points each)*

On the line provided, write the letter of the *best* answer to each of the following items.

_____ **1.** When Monsieur Lantin first meets his wife-to-be, he likes her —

    A love of imitation jewelry

    B simple beauty

    C wealth

    D naive honesty

_____ **2.** Monsieur Lantin's life with his wife is happy *except* that she —

    F is moody

    G is not a good manager of the household expenses

    H drags him to the theater in the evenings

    J keeps having to sell her jewels in order to pay the rent

_____ **3.** When Madame Lantin dies, Monsieur Lantin —

    A is overcome with grief

    B is relieved

    C sells the jewels immediately

    D remarries immediately

_____ **4.** Monsieur Lantin attempts to sell one of his wife's jewels because —

    F he cannot live on his income and has almost no money left

    G in her will, his wife advised him to

    H he cannot stand the painful memories they arouse

    J a friend at the Ministry offers him a great deal of money for them

_____ **5.** Why is Monsieur Lantin surprised when the jeweler names his price for the necklace?

    A He thinks he deserves more money than was offered for the necklace.

    B He had thought the necklace was fake, not real jewelry.

    C Monsieur Lantin has no desire to sell the necklace.

    D The jeweler has read Monsieur Lantin's mind precisely.

_____ **6.** After selling all the jewels, Monsieur Lantin is —

    F torn with regret at having parted with his mementos of his beloved wife

    G coldly, furiously bitter at having been financially cheated

    H ashamed to have been so desperate as to sell them

    J boldly, extravagantly, recklessly boastful about his fortune

_____ **7.** When Monsieur Lantin marries a second time —

    A the same thing happens as when he married his first wife

    B his new wife makes him so happy that he forgets his first wife

    C his new wife's bad temper causes him much unhappiness

    D he cannot be happy because he cannot leave behind the memory of his first marriage

_____ **8.** Which of the following aspects of the story is *not* ironic?

    F Monsieur Lantin's salary is barely enough to keep him going.

    G Madame Lantin at first seems to be simple and virtuous but later turns out to have been immoral.

    H Although Madame Lantin was unfaithful, she was still an ideal wife in every other respect.

    J Where Lantin's first wife's dishonesty made him happy, his second wife's virtuousness makes him miserable.

_____ **9.** The jeweler's assistants are amused by Monsieur Lantin because they —

    A find ministry officials ridiculous

    B know what his late wife was doing

    C know he's being cheated by the jeweler

    D think he's been wearing the jewels himself

_____ **10.** Which of the following issues is *not* dealt with in "The Jewels"?

    F Honesty between husband and wife

    G Conventional versus individual morality

    H The economics of survival for a middle-class French couple in the late 1800s

    J Weaknesses of the French educational system, then and now

LITERARY FOCUS: THEME *(15 points; 5 points each)*
On the line provided, write the letter of the *best* answer to each of the following items.

_____ **11.** The reader is as surprised by the events of "The Jewels" as Monsieur Lantin is because the narrator —

    A tells the story from the wife's point of view

    B distracts the reader with descriptions of the flashy jewels

    C tells nothing about the wife her husband doesn't know

    D emphasizes the strict morals of the wife

_____ **12.** Monsieur Lantin's reaction to learning what his wife had done is one of —

    F fury and self-destruction

    G sorrow and embarrassment

    H disbelief and exasperation

    J exhilaration and release

_____ **13.** The themes of "The Jewels" —

    A center on corruption

    B involve what people will do for money

    C concern what produces happiness

    D deal directly with marriage

READING SKILLS: MAKING INFERENCES *(5 points)*

On the line provided, write the letter of the *best* answer to the following item.

_____ **14.** Readers are expected to infer that Madame Lantin obtained the jewels —

    F in robberies

    G as presents from men

    H by working secretly in a shop

    J from Monsieur Lantin's office superior

VOCABULARY DEVELOPMENT *(20 points; 4 points each)*

Match the definition on the left with the Vocabulary word on the right. On the line provided, write the letter of the Vocabulary word.

_____ **15.** scornful

_____ **16.** brought upon oneself

_____ **17.** modest

_____ **18.** ease; calm

_____ **19.** sneakily or stealthily

  a. unpretentious

  b. assuage

  c. incurred

  d. surreptitiously

  e. contemptuous

CONSTRUCTED RESPONSE *(20 points)*

20. Assuming that Maupassant's views and perceptions were accurate, what can you conclude about middle-class society in late-nineteenth-century France from "The Jewels"? Write your answer on a separate sheet of paper. Support your analysis with textual evidence.

COLLECTION 6 SUMMATIVE TEST ███████████

The Victorian Period 1832–1901: Paradox and Progress

Read the following poem carefully, and then answer the questions that follow.

To Marguerite—Continued
by Matthew Arnold

Yes! in the sea of life enisled,
With echoing <u>straits</u> between us thrown,
Dotting the shoreless watery wild,
We mortal millions live *alone*.
5   The islands feel the enclasping flow,
And then their endless bounds they know.

But when the moon their hollows lights,
And they are swept by balms of spring,
And in their glens, on starry nights,
10   The nightingales divinely sing;
And lovely notes, from shore to shore,
Across the sounds and channels pour—

Oh! then a longing like despair
Is to their farthest caverns sent;
15   For surely once, they feel, we were
Parts of a single continent!
Now round us spreads the watery plain—
Oh, might our marges meet again!

Who ordered, that their longing's fire
20   Should be, as soon as <u>kindled</u>, cooled?
Who <u>renders</u> vain their deep desire?
A God, a god their severance ruled!
And bade betwixt their shore to be
The <u>unplumbed</u>, salt, estranging sea.

VOCABULARY SKILLS *(20 points; 5 points each)*
Each of the underlined words below has also been underlined in the selection. Re-read those passages in which the underlined words appear, and then use context clues and your prior knowledge to help you select an answer. On the line provided, write the letter of the word or words that *best* complete each sentence.

_____ **1.** Straits of water are —

    A puddles

    B narrow passageways

    C icicles

    D dry creeks

_____ **2.** When a fire is <u>kindled</u>, it is —

    F extinguished

    G ignited

    H abandoned

    J dying

_____ **3.** If an event <u>renders</u> a person speechless, the person is —

    A made speechless by the event

    B almost speechless, but not quite

    C released from speechlessness by the event

    D choosing to be speechless

_____ **4.** An <u>unplumbed</u> sea is —

    F unclear and polluted

    G uncertain and unbelievable

    H unnoticed and untouched

    J unmeasured and unexplored

COMPREHENSION *(20 points; 4 points each)*

On the line provided, write the letter of the *best* answer to each of the following items.

_____ **5.** The speaker in this poem is —

    A "the sea of life"

    B the nightingale

    C one of the "mortal millions"

    D "a single continent"

_____ **6.** The tone of the poem is —

    F regretful

    G humorous

    H violent

    J joyous

_____ **7.** The speaker claims that everyone lives —

    A unthinkingly from day to day

    B in isolation

    C in small, closely knit communities

    D in desperate need of solitude

_____ **8.** When individuals hear the nightingales' songs, the people feel —

    F annoyed

    G astonished by the songs' beauty

    H inspired to set off for new lands

    J certain that they were once united

_____ **9.** In lines 19–20, the speaker suggests that someone has ordered —

    A love's passion to live forever

    B a unity of all living beings

    C the longing for connection to fade as soon as it is felt

    D a universe in which no meaning or purpose can be discerned

READING SKILLS AND STRATEGIES *(10 points; 5 points each)*

Identifying Contrasting Images

_____ **10.** The meaning at the center of "To Marguerite—Continued" is developed by contrasting images of —

    F separation and connection

    G fire and ice

    H love and hate

    J frustration and satisfaction

Drawing Inferences from Textual Clues

_____ **11.** Which passage from the poem is an example of Victorian knowledge of and interest in the natural sciences?

    A "Dotting the shoreless watery wild, / We mortal millions live *alone*."

    B "And lovely notes, from shore to shore, / Across the sounds and channels pour —"

    C "For surely once, they feel, we were / Parts of a single continent!"

    D "Who ordered, that their longing's fire / Should be, as soon as kindled, cooled?"

LITERARY FOCUS: CONSTRUCTED RESPONSE *(50 points)*
Identifying Theme *(10 points)*

12. What **theme** can you infer from the speaker's comments in this poem? From the following options, choose the one you think is the *best* response to this question. Then, on a separate sheet of paper, write the letter of the answer you choose and briefly defend your choice. Use at least one example from the poem to support your ideas.

    a. People are essentially alone but long for connection with one another.

    b. The human condition is part of an unfathomable divine plan.

    c. Love is not enough to bridge the gap between one person and another.

    d. All of life is essentially tragic; even beauty is essentially tragic.

Analyzing Mood *(10 points)*

13. The speaker of the poem mourns the unavoidable separateness of human beings. What is the poet's **purpose** in creating this mournful mood? What descriptive details, sounds, and figures of speech does Matthew Arnold use to create this mood? On a separate sheet of paper, write a paragraph answering these questions with the help of examples from the poem.

Evaluating Imagery *(10 points)*

14. How does **imagery** help evoke emotions in this poem? Choose three images from the poem, and list them on the left side of the following chart. On the right side, describe an emotion the image calls forth. Briefly elaborate on how each emotion connects with the particular image.

▶ Image	▶ Emotion Evoked by the Image

Evaluating Style, Technique, and Historical and Social Influences *(20 points)*

15. On a separate sheet of paper, discuss at least two ways in which "To Marguerite—Continued" is identifiably a product of the Victorian era. Among the elements you may wish to examine are style, technique, theme, and historical or social influences.

The Modern World
1900 to the Present:
A Remarkable Diversity

On the line provided, write the letter of the *best* answer to each of the following items.
(*100 points; 5 points each*)

_____ 1. Which of the following words or phrases is an example of an **oxymoron**?

    A sounding board

    B sweet sorrow

    C pitter-patter

    D scarecrow

_____ 2. Which of the following statements about **allusions** is *false*?

    F Allusions can evoke associations and emotions.

    G Writers use allusions to convey ideas and themes.

    H Allusions are stories with symbolic meaning.

    J When writers refer to people or events from literature or art, they are using allusions.

_____ 3. A **memoir** is a type of —

    A biography

    B short story

    C autobiography

    D letter

_____ 4. Which of the following statements about **setting** is *false*?

    F Writers can use imagery and dialogue to create setting.

    G Sometimes the time or place in which a story occurs is implied, not stated.

    H The setting of a story does not contribute to a story's theme.

    J A story's setting can reflect the political and social forces of a particular historical period.

_____ 5. In the **third-person-limited point of view,** the narrator —

    A tells the story from the vantage point of only one character

    B is the main character in the story

    C is unreliable and may lie

    D recounts the story from the viewpoint of the author

_____ **6. Dramatic irony** occurs when —

    F a character says the opposite of what he or she means

    G the reader or audience is aware of something that a character doesn't know

    H a character makes a sarcastic comment about another character

    J the reader is surprised by the outcome of the story

_____ **7.** A writer might use a **symbol** for all of the following purposes *except* —

    A to suggest emotions and themes

    B to build meaning in the course of a work

    C to stand both for itself and for something beyond itself

    D to state a main idea in a literal manner

_____ **8. Assonance** refers to —

    F the repetition of similar vowel sounds in words that are close together

    G a regular pattern of stressed and unstressed syllables

    H words whose sounds suggest their meanings

    J recurring rhymes in a poem

_____ **9.** Writers use **flashbacks** to do all of the following *except* —

    A provide background information about characters

    B tell about events that took place at an earlier time

    C explain the effects of the past on the present

    D describe the future lives of characters

_____ **10.** Writers use an **omniscient narrator** to —

    F make their voice in a story more formal

    G simplify the plot of a story

    H enter the minds of different characters

    J give a story universal appeal

_____ **11.** Why do writers use **foreshadowing**?

    A To arouse the reader's curiosity and build suspense

    B To create round characters

    C To make their stories realistic

    D To establish a distinctive style and tone in their works

_____ **12.** What is the difference between a **metaphor** and an **extended metaphor**?

    F An extended metaphor is a metaphor that is developed over several lines of writing or throughout an entire poem.

    G An extended metaphor is a metaphor that is commonly used.

    H An extended metaphor mixes several different types of metaphors in one poem.

    J An extended metaphor, unlike a metaphor, compares two seemingly unlike things.

_____ **13. Diction** refers to —

    A the subject of a story

    B an author's choice of words

    C a story's mood

    D a type of dialogue

_____ **14.** Which of the following statements about **refrains** is *false*?

    F Poets rely on refrains to give their work figurative meaning.

    G Refrains are repeated words, phrases, or lines in poetry.

    H Refrains are used to create rhythm in poetry.

    J Poets use refrains to emphasize important ideas.

_____ **15.** What is **lyric poetry**?

    A Poetry that tells a story

    B Poetry that focuses on expressing thoughts or emotions

    C Poetry that rhymes

    D A poetic form that pays tribute to a person

_____ **16.** How do authors' **implicit** beliefs differ from their **explicit** beliefs?

    F Unlike explicit beliefs, implicit beliefs are presented in great detail.

    G Implicit beliefs, unlike explicit ones, are suggested, but not directly stated.

    H Explicit beliefs, in contrast to implicit ones, are used to influence the reader.

    J Explicit beliefs are shared by a community, but implicit beliefs are personal ones.

_____ **17.** Relying on reason to create an **argument**, writers use —

    A repetition

    B exposition

    C logical appeals

    D calls to action

_____ **18.** Which of the following statements is the *best* example of an **emotional appeal**?

    F Americans are spending more on health care than ever before.

    G It is every person's civic duty to obey this law.

    H We must put an end to injustice.

    J People are sick and tired of seeing their strenuous efforts go to waste.

_____ **19.** Words with different **connotations** may —

    A differ in intensity or have different associations

    B have different roots but exactly the same meaning

    C sound alike but be spelled differently

    D have the same spelling but differ in meaning

_____ **20.** To complete a **word analogy,** you —

    F make sure that the words in one pair have the same relationship as the words in a second pair

    G look for four words that have the same meaning

    H explain the meaning of a figure of speech

    J define the words in the pairs

The Modern World 1900 to the Present: A Remarkable Diversity

COMPREHENSION *(100 points; 10 points each)*

On the line provided, write the letter of the *best* answer to each of the following items.

_____ **1.** The Victorian writer Rudyard Kipling celebrated the British character as essentially —

    A heroic

    B patriotic

    C dull

    D unpatriotic

_____ **2.** What did Charles Darwin, Karl Marx, and Sigmund Freud have in common?

    F They tried to answer the question, "How did human life originate?"

    G They lived during the twentieth century.

    H Their works contributed to overturning accepted Victorian ideas.

    J Despite their intellectual differences, they were loyal British subjects.

_____ **3.** Which of the following statements *best* describes artistic experimentation in the first half of the twentieth century?

    A The painters exhibiting in 1905 were called the Fauves.

    B New uses of line, color, rhythm, and harmony challenged traditional notions of beauty and order.

    C Crowds rioted after seeing Synge's *The Playboy of the Western World* and Stravinsky's *The Rite of Spring*.

    D Publishers refused to print James Joyce's *Dubliners* for many years.

_____ **4.** Which of the following statements is *false*?

    F Virginia Woolf perfected the technique of chronological storytelling.

    G D. H. Lawrence's novels show his resentment of the British class system.

    H James Joyce's novels draw upon Freudian insights into the mind.

    J Introspective analysis of individual characters is found in the fiction of Joseph Conrad.

_____ **5.** Which of the following is *not* true of James Joyce's 1922 novel *Ulysses*?

    A It is based on Homer's *Odyssey*.

    B It narrates the events of a single day.

    C It draws on myth and symbol.

    D It solves the mind/body problem.

_____ **6.** Postmodern writing usually deals either directly or indirectly with all of the following issues *except* —

    F royal lineage

    G nuclear destruction

    H multiculturalism

    J the environment

_____ **7.** The 1953 novel *Lucky Jim* by Kingsley Amis is a(n) —

    A satire of British university life

    B epic poem set in King James' time

    C lecture on the Angry Young Men

    D series of 154 sonnets

_____ **8.** Contemporary British literature is marked by great diversity, though the dominant mode is still —

    F farce

    G tragedy

    H elegy

    J satire

_____ **9.** In post–World War II Britain —

    A the younger generation of writers called for expansion of the British Empire

    B English literature portrayed middle-class life as vibrant and exciting

    C a group dubbed the Angry Young Men criticized the bland lives of the middle class

    D literature stagnated in an atmosphere of comfortable complacency

_____ **10.** Which of the following statements *best* describes world literature today?

    F Most plots are no longer written in chronological order.

    G Literature is either satirical or ironic.

    H Political concerns are rarely addressed.

    J Works from former colonies of European nations are read the world over.

| SELECTION TEST | LITERARY RESPONSE AND ANALYSIS |

Dulce et Decorum Est . Wilfred Owen
The Rear-Guard Siegfried Sassoon

COMPREHENSION *(40 points; 4 points each)*

On the line provided, write the letter of the *best* answer to each of the following items.

_____ **1.** Which of the following statements *best* describes the theme, or central idea, of "Dulce et Decorum Est"?

   A War is tough, but you get used to it.

   B Going to war for one's country is a noble act.

   C War teaches soldiers to look unemotionally at death.

   D War is horrifying and demoralizing.

_____ **2.** The speaker refers to the "old Lie" because he wants the reader to realize that —

   F glory is difficult to attain

   G there is no glory in war

   H war is inevitable

   J war always results in confusion

_____ **3.** The soldiers in "Dulce et Decorum Est" can *best* be described as —

   A exhausted and delirious

   B wandering and lost

   C afraid and hesitant

   D careful and calculating

_____ **4.** What is the crucial event in "Dulce et Decorum Est"?

   F A soldier foresees his own death.

   G British troops are attacked with poisonous gas.

   H The speaker descends into an underground tunnel.

   J The main character is killed just before the war ends.

_____ **5.** Whom does the speaker address in the last four lines of the poem?

   A His enemy

   B His conscience

   C His dead buddy

   D The reader

_____ **6.** Wilfred Owen's *main* rhetorical purpose in the poem is to —

   F entertain the reader

   G explain the procedure for defense against poisonous gas

   H impress the panel of judges for a literary prize

   J make the reader understand a soldier's experiences

_____ **7.** Which of the following images reflects the Trench Poets' attitudes toward war?

    A A soldier dies for his country with grace and dignity.

    B Children sing a song of praise to war heroes.

    C Young men are senselessly slaughtered in wars they have no control over.

    D Young men stand in line, waiting to enlist.

_____ **8.** The term *trench poetry* means that —

    F the characters in the poems never leave their trenches

    G the poems were written while the poets were actually under fire

    H such poems were distributed by the British Army as reading material for soldiers

    J the poems were written by combat veterans of the eastern front of World War I

_____ **9.** In "The Rear-Guard" the man who kicks the soldier does not realize that the soldier is —

    A a hero

    B dead

    C wounded

    D sleeping

_____ **10.** The imagery in "The Rear-Guard" —

    F emphasizes differences between modern war and medieval war

    G conveys the poet's belief in his army's cause

    H stresses the horror of war

    J contrasts war and peace

LITERARY FOCUS: FIGURES OF SPEECH *(40 points; 10 points each)*

On the line provided, write the letter of the *best* answer to each of the following items.

_____ **11.** Which type of figure of speech combines apparently contradictory ideas?

    A Simile

    B Metaphor

    C Symbol

    D Oxymoron

_____ **12.** Which of the following phrases from "Dulce et Decorum Est" is *not* a simile?

    F "Drunk with fatigue"

    G "Bent double, like old beggars under sacks"

    H "Obscene as cancer"

    J "His hanging face, like a devil's sick of sin"

_____ **13.** Which of the following phrases from "The Rear-Guard" is an oxymoron?

    A "blackening wound"

    B "stinking place"

    C "rosy gloom"

    D "unanswering heap"

_____ **14.** In line 6 of "Dulce et Decorum Est," the metaphor "blood-shod" compares —

    F soldiers to ghosts

    G blood on feet to shoes on feet

    H injuries from poison gas to bullet wounds

    J shed blood to unshed blood

CONSTRUCTED RESPONSE *(20 points)*

15. Choose a one- or two-line passage containing a figure of speech from "Dulce et Decorum Est." On a separate sheet of paper, explain how the figure of speech and other aspects of the passage's style and tone convey Owen's view of war.

SELECTION TEST ████████   LITERARY RESPONSE AND ANALYSIS

The Hollow Men T. S. Eliot

COMPREHENSION *(60 points; 6 points each)*

On the line provided, write the letter of the *best* answer to each of the following items.

_____ **1.** One paradox about the hollow men is that they are —

    A sightless and seeing

    B faithless and faithful

    C hollow and stuffed

    D intelligent and well-read

_____ **2.** The speaker of the poem —

    F is one of the hollow men

    G is afraid of becoming one of the hollow men

    H feels he is being chased by the hollow men

    J wishes to destroy the hollow men

_____ **3.** The place where the hollow men are gathered is described as a(n) —

    A hell of eternal torment

    B paradise of bliss

    C dry, twilit limbo

    D everyday real world

_____ **4.** What is the dominant form of vegetation in the poem's landscape?

    F Garden roses

    G Cacti

    H Fruit trees

    J Colorful autumn leaves

_____ **5.** In a figure of speech the hollow men's voices are compared to the —

    A sound of rats' feet on broken glass

    B eyes of God

    C voices of angels

    D sound of exploding bombs

_____ **6.** In a metaphor the valley of the hollow men is compared to a —

    F passage from Shakespeare's *Julius Caesar*

    G scarecrow

    H rose full of thorns

    J broken jaw

_____ **7.** The visual imagery of the poem is dominated by —

    A vivid color

    B expressions of love

    C dry, quiet sounds

    D shadows

_____ **8.** What is the *main* emotion the speaker expresses in the poem?

    F Religious faith

    G Despair at life

    H Fear of death

    J Longing for love

_____ **9.** Lines 66–67, "The hope only / Of empty men," refer to the hope for —

    A spiritual salvation

    B long life

    C health, wealth, and prosperity

    D artistic achievement

_____ **10.** In Section V, the three stanzas beginning with the word *between* all convey —

    F a feeling that the speaker has at last achieved peace of mind

    G a sense of spontaneity and discovery after the doubts of previous stanzas

    H the fatal gap between what people think, hope, or imagine and what they do

    J the speaker's trust in his fellow human beings as a source of reassurance

LITERARY FOCUS: ALLUSION *(15 points; 5 points each)*

On the line provided, write the letter of the *best* answer to each of the following items.

_____ **11.** Another word for **allusion** is —

    A unreality

    B reference

    C mystery

    D content

_____ **12.** "The Hollow Men" contains allusions to all of the following *except* —

    F Karl Marx and Charles Darwin

    G Shakespeare and Dante

    H British history and nursery rhymes

    J ancient Greek philosophy and Christian beliefs

_____ **13.** T. S. Eliot would prefer that readers *not* make inferences about the —

    A meaning of the phrase "hollow men"

    B influence of Eliot's life on the poem "The Hollow Men"

    C religious symbolism of the eyes in the poem

    D significance of the quotation from Joseph Conrad's *Heart of Darkness*

READING SKILL: ANALYZING THE AUTHOR'S PHILOSOPHICAL ARGUMENTS (5 *points*)

On the line provided, write the letter of the *best* answer to the following item.

_____ **14.** Which of the following statements from T. S. Eliot contains a direct expression of a philosophical view?

    F "the immense panorama of futility and anarchy which is contemporary history . . ."

    G "There are no eyes here. . . . "

    H "Rat's coat, crowskin, crossed staves . . ."

    J "Here we go round the prickly pear. . . ."

CONSTRUCTED RESPONSE (20 *points*)

15. The famous last four lines of "The Hollow Men" directly state a philosophical view. What is this view, and how is it also conveyed in other passages of the poem? On a separate sheet of paper, analyze at least two passages containing imagery or figures of speech that, in your view, support the concluding lines.

On the Bottom *from* Survival in Auschwitz   Primo Levi
translated by Stuart Woolf

COMPREHENSION *(40 points; 4 points each)*

On the line provided, write the letter of the *best* answer to each of the following items.

_____ **1.** Above the concentration camp entrance was a sign in German meaning —

     A "Abandon all hope, ye who enter here."

     B "To the Glory of the Thousand-Year Reich"

     C "Work gives freedom."

     D "Victory is certain."

_____ **2.** Levi's image of a modern-day hell is —

     F a large empty room with a dripping tap of undrinkable water

     G an endless lake of ice upon which demons cavort

     H the all-consuming fire of an atomic bomb

     J a waiting room in which the deceased must sit forever without being called

_____ **3.** All of the following details are cruel jokes played on the prisoners *except* the —

     A sign forbidding thirsty people to drink water

     B warning to the prisoners not to let their shoes be stolen

     C officer's comment that one man can use another man's truss

     D four days the prisoners have spent without water

_____ **4.** Throughout the events in this selection, Primo Levi feels as if he is —

     F responsible for his own sufferings

     G watching an insane stage play

     H dreaming and about to wake up

     J back home at peace in Italy

_____ **5.** Why does Flesch, the interpreter, refuse to translate some of what the prisoners and the German officer say?

     A He knows it would be useless.

     B His Italian is not really as good as he pretends.

     C His German is not really as good as he pretends.

     D The officer's replies are so insulting that Flesch is afraid violence will result.

_____ **6.** What does the Hungarian doctor mean when he says that "there is work and work"?

     F Some jobs make more money than others.

     G The work of the German soldiers is very different from that of the prisoners.

     H Some of the guards are harsher, more sadistic, than others.

     J Some jobs in camp help keep a prisoner alive while most lead to death.

_____ **7.** Because the Hungarian doctor is a criminal rather than a Jew, —

    A he has received a longer sentence than the other prisoners

    B his treatment has not been as harsh as most other prisoners

    C he lacks a conscience that would enable him to pity his fellow human beings

    D he is allowed to work as the camp dentist

_____ **8.** The new prisoners find it unbelievable when the doctor tells them that —

    F almost all of them will die in the camp

    G they will see their women and children again

    H there are concerts and sports events in the camp

    J the soup is so thin it will quench their thirst like water

_____ **9.** After they have been showered and clothed, what do the prisoners dare not to do?

    A Ask for food

    B Ask whether they are going to be killed

    C Look into one another's faces

    D Drink the foul tasting water

_____ **10.** The last three paragraphs of the selection are different from what came before in that they —

    F express Levi's thoughts rather than narrating events and describing scenes

    G offer a tone of hope after several pages of bleak despair

    H look at the Holocaust from the standpoint of non-Jews

    J tell the reader what happened to Levi after the camp was liberated

LITERARY FOCUS: MEMOIR *(15 points; 5 points each)*

On the line provided, write the letter of the *best* answer to each of the following items.

_____ **11.** How are most **memoirs** different from most **autobiographies**?

    A Memoirs are about mass experiences rather than individual experiences.

    B Autobiographies are written by authors; memoirs are written by the subjects themselves.

    C Memoirs focus on one important time rather than on a whole life.

    D Memoirs usually have more literary prestige than autobiographies.

_____ **12.** Which aspect of "On the Bottom" indicates that it is a memoir and not a history?

    F The author narrates his own experiences in the first person.

    G It concerns events that some living people still remember.

    H It is about the Nazi Holocaust.

    J It describes specific events in the lives of specific individuals.

_____ **13.** Which is *least* important for understanding this selection?

    A The rise of Nazism in Germany in the 1930s

    B Primo Levi's life as a science student before being arrested

    C The historical position of Jews in Europe before World War II

    D German-Italian relations during and after World War I

READING SKILLS: EVALUATING HISTORICAL CONTEXT *(5 points)*

On the line provided, write the letter of the *best* response to the following item.

_____ **14.** Which of the following facts is part of the historical context of "On the Bottom"?

    F The prisoners take a short train journey in order to teach at the camp.

    G The narrator is one of millions whom the Nazis send to concentration camps.

    H The room contains a sign forbidding the prisoners to drink the water.

    J The Hungarian doctor has been in the camp for four and a half years.

VOCABULARY DEVELOPMENT *(20 points; 4 points each)*

On the line provided, write the Vocabulary word from below that *best* completes the sentence.

    tepid   taciturn   sordid   demolition   affinity

15. "On the Bottom" describes the _____ of the human soul.

16. The events described in "On the Bottom" are so _____, they are shocking.

17. The prisoners were given water that was _____ and bad tasting.

18. The Nazi guards seemed to feel no _____ for the prisoners as fellow human beings.

19. The interpreter was a _____ man rather than a talkative one.

CONSTRUCTED RESPONSE *(20 points)*

20. According to the selection and what you have read about Primo Levi, what influence do you think his concentration camp experiences had on his view of life? Write your answer on a separate sheet of paper.

SELECTION TEST ▮▮▮▮▮▮ **INFORMATIONAL READING**

from The War Marguerite Duras *translated by* Barbara Bray
Never Shall I Forget Elie Wiesel
Kristallnacht
The United States Holocaust Memorial Museum

COMPREHENSION *(100 points; 10 points each)*

On the line provided, write the letter of the *best* answer to each of the following items.

_____ 1. What is the basic situation in the excerpt from Duras's *The War*?

    A A concentration camp survivor recalls his bitterest experiences.

    B A former camp guard tries to defend his innocence.

    C A prisoner's wife describes his death in a concentration camp.

    D A prisoner's wife describes his liberation from a concentration camp.

_____ 2. What was the situation in Dachau when Robert L.'s friends got him out?

    F Robert L. was the last survivor.

    G The war was on and the camp was in German hands.

    H The war was over and the camp was in American hands.

    J The camp had been emptied before Robert L.'s friends arrived.

_____ 3. What were the people in the camp most afraid of at the time Robert L.'s friends arrived?

    A Disease

    B Nazis

    C The American army

    D The French Resistance

_____ 4. What does François Morland mean when he says, "If they tried to do it officially they'd arrive too late"?

    F If they asked for German permission to enter the camp, they would be arrested or shot.

    G If they asked for American permission to enter the camp, they would be refused.

    H If they waited for American permission to enter, Robert L. would probably die.

    J If they pretended to be Nazi officers, they would be unmasked and killed.

_____ 5. Whom does Robert L. blame for his sufferings?

    A Germany

    B The United States

    C France

    D All governments

_____ **6.** Why do Robert L.'s friends and loved ones not allow him to eat dessert after he returns home?

    F If the Nazis find evidence that he has been fed, they will kill everyone present.

    G People have died from overeating soon after release from concentration camps.

    H Robert L. has diabetes and cannot eat sweets.

    J No clear explanation is given in the text.

_____ **7.** In "Never Shall I Forget," when Elie Wiesel describes children's bodies being turned into wreaths of smoke, he is —

    A stating a literal fact

    B personifying smoke as if it were human

    C exaggerating, for the children were not completely burned

    D metaphorically comparing human beings to smoke

_____ **8.** Lines 16–18 reveal that Wiesel sees life as —

    F a torment without spiritual meaning

    G an unanswerable puzzle posed by God

    H too cruelly short to achieve all the things he dreams of doing

    J a fortunate blessing that has been granted by sheer luck

_____ **9.** November 9, 1938, or Kristallnacht, is the night when —

    A thousands of Jewish-owned businesses in Germany were vandalized

    B the last remaining Jews in Germany were rounded up and taken to the camps

    C the American army crossed into Germany

    D Adolf Hitler was elected Chancellor of Germany

_____ **10.** The word *pogroms,* used in the Kristallnacht Web page, refers to —

    F concentration camps

    G survivors of the Holocaust

    H the selection of prisoners to be killed

    J organized mass attacks upon Jews

SELECTION TEST

LITERARY RESPONSE AND ANALYSIS

Blood, Sweat, and Tears Winston Churchill

COMPREHENSION *(50 points; 10 points each)*
On the line provided, write the letter of the *best* answer to each of the following items.

_____ **1.** What was the specific occasion for this speech?

    A The German attack on Poland

    B The Japanese attack on Pearl Harbor

    C Churchill's forming of a new British government

    D Hitler's bombing of London

_____ **2.** The first paragraph of the speech provides information about —

    F the progress of the military campaign

    G Churchill's qualifications for office

    H the identities of the top officials in Churchill's cabinet

    J procedures Churchill followed in forming his government

_____ **3.** The "House" that Churchill refers to in the second paragraph is the —

    A House of Commons

    B House of Representatives in Congress

    C White House

    D Prime Minister's official residence

_____ **4.** According to Churchill, why is victory for Britain absolutely necessary?

    F It's an all or nothing situation: if Britain loses, it won't survive as a free nation.

    G Britain has never lost a war and to lose to Germany would be disgraceful.

    H Britain must retain its overseas colonies or cease to be a world power.

    J The Nazis are evil, and evil must be opposed wherever and whenever it arises.

_____ **5.** By saying, "I have nothing to offer but blood, toil, tears, and sweat," Churchill is implying that —

    A he is not fully qualified to be prime minister

    B he expects the United States to provide the material means to fight the war

    C Britain must make up with effort what it lacks in military and industrial power

    D he does not really believe that Britain can win the war

VOCABULARY DEVELOPMENT *(50 points; 10 points each)*

Fill in each blank below with the Vocabulary word that *best* completes the analogy.

_____ **6.** PESSIMISM : DEPRESSION :: OPTIMISM :   **a.** rigor

_____ **7.** HEROIC : COWARDLY :: LAUDABLE :   **b.** provision

_____ **8.** WONDERFUL : BREATHTAKING :: TERRIBLE :   **c.** grievous

_____ **9.** REQUIREMENT : OBLIGATION :: CONDITION :   **d.** lamentable

_____ **10.** SOFT : HARD :: FLEXIBILITY :   **e.** buoyancy

The Silver Fifty-Sen Pieces

Yasunari Kawabata *translated by* **Lane Dunlop** *and* **J. Martin Holman**

COMPREHENSION *(40 points; 4 points each)*

On the line provided, write the letter of the *best* answer to each of the following items.

_____ **1.** Yoshiko did *not* —

    A work in an office

    B live alone before the war

    C marry a Yokohama man

    D get an allowance from her mother

_____ **2.** Yoshiko spends her money —

    F wastefully, on things she doesn't need

    G generously, for the war effort

    H charitably, giving it to beggars

    J frugally, on a few selected items

_____ **3.** Yoshiko's mother says that Yoshiko's carefully made purchase of the paperweight made Yoshiko seem —

    A silly

    B lovable

    C meticulous

    D discriminating

_____ **4.** The second major incident of the story occurs in —

    F the bargain-basement of a department store

    G a sheet metal shack

    H a subway station

    J a Tokyo office complex

_____ **5.** Both of the first two sections of the story —

    A include dialogue between Yoshiko and her sister

    B explain how the people of Japan feel about the war

    C deal with shopping incidents

    D focus on the men in Yoshiko's family

_____ **6.** Yoshiko's mother shows awareness of Yoshiko's feelings by buying —

    F a birthday present for Yoshiko

    G new kitchen utensils

    H a colorful umbrella for Yoshiko

    J stationery for her

_____ **7.** Yoshiko and her mother leave the store —

    A feeling comfortable with each other

    B arguing about the lack of a purchase

    C with no money left

    D loaded down with large bags of items

_____ **8.** What reminds Yoshiko of the shopping expedition?

    F The voices of the girls in her new neighborhood

    G The sight of the glass paperweight

    H Rain pounding on the sheet-metal roof

    J A bomber flying overhead

_____ **9.** Since the shopping expedition, which of the following events has *not* happened to Yoshiko in the story?

    A She became a mother.

    B Her house burned down.

    C Her mother died.

    D She became poor.

_____ **10.** How much time passes between the earlier sections of the story and the final section?

    F A day

    G A few months

    H A year

    J Seven years

LITERARY FOCUS: THEME *(15 points; 5 points each)*

On the line provided, write the letter of the *best* answer to each of the following items.

_____ **11.** What is the difference between a **theme** and a **topic**?

    A A theme is a large subject; a topic is smaller than a subject.

    B A topic is a subject; a theme is an idea about a subject.

    C A theme can be stated more concisely than a topic.

    D There is little or no difference between the two.

_____ **12.** Which of the following statements is *least* probable as a theme of "The Silver Fifty-Sen Pieces"?

    F Lives of comfort can be suddenly shattered by outside violence.

    G The small events of everyday life can take on unexpected, large significance.

    H Material things may vanish, but memory preserves love.

    J The internment of Japanese-Americans during World War II was wrong.

_____ **13.** All of the following objects might be symbols of peacetime innocence in the story, *except* the —

    A paperweight

    B umbrella

    C sheet-metal shack

    D fifty-sen coins

READING SKILLS: MAKING INFERENCES *(5 points)*

On the line provided, write the letter of the *best* answer to the following item.

_____ **14.** An inference about a symbol —

    F must be expressed in terms of another symbol

    G is usually not based on much evidence

    H can lead to insights about theme

    J is always also an insight about character

VOCABULARY DEVELOPMENT *(20 points; 4 points each)*

On the line provided, write the letter of the *best* answer to each of the following items.

_____ **15.** To be spurned is to be —

    A accepted

    B rejected

    C removed

    D acquired

_____ **16.** What kind of beauty does the word exquisite connote?

    F strong and durable

    G delicate

    H in the eye of the beholder

    J universal

_____ **17.** The opposite of meticulous is —

    A careless

    B refined

    C painstaking

    D natural

_____ **18.** Discrimination is the ability to —

    F make fine distinctions

    G overcome prejudice

    H see at a distance

    J excuse hatred

The Silver Fifty-Sen Pieces

_____ **19.** If two people feel <u>antipathy</u> for each other, they will probably —

    A get married

    B praise each other

    C work together

    D avoid each other

CONSTRUCTED RESPONSE *(20 points)*

20. Choose one of the thematic statements below for "The Silver Fifty-Sen Pieces."
On a separate sheet of paper, use that statement and supporting evidence you
find in the story to describe author Kawabata's view of life.

    a. Happiness and beauty are fleeting but nevertheless real and important.

    b. War changes everything, making the comforts of peacetime seem irrelevant.

SELECTION TEST █████████   LITERARY RESPONSE AND ANALYSIS

The Destructors Graham Greene

COMPREHENSION *(40 points; 4 points each)*

On the line provided, write the letter of the *best* answer to each of the following items.

_____ **1.** Of the following events in the story, which happens first?

    A Mr. Thomas shows T. the interior of the house.

    B T. joins the Wormsley Common gang.

    C Blackie surrenders to the new leader.

    D Mr. Thomas gives the boys chocolates.

_____ **2.** Mr. Thomas's house reflects the character of the postwar era because it —

    F was used to house refugees during the war

    G is in a state of decline

    H is well maintained

    J has been repaired after being bombed

_____ **3.** T. admits that he —

    A approves of stealing and bribery

    B values friendship based on mutual interests

    C relishes destruction because he wants revenge

    D does not hate Mr. Thomas

_____ **4.** T.'s plea for help in finishing the destruction of the house —

    F is ridiculed by another boy in the gang

    G strikes the other boys as professional and mature

    H is ignored by Blackie

    J confirms T.'s absolute authority as leader

_____ **5.** T. might *best* be described as —

    A personable and likable

    B always late to the gang's meetings

    C mysterious and determined

    D talkative and funny

_____ **6.** Which of the following events reveals that T. is a destructor?

    F He burns Mr. Thomas's savings.

    G He joins the army and goes to war.

    H He beats up Blackie to become gang leader.

    J He beats up his own father.

_____ **7.** T. knows what the interior of Mr. Thomas's house looks like because he —

    A was invited in by Mr. Thomas

    B sneaked in when the house was empty

    C was shown pictures of the floor plan by his father, an architect

    D has looked through the windows of the house with the rest of the gang

_____ **8.** Blackie loses his leadership of the gang when he —

    F is physically ousted by T.

    G has a plan that loses the vote to T.'s plan

    H resigns because he is tired of taking the blame for things that go wrong

    J is humiliated when the other members make fun of his name

_____ **9.** Blackie goes along with T.'s plan because he —

    A wants the gang to become famous

    B likes T. and considers him a friend

    C knows that T. will be a better leader than he was

    D secretly plans to get his leadership back when T.'s plan fails

_____ **10.** When the lorry driver realizes that the house has suddenly come down, he laughs because he —

    F doesn't like Mr. Thomas either

    G is surprised and impressed by the event

    H thinks Mr. Thomas looks funny wrapped in the blanket

    J remembers pulling the same kinds of pranks when he was a boy

LITERARY FOCUS: SETTING (15 points; 5 points each)

On the line provided, write the letter of the *best* answer to each of the following items.

_____ **11.** The opening paragraph states that the gang's newest member becomes its leader. Why would the gang allow this to happen?

    A It is the gang's custom to place newcomers in the seat of honor.

    B The newest member happens also to be the oldest in age.

    C The gang is about to break up, so no one cares who is the official leader.

    D The new member has an idea that poses an interest to the others.

_____ **12.** Which of the following elements does *least* to establish setting in this story?

    F   Physical details

    G Historical details

    H Comic characterizations

    J   Imagery and word choice

_____ **13.** The setting of this story can *best* be described as —

    A beautiful and spectacular

    B comfortable and cozy

    C drab and decaying

    D dainty and exquisite

READING SKILL: INFERRING MOTIVES *(5 points)*

On the line provided, write the letter of the *best* answer to the following item.

_____ **14.** To infer a motive is to —

    F   predict what will happen later in a story

    G confirm that an earlier prediction had been correct

    H analyze the impact of setting upon character

    J   make a guess, based on evidence, about a character's reasons for doing something

VOCABULARY DEVELOPMENT *(20 points; 4 points each)*

On the lines provided, fill in the Vocabulary word from below that *best* completes each sentence.

impromptu   **exploit**   **daunted**   **exhilaration**   **stealthy**

15. The destructors had to be careful, quiet, and _____ so that no one would hear them.

16. For the boys in the story, destroying things creates a mood of _____.

17. The young destructors in the story are not at all _____ by dealing with older, bigger people.

18. T. and his friends see the destruction of the house as a bold _____.

19. Destroying the house was not done _____ , but after careful discussion and planning.

CONSTRUCTED RESPONSE (20 points)

20. Imagine that "The Destructors" takes place not in postwar London, but in a peaceful, affluent suburb in present-day United States. What political or social influences would shape the characters in this changed setting, as opposed to the setting Graham Greene worked with? How would the view of life of the American story be different as a result? Write your answer on a separate sheet of paper, and be sure to refer to Greene's story and themes as well as your imagined version.

SELECTION TEST　　　　　　　　　　　　　　　**LITERARY RESPONSE AND ANALYSIS**

In the Shadow of War Ben Okri
The End and the Beginning Wisława Szymborska
translated by **Stanislaw Baranczak** *and* **Clare Cavanagh**

COMPREHENSION *(40 points; 4 points each)*
On the line provided, write the letter of the *best* answer to each of the following items.

_____ **1.** The setting of the story is —

    A present-day Nigeria

    B an Ibo village during colonial times

    C a Nigerian village during that nation's civil war

    D Nigeria during its struggle for independence from Britain

_____ **2.** Omovo's father tries to protect him from the dangers surrounding them by —

    F giving Omovo a weapon

    G telling Omovo to make friends with the soldiers

    H trying to scare Omovo into staying indoors

    J staying home with Omovo

_____ **3.** The woman in the story is mysterious for all the following reasons *except* that —

    A her face is hidden by a veil

    B her purpose is not known to the other characters

    C she may or may not be Omovo's mother

    D Omovo is not sure whether she is mortal or supernatural

_____ **4.** The woman with the black veil turns out to be —

    F a journalist

    G a ghost

    H helping the people in hiding

    J the wife of the village leader

_____ **5.** What is the *most* likely reason Omovo doesn't take the ten kobo the soldiers offer him?

    A His father has already given him money.

    B He wants to insult the soldiers because they are murderers.

    C He doesn't want to be seen accepting money.

    D He doesn't want to have to tell the soldiers he has seen the woman.

_____ **6.** What do the soldiers want from the woman?

    F Information about their enemies

    G Bribe money

    H Support for their side of the war

    J The contents of her basket

_____ **7.** Omovo is overcome with fear when —

    A the fat soldier shoots the woman

    B he cannot find his way out of the forest

    C the soldiers start shooting at him

    D the soldiers threaten his father

_____ **8.** How does Omovo get out of the forest?

    F The woman shows him the way.

    G He crawls on all fours in the dark.

    H His father comes to rescue him.

    J The soldiers carry him home.

_____ **9.** The society depicted in this story is a —

    A young nation in violent conflict

    B prosperous, rapidly industrializing country

    C stable, traditional culture cut off from the outside world

    D native society ruled by white colonizers

_____ **10.** What is the *most* likely reason that Omovo's father carries him to bed at the end of the story?

    F He knows that Omovo is exhausted from his adventures.

    G He is afraid Omovo will blurt out something that will anger the soldiers.

    H Furious with Omovo for getting lost, he wants to banish the boy to his room.

    J Omovo has school the next day and must go to bed even if he is not tired.

LITERARY FOCUS: POINT OF VIEW *(15 points; 5 points each)*

On the line provided, write the letter of the *best* answer to each of the following items.

_____ **11.** What point of view is used to narrate "In the Shadow of War"?

    A First person

    B Second person

    C Third person omniscient

    D Third person limited

_____ **12.** What point of view is used to narrate "The End and the Beginning"?

    F Third person omniscient

    G Second person

    H Third person limited

    J First person

_____ **13.** Which of the following predictions about "In the Shadow of War" could *not* come true?

    A The soldiers who are now chatting with Omovo's father will later kill him.

    B Omovo and his father will be killed in the war.

    C The veiled woman will return the next day.

    D Omovo will survive to manhood.

READING SKILLS: MAKING PREDICTIONS *(5 points)*

On the line provided, write the letter of the *best* answer to the following item.

_____ **14.** A **prediction** is always a statement about —

    F a character

    G the past

    H the present

    J the future

VOCABULARY DEVELOPMENT *(20 points; 4 points each)*

Match the definition on the left with the Vocabulary word on the right. On the line provided, write the letter of the Vocabulary word.

_____ **15.** dulling the mind and the senses   **a.** oppressive

_____ **16.** hard to bear   **b.** succumbed

_____ **17.** showy   **c.** dementedly

_____ **18.** yielded; gave way to   **d.** stupefying

_____ **19.** madly; wildly   **e.** ostentatious

CONSTRUCTED RESPONSE *(20 points)*

20. In "In the Shadow of War" and "The End and the Beginning," the authors use different styles to convey their feelings about war. On a separate sheet of paper, compare and contrast the two works' ideas and the authors' stylistic means of conveying them. Give specific examples from both texts.

SELECTION TEST

LITERARY RESPONSE AND ANALYSIS

Shakespeare's Sister *from* A Room of One's Own   Virginia Woolf

COMPREHENSION *(40 points; 4 points each)*

On the line provided, write the letter of the *best* answer to each of the following items.

_____ **1.** In describing the life of Judith Shakespeare, Virginia Woolf —

    A uses facts she has researched about that woman

    B follows in the footsteps of others who have written about Shakespeare's sister

    C relies on her personal knowledge of the Shakespeare family

    D fictionalizes about someone whose existence she is uncertain of

_____ **2.** The tone of Woolf's description of the old gentleman who gives his opinion about women writers and cats is —

    F respectful

    G loving

    H satirical

    J objective

_____ **3.** Woolf describes Judith Shakespeare's parents as —

    A typical middle-class parents of their time

    B uninterested in a mere daughter

    C ambitious for their daughter to marry a nobleman

    D encouraging of Judith's talent

_____ **4.** What do Woolf and the old gentlemen agree about?

    F Cats do not have souls.

    G No English woman in Shakespeare's time could have written Shakespeare's plays.

    H Women cannot be literary geniuses.

    J The old gentlemen's writings helped reduce the ignorance of the public.

_____ **5.** In Woolf's vision of Judith Shakespeare's life, Judith does *not* —

    A travel to London to make her fortune as her brother did

    B have an illegitimate child by an actor

    C room with her brother Will and ask for his help

    D kill herself, to be buried unknown and in poverty

_____ **6.** In order to live a free life in London, Woolf asserts that Judith Shakespeare would have had to give up her —

    F dignity

    G long hair

    H brother

    J children

_____ **7.** Woolf says that female writers were treated with —

    A respect and even adoration

    B special programs to compensate for past discrimination

    C the same indifference accorded to men

    D hostility and derision

_____ **8.** Why couldn't Judith Shakespeare have acted in her brother's plays?

    F Women were not permitted to act onstage in England at that time.

    G William Shakespeare did not get along with his sister.

    H Because of their age difference, Judith and William were not in London at the same time.

    J Judith was not able to find an acting teacher willing to take her on as a student.

_____ **9.** Woolf says that women writers in the past were "debarred from such alleviations as came even to Keats or Tennyson or Carlyle, all poor men." In other words, women —

    A writers were not as bold in personality as such men

    B did not have opportunities for independent travel and solitude

    C did not have as much money as men did

    D often had more strife in marriage than men

_____ **10.** Which virtues does Woolf see as having had a negative impact upon the ability of women writers to become recognized?

    F Patience and kindness

    G Sloth and avarice

    H Faith and hope

    J Modesty and chastity

LITERARY FOCUS: ESSAY *(15 points; 5 points each)*
On the line provided, write the letter of the *best* answer to each of the following items.

_____ **11.** What kind of essay is "Shakespeare's Sister"?

    A A formal essay, because it is written in formal English and carefully organized around a factual structure

    B An informal essay, because it is humorous and casual in tone

    C A formal essay, because it is on a serious topic of great public importance

    D An informal essay, because it is subjective, expressing the author's individual ideas and feelings

_____ **12.** An **essay** has all the following traits *except* it —

    F uses a specific point of view

    G is short

    H examines one topic

    J is fictional

_____ **13.** Which of the following statements supports Woolf's belief that many of the unknown writers referred to as "anonymous" were women?

    A Shakespeare's sister, Judith, never appears in history or literature books.

    B Until Woolf's lifetime, women were legally barred from publishing in England.

    C Women naturally prefer to refuse credit for their work and to give it to men instead.

    D As late as the mid–nineteenth century, many women used male pen names.

READING SKILL: IDENTIFYING THE AUTHOR'S BELIEFS *(5 points)*

On the line provided, write the letter of the *best* answer to the following item.

_____ **14.** Which of the following is *not* a belief of Virginia Woolf's in this essay?

    F No special obstacles have stood in the way of female literary geniuses.

    G Unknown female geniuses have existed.

    H Material circumstances pose an obstacle to most genius writers.

    J Unknown male geniuses have existed.

VOCABULARY DEVELOPMENT *(20 points; 4 points each)*

On the line before each sentence, write the Vocabulary word from the list below that has a similar meaning to the boldface word or phrase in the sentence.

servile   **suppressed**   **propitious**   **notorious**   **formidable**

_____ **15.** According to Woolf, what conditions are **favorable** for the development of genius?

_____ **16.** The talents of many gifted women and many gifted poor people have been **kept down** throughout history.

_____ **17.** Women who were in public life in the nineteenth century were often **unfavorably famous**.

_____ **18.** For most people today, the restrictions confronting women during the Renaissance would be **difficult to handle.**

_____ **19.** When meeting a genius, one should be respectful but not **slavish.**

CONSTRUCTED RESPONSE *(20 points)*

20. Choose any of the author's beliefs that you have identified as appearing in "Shakespeare's Sister." On a separate sheet of paper, discuss how that belief reflects themes and issues of Virginia Woolf's era.

SELECTION TEST ████████████   **LITERARY RESPONSE AND ANALYSIS**

Shooting an Elephant   George Orwell

COMPREHENSION *(40 points; 4 points each)*

On the line provided, write the letter of the *best* answer to each of the following items.

_____ **1.** The country in which the events in the essay occurred is now called —

    A Sri Lanka

    B Vietnam

    C Cambodia

    D Myanmar

_____ **2.** Orwell's elephant-shooting experience occurred —

    F during World War II

    G after World War II

    H between World War I and World War II

    J before World War I

_____ **3.** Why is Orwell the person called upon to kill the elephant?

    A Orwell is the most experienced elephant hunter in the area.

    B The natives have more respect for Orwell than for other local colonial officers.

    C Orwell is the British policeman within whose territory the elephant is located.

    D The natives want to test Orwell's courage.

_____ **4.** What has the elephant done to warrant being killed?

    F Nothing—the elephant is merely in the wrong place at the wrong time.

    G The elephant has killed a man and a cow and caused property damage.

    H The elephant has trespassed on sacred ground.

    J The innocent elephant was mistaken for a different, truly dangerous elephant.

_____ **5.** At first, Orwell thinks he should not shoot the elephant because he —

    A is afraid

    B is morally opposed to killing animals

    C thinks the Burmese people will turn against him if he kills it

    D thinks the elephant's rampage has ended

_____ **6.** Orwell's attitude toward the elephant is —

    F sympathetic

    G coldly indifferent

    H hostile, hateful

    J superstitious

_____ **7.** The Burmese hate Orwell because he—

    A treats them as inferiors

    B is a fierce supporter of British colonialism

    C shoots the elephant

    D is a British police officer

_____ **8.** Orwell finally decides to shoot the elephant —

    F because the elephant has killed a person

    G so that he can have the tusks

    H in order to save himself from humiliation

    J for reasons he does not reveal

_____ **9.** What is the older Orwell's attitude toward the moment when, as a youth, he shot the elephant?

    A He defiantly approves of his past actions.

    B He regrets his actions.

    C He does not understand his actions.

    D He does not give the matter much thought.

_____ **10.** What paradox, or seeming contradiction, does Orwell point out concerning his behavior in front of the crowd?

    F Although he was experienced in college dramatics, he was very nervous in front of the crowd.

    G Although he was the person with the elephant gun, he did a very clumsy job of shooting the elephant.

    H Although he was a very efficient colonial officer, he hated colonialism.

    J Although he seemed to be in the position of leader, he only acted because the crowd expected him to.

LITERARY FOCUS: IRONY *(15 points; 5 points each)*

_____ **11.** Orwell effectively uses irony, which can be defined as —

    A a discrepancy between expectations and reality

    B language that appeals to the senses

    C a descriptive phrase used to characterize a person, place, or thing

    D a word's sound suggesting its meaning

_____ **12.** Which of the following descriptions from "Shooting an Elephant" is an example of situational irony?

    F People give Orwell conflicting accounts of the elephant's activities.

    G Armed to encounter a violent animal, Orwell confronts a quietly grazing elephant.

    H After Orwell sends for the elephant gun, the townspeople expect him to shoot the elephant.

    J The elephant kills a cow and a man.

_____ **13.** Which of the following passages from "Shooting an Elephant" is an example of verbal irony?

    A "Never tell me, by the way, that the dead look peaceful. Most of the corpses I have seen looked devilish."

    B "In Moulmein, in Lower Burma, I was hated by large numbers of people—the only time in my life that I have been important enough for this to happen to me."

    C "One day something happened which in a roundabout way was enlightening."

    D "[I]t was a damn shame to shoot an elephant for killing a coolie, because an elephant was worth more than any damn Coringhee coolie."

READING SKILL: IDENTIFYING THE AUTHOR'S PURPOSE *(5 points)*

On the line provided, write the letter of the *best* answer to the following item.

_____ **14.** Orwell's *most* likely purpose for writing "Shooting an Elephant" was probably to —

    F share his reflections on the nature of colonial power

    G provide his individual perspective on a major event in Burmese-British history

    H entertain readers with an exciting elephant hunting story

    J advise colonial officials on how to act in front of natives

VOCABULARY DEVELOPMENT *(20 points; 4 points each)*

On the line provided, write the letter of the *best* answer to each of the following items.

_____ **15.** Which of the following sentences uses the word **supplant** correctly?

    A Over time, more advanced weapons tend to supplant more primitive ones.

    B Salt is an important supplant that goes well with many foods.

    C A colonial officer's duty is to supplant the natives by enforcing laws.

    D When a colonial power defeats a native kingdom, the native kingdom must supplant it.

_____ **16.** Which of the following *best* describes a **labyrinth**?

    F dirty

    G immoral

    H complex

    J outdoors

_____ **17.** **Squalid** is a synonym for all of the following words except —

    A wretched

    B splendid

    C foul

    D unclean

_____ **18.** If you give someone a **pretext,** you give him or her a(n) —

    F examination

    G lesson

    H salary

    J excuse

_____ **19.** The word **maze** is a synonym for the word —

    A supplant

    B labyrinth

    C squalid

    D pretext

CONSTRUCTED RESPONSE *(20 points)*

20. What political, ethical, or social influences of the period led to the younger Orwell's becoming a colonial officer? What political, ethical, or social influences do you think led to the older Orwell's criticisms of colonialism? Write your response on a separate piece of paper.

SELECTION TEST ▬▬▬▬▬▬▬ LITERARY RESPONSE AND ANALYSIS

No Witchcraft for Sale Doris Lessing

COMPREHENSION *(40 points; 4 points each)*
On the line provided, write the letter of the *best* answer to each of the following items.

_____ **1.** Mrs. Farquar seems to raise Gideon's wages —

    A each time he shows affection for the Farquars

    B after he shows Teddy how to ride the scooter

    C when he cooks an excellent meal

    D annually

_____ **2.** Why is Gideon angry with Teddy?

    F Teddy refuses to obey Gideon.

    G Teddy is a cruel boss to the workers on his farm.

    H After being healed by Gideon, Teddy turns against him.

    J Teddy insults Gideon's son.

_____ **3.** When Teddy is six years old, his behavior toward Gideon changes, and the boy —

    A begins to act more affectionate

    B stops trusting Gideon's medicines

    C acts like a master addressing a servant

    D begins to show fear of Gideon

_____ **4.** An accident befalls Teddy when a —

    F snake spits poison in his eye

    G snake bites him in the leg

    H lion bites him in the leg

    J lion gashes his face severely

_____ **5.** To prepare the root for medicinal use, Gideon —

    A simmers it in water for one hour

    B chews it, to flatten it

    C chews it, to mix it with saliva

    D burns it to make use of the ash

_____ **6.** When the Farquars ask Gideon to identify the root, they —

    F believe they are acting to benefit humanity

    G show respect for Gideon's medical knowledge

    H are desperate to use the plant again

    J know Gideon won't be able to find the plant again

_____ **7.** Before the events of this story, the Farquars do not know that Gideon —

    A planned a revolt against the colonists

    B had attended school in England

    C is not sincerely religious and has deceived the missionaries

    D is respected by his people as a healer and the son of a great man

_____ **8.** Which of the following motivations is *not* one of the interests the scientist has in finding the root?

    F To aid European humanity by introducing a new medicine

    G To make money from developing a product

    H To give black Africans credit for knowing the use of the plant

    J To increase his scientific reputation

_____ **9.** To *best* describe the Farquars, you might say that they —

    A are hostile toward everyone they encounter

    B are devoted to Africans but are afraid to show it

    C want to do all they can to improve the lives of Africans

    D accept their roles and are not very involved with their servants

_____ **10.** According to the story, the African veld is a place —

    F where rich people live, love, work, and raise their children

    G where powerful, potentially lifesaving plants grow

    H of dread and horror, where everyone suffers terribly

    J where most people disapprove of superstition

LITERARY FOCUS: THEME *(15 points; 5 points each)*

On the line provided, write the letter of the *best* answer to each of the following items.

_____ **11.** Which of the following sentences is a possible statement of the story's theme?

    A Cultural differences can easily be overcome if everyone makes an effort to be sensitive.

    B People should always say what they mean regardless of their words' potential effects.

    C European medicine has no place in Africa, and African medicine has no place in Europe.

    D Racism is deeply divisive and can prevent people from understanding one another.

_____ **12.** The behavior of the Farquars and of the scientist can be seen as typical of colonial attitudes in that they —

    F treat Gideon abusively

    G assume they can easily get information from a culture they consider inferior

    H believe that Gideon's cure has potentially harmful effects

    J make a point of talking to servants only when necessary

_____ **13.** The story takes place in a country that used to be called _____ and is now called_____.

    A Southern Rhodesia; Zimbabwe

    B South Africa; South Africa

    C the Belgian Congo; Congo

    D Tanganyika; Tanzania

READING SKILL: IDENTIFYING HISTORICAL CONTEXT *(5 points each)*

On the line provided, write the letter of the *best* answer to the following item.

_____ **14.** When Doris Lessing was a child, she was a member of a —

    F colonized majority

    G colonized minority

    H colonialist minority

    J colonialist majority

VOCABULARY DEVELOPMENT *(20 points; 4 points each)*

Match the definition on the left with the Vocabulary word on the right. On the line provided, write the letter of the Vocabulary word.

_____ **15.** effectiveness

_____ **16.** halfhearted; indifferent

_____ **17.** did away with; canceled

_____ **18.** disagreeably; contrarily

_____ **19.** with deep respect, love, or awe, as for something sacred

    a. perfunctory

    b. perversely

    c. reverently

    d. annulled

    e. efficacy

CONSTRUCTED RESPONSE *(20 points)*

20. What do you think Doris Lessing is saying about colonialism in this story? Elaborate on your answer on a separate piece of paper, providing details from the text.

SELECTION TEST

"I Believe in a British Empire" Joseph Chamberlain
"The Noble Mansion of Free India" Jawaharlal Nehru

COMPREHENSION *(60 points; 6 points each)*

On the line provided, write the letter of the *best* answer to each of the following items.

_____ **1.** The author of "I Believe in a British Empire" was —

    A prime minister of Great Britain

    B a popular journalist of the early 1900s

    C British colonial secretary during the Boer War

    D a novelist who previously served in the colonial service in South Africa

_____ **2.** Which headline below most accurately summarizes the first paragraph of Chamberlain's speech?

    F "Britain Loses Boer War"

    G "Protest Movement Rises Against Boer War"

    H "Many from Britain Emigrating to U.S."

    J "Britons Still Patriotic in England and Abroad"

_____ **3.** Which of the following is *not* one of Chamberlain's goals for the British Empire?

    A Ceasing to do business with other empires

    B Achieving friendship with all other nations

    C Resisting competition from challengers

    D Achieving self-reliance

_____ **4.** What past policy of England does Chamberlain criticize?

    F Isolation

    G Colonialism

    H Giving up the American colonies

    J Going to war against the Boers in South Africa

_____ **5.** What does Chamberlain propose for colonized native peoples in the British Empire?

    A He feels they are the equals of English people.

    B He feels they should be educated and trained until they are capable of replacing English people in running their own nations.

    C He feels they should remain the responsibility of their British rulers.

    D He feels they should be restricted within traditional cultures and not educated in English ways.

_____ **6.** In Jawaharlal Nehru's speech the phrase "the achievement we celebrate today" refers to —

    F victory in World War II

    G India's independence from Britain

    H Nehru's election as Prime Minister of India

    J India's defeat of Pakistan

_____ **7.** Nehru invites the people of India to look forward to a future of —

    A growth and responsibility under the wing of the British Empire

    B ease and plenty under Indian self-rule

    C political freedom and ceaseless striving to solve social problems

    D revolutionary war to achieve liberty from colonialism

_____ **8.** In the world according to Nehru, how should nations interact?

    F They should work together to achieve peace, freedom, and prosperity, and avoid disaster.

    G They should pursue their individual goals beneath the protective umbrella of Great Britain.

    H They should adopt an increasingly Americanized world culture of free market individualism.

    J Each nation should take care of its own problems and not interfere in the problems of others.

_____ **9.** "The ambition of the greatest man of our generation has been to wipe every tear from every eye," says Nehru. Which great man is he referring to?

    A Nehru

    B Gandhi

    C Churchill

    D Roosevelt

_____ **10.** The phrase "the noble mansion of free India where all her children may dwell" implies that in Nehru's view, India should be —

    F a socialist nation

    G divided between Hindu India and Muslim Pakistan

    H a diverse multicultural nation

    J aligned with the United States against the Soviet Union

LITERARY FOCUS: COMPARING MAIN IDEAS ACROSS TEXTS *(20 points; 5 points each)*
On the line provided, write the letter of the *best* answer to each of the following items.

_____ **11.** Which of the four authors in Political Points of View did *not* observe the British Empire from the standpoint of a colonizer?

    A George Orwell

    B Doris Lessing

    C Joseph Chamberlain

    D Jawaharlal Nehru

_____ **12.** Which of the four authors is most pro-empire?

    F George Orwell

    G Doris Lessing

    H Joseph Chamberlain

    J Jawaharlal Nehru

_____ **13.** An important difference between Chamberlain and Nehru is that —

    A Chamberlain is British, while Nehru is Indian.

    B Chamberlain is a patriot, while Nehru is not.

    C Nehru is a patriot, while Chamberlain is not.

    D Only one of the two men is a government official.

_____ **14.** Which of the following statements would *most* likely be agreed with by both Chamberlain and Nehru?

    F "Britain's destiny is to rule wisely and benevolently over foreign peoples."

    G "In the future England will be a multicultural society with a large population of African and Asian immigrants."

    H "Freedom for colonized peoples is inevitable."

    J "I know what is best for my country."

CONSTRUCTED RESPONSE *(20 points)*

15. Imagine that Joseph Chamberlain and Jawaharlal Nehru come back to life today and have a conversation about the present state of Britain and its former colonies. Write their dialogue on a separate sheet of paper. Base their comments on the views they express in their selections. Write at least three comments per speaker.

SELECTION TEST LITERARY RESPONSE AND ANALYSIS

Once upon a Time Nadine Gordimer

COMPREHENSION (40 points; 4 points each)

On the line provided, write the letter of the *best* answer to each of the following items.

_____ **1.** The narrator of "Once upon a Time" is —

    A one of the members of the family

    B one of the servants

    C a writer who thinks of a bedtime story

    D not identified

_____ **2.** Though the family's home has never been broken into —

    F the father has been mugged

    G their fears of such an assault grow

    H they become suspicious of their servants

    J they plan to move to a safer neighborhood

_____ **3.** The installation of alarm systems and bars on the windows —

    A is too expensive for many people in the neighborhood

    B effectively deters potential burglars

    C has a calming effect on the neighborhood

    D does not seem sufficiently effective to the family

_____ **4.** On walks through the increasingly barricaded neighborhood, the —

    F parents no longer admire rose bushes but compare security devices

    G family finds the streets blocked off

    H little boy plays with neighboring children

    J pet dog disappears

_____ **5.** To make their home safer, the parents finally —

    A dig a cellar where the entire household can hide

    B hire a guard to patrol the property

    C install a coil of barbed wire on top of the security wall

    D buy enough guns and ammunition for a small army

_____ **6.** In the final paragraph of the story, the boy is killed —

    F by one of the servants who goes mad and attacks the family

    G by an electronic security robot run amok

    H pretending to be the hero in a fairy tale

    J accidentally by his father's gun

_____ **7.** The tone of the story's final paragraph differs from the tone of the rest of the story in that the final paragraph is more —

    A satirical than the rest of the story

    B snobbish than the rest of the story

    C otherworldly than the rest of the story

    D horrifying than the rest of the story

_____ **8.** "Once upon a Time" is *primarily* a commentary on the —

    F silly endings of fairy tales

    G futility of security devices

    H evils of apartheid in South Africa

    J effectiveness of advertising

_____ **9.** The use of parody in this story —

    A has a serious as well as a humorous quality

    B makes the story less troubling

    C ensures that the story will have a happy ending

    D interferes with the plot of the story

_____ **10.** According to the narrator, she shares with the characters in this story their —

    F interest in buying security devices

    G family structure: two parents, a child, and a cat

    H belief in the justice of the white South African cause

    J fears of violence

LITERARY FOCUS: SYMBOLISM *(15 points; 5 points each)*
On the line provided, write the letter of the *best* answer to each of the following items.

_____ **11.** The security system in the story could symbolize all of the following concepts *except* the —

    A family's feeling of insecurity

    B racial barrier between blacks and whites under apartheid

    C actual security of the setting in which the characters live

    D modern obsession with safety and privilege

_____ **12.** The boy's death at the end of the story *most* likely symbolizes the —

    F harm that can come from reading fairy tales

    G punishment that befalls those who live by violence

    H imperfections of present-day security systems

    J parents' hatred of their child

_____ **13.** What aspect of the family in the story suggests a fairy tale?

    A They live in a house in a suburb.

    B They buy security devices.

    C They have servants.

    D They "were living happily ever after."

READING SKILL: IDENTIFYING LANGUAGE STRUCTURES *(5 points)*

_____ **14.** Which of the following details is *not* a clue to the story's fairy tale genre?

    F The presence of a "wise old witch"

    G A "concentration-camp style" security

    H The unspecified, generic setting

    J The "terrible thicket of thorns"

VOCABULARY DEVELOPMENT *(20 points; 4 points each)*

On the line provided, write the letter of the *best* answer to each of the following items.

_____ **15.** If the pupils of your eyes distend with concentration, they —

    A widen

    B narrow

    C become red

    D become teary

_____ **16.** An itinerant gardener is a gardener who —

    F only works part-time

    G has great skill

    H travels from job to job

    J has little skill

_____ **17.** Audaciously means —

    A ungratefully

    B boldly

    C gently

    D wickedly

_____ **18.** If you buy a car for reasons of <u>aesthetics</u>, you are buying it for —

    F the way it handles

    G its low price

    H its safety features

    J the way it looks

_____ **19.** Which of the following objects usually has a <u>serrated</u> edge?

    A ruler

    B dagger

    C saw

    D screwdriver

CONSTRUCTED RESPONSE *(20 points)*

20. On a separate sheet of paper, explain what you think Nadine Gordimer's purpose was in writing this story. Citing details from the story, show how Gordimer uses style, language, and irony to help achieve that purpose.

SELECTION TEST ████████████ LITERARY RESPONSE AND ANALYSIS

Marriage Is a Private Affair Chinua Achebe

COMPREHENSION *(40 points; 5 points each)*

On the line provided, write the letter of the *best* answer to each of the following items.

_____ **1.** A trait that Okeke and Nnaemeka share is —

    A frailty

    B stubbornness

    C adventurousness

    D selfishness

_____ **2.** Before telling Okeke about his engagement, Nnaemeka —

    F tells Okeke he doesn't want to see him anymore

    G asks Okeke for money

    H asks Okeke for forgiveness

    J introduces Nene to Okeke

_____ **3.** The *strongest* objection Okeke has to his son's marriage is that —

    A Nnaemeka hasn't first consulted him

    B Nene is from another tribal group

    C Okeke has not yet been introduced to his son's fiancée

    D Nnaemeka plans to leave his father out of all the arrangements

_____ **4.** Compared with social attitudes in the village where Okeke lives, social attitudes in Lagos are —

    F modern

    G old-fashioned

    H the same

    J rural

_____ **5.** Nnaemeka tries to get his father to accept his marriage to Nene by —

    A arguing with him strenuously throughout the years

    B bringing Nene to the village to meet Okeke

    C sending a friend to intercede on Nnaemeka's behalf

    D first arguing with him and then waiting patiently

_____ **6.** After their marriage, Nnaemeka and Nene —

    F successfully withstand the prejudices of people in Lagos

    G are snubbed by everyone

    H move to another country where they can live peacefully

    J give in to social pressure and separate

_____ **7.** At the end of the story, Nene —

    A decides to confront her father-in-law in person

    B writes to her father-in-law to tell him that he has ruined her life

    C does not tell her sons that they have a grandfather

    D writes to her father-in-law, asking him to let his grandsons meet him

_____ **8.** Why does Okeke have trouble sleeping at the end of the story?

    F The rain keeps him awake.

    G He is angry that Nene has tried to communicate with him.

    H He worries that his behavior may have caused his grandsons to suffer.

    J He fears that Nnaemeka and Nene may never speak to him again.

LITERARY FOCUS: VERBAL IRONY *(20 points; 5 points each)*

On the line provided, write the letter of the *best* answer to each of the following items.

_____ **9.** In **verbal irony** a statement —

    A means the opposite of what it says

    B means what it says

    C means what it says and stands for another statement

    D confuses the reader as to its meaning

_____ **10.** If the title "Marriage Is a Private Affair" is ironic, what does it really mean?

    F Marriage is a matter of concern for a group.

    G Marriage is a ceremony regulated by church and state.

    H Children as well as parents may be affected by a marriage.

    J A couple's marriage is something that only concerns them.

_____ **11.** What is ironic about the old man's comment "It is the beginning of the end"?

    A Nnaemeka's marriage to Nene threatens the traditional Ibo ways.

    B The marriage of Nnaemeka and Nene is actually the beginning of a new way of life.

    C The old man is not personally acquainted with the married couple.

    D The old man's own marriage was not a happy one.

_____ **12.** Which statement from Okeke's letter does Achebe mean to be ironic?

    F "It amazes me that you could be so unfeeling as to send me your wedding picture."

    G "I would have sent it back."

    H "But on further thought I decided just to cut off your wife and send it back to you. . . ."

    J "How I wish that I had nothing to do with you either."

VOCABULARY DEVELOPMENT *(20 points; 4 points each)*

On the line provided, write the Vocabulary word from the list below that has a similar meaning to the italicized word or phrase in the sentence. One word is used twice.

    cosmopolitan   **rash**   **commiserate**   **persevered**

_____ **13.** Nene believes that she is a *worldly* person and at first does not take Nnaemeka's objections seriously.

_____ **14.** Okeke *obstinately continued* in his opposition to the marriage.

_____ **15.** Friends *sympathize* with Okeke about his son's unusual marriage.

_____ **16.** People in his home village think that Nnaemeka's marriage is a *reckless, hasty, ill-considered* mistake.

_____ **17.** The narrator of "Marriage Is a Private Affair" takes a *sophisticated* view of the characters and their behaviors.

CONSTRUCTED RESPONSE *(20 points)*

18. Based on the story, what do you feel is Chinua Achebe's view of race? On a separate sheet of paper, elaborate on your answer with examples from the text.

SELECTION TEST ████████████ **LITERARY RESPONSE AND ANALYSIS**

Telephone Conversation Wole Soyinka

COMPREHENSION *(60 points; 6 points each)*
On the line provided, write the letter of the *best* answer to each of the following items.

_____ **1.** The poem takes place in —

  A Africa at the end of colonial times

  B Africa in the era of independence

  C London in the 1950s

  D England in the early 2000s

_____ **2.** The speaker tells the landlady, "I am African," because he —

  F suspects that she is African, too

  G thinks she will be pleased that he is African

  H dislikes people of other races

  J hopes to avoid a needless trip to meet a racist landlady

_____ **3.** The description of the landlady's lipstick and cigarette holder in lines 8–9 is based on —

  A what the speaker sees

  B what the landlady tells the speaker

  C a photograph accompanying the rental ad

  D the landlady's voice and the speaker's imagination

_____ **4.** What fact about telephone conversations is central to this poem?

  F Telephone conversations are usually impersonal and brief.

  G The people talking cannot see each other.

  H It is difficult to hear someone talking through a pay phone on a busy street.

  J British phone booths have separate buttons for listening and for talking.

_____ **5.** What do the landlady's words reveal about her character?

  A She is racist.

  B She pretends to like foreigners, but she really doesn't.

  C She has a wry, irrepressible sense of humor.

  D She is compassionate and sensitive.

_____ **6.** In lines 10–14, the speaker —

  F describes to the landlady the location from which he is calling

  G studies the phone booth while waiting for the landlady to speak

  H studies his surroundings to make sure he isn't dreaming

  J remembers a dream he had

_____ **7.** By the end of the poem, the speaker's tone has become —

    A solemn and moody

    B irritable and petty

    C gentle and thoughtful

    D ironic and sarcastic

_____ **8.** The third and fourth stanzas show the speaker's —

    F attempts to answer the landlady's question while combating its offensiveness

    G considerable sympathy for the landlady's perspective

    H lack of understanding of the landlady's question

    J desire to be as helpful as possible to the landlady

_____ **9.** The *best* description of the speaker's feelings is —

    A confused, weary, and resigned

    B romantic, passionate, and perplexed

    C angry, embarrassed, and amused

    D annoyed, doubtful, and caring

_____ **10.** What justification does the landlady give for her attitude toward the speaker?

    F She believes Africans are inferior to Europeans.

    G She believes that all people should be treated equally.

    H She believes that apartments should be rented on the basis of merit and money.

    J She gives no justification for her attitude.

LITERARY FOCUS: SATIRE *(20 points; 5 points each)*

On the line provided, write the letter of the *best* answer to each of the following items.

_____ **11.** The essential quality of **satire** is that it —

    A opposes racism and injustice

    B endures after the issues it addresses have passed

    C does not survive very long since it deals with current topics

    D ridicules human folly

_____ **12.** Which of the following is *not* a purpose of **satire**?

 F To exaggerate for purposes of comedy

 G To change things that are wrong in society

 H To support the accepted way of doing things

 J To make readers laugh and think

_____ **13.** What does the discussion of chocolate in line 19 satirize?

 A People's concern with skin color

 B People's different tastes in food

 C The idea that chocolate is better than vanilla

 D The premise that a person in desperate search of an apartment would pause to eat chocolate

_____ **14.** Which of the following people is the *main* object of satire in this poem?

 F The speaker

 G The landlady

 H The reader

 J Wole Soyinka

CONSTRUCTED RESPONSE *(20 points)*

15. What comment is author Wole Soyinka making by means of the conversation between the speaker and the landlady? Write your answer on a separate sheet of paper, and support it by using at least two references from the poem.

SELECTION TEST ████████ LITERARY RESPONSE AND ANALYSIS

The Second Coming William Butler Yeats

COMPREHENSION *(40 points; 4 points each)*
On the line provided, write the letter of the *best* answer to each of the following items.

_____ **1.** What is the gyre in line 1?

    A A hunting falcon

    B A person who hunts with a falcon

    C Spirits of the dead

    D A cycle of history

_____ **2.** The image of the falconer losing control of the falcon in line 2 probably stands for —

    F the tendency of people to rebel against what is good for them

    G the difficulty of really mastering any art, such as poetry

    H the human desire to be free and wild rather than tame and civilized

    J the inability of people to stop civilization's descent into chaos

_____ **3.** Lines 3–4 describe a(n) —

    A house falling down

    B society in collapse

    C individual growing old

    D economy in recession

_____ **4.** Images of a "blood-dimmed tide" and of drowned innocence in lines 5–6 were probably affected by the events of —

    F the Boer War

    G the Victorian era

    H World War I

    J World War II

_____ **5.** "The best lack all conviction, while the worst / Are full of passionate intensity" (lines 7–8) is a criticism of people who —

    A remain neutral in times of crisis

    B have good intentions but no passion

    C feel things too passionately

    D know how to get what they want

_____ **6.** The second stanza of the poem introduces an extended allusion to —

    F Christian scripture

    G English folk legend

    H Victorian literature

    J Greek mythology

_____ **7.** In lines 13–16, the speaker's vision of a happy time is displaced by the vision of a —

    A ghost ship

    B stone sphinx

    C masked murderer

    D battlefield strewn with skeletons

_____ **8.** In lines 18–19, the sleeper is —

    F Christianity

    G the spirit of the world, or "Spiritus Mundi"

    H eternal truth

    J the spirit of pagan savagery

_____ **9.** What is ironic about the allusion to Bethlehem in the last line?

    A The event described is the opposite of Christian salvation.

    B Yeats was a devotee of pre-Christian theology.

    C Jesus had already been born two thousand years earlier.

    D The Second Coming will happen when you least expect it.

_____ **10.** The *main* feeling conveyed by the speaker in this poem is one of —

    F hope

    G dread

    H frivolity

    J vengefulness

LITERARY FOCUS: THEME *(40 points; 10 points each)*

On the line provided, write the letter of the *best* answer to each of the following items.

_____ **11.** A **theme** in literature reflects an author's —

    A intuition

    B purpose

    C insight

    D individuality

_____ **12.** Which of the following topics is *not* relevant to "The Second Coming"?

    F The economic boom of the 1920s

    G The movement away from Victorian views and customs

    H Religious uncertainty

    J War and revolution

_____ **13.** How is prophecy reflected in the poem?

    A The poem's ideas and imagery come from a biblical prophecy.

    B The poet claims that he himself is a prophet.

    C The poem tells of an ancient Egyptian curse that comes true.

    D The poet denies that prophecy is a valuable tool.

_____ **14.** What is Yeats's prophecy for modern civilization?

    F World War II will kill millions of civilians and soldiers.

    G The United States will become the dominant world power.

    H Western civilization will enter a period of decline.

    J Science will find cures for many previously fatal diseases.

CONSTRUCTED RESPONSE *(20 points)*

15. On a separate sheet of paper, analyze the use of irony in "The Second Coming," discussing how irony helps convey the poem's themes. Examine at least two examples of irony.

LITERARY RESPONSE AND ANALYSIS

The Lake Isle of Innisfree William Butler Yeats

COMPREHENSION *(40 points; 4 points each)*

On the line provided, write the letter of the *best* answer to each of the following items.

1. What does Innisfree represent for the speaker?

 A Adventure and excitement

 B Learning, poetry, and culture

 C Untouched wilderness

 D Ideal peace and rural beauty

2. The speaker of this poem is probably —

 F the poet himself

 G a young girl

 H a sailor

 J an unknown caretaker

3. What role does Innisfree play in the speaker's life?

 A It is a weekend getaway spot.

 B It is a disturbing vision of isolation.

 C It is the promise of a pleasant retreat.

 D It is a memory of a place he will never see again.

4. The second stanza mentions morning, noon, evening, and midnight, and yet all these are described through the imagery of —

 F a celebration

 G sounds, movements, and colors

 H light

 J birds' wings

5. In the last stanza the speaker reveals that —

 A he has suffered greatly in his life

 B the sound of the lake is with him wherever he goes

 C he cannot live far away from a body of water

 D there is a good chance he will fulfill his dream

6. Which of the following statements about the poem is *not* true?

 F The speaker intends to build a cabin.

 G The speaker wants to start a dairy farm.

 H The speaker dreams of making honey with his own bees.

 J The speaker plans to live alone.

Holt Assessment: Literature, Reading, and Vocabulary

7. When he shares his vision of Innisfree with the reader, where is the speaker?

    A At Innisfree

    B On the ferry to Innisfree

    C On the city pavement

    D On a battlefield

8. How is rhyme used in this poem?

    F There is no regular rhyme scheme.

    G The rhyme scheme is *abab abab abab*.

    H The rhyme scheme is *aabb ccdd eeff*.

    J The rhyme scheme is *abab cdcd efef*.

9. The tone of this poem could *best* be described as —

    A irritable

    B serene

    C ironic

    D anguished

10. Which passage in the poem contains the most obvious allusion to Henry David Thoreau's *Walden*?

    F "I will arise and go now, and go to Innisfree . . ."

    G "And evening full of the linnet's wings."

    H "And a small cabin build there . . . / Nine bean-rows will I have there . . ."

    J "While I stand on the roadway, or on the pavements gray . . ."

LITERARY FOCUS: ASSONANCE AND ALLITERATION *(40 points; 10 points each)*

On the line provided, write the letter of the *best* answer to each of the following items.

11. What is the difference between **assonance** and **alliteration**?

    A Assonance refers to vowels; alliteration refers to consonants.

    B Assonance refers to consonants; alliteration refers to vowels.

    C Alliteration appears at the ends of lines; assonance can appear anywhere.

    D Alliteration appears at the beginnings of words; assonance can appear anywhere.

12. The effect of the alliteration in line 10 is to re-create the sound of —

    F the lake

    G the night

    H Innisfree

    J the cricket's song

The Lake Isle of Innisfree   **343**

_____ **13. Assonance** has to do with a poem's —

    A organization

    B rhyme

    C rhythm

    D music

_____ **14.** Yeats seems to favor vowel sounds over hard consonants in this poem. This emphasis conveys to the reader a sense of —

    F detachment

    G freedom

    H harshness

    J austerity

CONSTRUCTED RESPONSE *(20 points)*

15. On a separate sheet of paper, describe Yeats's style in "The Lake Isle of Innisfree." What techniques does he use to achieve that style, and what is the overall effect on the reader?

SELECTION TEST

The Wild Swans at Coole William Butler Yeats
The Swan Rainer Maria Rilke *translated by* Robert Bly

COMPREHENSION *(40 points; 4 points each)*

On the line provided, write the letter of the *best* answer to each of the following items.

_____ **1.** How much time has elapsed since Yeats's speaker first saw the swans?

    A A week

    B Two years

    C Nineteen years

    D Fifty-nine years

_____ **2.** The first stanza tells you that the poem takes place during the —

    F fall

    G winter

    H spring

    J summer

_____ **3.** While watching the swans the speaker feels —

    A angry

    B proud

    C nostalgic

    D aloof

_____ **4.** Throughout the poem the speaker contrasts —

    F swans of the past with those of the present

    G the swans' constancy with his own inconstancy

    H the death of the swans with his own death

    J the swans' behavior with that of other birds

_____ **5.** The figure of speech "the bell-beat of their wings" in line 17 suggests all of the following interpretations *except* that —

    A the swans' wings beat loudly

    B the swans give him a feeling of spirituality

    C the swans have all gone away

    D swans are a way of measuring time

_____ **6.** In line 18, "trod with a lighter tread" implies that —

    F human beings are lighter in weight than swans

    G swans are lighter in weight than human beings

    H the speaker spoke more softly in the past

    J the speaker walked more cheerfully in the past

The Wild Swans at Coole / The Swan

_____ **7.** Lines 19–20, "Unwearied still, lover by lover, / They paddle . . . ," convey an image of swans as —

    A playful and lighthearted

    B tricky and undependable

    C fickle and lacking in morals

    D strong and faithful

_____ **8.** When the speaker observes in line 22, "Their hearts have not grown old," he implies that —

    F swans do not live very long

    G this group of swans is young

    H his heart has grown old

    J the swans are the same ones he'd seen before

_____ **9.** In the last four lines the speaker wonders —

    A where the swans will travel next

    B whether other people like swans as much as he does

    C when his feelings will awaken from their sleep

    D where the swans have come from, and what they have suffered

_____ **10.** The overall feeling of the poem is *best* described as —

    F anger at the destruction of nature by humans

    G sorrow for the swans' plight

    H a man's joy at recapturing his youth

    J an unsettled mind viewing a peaceful, serene landscape

LITERARY FOCUS: SYMBOL *(40 points; 10 points each)*
On the line provided, write the letter of the *best* answer to each of the following items.

_____ **11.** A **symbol** is —

    A a figure of speech because it is original and well written

    B a figure of speech because it should be taken figuratively as well as literally

    C not a figure of speech because it is not a comparison

    D not a figure of speech because it is not spoken

_____ **12.** The swans in "The Wild Swans at Coole" *most* likely symbolize —

    F faithlessness and distrust

    G fragility and purity

    H the flight from life's problems

    J beauty and timelessness

_____ **13.** In the fourth stanza the swans specifically symbolize —

    A enduring love

    B an artistic life

    C old age

    D youth

_____ **14.** In Rainer Maria Rilke's "The Swan," what important life experiences do the movements of the swans symbolize?

    F Living and dying

    G Waking and sleeping

    H Laughing and crying

    J Loving and hating

CONSTRUCTED RESPONSE *(20 points)*

15. On a separate piece of paper, compare and contrast the use of swans as symbols in Yeats's "The Wild Swans at Coole" and Rilke's "The Swan."

SELECTION TEST ███████████ **LITERARY RESPONSE AND ANALYSIS**

Araby James Joyce

COMPREHENSION *(40 points; 4 points each)*

On the line provided, write the letter of the *best* answer to each of the following items.

_____ **1.** The story takes place —

    A on a dairy farm in present-day Wales in the summer

    B in Dublin, Ireland, about a hundred years ago

    C in London during the air raids of World War II

    D in a Scottish fishing village, around Christmas

_____ **2.** The story is narrated by —

    F the main character at the time the events occur

    G the main character later in his life

    H a first-person narrator who is not the main character

    J an omniscient third-person narrator

_____ **3.** What the main character wants *most* in life is to be —

    A loved by Mangan's sister

    B treated well by his aunt and uncle

    C an older adolescent

    D an adult

_____ **4.** In this story the word *Araby* refers *primarily* to a —

    F crowded city

    G romantic interlude

    H book or story title

    J fair or bazaar

_____ **5.** Which of the following events happens *first* in the story?

    A The boy is disappointed by the bazaar.

    B The boy promises to buy Mangan's sister a gift.

    C The boy's uncle arrives home late.

    D Mangan's sister speaks to the boy.

_____ **6.** The boy's desperation about going to the bazaar is heightened when the —

    F uncle comes home late and the trains move slowly

    G boy bursts into fits of uncontrollable crying

    H aunt and uncle refuse to let the boy go to the bazaar, so he sneaks out

    J boy gets lost on the way to the bazaar

_____ **7.** The boy learns all of the following truths *except* that —

    A his love for Mangan's sister is in vain

    B Mangan's sister has feelings for him, too

    C Araby is not an exotic event

    D he will not be able to buy Mangan's sister a gift

_____ **8.** The boy's experience at the stall of the young lady adds to the story because the incident —

    F illustrates that the boy is too young to enjoy the bazaar

    G characterizes the bazaar as drab, seedy, and ordinary

    H emphasizes the bazaar's air of excitement

    J creates a satisfying resolution to the story

_____ **9.** The emotion that the boy does *not* feel at the end of the story is —

    A anguish

    B anger

    C shame

    D jealousy

_____ **10.** Which statement *best* summarizes the story?

    F Confusion eventually leads to depression.

    G Dreams often end in disillusionment.

    H Hatred and love are two sides of the same coin.

    J Despair usually gives way to hope.

LITERARY FOCUS: EPIPHANY AND IRONY *(16 points; 4 points each)*
On the line provided, write the letter of the *best* answer to each of the following items.

_____ **11.** In literature the term **epiphany** refers to —

    A a holiday shortly after Christmas

    B a church ceremony

    C a moment of sudden insight

    D the appearance of something that had previously been invisible

_____ **12.** For the boy in the story, his epiphany brings him —

    F a gift from the bazaar

    G renewed appreciation of the value of traditional beliefs

    H the knowledge that his desires have been vain and foolish

    J a seething resentment against his aunt and uncle

Araby

_____ **13.** Which type of irony is represented by the boy's disillusionment at the bazaar?

    A   Verbal irony

    B   Historical irony

    C   Dramatic irony

    D   Ironic contrast between romance and reality

_____ **14.** Which of the boy's feelings or thoughts is ironic?

    F   He worries that he is going to be late for the bazaar.

    G   He has a crush on Mangan's sister.

    H   He is anxious for his uncle to return home.

    J   He thinks of the package in his arms as a sacred chalice.

READING SKILLS: COMPARING AND CONTRASTING   (8 points; 4 points each)

On the line provided, write the letter of the *best* answer to each of the following items.

_____ **15.** The comparisons and contrasts implied in "Araby" are largely between —

    A   imagination and reality

    B   health and illness

    C   youth and old age

    D   emptiness and fulfillment

_____ **16.** In contrast to the boy who is the main character, the narrator of "Araby" —

    F   is female

    G   is wealthy

    H   is a priest

    J   is older

VOCABULARY DEVELOPMENT   (20 points; 4 points each)

On the line provided, write the Vocabulary word from the list below that *best* completes each sentence.

imperturbable	**somber**	**impinge**	**annihilate**
monotonous	**garrulous**	**improvised**	**pervades**

17. The rain fell with a(n) _____ sound, the same drizzling dribble for hours on end.

18. The mood of "Araby" is gloomy, dank, cheerless—in short, utterly _____.

19. A gloomy, dank, cheerless mood _____ "Araby."

20. Since there is very little dialogue in "Araby," it would be difficult to prove any of the characters _____.

21. It seems to the boy that the houses on his street are like _____ faces, unchanging no matter what happens within them or outside them.

CONSTRUCTED RESPONSE *(16 points)*

22. On a separate sheet of paper, explain how Joyce uses irony to heighten the epiphany in this story. Cite details from the text to support your ideas.

SELECTION TEST ████████   LITERARY RESPONSE AND ANALYSIS

The Rocking-Horse Winner D. H. Lawrence

COMPREHENSION (40 points; 4 points each)

On the line provided, write the letter of the *best* answer to each of the following items.

_____ 1. The opening paragraphs of the story describe a family that is —

    A happy but financially troubled

    B anxious about money, though obviously not living in poverty

    C about to fall apart because of the mother's inattentiveness

    D in mourning for the loss of a relative

_____ 2. Mainly in the first paragraph the story uses the style of —

    F a science fiction story

    G a mystery

    H a horror story

    J a fairy tale

_____ 3. Paul's mother blames the family's troubles on —

    A the Depression

    B Uncle Oscar, who loses money gambling

    C family members who wasted their inheritance

    D Paul's father, who has no luck

_____ 4. Paul's technique for picking horses is to —

    F just guess

    G read the racing forms obsessively

    H learn the horse's name while in an excited trance

    J choose the horses based on their names

_____ 5. How often do the horses Paul bets on turn out to be winners?

    A Always

    B Sometimes

    C Once

    D Rarely

_____ 6. When Paul's mother gets news that she has received money from a relative, she reacts by —

    F being happy and grateful

    G being insulted that the relative thinks she cannot manage by herself

    H greedily asking to receive all the money at once

    J ruining everything by trying to find out the identity of the relative

_____ **7.** Why does Paul place bets?

    A To make his mother happy

    B To earn extra money

    C Because the gardener orders him to

    D To rebel against his parents

_____ **8.** At the end of the story, Paul —

    F dies from exhaustion

    G is able to go to the best college in England

    H is poor and disillusioned

    J has learned an important lesson

_____ **9.** At the end of the story, Paul's mother —

    A is rich

    B is poor

    C appreciates what she has

    D has left her husband

_____ **10.** Which of the following sentences *best* states the main idea, or theme, of the story?

    F Love conquers all.

    G Greed destroys.

    H Honesty is the best policy.

    J Power corrupts.

LITERARY FOCUS: SYMBOL *(20 points; 5 points each)*
On the line provided, write the letter of the *best* answer to each of the following items.

_____ **11.** Which statement about **symbolism** is *true*?

    A Symbols are necessary in any work of literature.

    B A symbol's meaning is always unclear to the reader.

    C A symbol stands both for itself and for something else.

    D A symbol must be an inanimate, nonliving object.

_____ **12.** Which statement about **symbolism** is *false*?

    F An event can be a symbol.

    G A place can be a symbol.

    H A symbol may stand for an idea or emotion.

    J A symbol is usually taken from the writer's childhood.

_____ **13.** The rocking horse in the story *most* likely symbolizes —

    A jealousy

    B materialism

    C evil

    D anger

_____ **14.** How does horse racing symbolize the family's plight?

    F Paul's parents are in an endless race for material fulfillment.

    G Paul's father lost all his money betting on horses.

    H The family members are very competitive with each other.

    J The family puts its faith in Uncle Oscar to save the day.

VOCABULARY DEVELOPMENT *(20 points; 4 points each)*

On the line provided, write the letter of the *best* answer for each of the following items.

_____ **15.** The opposite of <u>obscure</u> is —

    A unknown

    B strong

    C famous

    D weak

_____ **16.** The opposite of <u>uncanny</u> is —

    F weird

    G ordinary

    H foolish

    J humorous

_____ **17.** Someone who is <u>overwrought</u> is —

    A studious

    B calm

    C shy

    D agitated

_____ **18.** An <u>iridescent</u> object —

    F is gaudy

    G melts at low temperatures

    H sparkles

    J is see-through

_____ **19.** If a fact is <u>asserted</u>, it is —

    A declared

    B doubted

    C questioned

    D denied

CONSTRUCTED RESPONSE *(20 points)*

20. On a separate sheet of paper, explain what comment about life you think D. H. Lawrence is making in this story. How does he use symbolism to make this comment? You may cite "D. H. Lawrence on Money" as well as "The Rocking-Horse Winner" in your answer.

SELECTION TEST   **LITERARY RESPONSE AND ANALYSIS**

Lot's Wife *translated by* Richard Wilbur
All the unburied ones *translated by* Judith Hemschemeyer
I am not one of those who left the land
translated by Stanley Kunitz
Anna Akhmatova

COMPREHENSION *(40 points; 4 points each)*
On the line provided, write the letter of the *best* answer to each of the following items.

_____ **1.** Lot and his wife leave their home in Sodom because —

     A they hope for better economic opportunities elsewhere

     B they are not free to practice their religion in Sodom

     C they are horrified by the wickedness of Sodom

     D God warns them of the destruction of Sodom

_____ **2.** What fatal action occurs on the road out of Sodom?

     F Lot looks back, disobeying God's warning.

     G Lot's wife looks back, disobeying God's warning.

     H Lot's wife decides not to leave Sodom.

     J Lot sends his wife back to Sodom on her own.

_____ **3.** Which of the following reasons for Lot's wife's fatal action is suggested in the poem?

     A Lot tricks his wife into turning back toward Sodom.

     B Lot's wife longs for a last glimpse of her native city.

     C Lot's wife stubbornly refuses to believe the warning.

     D Lot asks his wife to turn around to see if anyone is following them.

_____ **4.** What does the speaker of the poem feel about Lot's wife?

     F Lot's wife was a person worth remembering, one who sacrificed much.

     G It would have been better if Lot's wife had survived and Lot had been turned into a pillar of salt.

     H Lot's wife went to her death because of her own folly, so she is not worth mourning for.

     J Lot's wife was an evil resident of a corrupt city and deserved to die.

_____ **5.** In view of Anna Akhmatova's history, it is likely that Sodom in the poem stands for —

     A New York

     B Berlin

     C Russia

     D Hiroshima

6. The dominant emotions expressed in "Lot's Wife" are —

    F love and faith

    G hope and despair

    H determination and courage

    J grief and nostalgia

7. "All the unburied ones" does *not* address the speaker's —

    A weariness after years of mourning

    B faith that she will be remembered after her death

    C anxiety about who will be left to mourn for her

    D pride in her own survival

8. When the speaker speaks of herself as having buried the "unburied ones," she means that she —

    F buried the bodies of her friends murdered by Soviet tyranny

    G only imagined she was burying the unburied

    H has mourned the deaths of many victims

    J wasn't sure who had been killed and who hadn't

9. In the line "I am not one of those who left the land," who are the people who left the land?

    A The Soviets, when they lost the Cold War

    B Lot and his wife, leaving Sodom

    C Those who fled Russia to escape the revolution in 1917

    D The Nazis, when they were driven out of Russia in 1940

10. The speaker's attitude toward "those who left the land" is one of —

    F scorn

    G sympathy

    H indifference

    J love

LITERARY FOCUS: THEME *(40 points; 10 points each)*

On the line provided, write the letter of the *best* answer to each of the following items.

_____ **11.** Which of the following strategies would *not* help you to identify the **theme** in a poem?

    A Tracing the plot, or flow of events

    B Reading and re-reading the poem carefully

    C Asking yourself questions about the poem

    D Identifying what is being said about the subject

_____ **12.** The themes of "Lot's Wife" have *least* to do with the —

    F relationship of a husband and wife

    G longing for one's homeland

    H temptation to disobey a command

    J feelings onlookers have about a victim

_____ **13.** One theme of "All the unburied ones" could be restated as —

    A "Let the dead bury the dead."

    B "In the midst of grief, life must go on."

    C "Those who grieve for others, must someday themselves be grieved for."

    D "Death is not the tragedy it seems to be, but a passage to another state of being."

_____ **14.** The poem "I am not one of those who left the land" implies that —

    F everyone has the right to try to save his or her own life

    G people who remain behind to live under tyranny are better than those who flee to freedom

    H one person's tyranny is another person's revolution

    J justice and mercy demand that we deal fairly with those who differ from us

CONSTRUCTED RESPONSE *(20 points)*

15. Judging from the three poems and from the background information accompanying this selection, how do you think Akhmatova's themes reflect the historical period in which she lived? Write your answer on a separate sheet of paper.

SELECTION TEST   **LITERARY RESPONSE AND ANALYSIS**

The Demon Lover   Elizabeth Bowen

COMPREHENSION *(40 points; 4 points each)*

On the line provided, write the letter of the *best* answer to each of the following items.

_____ **1.** Why is Mrs. Drover's house in London shut up?

 A She can no longer afford to pay property taxes on it.

 B She has moved out because of the bombings.

 C She has left London for the summer season to go to the country.

 D Everyone in the family has gone off to serve in the war.

_____ **2.** Mrs. Drover is —

 F a widow with no children

 G a landlady whose past is a mystery

 H the faithless wife of a cad

 J a middle-aged woman with a husband and three children

_____ **3.** The letter Mrs. Drover finds on the table tells her of —

 A the anniversary of a bygone relationship

 B her birthday

 C news that her fiancé is presumed missing

 D her husband's plans to come home late from work

_____ **4.** Kathleen married William Drover after —

 F many men proposed to her

 G she had broken her engagement to her fiancé

 H she had a fight with her fiancé

 J her fiancé was reported missing and presumed dead

_____ **5.** Kathleen's first fiancé is described as —

 A callous and cold

 B adoring and gracious

 C evil and brilliant

 D hysterical and nervous

_____ **6.** In response to the note she finds in the house, Mrs. Drover decides to —

 F leave in order to avoid a confrontation with her former fiancé

 G confront the letter-writer at the appointed hour

 H call the police

 J seek shelter at a neighbor's house

_____ **7.** Throughout the story, Mrs. Drover is —

    A humming a tune

    B absorbed by loving memories of her first fiancé

    C thinking of her children

    D alone with her thoughts and feelings

_____ **8.** Which of the following statements *best* characterizes the plot of this story?

    F A married woman wonders what it would have been like to have married someone else.

    G An ordinary woman's life changes with the sudden reappearance of a supposedly dead suitor.

    H A woman runs into her former fiancé.

    J An older woman recalls the difficulties of her youth.

_____ **9.** Of the following events, which does Mrs. Drover do *last* in the story?

    A Find a letter

    B Remember her last encounter with the "demon lover"

    C Recognize the taxi driver

    D Pack the items she needs

_____ **10.** The mood of the story can *best* be described as —

    F blissful

    G ominous

    H careless

    J humorous

LITERARY FOCUS: FLASHBACK *(15 points; 5 points each)*

On the line provided, write the letter of the *best* answer to each of the following items.

_____ **11.** **Flashback** is a device that —

    A interrupts the action to describe something that happened earlier

    B prevents the reader from understanding the plot

    C has been little used by writers since World War II

    D breaks the rules of grammar

_____ **12.** Which of the following details about Mrs. Drover is *not* revealed in the story's central flashback?

    F Her former fiancé was a soldier.

    G She was cut by a button on the soldier's uniform.

    H Her fiancé was unwilling to wait for her until the war's end.

    J Her family supported her after her fiancé was presumed dead.

_____ **13.** The use of flashbacks in this story —

    A clearly lays out Mrs. Drover's childhood

    B reveals important historical information about World War I

    C gives you a picture of Mrs. Drover over the years

    D explains the lover's reasons for pursuing Mrs. Drover

READING SKILLS: MODIFYING YOUR PREDICTIONS (5 points)
On the line provided, write the *best* answer to the following item.

_____ **14.** To modify a prediction is to —

    F confirm what you thought would happen

    G adjust or change a guess you made about the plot

    H rewrite a story so that the setting or characters are different

    J be unable to figure out what is going to happen next

VOCABULARY DEVELOPMENT (20 points; 4 points each)
Match the definition on the left with the Vocabulary word on the right. On the line provided, write the letter of the Vocabulary word.

_____ **15.** flowed; came forth   **a.** assent

_____ **16.** ordinary; dull   **b.** emanated

_____ **17.** calmly; indifferently   **c.** prosaic

_____ **18.** acceptance   **d.** intermittent

_____ **19.** starting and stopping at intervals; periodic   **e.** impassively

CONSTRUCTED RESPONSE (20 points)
20. On a separate sheet of paper, explain how Elizabeth Bowen makes use of the literary device of **flashback** to tell her story and make it more effective. Give some examples, and discuss how her development of time and sequence suggests a view or comment about life.

SELECTION TEST ████████████   **LITERARY RESPONSE AND ANALYSIS**

Axolotl   Julio Cortázar *translated by* Paul Blackburn

COMPREHENSION *(40 points; 4 points each)*

On the line provided, write the letter of the *best* answer to each of the following items.

_____ **1.** An axolotl is a kind of —

    A fish

    B bird

    C frog

    D salamander

_____ **2.** The narrator finds axolotls in —

    F a pond

    G Mexico

    H an aquarium

    J his back yard

_____ **3.** The faces of the axolotls are repeatedly described as —

    A bright red

    B lacking expression

    C demonic

    D unintelligent

_____ **4.** Which of the following traits or qualities does the narrator *not* find in the axolotls?

    F A yearning to be saved

    G Saintliness

    H Cruelty

    J Suffering

_____ **5.** The world in which the axolotls move is described as —

    A infinitely slow and remote

    B alive with mystery

    C unpredictable, magical, ever-changing

    D hilariously comic

_____ **6.** When the narrator describes the axolotls' "secret will, to abolish space and time with an indifferent immobility," he is describing the fact that the axolotls —

    F are fierce predators of small fish

    G mate in unusual ways

    H understand more than people do

    J spend a lot of time doing nothing

362

_____ **7.** What does the narrator feel toward the axolotls?

    A A deep, mysterious attraction and sense of kinship

    B A revulsion that he must force himself to overcome

    C Amusement because of their cuteness and liveliness

    D Despair that no one will ever understand them

_____ **8.** At the crucial moment when the narrator turns into an axolotl, he —

    F feels himself growing gills

    G screams in horror

    H is grateful to be an axolotl rather than a man

    J feels no change in himself

_____ **9.** The narrator learns that the other axolotls in the tank —

    A are lacking in his human intelligence and awareness

    B have consciousness just as he does

    C are cannibals and plan to eat him when he isn't looking

    D communicate by means of jolts of electricity sent through the water

_____ **10.** At the end of the story, the narrator finds consolation when he —

    F hopes to resume his human form one day

    G imagines that the human watching him will write a story about him

    H knows that the life span of an axolotl is longer than that of a human being

    J realizes he can turn back into a man whenever he wants

LITERARY FOCUS: MAGIC REALISM *(15 points; 5 points each)*

On the line provided, write the letter of the *best* answer to each of the following items.

_____ **11.** Julio Cortázar defines **magic realism** as —

    A that which is neither real nor unreal

    B that which is both true and false

    C an invasion by the imaginary

    D a departure from the everyday

Axolotl

_____ **12.** Which aspect of the story *most* clearly shows that it is a work of magic realism?

    F The Latin name for axolotl is *Ambystoma*.

    G The axolotl is actually a larval, or immature, creature rather than an adult.

    H The narrator is an axolotl.

    J The axolotls spend much of their time with their eyes pressed to the glass.

_____ **13.** Writers like Cortázar believe that magic realism can be used to expand our rigid concept of —

    A magic

    B reality

    C literature

    D religion

READING SKILLS: IDENTIFYING POINT OF VIEW *(5 points)*

On the line provided, write the letter of the *best* answer to the following item.

_____ **14.** What is unusual about the point of view of the narrator in this story?

    F There is no narrator or point of view.

    G The narrator is an axolotl.

    H It's unclear who or what is narrating the story.

    J The author is also the narrator.

VOCABULARY DEVELOPMENT *(20 points; 4 points each)*

On the line provided, write the letter of the *best* answer to each of the following items.

_____ **15.** If a sheet of paper is <u>translucent</u>, —

    A you can see clear through it

    B you can see partly through it

    C you can't see through it at all

    D it reflects rainbow colors

_____ **16.** A <u>diminutive</u> person is —

    F short

    G old

    H famous

    J forgotten

_____ **17.** A <u>tentative</u> appointment is one that —

    A is very far in the future

    B may be changed

    C intrudes into one's personal time

    D has been canceled

_____ **18.** If you are bothered by the <u>proximity</u> of an animal, you are bothered by its —

    F smell

    G poisonous bite

    H loud noise

    J closeness to you

_____ **19.** Which of these Vocabulary words is a noun rather than an adjective?

    A translucent

    B diminutive

    C tentative

    D proximity

CONSTRUCTED RESPONSE *(20 points)*

20. On a separate sheet of paper, explain how the use of magic realism enhances the meaning of this story. Refer to a specific view or comment on life that you think Cortázar expresses in this story and to the specific "magical" details that help express it.

SELECTION TEST ███████████   LITERARY RESPONSE AND ANALYSIS

The Book of Sand Jorge Luis Borges *translated by* Andrew Hurley

COMPREHENSION *(40 points; 4 points each)*

On the line provided, write the letter of the *best* answer to each of the following items.

_____ **1.** At the beginning of the story, the narrator declares that his tale is —

    A true

    B tragic

    C fictional

    D ironic

_____ **2.** The stranger who comes to the narrator's door is a —

    F seller of Bibles

    G fan of the author's

    H writer of paradoxes

    J criminal on the run

_____ **3.** In approaching the narrator, the stranger's *real* purpose is to —

    A rob him

    B drive him mad

    C get rid of the Book of Sand

    D learn the narrator's secrets

_____ **4.** "The Book of Sand" is written in a language —

    F the narrator has seen in a dream

    G made up entirely of numerals

    H that the narrator can recognize as Arabic

    J whose characters are unfamiliar to the narrator

_____ **5.** Which of the following statements is *not* true about the book?

    A The book consists of an infinite number of pages.

    B A secret code is embedded in the text.

    C Once a page has been turned, relocating it is almost impossible.

    D New pages spring into place at the beginning and end of the book.

_____ **6.** Why is the book called the Book of Sand?

    F The book is literally made of sand.

    G There are as many pages in the book as there are grains of sand on a beach.

    H Neither sand nor the book has a beginning or an end.

    J Only those who understand the nature of sand can understand the book.

_____ **7.** What does the narrator learn from the text of the book?

    A The day of his death

    B The history of the book from the infinite past to the infinite future

    C That everything in the story he is writing is predicted in the Book of Sand

    D Nothing, since he cannot read the words

_____ **8.** What happens to the narrator after he buys the Book of Sand?

    F He becomes obsessed by the book, then disgusted by it.

    G His wishes come true—but at a heavy price.

    H He kills the stranger who sold it to him.

    J His life is ruined forever.

_____ **9.** Why does the narrator decide not to burn the book?

    A He is hopelessly enslaved by it.

    B He still hopes to learn from it.

    C He promised the stranger he would not destroy it.

    D It might cause a fire that would burn for all eternity.

_____ **10.** In this story, Borges —

    F playfully speculates about infinity and knowledge

    G avoids the use of a plot

    H uses a narrator who lacks any identifying traits

    J claims that all books are infinite

LITERARY FOCUS: PARADOX *(15 points; 5 points each)*
On the line provided, write the letter of the *best* answer to each of the following items.

_____ **11.** A **paradox** is a statement that —

    A is both new and old at the same time

    B contains two seemingly contradictory truths

    C can be believed but not proven

    D is so mysterious it can't be solved

_____ **12.** What is the key paradox in "The Book of Sand"?

    F The book turns out to be made of sand.

    G The book both does and does not belong to the narrator.

    H The book is finite but has an infinite number of pages.

    J The narrator feels he is as monstrous as the book.

_____ **13.** The narrator sees a paradox in the fact that —

    A he loves and hates the book at the same time

    B he cannot understand the book until he understands it

    C the book is not made of sand yet it is like sand

    D the book is true and also not true

READING SKILLS: MAKING PREDICTIONS *(5 points)*

On the line provided, write the letter of the *best* answer to the following item.

_____ **14.** Based on the ending of the story, what is the *most* likely prediction about what will happen to the Book of Sand?

    F The narrator will keep it.

    G Years, even decades, will pass before anyone finds the book.

    H The narrator will give it to a stranger he sees on the street.

    J The book will be destroyed when an earthquake destroys the library.

VOCABULARY DEVELOPMENT *(25 points; 5 points each)*

On the line provided, write the Vocabulary word from the list below that *best* completes each statement.

pedantic	**discomfiture**	**caste**	**defiled**
diabolic	**bibliophile**	**misanthropy**	**artifice**

15. The narrator, a dry, learned, very correct person, is aware that his own tone is

sometimes _____.

16. The narrator is a bookseller and book lover, and the stranger who visits him is also a

_____.

17. It may seem like _____ when a person lives alone, never going out, seeing no fellow human beings.

18. A magical creation such as the Book of Sand may seem to some to be threatening,

dangerous, even _____

19. The narrator came to feel that the Book of Sand was an obscene, nightmarish thing,

that it _____ reality.

368

Holt Assessment: Literature, Reading, and Vocabulary

CONSTRUCTED RESPONSE *(15 points)*

20. This story centers on paradox. On a separate piece of paper, describe how the author makes use of this literary device to convey his ideas. Choose two paradoxes from the story, and discuss their use. Cite specific examples from the story in your answer.

SELECTION TEST ▓▓▓▓▓▓ **LITERARY RESPONSE AND ANALYSIS**

B. Wordsworth V. S. Naipaul

COMPREHENSION *(40 points; 4 points each)*
On the line provided, write the letter of the *best* answer to each of the following items.

_____ **1.** The narrator first meets B. Wordsworth when the poet —

    A asks the narrator to do him a favor

    B teaches the narrator how to fish

    C begs a favor from the narrator's family

    D steals from the narrator's house

_____ **2.** What activity do the boy and B. Wordsworth first enjoy together?

    F Outwitting the boy's mother

    G Running through the woods

    H Writing poems

    J Observing nature

_____ **3.** How does the narrator's mother treat her son?

    A In a kindly way

    B In a strict way

    C Permissively

    D Neglectfully

_____ **4.** The narrator learns that B. Wordsworth lets his garden grow wild —

    F in memory of his wife and unborn child

    G in celebration of the wildness of nature

    H because this setting inspires him to write

    J because he has no time for unimportant things

_____ **5.** Of the following possibilities, which was *not* a lesson the narrator learned from B. Wordsworth?

    A Poets appreciate even the most ordinary things.

    B Poets get emotional over everything.

    C The narrator has poetry in him.

    D B. Wordsworth really was the world's greatest poet.

_____ **6.** *Most* likely the narrator thinks that B. Wordsworth is —

    F no different than other adults

    G awkward around people

    H interesting and kind

    J overbearing and harsh

_____ **7.** B. Wordsworth is writing his great poem —

    A carefully but quickly

    B image by image

    C one line per month

    D one word at a time

_____ **8.** B. Wordsworth's manner of speaking is —

    F careful and precise

    G filled with slang

    H metaphorical

    J difficult to understand

_____ **9.** The narrator is filled with wonder at B. Wordsworth's wisdom when B. Wordsworth —

    A recites the line, "The past is deep"

    B refuses to say whether a pin dropped into water will sink or float

    C swears the narrator to secrecy about the fruit trees

    D reveals how to make a living singing

_____ **10.** When B. Wordsworth dies, he gives the narrator his —

    F house and land

    G fame

    H influence

    J writings

LITERARY FOCUS: SETTING *(20 points; 5 points each)*

On the line provided, write the letter of the *best* answer to each of the following items.

_____ **11.** The setting of this story is a —

    A desert

    B mountain range

    C rain forest

    D tropical island

_____ **12.** How does the setting contribute to the story?

    F   B. Wordsworth's attentiveness to the world around him makes the setting an important part of the story.

    G   The setting is essential, since the story is about the history of Trinidad.

    H   The narrator's love of fresh mangoes is central to the story.

    J   The setting is used as a beautiful background that the characters never notice.

_____ **13.** How does dialogue help enhance the setting in this story?

    A   Most of the descriptions of the setting take place in the form of conversation.

    B   The narrator and his mother speak a vernacular which is particular to this setting.

    C   It is in dialogue that the name "Miguel Street" first appears in the story.

    D   B. Wordsworth and the narrator carry on an extended discussion about the merits of the place they live.

_____ **14.** Which literary element contributes *most* to establishing the setting in this story?

    F   Character

    G   Imagery

    H   Theme

    J   Plot

VOCABULARY DEVELOPMENT *(20 points; 4 points each)*

On the line provided, write the letter of the *best* answer to each of the following items.

_____ **15.** Botanical means having to do with —

    A   plants

    B   animals

    C   minerals

    D   sea life

_____ **16.** Which of the following activities is an example of a rite?

    F   Freedom of speech

    G   Communion at church

    H   Making a turn at a red light

    J   Waking up and getting dressed

_____ **17.** If you patronize a certain shop, you —

    A   avoid it

    B   own it

    C   work in it

    D   buy from it

_____ **18.** To <u>distill</u> an experience is to —

    F improve it

    G elaborate upon it

    H draw out its essence

    J express it in simple words

_____ **19.** Two possible antonyms for this word are _boycott_ and _shun_. What is the word?

    A botanical

    B rite

    C patronize

    D distill

CONSTRUCTED RESPONSE _(20 points)_

20. On a separate piece of paper, explain how you think the theme and the setting of this story are related. Do you think it would be the same story in another setting? Support your ideas with evidence from the text.

B. Wordsworth

SELECTION TEST ████████

LITERARY RESPONSE AND ANALYSIS

Half a Day Naguib Mahfouz *translated by* Denys Johnson-Davies

COMPREHENSION *(40 points; 4 points each)*
On the line provided, write the letter of the *best* answer to each of the following items.

_____ 1. Getting ready for his first day of school, the narrator feels —

    A expectant

    B proud

    C anxious

    D ashamed

_____ 2. The narrator's father takes him to school and tells the boy that he will now —

    F begin to live

    G learn a trade

    H learn to read

    J know fear

_____ 3. The woman in charge tells the children to think of school as —

    A a kind of prison

    B the best years of their lives

    C their new home

    D a lifeboat in a storm

_____ 4. The narrator's first reaction to school is to —

    F try to hide under a desk

    G feel like a stranger who is lost

    H think it looks familiar

    J dislike the teacher

_____ 5. As the school day goes on, the narrator learns that school is —

    A filled with danger

    B no place to sleep

    C like military training

    D difficult as well as fun

_____ 6. What happens when the narrator leaves school?

    F His father is not waiting for him.

    G He sees his father running toward him.

    H He sees his father in the distance.

    J His father is talking to his teacher.

_____ **7.** The walk to school and the walk away from school is the contrast between —

    A garden-lined streets and a huge city

    B garden-lined streets and bomb craters

    C a busy city and a desert

    D a city and a circus

_____ **8.** As the narrator walks toward home, he sees —

    F hills of garbage

    G high buildings

    H security troops

    J all of the above

_____ **9.** After school, a young man helps the narrator cross the street and calls him —

    A a baby

    B grandpa

    C stupid

    D a little soldier

_____ **10.** By the end of the story, the author makes half a day represent a —

    F whole day

    G school year

    H lifetime

    J war

LITERARY FOCUS: FORESHADOWING _(20 points; 5 points each)_

On the line provided, write the letter of the _best_ answer to each of the following items.

_____ **11. Foreshadowing** is the author's use of —

    A clues to what will happen later

    B vivid descriptions of settings

    C characters who reveal their thoughts and feelings

    D shifting time sequences in a plot

_____ **12.** Foreshadowing usually consists of either —

    F dialogue or characters' thoughts

    G a happy ending or an ending that results in insight

    H internal or external conflict

    J specific events or more subtle atmospheric touches

_____ **13.** What is foreshadowed by the fact that the children form "an intricate pattern in the great courtyard"?

    A The children have been told where to stand and how to behave.

    B The narrator is standing outside the pattern, observing.

    C The course of a life is complicated and is interrelated with other lives.

    D Some of the children will die young; others will live to old age.

_____ **14.** What do the "dust-laden winds and unexpected accidents" in the school yard foreshadow?

    F School will be dismissed early that day.

    G Life's lessons will include painful experiences as well as pleasant ones.

    H The teachers will not be able to control their classes.

    J The narrator's father will be late picking him up after school.

VOCABULARY DEVELOPMENT *(20 points; 4 points each)*

Match the definition on the left with the Vocabulary word on the right. On the line provided, write the letter of the Vocabulary word.

_____ **15.** lamentable

_____ **16.** undamaged; unspoiled

_____ **17.** benefit; advantage

_____ **18.** full of elaborate details or parts

_____ **19.** trash

a. unmarred

b. pitiable

c. intricate

d. avail

e. refuse

CONSTRUCTED RESPONSE *(20 points)*

20. Author Naguib Mahfouz uses two parallel time sequences in this very brief story. On a separate piece of paper, explain what they are and how Mahfouz uses them to make his story more meaningful.

SELECTION TEST   LITERARY RESPONSE AND ANALYSIS

Digging Seamus Heaney

COMPREHENSION *(40 points; 4 points each)*

On the line provided, write the letter of the *best* answer to each of the following items.

_____ 1. As he speaks, the speaker in "Digging" is —

    A digging up earth for potatoes

    B digging for valuable metals

    C conversing with his elders

    D sitting, looking out the window

_____ 2. The word in the title refers both to digging in the earth and to —

    F understanding, appreciating

    G plowing the seas

    H dissecting bodies

    J cutting harvest crops

_____ 3. The father and the grandfather described in the poem are —

    A poets

    B miners

    C farmers

    D unemployed laborers

_____ 4. The father and grandfather seem to be —

    F energetic and hard-working

    G thoughtful and creative

    H cautious and shy

    J hostile and dangerous

_____ 5. The speaker regards his ancestors with —

    A ironic disrespect

    B amazement and disbelief

    C embarrassment and shame

    D awe and admiration

_____ 6. In this poem the act of digging is described —

    F as if it were easy work

    G in minute physical detail

    H by an experienced digger

    J by someone who knows little about it

_____ **7.** Line 4, "When the spade sinks into gravelly ground," contains an example of —

    A alliteration

    B symbolism

    C conflict

    D rhyme

_____ **8.** Two lines that rhyme in this poem are —

    F 1 and 3

    G 1 and 2

    H 2 and 3

    J 3 and 4

_____ **9.** Which words from the poem alliterate *best* with the word *squat*?

    A pen/rests

    B nicking/neatly

    C rump/bends

    D scatter/squelch

_____ **10.** For the speaker, the act of writing —

    F is a betrayal of his father and grandfather

    G is not as honorable as the act of digging

    H honors his father and grandfather

    J is a way of fleeing from his past

LITERARY FOCUS: EXTENDED METAPHOR (40 points; 10 points each)

On the line provided, write the letter of the *best* answer to each of the following items.

_____ **11.** A **metaphor** is a kind of —

    A stanza

    B simile

    C comparison

    D poem

_____ **12.** An **extended metaphor** —

    F is a metaphor that cannot be expressed in words alone

    G is carried out over several lines or through a whole poem

    H is limited to a single sharp detail

    J must have rhythm and rhyme

_____ **13.** The extended metaphor in "Digging" is an implied comparison between the —

  A speaker's grandfather and father

  B beauty of a garden and the ugliness of a bog

  C speaker's work and the work of his father and grandfather

  D father's peat and the speaker's potatoes

_____ **14.** Two objects that figure *most* prominently in the extended metaphor in this poem are a —

  F hand and a mind

  G pen and a sword

  H spade and a pen

  J shovel and a rake

CONSTRUCTED RESPONSE *(20 points)*

15. Write a paragraph on a separate sheet of paper explaining how the extended metaphor in "Digging" conveys the author's meaning. Use at least two examples from the poem to illustrate what the speaker "unearths."

LITERARY RESPONSE AND ANALYSIS

The Doll's House Katherine Mansfield

COMPREHENSION (40 points; 4 points each)

On the line provided, write the letter of the *best* answer to each of the following items.

_____ **1.** What do the Burnell girls' parents dislike about the school their daughters attend?

    A It is too far for the girls to walk to.

    B The teachers do not have advanced degrees.

    C The grading system is too easy.

    D Girls and boys of all social classes go to the same school.

_____ **2.** Else Kelvey could be described as —

    F proud and haughty

    G simpleminded and meek

    H ordinary and kind

    J intelligent and forceful

_____ **3.** The *main* difference between the Burnells and the Kelveys is that the Kelveys —

    A are less polite

    B eat better

    C belong to a lower social class

    D do better in school

_____ **4.** In comparison to her sisters Isabel and Lottie, Kezia Burnell is —

    F more independent

    G richer

    H more snobbish

    J prettier

_____ **5.** Which of the following statements is the *clearest* example of snobbery in the story?

    A Students from the same area attend the same school.

    B The Burnell girls are not allowed to speak to the Kelvey girls.

    C Mrs. Hay sends the Burnells a doll's house.

    D Else finally is allowed to see the doll's house.

_____ **6.** The girls in the story consider the boys to be —

    F rough and rude

    G interesting and alien

    H fascinating and cute

    J puzzling and disturbing

Holt Assessment: Literature, Reading, and Vocabulary

_____ **7.** Why does Aunt Beryl feel better after she chases away the Kelveys and scolds Kezia?

    A She believes children should be scolded regularly.

    B It distracts her from her problems.

    C It will win the approval of Mrs. Burnell.

    D She enjoys disciplining children as well as adults.

_____ **8.** How does Lil act toward her younger sister Else?

    F She bullies Else.

    G She acts like a stranger to Else.

    H She treats Else as an equal.

    J She protects Else.

_____ **9.** Kezia sneaks out the back door of the house to —

    A go to school early

    B hide from Aunt Beryl

    C avoid having to meet company

    D steal the lamp from the doll's house

_____ **10.** Kezia's behavior toward the Kelveys is different than everyone else's because she —

    F has been friends with the Kelveys for a long while

    G wants to include the Kelveys while everyone else wants to exclude them

    H hates the Kelveys while everyone else is indifferent to them

    J wants to improve the Kelveys' lot in life

LITERARY FOCUS: SYMBOLISM AND THE MODERN SHORT STORY *(20 points; 5 points each)*
On the line provided, write the letter of the *best* answer to each of the following items.

_____ **11.** The Burnell girls eat mutton sandwiches, but the Kelvey girls eat jam sandwiches. The latter detail *most* likely symbolizes —

    A hunger

    B stinginess

    C poverty

    D thoughtlessness

_____ **12.** For the Kelvey girls, the doll's house probably symbolizes —

    F a beautiful, remote world of wealth

    G the smallness of their ordinary lives

    H the grownup world which they will someday enter

    J the carefree childhood they have left behind

_____ **13.** Like most modern short stories, "The Doll's House" —

    A has a fast-paced plot

    B uses a trick ending

    C is unrealistic

    D indirectly states psychological truths

_____ **14.** Dramatic irony, a common feature of the modern short story, occurs at the end of "The Doll's House" when —

    F the Kelveys accept Kezia's invitation

    G Kezia realizes she made a mistake by inviting the Kelveys

    H Kezia shows the Kelveys the doll's house

    J Aunt Beryl fails to understand Kezia's treatment of the Kelveys

VOCABULARY DEVELOPMENT *(20 points; 4 points each)*

On the line provided, write the Vocabulary word from the list below that has a similar meaning to the italicized word or phrase in the sentence. One word will be used twice.

    congealed   **conspicuous**   **flagged**   **clambered**

_____ **15.** Interest in the doll's house *declined* after almost everyone had seen it.

_____ **16.** The varnish had *thickened* on the door of the doll's house.

_____ **17.** The poverty of the Kelvey girls made them *attract attention*.

_____ **18.** Kezia *climbed clumsily* onto the gate.

_____ **19.** Aunt Beryl was very upset at first, but then her anxiety *lost its strength*.

CONSTRUCTED RESPONSE *(20 points)*

20. On a separate sheet of paper, explain how symbolism in "The Doll's House" shows Katherine Mansfield's view of life. Discuss two specific symbols.

SELECTION TEST ▮▮▮▮▮▮▮▮▮▮   **LITERARY RESPONSE AND ANALYSIS**

Musée des Beaux Arts   W. H. Auden

COMPREHENSION *(40 points; 4 points each)*

On the line provided, write the letter of the *best* answer to each of the following items.

_____ **1.** The title of this poem provides the reader with the —

     A   subject of the poem

     B   key to Auden's symbolism

     C   setting of the poem's inspiration

     D   idea that poetry belongs in museums

_____ **2.** The poem is a description of and response to —

     F   a shipwreck

     G   a painting

     H   the speaker's life

     J   European history

_____ **3.** Which word at the end of a line does *not* rhyme with any other end-word in this poem?

     A   wrong

     B   place

     C   away

     D   green

_____ **4.** A technical characteristic that marks this poem as modern is the —

     F   emphasis on human suffering

     G   respect for great art

     H   use of varying line lengths and flexible meter

     J   knowledge of Greek mythology

_____ **5.** The tone of this poem could *best* be described as —

     A   thoughtful

     B   anxious

     C   argumentative

     D   whimsical

_____ **6.** What is the main idea, or theme, that the poem expresses about life?

     F   Society in general is unconcerned about individual suffering.

     G   We are all brothers and sisters and must help one another.

     H   The idea "love thy neighbor" is powerful and is the subject of much great art.

     J   Martyrdom is not worth it and is only sought by confused, deluded people.

_____ **7.** The poem implies that great art makes the world seem —

  A pleasant and comfortable

  B endlessly horrible

  C both beautiful and terrible

  D cold and indifferent

_____ **8.** What does the poem say about the plowman?

  F He is unaware of Icarus's fall, or he would have gone to help.

  G He is an enemy of Icarus and is glad to see the boy fall.

  H It is possible he is aware of Icarus's fall but does not care about it.

  J The plowman is an unimportant detail added just to fill space.

_____ **9.** Which details contrast with, rather than reinforce, the poem's main point about suffering and indifference?

  A People laughing

  B People waiting for a miracle

  C Children joking

  D The sun rising

_____ **10.** What fact about this poem is actually a piece of evidence against the poem's main point about suffering?

  F The poem tries to make suffering seem unimportant or lighthearted.

  G The speaker himself takes suffering seriously and makes it the focal point of his poem.

  H The phrase "something amazing" implies that the people on the ship did see Icarus fall.

  J The poem's language is too delicately pretty to make suffering seem real.

LITERARY FOCUS: DICTION *(40 points; 10 points each)*
On the line provided, write the letter of the *best* answer to each of the following items.

_____ **11.** Another term for **diction** is —

  A imagery

  B figures of speech

  C rhythm

  D word choice

_____ **12.** W. H. Auden is known for diction that —

    F compares the ordinary to the bizarre

    G takes liberties with traditional English metric forms

    H tries to make the reader go to the dictionary

    J combines the everyday and the poetic levels of language

_____ **13.** The quotation that contains informal, down-to-earth diction is —

    A "About suffering they were never wrong"

    B "reverently, passionately waiting / For the miraculous birth"

    C "the sun shone / As it had to on the white legs disappearing into the green / Water"

    D "the dogs go on with their doggy life"

_____ **14.** The quotation that contains an example of formal, elegant diction is —

    F "the plowman may / Have heard the splash"

    G "the torturer's horse / Scratches its innocent behind on a tree"

    H "someone else is eating or opening a window"

    J "That even the dreadful martyrdom must run its course"

CONSTRUCTED RESPONSE *(20 points)*

15. Auden, writing in the middle of the twentieth century, used a Renaissance landscape painting as a topic for observations on human suffering. How well do you think his poem makes a comment on twentieth-century life, and why? What aspects of the poem might be as much about Auden's time as about Pieter Bruegel's? Discuss these topics on a separate sheet of paper.

| SELECTION TEST ▮▮▮ | LITERARY RESPONSE AND ANALYSIS |

Fear Gabriela Mistral *translated by* Doris Dana

COMPREHENSION *(40 points; 4 points each)*

On the line provided, write the letter of the *best* answer to each of the following items.

_____ **1.** The fear referred to in the title is felt by —

    A the mother

    B the daughter

    C people in the outside world

    D the reader

_____ **2.** The essential subject of the poem is a —

    F child's wish to escape her home

    G poor person's wish to escape poverty

    H poet's ambition to find exactly the right words for an emotion

    J mother's worry about her child growing up

_____ **3.** The speaker of the poem sees the world outside her community as —

    A hazardous

    B friendly

    C unimportant

    D wicked

_____ **4.** In saying that she doesn't want her little girl to become a swallow, the speaker means that she doesn't want —

    F to have to become a swallow, too

    G her little girl to travel far away from her

    H her little girl to be placed in a zoo for people to look at

    J her little girl to be less intelligent than she is now

_____ **5.** What disadvantage does the speaker see in being a princess?

    A A princess, being female, has relatively little chance of ruling a kingdom.

    B Princesses are generally married off to princes whom they have never met.

    C Princesses spend their childhoods in a "fishbowl," as objects of public attention.

    D A princess cannot play freely outdoors.

_____ **6.** Which of the following does the speaker *not* like to do for her daughter?

    F Comb her hair

    G Rock her

    H Sleep by her side

    J Try to advance her fortunes in the world

_____ **7.** According to the speaker, if her daughter became a queen, then —

    A the speaker would rescue her from the castle

    B the speaker would at last admit that it was a good thing

    C the speaker would never be able to see her daughter

    D her daughter would be the best queen their land had ever known

_____ **8.** "Fear" is a lyric poem because it —

    F is short

    G is intended to be sung to music

    H is about an individual's emotions

    J has a refrain

_____ **9.** The form of the poem is —

    A a sonnet

    B free verse

    C a ballad

    D a metrical ode

_____ **10.** The dominant tone or attitude of the speaker is —

    F anxious

    G joyous

    H sarcastic

    J grief-stricken

LITERARY FOCUS: REFRAIN *(40 points; 10 points each)*

On the line provided, write the letter of the *best* answer to each of the following items.

_____ **11.** Which of the following elements, when repeated, does not create a refrain?

    A A consonant sound

    B A word or phrase

    C A line

    D A group of lines

_____ **12. Refrains** are found —

    F only in the last lines of a poem or stanza

    G only in pre-modern poems

    H anywhere, but usually at the end of a stanza

    J in the couplets of sonnets

_____ **13.** How many lines in each stanza of "Fear" are used for the refrain?

    A Two

    B Four

    C Six

    D Eight

_____ **14.** The wording of the refrain in "Fear" —

    F varies slightly from stanza to stanza

    G is exactly the same in each stanza

    H changes in level of diction but not in meaning

    J changes in tone and mood

CONSTRUCTED RESPONSE *(20 points)*

15. On a separate piece of paper, compare and contrast the emotions of the speaker of this poem with the emotions evoked in you as a reader of the poem. Point to specific images and aspects of style that convey the speaker's emotions and that evoke your emotions.

SELECTION TEST   **LITERARY RESPONSE AND ANALYSIS**

Fern Hill Dylan Thomas

COMPREHENSION *(40 points; 4 points each)*

On the line provided, write the letter of the *best* answer to each of the following items.

_____ **1.** The speaker describes his childhood as being —

    A endless and boring

    B golden and carefree

    C harsh but happy

    D joyful despite his illness

_____ **2.** At the end of the poem, time is portrayed as —

    F friendly

    G merciless

    H forgiving

    J protective

_____ **3.** Which of the following statements *best* characterizes the speaker's depiction of a child's sense of being in the world?

    A The world is a child's playground.

    B The world's activities are overwhelming to a child.

    C A child is happiest among other children.

    D Children need to be provided with suitable entertainment by adults.

_____ **4.** "Fern Hill" concerns the speaker's childhood experiences —

    F in the woods

    G at the seashore

    H in the country

    J in the city

_____ **5.** Dylan Thomas plays with a common fairy-tale opening in his phrase —

    A "now as I was young and easy"

    B "once below a time"

    C "golden in the mercy of his means"

    D "it was running, it was lovely"

_____ **6.** In line 23, the phrase "simple stars" implies that —

    F a child's view of the world is simpler than an adult's

    G fewer stars were known to science during Thomas's childhood than in later years

    H most stars are made of a few simple chemical elements

    J the stars are actually complex—Thomas is being ironic

_____ **7.** What does "as I rode to sleep the owls were bearing the farm away" (line 24) mean?

    A Owls are predatory birds who may snatch small animals from farms.

    B Owls do not know or care about such human pursuits as farming.

    C When he heard the owls, the boy became more interested in them than in the farm.

    D The boy fell asleep and thus traveled "away" from the farm to the hooting of owls.

_____ **8.** Stanza four makes several allusions to the Biblical account of the creation of the world. Which of the following quotations from the stanza is *not* an allusion to that event?

    F "the farm, like a wanderer white / With the dew"

    G "it was all / Shining, it was Adam and maiden"

    H "So it must have been after the birth of the simple light"

    J "In the first, spinning place, . . . / On to the fields of praise."

_____ **9.** "My wishes raced through the house high hay" (line 41) is a figurative description of —

    A running through a new house for the first time

    B cutting hay on a farm

    C filling a house with hay

    D running among high haystacks

_____ **10.** The last two stanzas of the poem express the speaker's —

    F urgency about preserving nature

    G certainty that death can be conquered

    H childhood innocence

    J adult disillusionment

LITERARY FOCUS: LYRIC POETRY *(40 points; 10 points each)*

On the line provided, write the letter of the *best* answer to each of the following items.

_____ **11.** The characteristic of "Fern Hill" that is *most* typical of lyric poetry is —

    A metrical variation

    B a focus on emotions and thoughts

    C irregular rhyme scheme

    D an emphasis on storytelling

_____ **12.** Lines 28–32 express the speaker's feeling of being a child in that they —

    F depict the days as long and repetitive

    G express how day and night blur together

    H show how every day is new and fascinating

    J portray a child's deep suspicion of the world

_____ **13.** Thomas's phrases "all the sun long" (line 19) and "all the moon long" (line 25) are lyrical ways of saying —

    A "the sun is far away, and so is the moon"

    B "night and day are of different lengths at different times of year"

    C "all day" and "all night"

    D small children cannot tell time

_____ **14.** Which of the following lines contains both alliteration and assonance?

    F "And the sun grew round that very day."

    G "Up to the swallow thronged loft by the shadow of my hand, . . ."

    H "About the lilting house and happy as the grass was green, . . ."

    J "Golden in the mercy of his means, . . ."

CONSTRUCTED RESPONSE *(20 points)*

15. The last two stanzas turn the poem from its idyllic portrayal of childhood to a contrasting view. On a separate sheet of paper, analyze the meaning of the final stanza and how it adds a more complex view of life to the poem.

SELECTION TEST ███████████████   LITERARY RESPONSE AND ANALYSIS

Do Not Go Gentle into That Good Night Dylan Thomas

COMPREHENSION *(40 points; 4 points each)*

On the line provided, write the letter of the *best* answer to each of the following items.

_____ 1. This poem is addressed to the speaker's —

   A   mother

   B   father

   C   brother

   D   grandfather

_____ 2. The speaker states that wise men and good men —

   F   accept death peacefully

   G   pray before dying

   H   believe in life after death

   J   do not accept death without a fight

_____ 3. "Because their words have forked no lightning" (line 5) implies that —

   A   human wisdom has only a limited power

   B   even the strongest tyrant cannot control the weather

   C   words in the final analysis cannot really achieve anything

   D   beauty is less important than power

_____ 4. The lines "crying how bright / Their frail deeds might have danced in a green bay" is a figure of speech comparing human deeds to —

   F   lighthouses

   G   a body of water

   H   fishing lures

   J   sailboats

_____ 5. In this poem, light symbolizes —

   A   happiness

   B   change

   C   heat

   D   life

_____ 6. In lines 10–11, what do the wild men learn?

   F   That their glorious recklessness kept them alive

   G   That their wild ways hastened their death

   H   That escaping death is as impossible as catching the sun

   J   To sing about their own deaths

_____ 7. At the end of the day, the speaker asks his listener to —

    A cry before dying

    B curse the speaker rather than giving in to gentleness

    C avoid any negative feelings while dying

    D refuse to become sicker

_____ 8. According to the poem, to accept calmly the approach of death —

    F would be to give up on living

    G is the only realistic way to respond

    H is the choice of the wisest people

    J has been the practice of many cultures, including the ancient Welsh

_____ 9. Dylan Thomas uses the word *grave* in line 13 as a pun to mean both serious and —

    A headed for the grave

    B gravediggers

    C dead men

    D blind men with special powers

_____ 10. The "sad height" that is figuratively referred to in line 16 is the —

    F highest point of human endeavor

    G hills of Wales

    H cliff-edge of death

    J saddest day in the speaker's life

LITERARY FOCUS: ELEGY AND VILLANELLE (40 points; 10 points each)

On the line provided, write the letter of the *best* answer to each of the following items.

_____ 11. Traditionally an **elegy** is —

    A reserved for public figures

    B a poem of mourning

    C a poem with a strict rhyme scheme

    D an ancient Persian form

_____ 12. This poem is an example of an elegy because it —

    F is ironic

    G rhymes

    H expresses grief

    J expresses joy

_____ **13.** Which of the following items is *not* a feature of a **villanelle**?

    A The first and last stanzas of the poem are identical.

    B It contains nineteen lines.

    C The entire poem uses only two end-rhyme sounds.

    D The first and third lines of the poem are repeated at specified points.

_____ **14.** The last stanza of a villanelle is always different from the preceding stanzas in that it —

    F raises the poem to a new level of insight

    G summarizes or restates the main idea of the poem

    H uses a different meter than the other stanzas

    J has one more line than the other stanzas

CONSTRUCTED RESPONSE *(20 points)*

15. On a separate piece of paper, identify the main emotion or feeling of "Do Not Go Gentle into That Good Night," and describe how two or more figures of speech help evoke that feeling.

SELECTION TEST	██████████	LITERARY RESPONSE AND ANALYSIS

Sonnet 79 / Soneto 79 Pablo Neruda *translated by* Stephen Tapscott

COMPREHENSION *(40 points; 4 points each)*

On the line provided, write the letter of the *best* answer to each of the following items.

_____ **1.** In this poem the capitalized word *Love* refers to —

    A the ancient goddess Aphrodite, or Venus

    B love considered as an abstract idea

    C a person's name

    D the speaker's beloved

_____ **2.** In a simile in the first stanza, the speaker compares two hearts to —

    F two doves flying

    G two halves of a double drum

    H darkness and daylight

    J a double-trunked tree

_____ **3.** The image of pounding in the darkness, in the first stanza, appeals *mostly* to the sense of —

    A sight

    B hearing

    C touch

    D smell

_____ **4.** Which of the following is sleep *not* compared to in the second stanza?

    F Winter

    G Fire

    H Something that cuts

    J A railroad train

_____ **5.** The figures of speech for sleep in the second stanza combine to create a mood that could *best* be called —

    A eerie

    B calm

    C rollicking

    D careless

_____ **6.** According to the third stanza, why is the speaker so intent on being united in love?

    F He feels it is the only way to see into the eternal.

    G As an experienced diplomat, he is disgusted by the outside world.

    H He feels that a good marriage is necessary to a healthy emotional life.

    J He seeks love as a protection from what frightens him at night.

Holt Assessment: Literature, Reading, and Vocabulary

_____ **7.** In line 9, the "purer motion" is purer than the —

    A speaker's love

    B motion of the train in the previous stanza

    C rhythm of a sonnet

    D beating of swan's wings

_____ **8.** If you were translating this poem from Spanish into English, instead of *constancy* (line 10), you might have chosen any of the following words *except* —

    F firmness

    G fickleness

    H steadiness

    J faithfulness

_____ **9.** In the last stanza the speaker asserts that love —

    A answers the difficult questions of life and death

    B is not by itself a sufficient philosophy

    C exists only in certain times, places, and cultures

    D is hard to find and worth any sacrifice

_____ **10.** You can immediately tell that this poem is a Petrarchan sonnet because of its —

    F rhyme scheme

    G subject

    H form

    J tone

LITERARY FOCUS: METAPHOR *(40 points; 10 points each)*
On the line provided, write the letter of the *best* answer to each of the following items.

_____ **11.** Neruda's poem is full of **metaphors**, that are —

    A similes

    B figures of speech that cannot be proven

    C comparisons that do not use connecting words such as *like* or *as*

    D comparisons that use connecting words such as *like* or *as*

_____ **12.** Poets use metaphors in order to —

    F suggest more than a literal statement can say

    G make their poems more complex, requiring interpretation and criticism

    H make their poems longer so as to fill out the requirements of sonnet length

    J demonstrate that the essence of poetry cannot be translated

_____ **13.** Which of the following descriptions of sleep is *not* a metaphor?

    A "Night travel"

    B "black flame of sleep"

    C Snipping "the threads of the earth's grapes"

    D "punctual as a headlong train that would haul / shadows and cold rocks"

_____ **14.** In the final stanza the speaker metaphorically compares sleep to —

    F the questioning sky

    G a key

    H an open door

    J a shadow

CONSTRUCTED RESPONSE *(20 points)*

15. Choose a figure of speech that Neruda uses to describe himself and his lover in this poem. On a separate piece of paper, explain the figure of speech, and state whether or not you agree with its presentation of love, and why.

SELECTION TEST   **LITERARY RESPONSE AND ANALYSIS**

Like the Sun R. K. Narayan

COMPREHENSION *(40 points; 4 points each)*

On the line provided, write the letter of the *best* answer to each of the following items.

_____ **1.** At the beginning of the story, Sekhar resolves to —

     A tell the truth for the rest of his life

     B tell the truth to those people he cares most about

     C tell the truth for one day

     D be truthful to himself above all

_____ **2.** What is Sekhar's profession?

     F Musician

     G Teacher

     H Music critic

     J School principal

_____ **3.** Sekhar first tries out his experiment when he —

     A pretends he likes his wife's cooking

     B tells his children he cannot take them out that evening

     C asks the headmaster for extra time

     D tells his wife he does not like the meal she prepared for him

_____ **4.** Who does Sekhar tell about his experiment?

     F His wife

     G His children

     H The headmaster

     J No one

_____ **5.** Sekhar's resolution forces him to —

     A criticize a colleague who has just died

     B leave home for a day

     C shirk the task of grading papers

     D skip a concert he had looked forward to

_____ **6.** The headmaster's personality could be *best* described as —

     F brutally tyrannical

     G bossy but pathetic

     H not assertive

     J unreadable as a blank sheet of paper

_____ **7.** The headmaster practices music because he —

    A is very talented

    B makes a living at it

    C wishes to forget his troubles

    D comes from a family of fine musicians

_____ **8.** The author's attitude toward Sekhar and toward the headmaster could *best* be described as —

    F harshly critical

    G enthusiastically approving

    H sternly disapproving

    J affectionately mocking

_____ **9.** The title of the story means that —

    A the sun is the giver of all life

    B the ups and downs of human existence are as predictable as sunrise and sunset

    C truth, like the sun, is painful to look at directly

    D just as the sun's existence is a true fact, so is human folly

_____ **10.** At the story's end, who has lost or gained what?

    F Sekhar has lost a wife but gained influence at his job.

    G The headmaster has lost a musical instrument, and Sekhar has gained money.

    H The headmaster has lost an illusion and gained some free time.

    J Sekhar has lost all his friends and the chance for a promotion.

LITERARY FOCUS: IRONY *(20 points; 5 points each)*

On the line provided, write the letter of the *best* answer to each of the following items.

_____ **11. Situational irony** occurs when —

    A someone says the opposite of what he or she means

    B what actually happens is very different from what was expected

    C a character does not know as much as the reader knows

    D a character is caught in a situation he or she does not know how to get out of

_____ **12.** Much of the situational irony in "Like the Sun" stems from —

    F Sekhar's getting in trouble for virtuously telling the truth

    G Sekhar's not knowing as much about music as he claims

    H R. K. Narayan's sly habit of saying one thing and implying another

    J Sekhar's thinking himself a truthful man when he's really a liar

_____ **13.** An example of situational irony in the story comes when Sekhar —

    A talks to his wife about her cooking

    B is bluntly truthful about the headmaster's music and is thanked for it

    C criticizes his colleague while other colleagues scold him

    D does not wish to grade the students' papers even though it is his duty

_____ **14.** The final situational irony in the story comes when —

    F the headmaster expels Sekhar

    G Sekhar's wife receives him sullenly at home

    H the headmaster pays off the two musicians

    J Sekhar finds that grading a hundred papers in one night is a small price to pay

VOCABULARY DEVELOPMENT *(20 points; 4 points each)*

Match the definition on the left with the Vocabulary word on the right. On the line provided, write the letter of the Vocabulary word.

_____ **15.** to flinch or draw back   **a.** wince

_____ **16.** attacked; assaulted   **b** shirked

_____ **17.** resentful; gloomy   **c.** incessantly

_____ **18.** constantly or unendingly   **d.** assailed

_____ **19.** neglected or avoided a task or duty   **e.** sullen

CONSTRUCTED RESPONSE *(20 points)*

20. On a separate sheet of paper, explain how R. K. Narayan uses irony and tone to convey a view of truth in this story.

SELECTION TEST ▮▮▮▮▮ **LITERARY RESPONSE AND ANALYSIS**

Games at Twilight   Anita Desai

COMPREHENSION *(40 points; 4 points each)*
On the line provided, write the letter of the *best* answer to each of the following items.

_____ **1.** What game is crucial to the plot of this story?

    A Cricket

    B Soccer

    C Blind man's bluff

    D Hide-and-seek

_____ **2.** Which of the following scenes occurs *first* in the story?

    F Ravi tries to enter the garage.

    G The children beg to play outside.

    H The children break their promise to stay on the porch.

    J The children act out a funeral.

_____ **3.** According to the narrator, play is —

    A a regrettable distraction from schoolwork

    B dangerous if not supervised by adults

    C children's proper business

    D acceptable after all chores are completed

_____ **4.** The children in the story are related because they are —

    F brothers, sisters, and cousins

    G classmates of the same age and sex

    H classmates of different ages and sexes

    J neighbors

_____ **5.** The children's parents are —

    A wealthy

    B poor

    C typical British colonists of that era

    D average members of the Indian middle class

_____ **6.** The shed in which Ravi hides can be characterized —

    F as being filled with rats, anthills, dust, and spider webs

    G as confinement behind shutters that protect without cooling

    H by the wonderful aroma of water on parched soil

    J by long shadows and inky vegetation

Holt Assessment: Literature, Reading, and Vocabulary

_____ **7.** Which of the following motives is *most* important for Ravi in the story?

    A Because he is a secretive person, he usually hides his feelings.

    B He hopes to defeat the older, bigger boy, Raghu.

    C Because his mother wouldn't let him play outside, he wants to punish her.

    D He wants to duplicate his father's childhood popularity.

_____ **8.** Ravi's childhood can *best* be described as —

    F rebellious and irresponsible

    G joyless and grim

    H free and adventurous

    J sheltered and privileged

_____ **9.** The parents in this story —

    A participate happily in their children's games

    B quarrel bitterly

    C are distant figures of authority

    D have no role in their children's lives

_____ **10.** At the end of the story, Ravi —

    F feels victorious

    G has become mature enough to shrug off a loss in a game

    H feels defeated and insignificant

    J is pleased he has won the affection of the other children

LITERARY FOCUS: IMAGERY *(10 points; 5 points each)*

On the line provided, write the letter of the *best* answer to each of the following items.

_____ **11.** The use of **imagery** in this story —

    A makes the story seem fantastic and unreal

    B reveals the author's identification with Ravi

    C suggests that the story is an actual, faithfully recorded event

    D makes the story especially vivid

_____ **12.** Which of the following statements is an example of descriptive imagery in the story?

    F The children play outdoor games at dusk.

    G Their mother "would not open the door."

    H Birds droop "like dead fruit"; the trees are "papery tents."

    J Everyone forgets about Ravi.

READING SKILLS: ANALYZING DETAILS *(10 points; 5 points each)*

On the line provided, write the letter of the *best* answer to each of the following items.

_____ **13.** Which descriptive detail in the story is *most* likely to evoke an emotion of fear or eeriness?

    A The gravelike smell of the shed

    B Ravi smiling to himself at the thought of defeating Raghu

    C The light in the doorway turning "to a kind of crumbling yellow pollen"

    D The children staring at Ravi's reappearance

_____ **14.** The detail of the children's lungs stuffed with wool is intended to convey a feeling of —

    F relief

    G ease

    H oppression

    J friendliness

VOCABULARY DEVELOPMENT *(20 points; 4 points each)*

On the line provided, write the letter of the *best* antonym, or opposite, for each Vocabulary word below.

_____ **15.** maniacal

    A active

    B mental

    C sane

    D physical

_____ **16.** stridently

    F sweetly

    G angrily

    H harshly

    J boldly

_____ **17.** temerity

   A loudness

   B timidity

   C respect

   D ignorance

_____ **18.** dogged

   F unusual

   G tired

   H feline

   J halfhearted

_____ **19.** ignominy

   A honor

   B shame

   C embarrassment

   D foolhardiness

CONSTRUCTED RESPONSE *(20 points)*

20. Re-read the ending of the story. Interpret the meaning of this final scene. On a separate sheet of paper, explain what emotions Ravi is feeling, and what comment on life the author is making.

SELECTION TEST   LITERARY RESPONSE AND ANALYSIS

Next Term, We'll Mash You Penelope Lively

COMPREHENSION *(40 points; 4 points each)*

On the line provided, write the letter of the *best* answer to each of the following items.

_____ **1.** The basic situation of this story is —

     A a schoolboy protesting against his parents' choice of school for him

     B classmates ganging up on one outcast child and destroying him

     C a headmaster and his wife arguing about how to treat the students

     D a boy's parents taking him to investigate a school where he might go

_____ **2.** The story's first sentence, a description of the family car, shows the reader that —

     F the characters are not good with money

     G the family in the story is very conscious of material status

     H Charles is ungrateful for the good things his parents have given him

     J Charles's parents have neglected routine repairs and maintenance

_____ **3.** The Manders's style of speaking shows that they —

     A are people who try to keep up appearances

     B are ashamed of their lack of education

     C have no prior experience with boarding schools

     D secretly hate each other

_____ **4.** What is the *most* important characteristic that Charles's parents look for when choosing a school for him?

     F High standardized test scores

     G An upper-class image or atmosphere

     H An enthusiastic, inspired, committed faculty

     J A group of students with whom Charles will fit in

_____ **5.** Margaret Spokes, the headmaster's wife, can be described in one word: —

     A beautiful

     B brilliant

     C proper

     D bashful

_____ **6.** The description of the headmaster is ironic because —

     F he and his wife are not really well matched

     G he is not really very clean

     H his shoes are not really old

     J he is really condescending

_____ **7.** What attitude does the headmaster seem to take toward the students?

    A He is proud and supportive of their accomplishments.

    B Although a hard taskmaster, he cares greatly about them.

    C He views them as annoying nuisances.

    D He talks of them with undisguised loathing.

_____ **8.** Author Penelope Lively *first* shows the reader that the school is not as fine as it pretends to be when she —

    F informs the reader that the headmaster is late for the appointment

    G shows that Mrs. Spokes is a completely different person when talking to students than when talking to parents

    H describes "inky tables," "rungless chairs," and a "mangy carpet"

    J describes Charles's future class as "the Lower Third"

_____ **9.** At the high point of the plot, the title of the story —

    A turns out to have been a false clue, or "red herring"

    B suggests Charles's miserable fate at the school

    C identifies who is the real main character

    D reveals that the students at the school are friendly after all

_____ **10.** What are Charles's feelings as he rides away from the school at the end of the story?

    F Dread of returning

    G Eagerness to escape his parents

    H An irrepressible desire to tell his parents what he thinks

    J Fear that his parents will not choose this school after all

LITERARY FOCUS: THEME *(20 points; 5 points each)*

On the line provided, write the letter of the *best* answer to each of the following items.

_____ **11.** A literary work's **theme** can often be stated in a sentence as a(n) —

    A assumption

    B generalization

    C motivation

    D characterization

_____ **12.** Which is the *least* common way for modern writers to convey their themes?

    F Explicit statement

    G Development of a central conflict

    H Values and motivations of the characters

    J Thoughts of the characters

Next Term, We'll Mash You

_____ **13.** Which of the following items is *not* one of the subjects of this story?

    A The British educational system

    B Social class and snobbery

    C The sportsmanlike values of the cricket field

    D The cruelty of children

_____ **14.** Which of the following sentences could *not* be a statement of this story's theme?

    F A sheltered background can make a child a victim.

    G Parents really know little about their children's lives.

    H Appearances are not what count.

    J A tough school is the building ground for a strong character.

VOCABULARY DEVELOPMENT *(20 points; 4 points each)*

On the line provided, write the Vocabulary word from the list below that *best*
fits in the sentence.

    subdued   **geniality**   **untainted**   **condescension**

    indulgent   **amiable**   **inaccessible**   **haggard**

15. The atmosphere of the school was _____, with little
noise and no visible messes.

16. With his quick smile and hearty handshake, the headmaster was expert at faking

_____.

17. The parents wished the child's education to be the best, _____
by any hint of the second-rate.

18. One could tell from the child's neat appearance and polite answers that his

parents had been strict rather than _____.

19. The headmaster's office was private and _____ to students
except when they were called in for a conference.

CONSTRUCTED RESPONSE (20 points)

20. On a separate sheet of paper, discuss how Penelope Lively presents a view or comment on life through irony. Refer to two or more specific examples of irony in the story.

Saboteur Ha Jin

COMPREHENSION *(40 points; 4 points each)*

On the line provided, write the letter of the *best* answer to each of the following items.

_____ **1.** Muji City, where the story takes place, is evidently —

    A a vacation destination

    B an industrial center

    C the capital of China

    D where Mr. Chiu teaches

_____ **2.** Which of the following statements is *not* true of Mr. Chiu's situation at the beginning of the story?

    F He has just had his honeymoon.

    G He is recovering from a dangerous liver disease.

    H He is expecting the police to catch up with him.

    J He is tired.

_____ **3.** The key event that triggers the story's plot occurs when —

    A Mr. Chiu makes a speech insulting the ruling regime

    B Mr. Chiu's bride cries out for help

    C a police officer deliberately dumps tea on Mr. and Mrs. Chiu

    D the police investigation delays Mr. Chiu's meeting with his wife

_____ **4.** The official charge against Mr. Chiu accuses him of —

    F disrupting public order

    G attempting to blow up a government building

    H spreading an infectious disease

    J muttering comments against the Communist Party

_____ **5.** Mr. Chiu *first* tries to get out of jail by —

    A threatening to go to the press and to higher authorities

    B swiping a key when the guards are not looking

    C trying to reason with the chief of the bureau and almost succeeding

    D phoning his employers and having them send a member of their legal staff

_____ **6.** What motive does the story give for the police's hostility against Mr. Chiu?

    F Mr. Chiu is not a member of the Communist Party, so he is fair game.

    G The police resent Mr. Chiu's better education and higher social status.

    H The police have been given orders to arrest anyone on any grounds who seems pro-democratic.

    J The story gives no motive for the police's hostility.

_____ **7.** How does Mr. Chiu finally get out of jail?

    A The police are forced to release him when the press take an interest in his case.

    B Mr. Chiu bribes the police to release him.

    C Mr. Chiu signs a confession even though he is innocent.

    D Mr. Chiu's students and colleagues sign petitions which influence the court.

_____ **8.** The story portrays Mr. Chiu as a(n) —

    F forgiving, almost saintly figure

    G ordinary man who turns nasty when wronged

    H faceless member of the bureaucracy

    J doting husband who can scarcely make a move without his wife's consent

_____ **9.** The ending of the story could *not* be called —

    A morally wrong

    B an act of vengeance

    C a comic comeuppance

    D a frightening resolution

_____ **10.** A theme of the story might be that —

    F life in a cruel state makes its citizens cruel

    G marriage is not advisable for those suffering from infectious diseases

    H Muji City is a notorious nest of police corruption

    J governments that oppress their citizens are sure to fall

LITERARY FOCUS: IRONY *(10 points; 5 points each)*
On the line provided, write the letter of the *best* answer to each of the following items.

_____ **11.** There are several types of **irony**, but they all involve —

    A satire aimed at social conditions

    B an attempt to improve the world

    C a discrepancy between appearance and reality or expectation and reality

    D opposition between what is said and what is really meant

_____ **12.** Which detail of the description of Muji Train Station is intended ironically?

    F Mr. Chiu and his bride drink soda and eat from paper boxes.

    G Peasants and pigeons use the statue of Chairman Mao as a rest stop.

    H Police officers and civilians eat at the same café.

    J Young women hold up signs advertising local hotels.

READING SKILLS: IDENTIFYING POLITICAL INFLUENCES *(10 points; 5 points each)*

On the line provided, write the letter of the *best* answer to each of the following items.

_____ **13.** Which aspect of the story is *most* clearly a result of the political situation in the story's historical period?

    A Mr. Chiu suffers from heart disease and hepatitis.

    B Mr. Chiu turns out to be a vengeful person.

    C The police imprison Mr. Chiu's lawyer without good cause.

    D Mr. Chiu's bride sends the wrong person to argue his case.

_____ **14.** Which word or phrase in the story is a signal of a specific political situation in China?

    F Millet

    G Muji Train Station

    H Hepatitis

    J Marxist materialism

VOCABULARY DEVELOPMENT *(20 points; 4 points each)*

Match the definition on the left with the Vocabulary word on the right. On the line provided, write the letter of the Vocabulary word.

_____ **15.** caused; brought about   **a.** coherent

_____ **16.** with disdain or scorn   **b.** induced

_____ **17.** logical; orderly; understandable   **c.** contemptuously

_____ **18.** abundantly; excessively   **d.** profusely

_____ **19.** demolished   **e.** razed

CONSTRUCTED RESPONSE *(20 points)*

20. What view or comment on life does author Ha Jin seem to make in this story, and how do you think that view has been affected by political influences in Ha Jin's world? In making your case, refer to specific details from the story. Write your answer on a separate sheet of paper.

SELECTION TEST

from the Universal Declaration of Human Rights
United Nations Commission on Human Rights

from The Question of South Africa Desmond Tutu

from Towards a True Refuge Aung San Suu Kyi

COMPREHENSION *(40 points; 4 points each)*

On the line provided, write the letter of the *best* answer to each of the following items.

_____ **1.** The **preamble** to a document is its —

    A introduction

    B table of contents

    C main text

    D conclusion

_____ **2.** The repeated word *whereas* in the Preamble to the Universal Declaration of Human Rights indicates that the text will —

    F take a long time to read

    G contain a rationale of why the document is necessary

    H be written in several languages

    J be honest but controversial

_____ **3.** The Universal Declaration of Human Rights is —

    A a standard toward which all nations should strive

    B international law which is enforced in courts

    C a copy of the American Bill of Rights

    D a dream that has never been actually approved by the nations of the world

_____ **4.** The Preamble states all of the following reasons for presenting the Declaration *except* —

    F human beings have fundamental, equal dignity and worth

    G nations should have friendly relations with one another

    H barbarous tyranny must be stopped

    J the United States has become a light of freedom for other nations of the world

_____ **5.** At the time Desmond Tutu made his speech "The Question of South Africa," what was the condition of South Africa?

    A Apartheid was in place, mandating segregation between the races.

    B Black citizens had overturned apartheid and established majority rule.

    C English colonists were furiously debating the future of their colony.

    D South Africa was technically no longer segregated but in practice whites still ruled.

_____ **6.** What attitude does Tutu express toward white South Africans?

    F He is willing to share a democratic, nonviolent South Africa with them.

    G He demands that they repay blacks for the years of oppression.

    H He yearns for them all to return quietly to Europe.

    J He calls for an armed uprising and the burning of whites' farms.

_____ **7.** Tutu mentions all of the following grievances of black South Africans *except* —

    A enforced separations of husbands from wives

    B police violence against black children

    C a deliberately inferior educational system for black students

    D impossibility of blacks' obtaining jobs as diamond miners

_____ **8.** According to Aung San Suu Kyi, the *major* threat to security for the nations of the world comes from —

    F famine

    G disease

    H the arms race

    J disregard for human rights

_____ **9.** Aung San Suu Kyi agrees with the idea that —

    A rights and liberties are a luxury that only rich nations can afford

    B in spite of idealistic statements to the contrary, prosperity is more important than democracy

    C every nation should strive for economic prosperity and the happiness of its people

    D when a nation is economically successful, freedom automatically benefits

_____ **10.** Closing her speech, Aung San Suu Kyi argues that —

    F the light of freedom will conquer the darkness of tyranny

    G she will continue to work for her people even though she knows the cause is hopeless

    H darkness is stronger than light because one candle cannot light up a darkened stadium

    J her Western audience cannot truly appreciate the suffering of her people

READING SKILLS: COMPARING MAIN IDEAS ACROSS TEXTS *(40 points; 10 points each)*
On the line provided, write the letter of the *best* answer to each of the following items.

_____ **11.** What is the *most* significant difference between the three texts in this selection and Ha Jin's "Saboteur"?

  A "Saboteur" is about a different continent.

  B "Saboteur" is fiction and the other three are nonfiction.

  C "Saboteur" shows the influence of living under a dictatorship while the others do not show specific political influences on individuals.

  D The Universal Declaration of Human Rights was drafted by a committee while the other three texts were written by individuals.

_____ **12.** What is the difference between the Universal Declaration of Human Rights and the speeches by Desmond Tutu and Aung San Suu Kyi?

  F The Declaration shows a greater devotion to Western ideals of democracy and freedom.

  G The two speeches are easier to read because they were written to be spoken.

  H The speeches are not official documents; the Declaration is.

  J The ideals of the Declaration are more realistic than those of the two speeches.

_____ **13.** Which statement about the rhetoric of the three texts in this selection is *true*?

  A The Universal Declaration of Human Rights is written in a deliberately obscure style in order to confuse censors.

  B Desmond Tutu's experience as a clergyman has enriched his sentence rhythms and his imagery.

  C Tailoring her speech for a mass audience, Aung San Suu Kyi has used short, crisp sentences and simple words.

  D All three documents are written in essentially the same impersonal prose style.

_____ **14.** Which work is written using the first-person ("I") point of view?

  F "Saboteur"

  G Universal Declaration of Human Rights

  H "The Question of South Africa"

  J "Towards a True Refuge"

CONSTRUCTED RESPONSE *(20 points)*
15. Review the three nonfiction works in this selection. On a separate piece of paper, describe a world which, in your opinion, the authors of the three texts would hail as a just world. Use references to the texts to support your claim.

The Modern World 1900 to the Present: A Remarkable Diversity

Heart of Darkness, by Joseph Conrad, is considered to be one of the greatest short novels written in English. The narrator, a middle-aged man named Marlow, describes a journey up the Congo River that he makes as a young steamboat captain. After a difficult, unpleasant journey to the "heart of darkness," he encounters Kurtz, a European ivory trader who has become a mad caricature of a tribal chief. As Marlow tells his tale, he broods about his experience in Africa, where, at the time of his visit, traditional cultures struggle against European colonization. Read the following excerpt from *Heart of Darkness* and answer all the questions that come after it.

FROM **Heart of Darkness**

by Joseph Conrad

Going up that river was like traveling back to the earliest beginnings of the world, when vegetation rioted on the earth and the big trees were kings. An empty stream, a great silence, an impenetrable forest. The air was warm, thick, heavy, sluggish. There was no joy in the brilliance of sunshine. The long stretches of the waterway ran on, deserted, into the gloom of overshadowed distances. On silvery sandbanks hippos and alligators sunned themselves side by side. The broadening waters flowed through a mob of wooded islands; you lost your way on that river as you would in a desert, and butted all day long against shoals, trying to find the channel, till you thought yourself bewitched and cut off forever from everything you had known once—somewhere—far away—in another existence perhaps. There were moments when one's past came back to one, as it will when you have not a moment to spare to yourself; but it came in the shape of an unrestful and noisy dream, remembered with wonder amongst the overwhelming realities of this strange world of plants, and water, and silence. And this stillness of life did not in the least resemble a peace. It was the stillness of an implacable force brooding over an inscrutable intention. It looked at you with a vengeful aspect. I got used to it afterwards; I did not see it any more; I had no time. I had to keep guessing at the channel; I had to discern, mostly by inspiration, the signs of hidden banks; I watched for sunken stones; I was learning to clap my teeth smartly before my heart flew out, when I shaved by a fluke some infernal sly old snag that would have ripped the life out of the tin-pot steamboat and drowned all the pilgrims; I had to keep a look-out for the signs of dead wood we could cut up in the night for next day's steaming. When you have to attend to things of that sort, to the mere incidents of the surface, the reality—the reality, I tell you—fades. The inner truth is hidden—luckily, luckily.

VOCABULARY SKILLS (*20 points; 4 points each*)

Each of the following underlined words has also been underlined in the selection. Re-read those passages, and use context clues and structural clues to help you select an answer. On the line provided, write the letter of the word or phrase that *best* completes each sentence.

_____ **1.** An <u>impenetrable</u> forest is one that cannot be —

    A passed through

    B cut for timber

    C forgotten

    D occupied by animals

_____ **2.** <u>Shoals</u> are —

    F seashells

    G ships

    H sandbars

    J boats

_____ **3.** An <u>implacable</u> force cannot be —

    A accelerated

    B described

    C pacified

    D improved

_____ **4.** An <u>inscrutable</u> glance is —

    F expensive

    G unintentional

    H understandable

    J mysterious

_____ **5.** When Marlow attempts to <u>discern</u> the hidden banks, he is trying to —

    A land on them

    B recognize them

    C reject them

    D hit them

COMPREHENSION *(20 points; 4 points each)*
On the line provided, write the letter of the *best* answer to each of the following items.

_____ **6.** The mood of the excerpt is —

    F ominous

    G thrilling

    H humorous

    J peaceful

_____ **7.** In this excerpt the narrator sees his surroundings as —

    A terrifying

    B strangely beautiful

    C exotic and luxurious

    D threatening

_____ **8.** In Marlow's view the contradiction that characterizes the African river landscape is that it is —

    F forested but lifeless

    G sunny but strangely cold

    H quiet and sunny, but not peaceful or joyous

    J full of danger, yet it makes Marlow feel safe

_____ **9.** Marlow finds it difficult to contemplate his surroundings because —

    A doing so unnerves him

    B he has his hands full trying to navigate the waters

    C his passengers and crew distract him

    D he spends most of his time filling out reports

_____ **10.** In the last two lines of the excerpt, —

    F the present tense replaces the past tense, creating an interesting emphasis

    G Marlow begins to relax and enjoy himself

    H night falls and the surrounding scenery fades from view

    J the imagery is especially lush

READING SKILLS AND STRATEGIES: CONSTRUCTED RESPONSE

Making Inferences *(8 points)*

11. What can be inferred about Marlow's character from the excerpt you have read? In the left-hand column of the following chart, list five character traits that you can infer about Marlow. In the right-hand column, list evidence from the excerpts that supports your ideas.

▶ Character Traits	▶ Evidence

Analyzing Details *(8 points)*

12. Conrad uses carefully chosen details to help readers imagine clearly the African forest environment. In the left-hand column of the following chart, describe an unusual detail that Conrad describes. In the middle column, write the exact words Conrad uses to describe the detail. In the right-hand column, write a phrase or sentence that describes the feeling the detail evokes.

▶ Detail	▶ Description	▶ Feeling

Analyzing Setting (20 points)

13. What images are used to describe the setting of the Congo River? How does the setting help imply a clash between African and European cultures or worldviews? Write a paragraph on a separate sheet of paper answering these questions, using at least two examples from the excerpt to support your ideas.

Identifying Aesthetic Devices (4 points)

On the line provided, write the letter of the *best* answer to the following item.

_____ **14.** The sentence "On silvery sandbanks hippos and alligators sunned themselves side by side" uses —

     F iambic pentameter and rhyme

     G onomatopoeia and parody

     H assonance and alliteration

     J personification and simile

LITERARY FOCUS: CONSTRUCTED RESPONSE (20 points)

15. The Nigerian novelist Chinua Achebe ("Marriage Is a Private Affair") wrote an influential article criticizing Conrad's *Heart of Darkness* for showing Africa through the eyes of a European colonialist, rather than through African eyes. How might African readers perceive Africa differently from the way Conrad's Marlow perceives it? Do you agree with Achebe's criticism that *Heart of Darkness* deserves to be condemned for this trait? Write your answer on a separate sheet of paper. Support your argument with reasons.

Reading and Literary Analysis

DIRECTIONS Read the passage below, and answer the following questions.

SAMPLE

If you love comic books, you've probably heard of Stan Lee. Stan Lee is a visionary writer and editor whose work has become the model for the modern superhero. Lee was born in New York City in 1922 and began working for Marvel Comics at age seventeen. He rose through the ranks at Marvel, ultimately becoming the company's publisher and editorial director.

Marvel's competition, DC Comics, promoted a stoic and virtuous classic superhero, such as Batman and Superman. Lee, on the other hand, wanted his superheroes to retain their human qualities. His characters, such as Spiderman, go through the same emotions and insecurities that regular, everyday people experience. This distinction has made Lee's superheroes some of the most endearing fictional characters in American culture.

A This passage is —

    A   poetic

    B   biographical

    C   analytical

    D   autobiographical

B Stan Lee's superheroes were different from other superheroes in that they —

    F   worked at Marvel Comics

    G   had no emotions

    H   were able to fly

    J   had human qualities

Reading and Literary Analysis

DIRECTIONS Read the poem below, and answer the following questions.

The Unknown Citizen
W. H. Auden

(To JS/07/M/378
This Marble Monument
Is Erected by the State)

He was found by the Bureau of Statistics to be
One against whom there was no official complaint,
And all the reports on his conduct agree
That, in the modern sense of an old-fashioned word, he was a saint,

5 For in everything he did he served the Greater Community.
Except for the War till the day he retired
He worked in a factory and never got fired,
But satisfied his employers, Fudge Motors Inc.
Yet he wasn't a scab or odd in his views,

10 For his Union reports that he paid his dues,
(Our report on his Union shows it was sound)
And our Social Psychology workers found
That he was popular with his mates and liked a drink.
The Press are convinced that he bought a paper every day

15 And that his reactions to advertisements were normal in every way.
Policies taken out in his name prove that he was fully insured,
And his Health-card shows he was once in hospital but left it cured.
Both Producers Research and High-Grade Living declare
He was fully sensible to the advantages of the Installment Plan

20 And had everything necessary to the Modern Man,
A phonograph, a radio, a car and a frigidaire.
Our researchers in Public Opinion are content
That he held the proper opinions for the time of year;
When there was peace, he was for peace; when there was war, he went.
25 He was married and added five children to the population,
Which our Eugenist says was the right number for a parent of his generation,
And our teachers report that he never interfered with their education.
Was he free? Was he happy? The question is absurd:
Had anything been wrong, we should certainly have heard.

1 This poem is a satire because it —

  A   pokes fun at bureaucratic society

  B   makes fun of the unknown citizen

  C   compares the citizen to a statistic

  D   develops a many-faceted character

2 The light tone and end rhymes of the poem —

  F   match the poem's intent of light entertainment

  G   act as a foil for the serious message at the end

  H   make the reader forget the poem's serious intent

  J   encourage a songlike recitation of the poem

3 The diction, rhythm, and rhyme scheme all contribute to the reader's —

  A   comprehension

  B   disinterest

  C   vocalization

  D   amusement

4 The poem's details of the unknown citizen's outward qualities —

  F   offer a contrast to the more important inner qualities

  G   demonstrate the citizen's importance in the world

  H   enable the reader to appreciate his true character

  J   evoke the unknown citizen's unhappy, sterile life

5 The information about the unknown citizen that indicates his era is that he —

  A   worked in a factory most of his life

  B   belonged to a union and paid his dues

  C   owned a phonograph and a frigidaire

  D   was for peace when there was peace

6 What is ironic about the speaker's response to the two questions posed in line 28?

  F   The speaker is not concerned with the citizen's happiness or freedom.

  G   The citizen was unhappy.

  H   The speaker is the citizen himself.

  J   The citizen was happy and free.

GO ON

7 What theme of twentieth-century literature is represented by this poem?

A   The remarkable diversity in literature around the world

B   The anonymity of the individual in a bureaucratic world

C   The shocking experimentation in form and content

D   The response to war and government oppression

8 The unknown citizen is an example of the archetype of —

F   a hard worker

G   an interned body

H   a statistic

J   an everyman

9 The political and philosophical assumption *underlying* this poem is —

A   the importance of the individual

B   the necessity for strong government

C   the world belongs to the strong

D   the meek shall inherit the earth

10 The speaker of this poem is —

F   thoughtful and sympathetic

G   analytical, detached, and overconfident

H   angry and disillusioned with bureaucracy

J   pessimistic, mocking, and resentful

11 The word *psychology* is based on Greek roots meaning "spirit" and "word" and means —

A   "written communication"

B   "community advice"

C   "environmental studies"

D   "science of the mind"

12 The unknown citizen is to a phonograph and a radio as a twenty-first century person is to —

F   a hi-fi and a television

G   a juke box and a drive-in

H   an MP3 player and a DVD player

J   a gramophone and a portable CD player

GO ON

Reading and Literary Analysis *(continued)*

DIRECTIONS Read the selection below, and answer the following questions.

Oscar Arias Sánchez, the president of Costa Rica (1986–1990), received the Nobel Peace Prize in 1987 "for his work for peace in Central America, efforts which led to the accord signed in Guatemala." The peace accord signed by the five presidents of Costa Rica, Guatemala, El Salvador, Honduras, and Nicaragua was based on a plan Arias Sánchez had proposed.

from Nobel Acceptance Speech
December 10, 1987
Oscar Arias Sánchez

Peace is not a matter of prizes or trophies. It is not the product of a victory or command. It has no finishing line, no final deadline, no fixed definition of achievement.

Peace is a never-ending process, the work of many decisions by many people in many countries. It is an attitude, a way of life, a way of solving problems and resolving conflicts. It cannot be forced on the smallest nation or enforced by the largest. It cannot ignore our differences or overlook our common interests. It requires us to work and live together.

Peace is not only a matter of noble words and Nobel lectures. We have ample words, glorious words, inscribed in the charters of the United Nations, the World Court, the Organization of the American States and a network of international treaties and laws. We need deeds that will respect those words, honor those commitments, abide by those laws. We need to strengthen our institutions of peace like the United Nations, making certain they are fully used by the weak as well as the strong.

I pay no attention to those doubters and detractors unwilling to believe that a lasting peace can be genuinely embraced by those who march under a different ideological banner or those who are more accustomed to cannons of war than to councils of peace.

We seek in Central America not peace alone, not peace to be followed some day by political progress, but peace and democracy, together, indivisible, an end to the shedding of human blood, which is inseparable from an end to the suppression of human rights. We do not judge, much less condemn, any

GO ON

other nation's political or ideological system, freely chosen and never exported. We cannot require sovereign states to conform to patterns of government not of their own choosing. But we can and do insist that every government respect those universal rights of man that have meaning beyond national boundaries and ideological labels. We believe that justice and peace can only thrive together, never apart. A nation that mistreats its own citizens is more likely to mistreat its neighbors.

To receive this Nobel prize on the tenth of December is for me a marvelous coincidence. My son Oscar Felipe, here present, is eight years old today. I say to him, and through him to all the children of my country, that we shall never resort to violence, we shall never support military solutions to the problems of Central America. It is for the new generation that we must understand more than ever that peace can only be achieved through its own instruments: dialogue and understanding; tolerance and forgiveness; freedom and democracy.

---

13 Oscar Arias Sánchez's speech includes all of the following rhetorical devices *except* —

   A   repetition

   B   parallel structure

   C   relevant statistics

   D   personal anecdote

14 The meaning of this speech is made clear by —

   F   contrasting what peace is and what it is not

   G   repeating the same idea over and over again

   H   the use of simple, declarative sentences

   J   its organization of ideas in order of importance

15 The author's belief about peace is that it —

   A   is an idealistic and unattainable goal

   B   requires the work of many people

   C   can be achieved only by international law

   D   is embraced by those used to cannons of war

16 Which quote best sums up the author's argument?

   F   "Peace is not a matter of prizes or trophies."

   G   "Peace is a never-ending process. . . ."

   H   "Peace is not only a matter of noble words. . . ."

   J   "We seek in Central America . . . peace. . . ."

GO ON

Holt Assessment: Literature, Reading, and Vocabulary

17 Oscar Arias Sánchez urges world peace *mostly* through —

A measured appeals to reason

B passionate appeals to emotion

C angry denunciations of opponents

D descriptions of personal experiences

18 A word from the speech that is derived from Greek roots meaning "idea" and "word" is —

F international

G democracy

H institutions

J ideological

19 When Sánchez says, "We do not judge, much less condemn, any other nation's political or ideological system," he is using which rhetorical device?

A Argument by analogy

B Restatement

C Counterargument

D Appeal to authority

20 Sánchez mentions the charters of the United Nations, the World Court, and the Organization of the American States to —

F persuade these organizations to change

G impress people with his knowledge

H lend credibility to his speech

J anger his opponents

21 The first three paragraphs of the speech begin with "Peace is . . ." This is an example of what pattern of organization?

A Chronological order

B Parallelism

C An introductory statement

D A rhetorical question

22 Sánchez mentions his son in order to —

F recognize his birthday

G appeal to the emotions of his listeners

H pass on the job of peacekeeping

J inspire peace in other countries

GO ON

End-of-Year Test

END-OF-YEAR TEST

Reading and Literary Analysis *(continued)*

DIRECTIONS Read the poem below, and answer the following questions.

This sonnet was unpublished until after 1832, the year of the first great reform measures passed by the English parliament. The king in line 1 is George III, the same king who presided over the loss of the American colonies. His insanity had been acknowledged in 1811. The king died in 1820.

England in 1819
Percy Bysshe Shelley

> An old, mad, blind, despised, and dying King;
> Princes, the dregs of their dull race, who flow
> Through public scorn—mud from a muddy spring;
> Rulers who neither see nor feel nor know,
> 5   But leechlike to their fainting country cling
> Till they drop, blind in blood, without a blow.
> A people starved and stabbed in th'untilled field;
> An army, whom liberticide° and prey
> Makes as a two-edged sword to all who wield;
> 10   Golden and sanguine laws which tempt and slay;
> Religion Christless, Godless—a book sealed;
> A senate, time's worst statute, unrepealed—
> Are graves from which a glorious Phantom° may
> Burst, to illumine our tempestuous day.

---

8. **liberticide:** murder of liberty.

13. **Phantom:** spirit (of revolution).

23 "Leechlike to their fainting country cling" (line 5) is an example of —

A visual imagery

B vernacular

C understatement

D hyperbole

24 Princes who are "the dregs of their dull race" is an example of —

F parody

G apostrophe

H theme

J irony

25 A paradox in the poem is —

A people stabbed in a field

B a king facing life's end

C life bursting forth from the grave

D princes who are scorned

26 In lines 2–3, the comparison of princes to mud is an example of —

F metaphor

G simile

H personification

J hyperbole

27 Which quotation includes an example of parallelism?

A "Rulers who neither see nor feel nor know"

B "Leechlike to their fainting country cling"

C "A senate, time's worst statute"

D "to illumine our tempestuous day"

28 What event provides the *best* historical context for the poem?

F A massacre occurred at a rally for parliamentary reform.

G Queen Victoria was born.

H Spain ceded Florida to the United States.

J A steamship crossed the Atlantic for the first time.

29 "A book sealed," a reference to the Bible, is called an —

A allusion

B allegory

C anachronism

D epitaph

30 The number of lines and the rhyme scheme indicates that this text is a —

F villanelle

G sonnet

H dramatic monologue

J tanka

GO ON

Vocabulary

DIRECTIONS Choose the word that means the same, or about the same, as the underlined word. Then, mark the answer you have chosen.

Someone who is <u>benign</u> is —

   A authoritative

   B kind

   C foolish

   D proud

31 <u>Deference</u> means —

   A respect

   B dignity

   C curiosity

   D envy

32 Someone who is <u>unpretentious</u> is —

   F friendly

   G confident

   H modest

   J stealthy

33 <u>Superfluities</u> are —

   A worries

   B excesses

   C reasons

   D rules

34 Someone who is <u>frugal</u> is —

   F thrifty

   G stubborn

   H ambitious

   J bad-tempered

35 <u>Clemency</u> is another word for —

   A despair

   B cowardice

   C leniency

   D hostility

36 Something that is <u>compulsory</u> is —

   F denied

   G delicate

   H forgiven

   J required

GO ON

End-of-Year Test | *continued*

37 A **labyrinth** is a —

A   maze

B   shelter

C   horizon

D   excavation

38 **Persevere** means —

F   celebrate

G   neglect

H   hesitate

J   persist

39 **Dispassionately** means —

A   courageously

B   impartially

C   cheerfully

D   gradually

40 Something that is **inevitable** is —

F   ineffective

G   undesirable

H   unavoidable

J   insecure

STOP

ENTRY-LEVEL TEST

Answer Sheet

Reading and Literary Analysis/Vocabulary

Sample

A   Ⓐ   Ⓑ   Ⓒ   Ⓓ
B   Ⓕ   Ⓖ   Ⓗ   Ⓙ

1   Ⓐ   Ⓑ   Ⓒ   Ⓓ
2   Ⓕ   Ⓖ   Ⓗ   Ⓙ
3   Ⓐ   Ⓑ   Ⓒ   Ⓓ
4   Ⓕ   Ⓖ   Ⓗ   Ⓙ
5   Ⓐ   Ⓑ   Ⓒ   Ⓓ
6   Ⓕ   Ⓖ   Ⓗ   Ⓙ
7   Ⓐ   Ⓑ   Ⓒ   Ⓓ
8   Ⓕ   Ⓖ   Ⓗ   Ⓙ
9   Ⓐ   Ⓑ   Ⓒ   Ⓓ
10   Ⓕ   Ⓖ   Ⓗ   Ⓙ
11   Ⓐ   Ⓑ   Ⓒ   Ⓓ
12   Ⓕ   Ⓖ   Ⓗ   Ⓙ
13   Ⓐ   Ⓑ   Ⓒ   Ⓓ
14   Ⓕ   Ⓖ   Ⓗ   Ⓙ
15   Ⓐ   Ⓑ   Ⓒ   Ⓓ
16   Ⓕ   Ⓖ   Ⓗ   Ⓙ
17   Ⓐ   Ⓑ   Ⓒ   Ⓓ
18   Ⓕ   Ⓖ   Ⓗ   Ⓙ
19   Ⓐ   Ⓑ   Ⓒ   Ⓓ
20   Ⓕ   Ⓖ   Ⓗ   Ⓙ
21   Ⓐ   Ⓑ   Ⓒ   Ⓓ
22   Ⓕ   Ⓖ   Ⓗ   Ⓙ
23   Ⓐ   Ⓑ   Ⓒ   Ⓓ
24   Ⓕ   Ⓖ   Ⓗ   Ⓙ
25   Ⓐ   Ⓑ   Ⓒ   Ⓓ
26   Ⓕ   Ⓖ   Ⓗ   Ⓙ
27   Ⓐ   Ⓑ   Ⓒ   Ⓓ
28   Ⓕ   Ⓖ   Ⓗ   Ⓙ
29   Ⓐ   Ⓑ   Ⓒ   Ⓓ
30   Ⓕ   Ⓖ   Ⓗ   Ⓙ

Sample A

Ⓐ   Ⓑ   Ⓒ   Ⓓ

31   Ⓐ   Ⓑ   Ⓒ   Ⓓ
32   Ⓕ   Ⓖ   Ⓗ   Ⓙ
33   Ⓐ   Ⓑ   Ⓒ   Ⓓ
34   Ⓕ   Ⓖ   Ⓗ   Ⓙ
35   Ⓐ   Ⓑ   Ⓒ   Ⓓ
36   Ⓕ   Ⓖ   Ⓗ   Ⓙ

Sample B

Ⓐ   Ⓑ   Ⓒ   Ⓓ

37   Ⓐ   Ⓑ   Ⓒ   Ⓓ
38   Ⓕ   Ⓖ   Ⓗ   Ⓙ
39   Ⓐ   Ⓑ   Ⓒ   Ⓓ
40   Ⓕ   Ⓖ   Ⓗ   Ⓙ

Holt Assessment: Literature, Reading, and Vocabulary

Answer Sheet

**Reading and Literary
Analysis/Vocabulary**

Sample A

    Ⓐ Ⓑ Ⓒ Ⓓ

Sample

A Ⓐ Ⓑ Ⓒ Ⓓ
B Ⓕ Ⓖ Ⓗ Ⓙ

1 Ⓐ Ⓑ Ⓒ Ⓓ
2 Ⓕ Ⓖ Ⓗ Ⓙ
3 Ⓐ Ⓑ Ⓒ Ⓓ
4 Ⓕ Ⓖ Ⓗ Ⓙ
5 Ⓐ Ⓑ Ⓒ Ⓓ
6 Ⓕ Ⓖ Ⓗ Ⓙ
7 Ⓐ Ⓑ Ⓒ Ⓓ
8 Ⓕ Ⓖ Ⓗ Ⓙ
9 Ⓐ Ⓑ Ⓒ Ⓓ
10 Ⓕ Ⓖ Ⓗ Ⓙ
11 Ⓐ Ⓑ Ⓒ Ⓓ
12 Ⓕ Ⓖ Ⓗ Ⓙ
13 Ⓐ Ⓑ Ⓒ Ⓓ
14 Ⓕ Ⓖ Ⓗ Ⓙ
15 Ⓐ Ⓑ Ⓒ Ⓓ
16 Ⓕ Ⓖ Ⓗ Ⓙ
17 Ⓐ Ⓑ Ⓒ Ⓓ
18 Ⓕ Ⓖ Ⓗ Ⓙ
19 Ⓐ Ⓑ Ⓒ Ⓓ
20 Ⓕ Ⓖ Ⓗ Ⓙ
21 Ⓐ Ⓑ Ⓒ Ⓓ
22 Ⓕ Ⓖ Ⓗ Ⓙ
23 Ⓐ Ⓑ Ⓒ Ⓓ
24 Ⓕ Ⓖ Ⓗ Ⓙ
25 Ⓐ Ⓑ Ⓒ Ⓓ
26 Ⓕ Ⓖ Ⓗ Ⓙ
27 Ⓐ Ⓑ Ⓒ Ⓓ
28 Ⓕ Ⓖ Ⓗ Ⓙ
29 Ⓐ Ⓑ Ⓒ Ⓓ
30 Ⓕ Ⓖ Ⓗ Ⓙ

31 Ⓐ Ⓑ Ⓒ Ⓓ
32 Ⓕ Ⓖ Ⓗ Ⓙ
33 Ⓐ Ⓑ Ⓒ Ⓓ
34 Ⓕ Ⓖ Ⓗ Ⓙ
35 Ⓐ Ⓑ Ⓒ Ⓓ
36 Ⓕ Ⓖ Ⓗ Ⓙ
37 Ⓐ Ⓑ Ⓒ Ⓓ
38 Ⓕ Ⓖ Ⓗ Ⓙ
39 Ⓐ Ⓑ Ⓒ Ⓓ
40 Ⓕ Ⓖ Ⓗ Ⓙ

Answer Key

Answer Key

Answer Key

Sample A C

Sample B G

Reading and Literary Analysis

1. A	16. H
2. H	17. B
3. D	18. J
4. J	19. A
5. B	20. H
6. H	21. D
7. D	22. F
8. G	23. B
9. A	24. J
10. F	25. A
11. C	26. F
12. F	27. D
13. B	28. G
14. F	29. B
15. C	30. H

Vocabulary

Sample A B	36. F
31. A	**Sample B** D
32. J	37. B
33. C	38. F
34. G	39. C
35. D	40. F

Collection 1

Collection 1 Diagnostic Test
Literature, Vocabulary, *page 15*

1. C	6. J
2. J	7. A
3. C	8. G
4. G	9. C
5. C	10. F

Literary Period Introduction Test,
page 17

1. D	6. F
2. G	7. A
3. B	8. J
4. H	9. C
5. D	10. H

from Beowulf, Part One

from Grendel
by John Gardner

Life in 999: A Grim Struggle
by Howard G. Chua-Eoan
from Time

from Beowulf, Part Two

Selection Test, *page 19*

Comprehension

1. A	6. F
2. J	7. A
3. C	8. F
4. H	9. B
5. A	10. J

Literary Focus

11. C	13. D
12. G	14. F

Vocabulary Development

15. resolute

16. vehemently

17. infallible

18. lavish

19. assail

Constructed Response

20. Students' responses will vary. A sample response follows:

The Anglo-Saxon age was a time of frequent warfare, involving ruthless marauding and ferocious attacks on peaceful settlements. The monsters' attacks on

Answer Key

human settlements may symbolically represent attacks by enemy nations. No doubt each side viewed the other side's warfare as monstrously bloodthirsty—each side demonized the other. Grendel commits wholesale slaughter at Herot, delighting in the blood he spills; Grendel's mother takes savage revenge; the dragon, furious because of the theft of his jewels, lays waste to all the land of the Geats. Each monster is relentless, merciless, and vicious, like an invading warrior. The image of a dragon jealously guarding his treasure makes this monster seems particularly like an archetype of the human enemy. The image of Grendel invading the hall while his enemies are asleep and blood spurting all around is also similar to something human warriors might have been seen doing.

from Gilgamesh: A Verse Narrative
retold by Herbert Mason

Selection Test, *page 23*

Comprehension

1. A	**6.** G
2. J	**7.** B
3. C	**8.** J
4. G	**9.** B
5. A	**10.** H

Literary Focus

11. D	**13.** D
12. F	**14.** G

Vocabulary Development

15. C	**18.** F
16. F	**19.** D
17. B	

Constructed Response

20. Students' responses will vary. A sample response follows:

By any standard, Gilgamesh and Enkidu are a superb hero-and-foil pair. Their personalities are glaringly different, but these differences don't affect them materially in their quest to pursue adventure and defeat evil. Fittingly, Enkidu, the foil, is the one who shows fear. His vulnerability enables the hero Gilgamesh's light to shine more brightly by contrast. Yet Enkidu shows valor in the fight, even though Gilgamesh has to rescue him from being killed by the monster. Enkidu's skill and empathy at interpreting Gilgamesh's dreams not only make him a better friend for Gilgamesh, but make him a more interesting character to the reader and help expand the psychological scope of the epic. His fear represents the fear of the ordinary person in the face of death, as opposed to the feelings of the epic hero. Yet Enkidu stoically deals with his own fear and refrains from voicing a fearful interpretation of Gilgamesh's dream. In contrast, Gilgamesh's response to fear is to feel pleasure in discovery. Fear teaches him about himself, and revitalizes him. These two characters are so well suited for each other and for their adventure and so well developed that they probably would not have to be changed for a modern epic except in external details, such as dress and weapons—and perhaps the addition of modern humor.

the Iliad, from Book 22, The Death of Hector
by Homer

Selection Test, *page 27*

Comprehension

1. C	**6.** F
2. F	**7.** D
3. D	**8.** G
4. G	**9.** B
5. A	**10.** H

Literary Focus

11. C	**13.** A
12. H	**14.** J

Answer Key

Vocabulary Development

15. gallant
16. scourge
17. fawning
18. groveling
19. groveling

Constructed Response

20. Students' responses will vary. A sample response follows:

Based on this selection, Homer seems to have admired his heroes for sheer ferocity and skill in battle. Personality traits seem not to have entered into the judgment of a hero, although Homer was well aware of the failings of each of his heroes. Hector had a cowardly streak, panicking and fleeing when attacked by Achilles, but this flaw does not prevent Hector from being extolled as the greatest of the Trojan heroes. Achilles is merciless, mean, and unforgiving in this selection, but these vices do not deprive him of the favor of the goddess Athena or of the undisputed position of greatest ancient Greek warrior. It sometimes seems as if Homer most admired the sheer excellence of combat skill and strength in his heroes, as if they were not men to be morally appraised but natural forces to be gazed at. It makes perfect sense, then, when Homer compares Achilles to a hound chasing a fawn or an eagle swooping down to catch a lamb. In nature such cruelty can often seem beautiful and not immoral. Homer's heroes act outside of morality, where the ability to make the kill is what really matters.

Collection 1 Summative Test,

page 31

Vocabulary Skills

1. C
2. J
3. A
4. G
5. C

Comprehension

6. F
7. D
8. F
9. D
10. H

Literary Focus: Constructed Response

11. Students' responses will vary. A sample response follows:

the hero: Is Like an Epic—is a man of high rank; has left the scene of a feud; has traveled from his homeland; *Is Unlike an Epic*—is apparently more of a merchant than a warrior
the events: Is Like an Epic—message from across the sea a plea to a loved one; solemn oaths; *Is Unlike an Epic*—intimate scale: a story of married love, not quest
the setting: Is Like an Epic—medieval Anglo-Saxon; involves sailing ships, mead-halls, bestowing of gifts upon knights; *Is Unlike an Epic*—emphasizes peacetime values of prosperity, family

"The Husband's Message" is not an epic because it is not about a quest; its hero is an ordinary (though prosperous and high-ranked) man of his times rather than a heroic ideal, and the subject is domestic and realistic life rather than adventure or ordeal.

Reading Skills and Strategies

Recognizing Archetypes

12. G

Answer Key

Identifying Literary Conventions

13. Students' responses will vary. Sample responses follow:

(1) Sample answers: commands/carry/cunningly-carved; sailed/south/salt-streams; feud/forced; wish/world/with/words.

(2) salt-streams

(3) "Just as soon as you hear the cuckoo's sad song,/ That mournful sound in the mountain woods."

Analyzing Literary Conventions

14. Most of the imagery in the poem is either of nature at peace ("the quiet waters," "Sharing one estate in the beautiful city") or of cultural luxury ("lady adorned with such lovely ornaments," "give rings once again to the men in the mead-hall"). There are no images of battle except possibly "won/ Wealth," and the images of the sea are placid rather than stormy (". . .the sea, the home of the gull;/ Sail south from here . . .") The kenning *salt-streams* implies a connection between the sea and human tears, emphasizing a lovelorn mood that pervades the poem. The overall feeling is one of melancholy yearning—of someone who longs for a distant love.

Using the Philosophical and Historical Approaches

15. Students' responses will vary. A sample response follows:

"The Husband's Message" shows an Anglo-Saxon world in which recognizable human beings with everyday interests and characteristics try to achieve love and prosperity, much like people of any era and setting. The husband has gone to sea in order to make money, not to slay a monster. He yearns for the security and comfort of marriage rather than for a romantic ideal. He is not a warrior. In contrast, *Beowulf* shows a world dominated by warriors and by the struggle against monsters—a strug-gle for honor. However, Beowulf, as a person, is probably most contented during the fifty-year interval between attacks by the monsters. So both poems show a keen awareness of the value of peace and prosperity.

16. Students' responses will vary. A sample response follows:

The oaths mentioned are probably marriage oaths, and perhaps other personal oaths or promises the husband and wife made to each other before parting, such as an oath of fidelity or a promise of reunion. The importance of oaths to the husband's plea shows the poem to be a product of a religious age in which legal formalities were given great weight—in other words, the Anglo-Saxon era, when both Christian vows and civil oaths involving allegiance were fundamental in the social order. Today, if a husband asks his wife to return home, he would probably place more emphasis on the personal benefits of being together rather than on the marital vows.

Collection 2

Collection 2 Diagnostic Test
Literature, Vocabulary, *page 37*

1. A	**6.** H
2. H	**7.** B
3. C	**8.** F
4. H	**9.** D
5. C	**10.** G

Literary Period Introduction Test,
page 39

1. B	**6.** J
2. F	**7.** D
3. C	**8.** J
4. F	**9.** C
5. B	**10.** G

Answer Key

Lord Randall
Get Up and Bar the Door

Selection Test, *page 41*

Comprehension

1. C	**6.** H
2. H	**7.** B
3. D	**8.** H
4. J	**9.** D
5. D	**10.** G

Literary Focus

11. D	**13.** A
12. G	**14.** F

Constructed Response

15. Students' responses will vary. A sample response follows:

The ballad genre in the Middle Ages appealed primarily to an audience of ordinary people, and these two ballads are no exceptions. The subject matter of "Get Up and Bar the Door"—marital squabbling between a husband and wife of middling means—is one that ordinary citizens of medieval England would have recognized and laughed at. And while the characters of "Lord Randall" are noble, this doesn't necessarily mean that the audience was noble. A mass audience traditionally takes an interest in melodramas of elite life, such as the modern television series *All My Children* and *The West Wing,* and the demise of the wealthy and powerful is frequently a theme that holds special interest to the lower classes. Moreover, ballad techniques, such as refrain, simple rhyme, and simple meter, originated in song; these elements, too, show that the ballads were used as early mass entertainment.

The Prologue *from* The Canterbury Tales
by Geoffrey Chaucer

Selection Test, *page 44*

Comprehension

1. C	**6.** G
2. F	**7.** A
3. B	**8.** H
4. G	**9.** C
5. C	**10.** J

Literary Focus

11. A	**13.** A
12. F	

Reading Skills

14. H

Vocabulary Development

15. c	**18.** e
16. d	**19.** b
17. a	

Constructed Response

20. Students' responses will vary. A sample response follows:

My favorite character so far is the Nun, or Prioress. She is a worldly person despite her religious calling and exemplifies genteel daintiness and courtly manners. She is sentimental, loves fine dining, and has a romantic streak. The detail of her French speech—in the Stratford style rather than the Parisian style—deftly shows her as an upper-middle-class aspirant toward aristocracy. The long description of her table manners shows that spirituality is not necessarily the dearest to her heart. Yet she is evidently a decent person—she speaks no strong oaths, and her sentimental weeping over animals' pain does show a warm heart. The motto on her bracelet, "*Amor vincit omnia,*" hints that despite her vow of chastity, romantic longings are important to her. In short, she represents the kind of well-bred woman who, given the con-

Answer Key

strained opportunities available in the Middle Ages, entered the Church as a place of refuge and of sociopolitical advancement. She may have been genuine in her religious devotion but did not completely renounce worldly things.

from The Pardoner's Tale
by Geoffrey Chaucer
Selection Test, *page 48*

Comprehension

1. B	**6.** G
2. J	**7.** B
3. A	**8.** J
4. G	**9.** A
5. A	**10.** H

Literary Focus

11. C	**13.** A
12. F	**14.** G

Vocabulary Development

15. prudent

16. avarice

17. transcend

18. adversary

19. absolve

Constructed Response

20. Students' responses will vary. A sample response follows:

The moral I find in "The Pardoner's Tale" that is most applicable today is that even sinners desire forgiveness and wish to lead better lives. This lesson is shown in the ironic contrast between the tale the Pardoner tells and the way he lives his life. His tale condemns greed; his life exemplifies greed. But it should not be inferred from this contradiction that the Pardoner disdains the moral lesson he is telling. He may accept it as a matter of religious doctrine and psychological truth, yet knows that he is unable to live up to it. He hides his despair behind a pose of worldly disrespect for goodness. The ultimate irony is that the Pardoner would secretly wish to be sincere—to live up to the moral of the tale that he seems to be mocking.

from The Wife of Bath's Tale
by Geoffrey Chaucer
Selection Test, *page 52*

Comprehension

1. C	**6.** J
2. F	**7.** B
3. B	**8.** F
4. J	**9.** D
5. C	**10.** H

Literary Focus

11. A	**13.** C
12. F	

Reading Skills

14. H

Vocabulary Development

15. D	**18.** H
16. F	**19.** A
17. B	

Constructed Response

20. Students' responses will vary. A sample response follows:

Based on "The Wife of Bath's Tale," Chaucer's view of life is good-humored and expansive, forgiving of human frailty and hopeful of human improvement. It is a view of life that applauds virtue, fairness, decency, and generosity wherever such qualities are found, whether in nobles or commoners. Despite Chaucer's high position in life, he is not taken in by the superficial virtues of wealth or nobility; he knows that true wealth and nobility are in the heart. So far, Chaucer's views as stated here are very similar to those of the Wife of Bath, who is, after all, Chaucer's creation. The Wife's long speech about virtue sounds sincere; it's hard to imagine the author not agreeing with it. Chaucer probably does not share the Wife's view of marriage, however.

Answer Key

She views it as a contest for power in which the wife is the rightful winner. Chaucer, being male, would probably not hold that view, but he gives his female characters—the Wife of Bath, the queen, and the old woman—such strength of character that it is equally hard to imagine him thinking that their husbands should be their masters. Chaucer's view is more likely shown in the outcome of the tale, when both spouses show each other their *best* qualities and learn from them.

Right-Mind and Wrong-Mind *from* the Panchatantra

Selection Test, *page 56*

Comprehension

1. B	**6.** J
2. H	**7.** C
3. A	**8.** H
4. G	**9.** C
5. A	**10.** F

Literary Focus

11. C	**13.** C
12. G	**14.** F

Vocabulary Development

15. c	**18.** a
16. d	**19.** b
17. e	

Constructed Response

20. Students' responses will vary. A sample response follows:

Most obviously, Chaucer would probably have written the story in verse, and would probably have set at least one of the levels of the action in England. Chaucer did set his tales in many different places and times, however, and did use beast fable. Chaucer, like the *Panchatantra*, was fond of frame devices, so that device wouldn't change. Perhaps the chief difference would be that Chaucer would have presented his characters more fully, as human personalities

rather than mere representatives of moral qualities, even if he also attempted to teach a moral lesson. Moreover, Chaucer's moral lessons, as in "The Pardoner's Tale," are more ambiguous.

from The Third Voyage of Sindbad the Sailor *from* The Thousand and One Nights

Selection Test, *page 59*

Comprehension

1. A	**6.** G
2. H	**7.** A
3. B	**8.** H
4. J	**9.** D
5. C	**10.** G

Literary Focus

11. D	**13.** B
12. H	**14.** J

Vocabulary Development

Students' responses will vary. Sample responses follow:

15. If you eat a meal disconsolately, you eat it glumly, without enthusiasm.

16. A corpulent person looks pudgy, fleshy, or fat.

17. I want people's approbation because I want them to like me and like the things I do.

18. He or she has not been nimble.

19. The sailor did succeed at escaping.

Constructed Response

20. Students' responses will vary. A sample response follows:

The archetype Sindbad belongs to might be called The Resourceful Sailor or The Sailor As Trickster. An obvious parallel is with Odysseus in Greek legend (Homer's *Odyssey*) who experiences an adventure very similar to that of Sindbad. (Odysseus and his crewmates are trapped by the one-eyed giant Cyclops until Odysseus blinds him.) The traits of this archetype include pluck, cleverness, quick intelligence, and a

Answer Key

flair for deception and disguise, combined with an essentially good heart, concern for his fellows—and a lot of sheer luck or divine favor. Sindbad is, however, a medieval Arabian version of the archetype. His ship's journey apparently goes down the coast of Africa, as real Arabian trading ships did during the Middle Ages. There is also a combination of boastfulness and innocence about Sindbad that seems characteristic of his time and place. Moreover, he is not the ship's captain but a rather scrawny sailor, someone who might have been plucked out of a bazaar and offered adventure.

Federigo's Falcon
from the Decameron
by Giovanni Boccaccio
Selection Test, *page 63*

Comprehension

1. D	**6.** J
2. F	**7.** B
3. A	**8.** F
4. H	**9.** B
5. D	**10.** G

Literary Focus

11. C	**13.** C
12. J	

Reading Skills

14. H

Vocabulary Development

15. A	**18.** H
16. F	**19.** B
17. C	

Constructed Response

20. Students' responses will vary. A sample response follows:

I think the fact that the tale of Federigo and Monna Giovanna is a love story is the reason for the story's existence. There would not have been a marriage at all had the story not taken place in its historical context, for the lady did not love Federigo and had no wish to marry. She agreed to marry only at the prolonged and insistent urgings of her brothers, pressure that would not have been needed or applied at another time. For Monna's part the only love in this love story is the love she had for her son, and surely that devotion exists regardless of its historical era.

Federigo's fruitless pursuit of her, resulting in the depletion of his fortune, might also occur in another historical period. His actions are especially appropriate to this era, for his wasting of his fortune for a distant, courtly love and his sacrifice of his favorite bird for her show him attempting to fulfill the ideals of a courtly gentleman. Which had greater influence on Monna to marry, love or historical era? I think the latter, because only after much pressure did the lady even think of Federigo. Only social and practical considerations provided the pretext for the union.

from The Day of Destiny
from Le Morte d'Arthur
by Sir Thomas Malory
retold by Keith Baines
Selection Test, *page 67*

Comprehension

1. C	**6.** F
2. H	**7.** B
3. D	**8.** F
4. J	**9.** B
5. A	**10.** H

Literary Focus

11. A	**13.** C
12. H	**14.** J

Vocabulary Development

15. b	**18.** c
16. e	**19.** d
17. a	

Answer Key

Constructed Response

20. Students' responses will vary. A sample response follows:

If I were living in the Middle Ages, I would find *Le Morte d'Arthur* to be an inaccurate portrayal of my era in terms of realistic detail, but accurate psychologically as a portrayal of the longings and nostalgic impulses that guide me. I might be a merchant in the city, a skilled craftsman, or a yeoman working on my own land; if so, none of these lifestyles would have a place in the world of King Arthur. Even if I were a knight in the real 1485, I wouldn't resemble a knight of the Round Table—as the life of Sir Thomas Malory itself shows. Rather than fighting evil, jousting, and championing chivalric virtues, Malory engaged in political squabbling and perhaps petty crime. As a real citizen of the Middle Ages, I would probably be a devout Catholic, and the mixture of Christianity and Druidism found in the Arthur tales might seem baffling or sacrilegious to me.

Collection 2 Summative Test,

page 70

Vocabulary Skills

1. D

2. G

3. C

4. F

5. C

Comprehension

6. J

7. B

8. F

9. D

10. H

Reading Skills and Strategies

Analyzing Style: Details

11. C

Interpreting Character

12. G

Evaluating Historical Context

13. A

Literary Focus: Constructed Response

Identifying the Characteristics of a Ballad

14. Students' responses will vary. A sample response follows:

"Ballade de Marguerite" is a song-like narrative poem, in other words a ballad. It includes typical ballad characteristics such as a question-and-answer dialogue format, a lack of details, and a couplet structure with strong rhythm and simple rhyme scheme. Although the subject of love is present here as in "Lord Randall," "Ballade de Marguerite" is more romantic in tone than that heroic ballad; and it is more serious in tone than the comic "Get Up and Bar the Door." An element of ballads that is not contained in this poem is a refrain.

Identifying and Evaluating Historical Content

15. Students' responses will vary. A sample response follows:

The story of "Ballade de Marguerite" is one of courtly love, involving a forester's son and a beautiful lady. This premise hints at a medieval setting, which the presence of knights in the marketplace confirms. Social relations in the poem feature a world of knights, ladies, squires, and of middling people who are beneath them, such as foresters. The sewing of tapestries is a classic medieval occupation for women. The vocabulary of the poem includes words and phrases such as *alack, arras, assoil, morte, chapelle, gramercy, stoop of ale,* and *sae,* which connote the Middle Ages. The ballad form, with its question-and-answer dialogue between mother and son, is also typical of that era. Thematically, the fact that the expression of courtly love is made by a forester's son mirrors perfectly the social changes accompanying the decline of feudalism and the rise of the middle class in the later Middle Ages.

Analyzing Irony

16. Students' responses will vary. A sample response follows:

Answer Key

Situational irony is a discrepancy between what is expected and what happens. The situational irony in this poem is that the young man is passionately drawn to, and discusses the possibility of courting, a young woman who is already dead.

Analyzing an Archetype

17. Students' responses will vary. A sample response follows:

The forester's son matches the archetype in that he is a forlorn young man who is desperately in love with a beautiful woman who is unattainable. In some cases she is married (often to the young man's king), but in this case she is above his station. Furthermore, at the end he learns she is dead. He departs from the archetype in that he is a middle-class youth rather than a knight, lord, or poet.

Collection 3

Collection 3 Diagnostic Test
Literature, Informational Text, Vocabulary, *page 75*

1. D	**6.** H
2. G	**7.** D
3. C	**8.** G
4. F	**9.** D
5. C	**10.** F

Literary Period Introduction Test, *page 77*

1. B	**6.** F
2. H	**7.** D
3. A	**8.** G
4. G	**9.** C
5. C	**10.** J

The Passionate Shepherd to His Love
by Christopher Marlowe

The Nymph's Reply to the Shepherd
by Sir Walter Raleigh

To the Virgins, to Make Much of Time
by Robert Herrick

To His Coy Mistress
by Andrew Marvell

Give Us This Day Our Daily Bread
from Shakespeare Alive!
by Joseph Papp and Elizabeth Kirkland

Selection Test, *page 79*

Comprehension

1. C	**6.** J
2. G	**7.** C
3. B	**8.** H
4. H	**9.** A
5. D	**10.** J

Literary Focus

11. B	**13.** A
12. J	**14.** H

Constructed Response

15. Students' responses will vary. A sample response follows:

My impression of life in Renaissance England is that it was a culture in which life could be very exciting if you were urban and middle class; upper class; or perhaps best of all, a poet. However, if you were a rural laborer, tied to the land, you were likely living in poverty, disease, and perhaps even starvation. The image of idle shepherds sitting on rocks in Marlowe's poem is quite different from the reality of rural workers anxiously wondering whether they would get enough work to feed themselves, as described in the article. Marlowe's pastoral characters craft the

Answer Key

finest cloth gowns and slippers with gold buckles, but the typical rural dweller settled for much plainer clothing. In fact, I wonder whether the real lives of privileged, urban English people in the Renaissance did not more often resemble the life shown in the article rather than that shown in pastoral poems.

Sonnet 29, Sonnet 30
by William Shakespeare
Selection Test, *page 82*

Comprehension

1. B	6. F
2. F	7. A
3. D	8. H
4. H	9. C
5. D	10. G

Literary Focus

11. A	13. D
12. G	14. J

Constructed Response

15. Students' responses will vary. A sample response follows:

The two emotions that pervade both sonnets are love and sadness. In both poems the speaker is sad when alone and thinking about his past or present, but he is cheered up by the thought of someone he loves—the person the poems are addressed to. In Sonnet 29, the figure of speech of the lark ascending clearly shows the transition from sorrow to joy at the thought of the beloved friend. In Sonnet 30, the use of rather grim metaphors from law and finance to represent the speaker's thought process reinforces the tone of emotional pain. The sound devices of repetition and alliteration, especially of long *o* and the consonants *d*, *p*, *g*, and *w*, produce a moaning, keening effect in the middle of Sonnet 30, after which the *e* sounds of the couplet bring respite.

Sonnet 71, Sonnet 73
by William Shakespeare
Selection Test, *page 85*

Comprehension

1. C	6. J
2. G	7. B
3. A	8. J
4. G	9. C
5. A	10. H

Literary Focus

11. D	13. A
12. J	14. H

Constructed Response

15. Students' responses will vary. A sample response follows:

I prefer Sonnet 73 because of the beauty of its melancholy mood, which is evoked by its images and sounds—images of the waning year and the waning day, especially as captured in the first four lines. Images of yellow leaves, bare birdless branches, and dying embers in a fireplace all contribute to beautifying the poet's sadness. Long *a* and *i* sounds and rhymes such as *behold/cold* and *hang/sang* contribute to the bittersweetness. In contrast, Sonnet 71 sounds bitter and nasty, complaining of "this vile world" and "vilest worms." Sonnet 71 sounds less sincere in its tone—it's hard to believe that the speaker isn't just taking a stance, rather than genuinely asking his beloved to forget him.

Answer Key

Sonnet 116, Sonnet 130
by William Shakespeare

Selection Test, *page 88*

Comprehension

1. D	**6.** G
2. G	**7.** B
3. C	**8.** J
4. H	**9.** C
5. A	**10.** G

Literary Focus

11. C	**13.** B
12. F	**14.** J

Constructed Response

15. Students' responses will vary. A sample response follows:

    The mood of Sonnet 130 is fondly affectionate; the poem has an atmosphere lightly charged with slight mocking. This effect is achieved by using stale, figurative conventions, of which the poet seems conflicted: He's tired of them, but at the same time perhaps fond of turning them inside out. The figures of speech often incorporated in a conventional love poem are all negated: his mistress's eyes are *not* like the sun, her complexion is *not* like a rose, and so on. The mood turns comical when the negative comparisons involve the mistress's breath and voice—here the poet-speaker nearly insults his mistress. The mood in the couplet changes to one of serious loving, for all the preceding comparisons are wiped away, declared false in comparison to the one true thing the poet knows: love.

Blow, Blow, Thou Winter Wind
by William Shakespeare

Fear No More the Heat o' the Sun
by William Shakespeare

Full Fathom Five
by William Shakespeare

Selection Test, *page 91*

Comprehension

1. A	**6.** J
2. G	**7.** C
3. D	**8.** G
4. H	**9.** B
5. D	**10.** J

Literary Focus

11. A	**13.** C
12. F	**14.** J

Constructed Response

15. Students' responses will vary. A sample response follows:

    The sheer vivacity and beauty of the songs' language are two demonstrations that the author loved life—or at least loved art, a part of life. More substantively, the metaphoric imagery of "Full Fathom Five" shows that even death is a transfiguration to be cherished, a "sea change/ Into something rich and strange." The father in this song has died but has become something precious, almost mystical. Similarly, in "Fear No More the Heat o' the Sun," the emphasis is obviously on the inevitability of death, but the title indicates a valid fearlessness, a jauntiness, which is echoed in the rhythms of the song. This tone is also found in the title "Blow, Blow, Thou Winter Wind," which acknowledges the harshness of life but also declares the singer's willingness to face it. Although it is possible to emphasize the morbid side of the songs— the "chimney sweepers, come to dust"—the songs also contain brilliant imagery of plea-

Answer Key

sure and learning and natural beauty— "Golden lads and girls," the "scepter, learning, physic," "th' all-dreaded thunder-stone"—which attest to the value of mortal life. If human ingratitude is criticized in "Blow, Blow, Thou Winter Wind," it is also laughingly tolerated.

To be, or not to be
by William Shakespeare

Tomorrow, and tomorrow, and tomorrow
by William Shakespeare

St. Crispin's Day Speech
by William Shakespeare

Our revels now are ended
by William Shakespeare

Selection Test, *page 94*

Comprehension

1. C	6. F
2. G	7. D
3. C	8. J
4. H	9. A
5. B	10. F

Literary Focus

11. D	13. C
12. J	14. H

Constructed Response

15. Students' responses will vary. A sample response follows:

   Macbeth, I think you're wrong about life. Human life *may* be short—may be, for after all, it's a lot longer than the lives of most creatures—but even so, it's not a "walking shadow." We are not illusions or shadows, we are the most real things in the universe. Our lives are serious and meaningful, not mere performances; we are not "poor player[s]" strutting and fretting upon the stage. Life does *not* signify nothing. We must be alive to experience meaning. It is not being

that signifies nothing. The one thing we can be sure of is that we ourselves can make meaning out of life.

Song
by John Donne

Selection Test, *page 97*

Comprehension

1. D	6. J
2. H	7. C
3. B	8. H
4. F	9. A
5. B	10. H

Literary Focus

11. C	13. A
12. G	14. J

Constructed Response

15. Students' responses will vary. A sample response follows:

   I disagree with the speaker's position. Both women and men can be honest or dishonest, and the speaker does not give any specific evidence for thinking women are worse than men. Actually, the very fact that he uses hyperbole instead of factual evidence could be held against him. It's obviously untrue that a virtuous woman does not exist, or that if one were found, she would become false (two or more times over) in the time it takes to walk next door to meet her. Finding an honest women is not as difficult as catching a falling star or getting a plant pregnant. Given that untruth, what basis do we have for believing Donne's argument? There's nothing in the poem to stand on; it only serves as reinforcment for those who already subscribe to this prejudice. Meanwhile, in Donne's own lifetime, England was ruled by a woman, Queen Elizabeth I, who was known for her many strengths and virtues—the greatest being her fidelity to her realm.

Answer Key

A Valediction: Forbidding Mourning
by John Donne
Selection Test, *page 100*

Comprehension

1. D	**6.** H
2. J	**7.** B
3. C	**8.** J
4. F	**9.** A
5. D	**10.** H

Literary Focus

11. A	**13.** D
12. G	**14.** H

Constructed Response

15. Students' responses will vary. A sample response follows:

I think the strong points of the conceit are its originality, its unusual quality, and its feeling of rightness. Probably few, if any, would go around thinking of themselves and their loved ones as two prongs of a compass, but, once the comparison has been made, it's not difficult to think of lovers in that way. In that sense the conceit is extremely effective. Perhaps the only way it is ineffective is that it is so far-fetched it can arouse inappropriate comedy. Human beings depicted as simple, small, metal objects is an idea that seems silly. But I think it works overall. Personally, I found the poem very moving, and the compass conceit especially so. Just as a circle is perfect, the love it describes is also perfect.

Meditation 17
by John Donne
Selection Test, *page 103*

Comprehension

1. D	**6.** F
2. G	**7.** A
3. B	**8.** H
4. J	**9.** C
5. A	**10.** H

Literary Focus

11. B	**13.** C
12. F	**14.** J

Constructed Response

15. Students' responses will vary. A sample response follows:

From "Meditation 17," I learned at least a partial answer to the "problem of pain," the age-old question of why God created suffering and evil. Donne thinks that the purpose of suffering is to mature us and, so, to bring us closer to God. I was especially impressed by the metaphor of gold and money. Gold is like pure, unexamined suffering—there is no use in hauling around a bar of gold if we are hungry, just as there is no use in living if we do not examine our souls. Just as we need to exchange money for goods, we need to exchange our suffering for thoughts about God if suffering is to be useful.

Answer Key

Death be not proud
by John Donne

from W;t
by Margaret Edson

Selection Test, *page 106*

Comprehension

1. D	**6.** F
2. G	**7.** C
3. A	**8.** J
4. G	**9.** C
5. D	**10.** H

Literary Focus

11. A	**13.** C
12. F	**14.** H

Constructed Response

15. Students' responses will vary. A sample response follows:

I think the argument in "Death be not proud" is extremely clever and well-formulated but not convincing. The argument rests largely on figures of speech and analogies, and they make for great reading, but they don't carry much logical weight. The fact that rest and sleep are welcome doesn't necessarily mean that death is also welcome. The fact that death is carried out through human or natural agencies doesn't make death any less final. By personifying death, Donne merely reduces it to a level where it seems like a less formidable foe—and thus falsifies it. In fact death is not a person or a thing. It is just the absence of life.

On My First Son
by Ben Jonson

Song: To Celia
by Ben Jonson

Selection Test, *page 109*

Comprehension

1. C	**6.** F
2. F	**7.** D
3. B	**8.** J
4. J	**9.** A
5. D	**10.** G

Literary Focus

11. D	**13.** B
12. H	**14.** G

Constructed Response

15. Students' responses will vary. A sample response follows:

The epigrams "On My First Son" and "Song: to Celia" are brief, but not extremely so. Clever they certainly are: the phrase "child of my right hand" and the lines "Here doth lie / Ben Jonson his best piece of poetry," and "As what he loves may never like too much" are clever enough to be both memorable and meaningful. The comparison of the child's life span to a loan is striking. The first two lines of "Song: To Celia" are also striking; they have become the lyrics of a famous popular song. The final wisecrack about the smell of the flowers in "Song: To Celia" is pointed and clever. I believe these are very successful epigrams.

Answer Key

Of Studies
by Francis Bacon

Axioms *from the* Essays
by Francis Bacon

Selection Test, *page 112*

Comprehension

1. C	**6.** H
2. G	**7.** A
3. D	**8.** J
4. G	**9.** C
5. B	**10.** H

Literary Focus

11. A	**13.** C
12. F	

Reading Skills

14. H

Vocabulary Development

15. d	**18.** c
16. e	**19.** a
17. b	

Constructed Response

20. Students' responses will vary. A sample response follows:

An underlying assumption behind Bacon's argument in "Of Studies" is that worldly success is of great importance. Almost every time Bacon claims a specific benefit for a specific kind of study, the benefit is a worldly one: judgment in business, development of "general counsels, and the plots and marshaling of affairs," and so on. He prescribes specific sorts of study for specific mental shortcomings, as if the latter were ailments to be cured: math for a wandering mind, the Schoolmen for trouble in making distinctions, and so on. Bacon explicitly compares this virtue of study to the virtue of physical exercise: "Bowling is good for the stone and reins." Lip service is given to studying for pleasure, but the matter is not as developed as are the practical advantages. Studying for enlightenment

is ignored: It is covered neither by "delight . . . ornament . . . [or] ability." So this assumption allows Bacon to overlook other reasons that some people, both then and now, might find equally persuasive.

Tilbury Speech
by Queen Elizabeth I

from Female Orations
by Margaret Cavendish, duchess of Newcastle

Selection Test, *page 116*

Comprehension

1. A	**6.** F
2. H	**7.** D
3. B	**8.** H
4. F	**9.** B
5. A	**10.** H

Literary Focus

11. D	**13.** B
12. H	**14.** F

Constructed Response

15. Students' responses will vary. A sample response follows:

Given that none of the four voices can be attributed to Cavendish herself, the obvious inference is that Cavendish held views and possessed abilities that enabled her to eloquently express all of these divergent views. She was aware of widely ranging positions, and she was herself an educated woman. Therefore, it is hard to believe that she would hold the views of Speaker III, for example, who disparages women. Most clearly, perhaps, the orations show that Cavendish values wide, open discourse. In that sense she seems to agree with Speaker I. The act of putting these orations together, in itself, implies that Cavendish must have believed in the value of female perceptions and of women taking active intellectual roles. The fact that all the orations are so skillfully presented is a clear and convincing demonstration that such values are valid.

Answer Key

Psalm 23
King James Bible

Psalm 137
King James Bible
Selection Test, *page 120*

Comprehension

1. C	**6.** G
2. F	**7.** D
3. D	**8.** J
4. H	**9.** A
5. B	**10.** F

Literary Focus

11. C	**13.** B
12. J	**14.** G

Constructed Response

15. Students' responses will vary. A sample response follows:

Numerous instances of parallelism can be found in these psalms. Two examples are found in Psalm 23, "He maketh me . . . He leadeth me . . . He restoreth" and in Psalm 137, "For there they that carried us away captive required of us a song; / And they that wasted us required of us mirth." The rhythmic repetition of these already solemn phrases enhances their solemnity and helps give them an air of sacredness, which was of course one of the psalmist's chief goals. The repetition of emotions increases their force, and the repeated statements of grief and anger in Psalm 137 also heighten those feelings. The pastoral metaphors repeated in parallel in Psalm 23 enhance the listeners' feeling of security in God's presence. Examples include the "He maketh me" lines and the metaphors of feasting and anointing stated in parallel in lines 9–10.

The Parable of the Prodigal Son
King James Bible
Selection Test, *page 123*

Comprehension

1. C	**6.** H
2. F	**7.** C
3. D	**8.** H
4. F	**9.** C
5. B	**10.** G

Literary Focus

11. A	**13.** C
12. J	**14.** H

Constructed Response

15. Students' responses will vary. A sample response follows:

If "The Parable of the Prodigal Son" was a realistic story, the younger son might leave without his inheritance (given what the Background feature says about ancient Israelite law) and on his return, the family's welcome might not be quite so effusive. That is, the father might still welcome him but without going overboard as in the parable. The effect of the exaggeration in the parable is to emphasize God's joy at the return of sinners and His forgiveness. Not only is the younger son allowed to return, he is positively feted. A realistic story might dwell in detail on the elder son's view; in the parable his viewpoint is swept aside. A realistic story would investigate subtleties and ambiguities, as opposed to the clearcut position set out in the parable.

Holt Assessment: Literature, Reading, and Vocabulary

Answer Key

Night *from the* Koran

from Philosophy and Spiritual Discipline *from the* Bhagavad-Gita

Zen Parables
compiled by Paul Reps

from The Analects of Confucius

from the Tao Te Ching
Laotzu

Taoist Anecdotes

Sayings of Saadi

African Proverbs
compiled by Charlotte and Wolf Leslau

Selection Test, *page 126*

Comprehension

1. B	**6.** H
2. G	**7.** C
3. B	**8.** F
4. F	**9.** C
5. D	**10.** J

Literary Focus

11. B	**13.** D
12. F	**14.** J

Constructed Response

15. Students' responses will vary. A sample response follows:

My two favorite passages are the Zen parable "The Moon Cannot Be Stolen" and the chapter from the *Tao Te Ching*. In form they are very different: One is a very short story and the other is a series of sayings, observations, or wise thoughts strung together. The parable shows a specific concrete human situation and narrates it without any explicit commentary, while the chapter from the *Tao* is all commentary and no specific concrete human narrative. I think of these two passages as two sides of a coin. Although the Zen master is not a Taoist, he seems to me to embody the spirit of the *Tao Te Ching*. He is simply himself, and he simply accepts others, even someone who tries to rob him. If you said to someone, "Make up a story to illustrate this chapter from the *Tao Te Ching*," he couldn't do much better than "The Moon Cannot Be Stolen."

The Fall of Satan *from* Paradise Lost
by John Milton

Selection Test, *page 129*

Comprehension

1. A	**6.** F
2. F	**7.** B
3. D	**8.** J
4. G	**9.** B
5. A	**10.** H

Literary Focus

11. A	**13.** D
12. J	**14.** F

Vocabulary Development

15. malice

16. impetuous

17. infernal

18. guile

19. contention

Constructed Response

20. Students' responses will vary. A sample response follows:

Elevated diction and blank verse (unrhymed iambic pentameter) are the two elements of Milton's style that seem to contribute most to the lofty tone that enhanced Milton's purpose. Blank verse, of all English meters, with its long lines and absence of rhyme is perhaps best suited for a serious, long poem on philosophical themes. Milton sets a pace that is stately and fluid, with enough variation to maintain interest. For instance, the first line of the poem has an extra syllable, but the next

Answer Key

three have perfect iambs. The elevated diction of phrases such as "Raised impious war in Heaven" or "To bottomless perdition, there to dwell / In adamantine chains and penal fire" makes the reader understand and feel the weight and importance of *Paradise Lost*'s tone toward its subject matter. The Latinate polysyllabics not only sound imposing, but they immensely aid the flow of the blank verse.

When I consider how my light is spent
by John Milton
Selection Test, *page 133*

Comprehension

1. B	**4.** G
2. J	**5.** D
3. B	

Literary Focus

6. H	**8.** F
7. D	**9.** C

Constructed Response

10. Students' responses will vary. A sample response follows:

I think Milton uses personification as a rhetorical strategy in order to create a somber and serious effect, one which would transmit the seriousness of Milton's intentions. Milton thinks of Patience as a concrete reality, having a human personality; the effect on the reader could be, "Wow, look at the company Milton keeps!" We may interact with our friends, but he interacts with Patience! Also, the personification increases the dramatic effect of the poem and enlivens it. Since Patience is a character who speaks dialogue, it creates in the poem action, personality, conflict; in contrast, if Milton were discussing Patience in the abstract, the poem might read like a sermon in verse.

from The Pilgrim's Progress
by John Bunyan
Selection Test, *page 136*

Comprehension

1. D	**6.** J
2. J	**7.** A
3. C	**8.** G
4. F	**9.** C
5. D	**10.** F

Literary Focus

11. B	**13.** B
12. H	**14.** G

Vocabulary Development

15. A	**18.** H
16. H	**19.** D
17. A	

Constructed Response

20. Students' responses will vary. A sample response follows:

The central philosophical idea of *The Pilgrim's Progress* is a Christian one. The reader should seek God, live a prayerful life, and avoid sin. This view permeates the entire book and is conveyed by the names of the characters: Christian, Faithful, and Hopeful are good characters; Mr. Cruelty and Mr. Hate-light are two of the villains. The world, as Vanity-Fair, is shown as an extravagant display of temptations, and it should be shunned, only traveled through on the way to the heavenly kingdom, given no more than a disgusted glance. The utter simplicity and lack of irony in the treatment of the main idea give it great charm that has not been lost over the centuries. Even today, Christian's journey still seems lively, amusing, and touching.

Answer Key

Collection 3 Summative Test,
page 140

Vocabulary Skills

1. B   **4.** F

2. H   **5.** B

3. A

Comprehension

6. G   **9.** A

7. C   **10.** G

8. J

Reading Skills and Strategies: Constructed Response

Analyzing Tone

11. Students responses will vary. A sample response follows:

The tone is both adoring and frustrated or seriously passionate and ironic. The speaker asserts his great love for the addressee, and this is demonstrated not only by his words but by his actions, such as waiting without chiding her. At the same time, however, by saying this, he *is* chiding her. I think he feels his frustration most deeply because if he were truly dedicated to being in love, he would not be calling himself a servant, a sad slave, and a fool.

Critiquing Summations

12. Students responses will vary. Sample responses follow:

a. It is never stated in the poem that the addressee has paid any attention whatsoever to the speaker. The speaker acts as if he were involved in a love affair, but his involvement may be entirely a matter of his own perception. It is clear that he is being ignored; exactly to what degree is not stated. What is indisputable is that the speaker is passionately infatuated with the addressee yet frustrated with her inattention.

b. Despite the sarcasm in the speaker's descriptions of waiting for his beloved, it is clear that he is very much in love. Since he seems to be rational, it is difficult to believe

he is deluded about the essential nature of the relationship.

Literary Focus: Constructed Response

13. Students' responses will vary. A sample response follows:

Image: The speaker is a slave who spends his every waking hour trying to tend to his beloved's desires.

Emotional Effect on Reader: The slave image makes me feel a lack of respect for the speaker even though I can understand his feelings. Most people know what it feels like to be dependent on a loved one, but the speaker carries it too far. He's humiliating himself, and he seems to enjoy it.

14. Students' responses will vary. A sample response follows:

Examples of irony can be found in the juxtaposition of slave and sovereign, such as in "I have no precious time . . . ," in which the speaker clearly thinks his time is precious and being wasted. Phrases such as "world-without-end hour" and "watch the clock for you" infer impatience, while he says he dares not complain. Another example of irony is in his saying, "Nor dare I question," when the entire sonnet represents a questioning.

15. Students' responses will vary. A sample response follows:

The sonnet shows love as a kind of derangement, a derangement of the mind and of people's social positions. An otherwise rational man becomes a slave to a woman who ignores him. The final couplet expresses the point clearly: "So true a fool is love. . . ." Love is folly, as is also demonstrated in the song "Blow, Blow, Thou Winter Wind," but a folly that may lead to fulfillment. Love defies reason: To the "will" (pun) of the lover, the beloved's mistreatment of him should not represent an "ill" (at least not ideally). In reality, as the poem implies, it is hard to overlook a beloved's slights.

Answer Key

Collection 4

Collection 4 Diagnostic Test
Literature, Informational Text, Vocabulary, *page 144*

1. A	**6.** H
2. H	**7.** B
3. C	**8.** J
4. J	**9.** B
5. A	**10.** G

Literary Period Introduction Test,
page 146

1. C	**6.** H
2. F	**7.** D
3. D	**8.** J
4. G	**9.** A
5. A	**10.** F

A Modest Proposal
by Jonathan Swift

Top of the Food Chain
by T. Coraghessan Boyle

Selection Test, *page 148*

Comprehension

1. A	**6.** J
2. J	**7.** C
3. B	**8.** G
4. H	**9.** C
5. A	**10.** G

Literary Focus

11. C	**13.** B
12. G	

Reading Skills

14. G

Vocabulary Development

15. c	**18.** d
16. a	**19.** b
17. e	

Constructed Response

20. Students' responses will vary. A sample response follows:

In *A Modest Proposal* the satire and verbal irony Swift uses to convince his audience takes the form of wild exaggeration and misstatement. For instance, the speaker claims to be civilized and well-meaning, but his solutions are brutal and inhumane. In making false claims and offensive suggestions, Swift demonstrates his essential strategy—saying the opposite of what he means to show the truth. Each point of his proposal is not only ridiculously impractical but meant to be deeply horrifying to the reader. Examples of obvious falsehoods include the claim that Americans are experienced cannibals. The use of this technique underscores the obvious rationality of the author's true views on the subject.

Heroic Couplets
by Alexander Pope

from An Essay on Man
by Alexander Pope

Selection Test, *page 152*

Comprehension

1. B	**6.** J
2. H	**7.** D
3. B	**8.** F
4. G	**9.** C
5. A	**10.** J

Literary Focus

11. C	**13.** B
12. G	

Reading Skills: Identifying the Writer's Stance

14. G

Constructed Response

15. Students' responses will vary. A sample response follows:

Pope's poetry emphasizes reason and moderation. As is stated in *An Essay on*

Answer Key

Man, mankind is in "a middle state," between animal and angel, between reason and error. The best course to take, then, is to "know then thyself" and use rational judgment, combined with the virtues Pope approves of: forgiveness, hope, learning, and artistic dedication. This advice applies even to the practice of satire, which is not supposed to be excessively harsh. The sound of Pope's poetry perfectly suits this "middle state" principle: His lines are beautifully balanced and paced, perfectly crafted, and lacking in any harshness, adventurousness, or deviation from the ideal.

from The Rape of the Lock
by Alexander Pope
Selection Test, *page 155*

Comprehension

1. D	**6.** F
2. H	**7.** A
3. A	**8.** G
4. J	**9.** C
5. A	**10.** J

Literary Focus

11. B	**13.** A
12. H	**14.** G

Vocabulary Development

15. exulting

16. repast

17. dejects

18. desist

19. recesses

Constructed Response

20. Students' responses will vary. A sample response follows:

Pope's tone is affectionately mocking of the foibles of the upper classes, and his wit, like the Baron's scissors, has a double edge. He glorifies the wealthy and insults them, but he does so in such a balanced way that

it is not clear which view is most prominent. This ambiguity ensures that the audience members—the very target of his wit—will be confused, not knowing whether to feel flattered or insulted by this description of their triviality. The sections in the text that seem most critical of society are found in the introductory passages, where Pope comments freely on topics such as politics and the law. Though Pope may not have lent much weight to the silly quarrel that inspired this work, he must have cared very deeply for the people involved. If he didn't, he wouldn't have spent so much time writing the poem. He must have known them well, for his approach brought them to their senses and averted a serious falling out.

from Candide
by Voltaire
Selection Test, *page 159*

Comprehension

1. C	**6.** F
2. H	**7.** D
3. B	**8.** G
4. J	**9.** C
5. C	**10.** F

Literary Focus

11. B	**13.** A
12. F	**14.** H

Vocabulary Development

15. A	**18.** F
16. G	**19.** C
17. C	

Constructed Response

20. Students' responses will vary. A sample response follows:

Voltaire's *Candide* seems less harsh than Swift's *A Modest Proposal* but harsher than Pope's *The Rape of the Lock*. There is nothing in this selection from *Candide* that is as disgusting as the cooking of babies in A *Modest*

Answer Key

Proposal; in addition, Swift's satire is not softened by the presence of a likable character such as Candide, or by a love story such as the one that occurs between Candide and Cunegonde. On the other hand, in *Candide* the tone is clearly one of disgust with human folly, whereas in *The Rape of the Lock* the tone is affectionate mockery. Swift obviously loathes the aristocracy, while Pope partly mocks and partly flatters them; Voltaire simply considers them, along with just about all of the rest of the world, to be dangerously mean-spirited.

from Don Quixote
by Miguel de Cervantes
Selection Test, *page 163*

Comprehension

1. B	**6.** F
2. H	**7.** D
3. D	**8.** J
4. J	**9.** B
5. B	**10.** G

Literary Focus

11. A	**13.** A
12. G	**14.** H

Vocabulary Development

15. b	**18.** d
16. c	**19.** a
17. e	

Constructed Response

20. Students' responses will vary. A sample response follows:

I agree with the assertion. *A Modest Proposal* parodies persuasive arguments; *The Rape of the Lock* parodies the epic; *Candide* parodies picaresque romantic novels; and *Don Quixote* parodies chivalric romances. It has already been established that *A Modest Proposal*, *The Rape of the Lock*, and *Candide* are satires; in addition, *Don Quixote* is a satire of, among other things, heroic idealism, machismo, and romantic

love. Tilting at windmills is certainly not heroic, but laughable; machismo in such a battle is equally foolish; and love of a lady who exists primarily in the imagination is folly.

from A Vindication of the Rights of Woman
by Mary Wollstonecraft
Selection Test, *page 166*

Comprehension

1. D	**6.** J
2. J	**7.** C
3. B	**8.** H
4. F	**9.** D
5. B	**10.** J

Literary Focus

11. A	**13.** B
12. G	

Reading Skills

14. F

Vocabulary Development

15. specious

16. insipid

17. fastidious

18. propensity

19. cursory

Constructed Response

20. Students' responses will vary. A sample response follows:

Wollstonecraft uses strong words and clear, unemotional language to argue that being a parent and homemaker is an honorable profession. It is a profession, she believes, that requires a great deal of intellect and strength of character. Training for this profession should be thorough and the work generously rewarded. Wollstonecraft's claim that upper-class British women of her time are ill-suited for motherhood and household management is supported by persuasive arguments, such

Answer Key

as the idea that women who have been treated solely as objects of desire cannot be expected to govern a family or to take care of the babies. The result, she says, is a degradation of women and a decline in the intelligence of the population as a whole. This eventuality occurs because oppressed women, as mothers, become "mere propagators of fools."

To the Ladies
by Mary, Lady Chudleigh

from The Education of Women
by Daniel Defoe

Selection Test, *page 170*

Comprehension

1. D	**6.** G
2. G	**7.** D
3. C	**8.** F
4. F	**9.** A
5. C	**10.** H

Constructed Response

11. Students' responses will vary. A sample response follows:

I think Chudleigh and Defoe would disagree about whether or not women should strive to be good companions for men. Defoe seems to see this role as a key reason for educating women; he repeatedly says he hopes to improve their conversation skills and make them presentable by learning various arts, such as dancing. Chudleigh, on the other hand, is opposed to the very idea of marriage, and she advises women to "despise" men and to hate "[a]ll the fawning Flatt'rers," by which she means men who court women. The differences between these points of view seem to stem from the differences in their circumstances: Defoe is a man, while Chudleigh is a woman who has suffered an unhappy marriage. It's not that Defoe sees women as inferior; rather, he considers women's rights from the rather selfish standpoint of how women's

education will benefit men. To be fair, it made sense at the time to appeal to men—they were, after all, the voters. However, I feel his argument is limited in scope and comes from a privileged position. He lacks the credibility of someone who had actually suffered from the effects of the existing system. I think Lady Chudleigh would set him straight in short order and that Defoe would defer, demurring gentlemanly, for the moment at least.

Collection 4 Summative Test,
page 172

Vocabulary Skills

1. A	**4.** F
2. F	**5.** C
3. B	

Comprehension

6. J	**9.** B
7. C	**10.** G
8. J	

Reading Skills and Strategies

11. C

Literary Focus: Constructed Response

Evaluating a Comment on Life

12. Students' responses will vary. A sample response follows:

Addison seems not to be as concerned with, or angry about, serious issues of women's rights as Wollstonecraft, Chudleigh, or Defoe. However, despite Addison's lightly mocking tone, he does present a view of London life in which educated women take a role in the political events of the day, and Wollstonecraft, Chudleigh, and Defoe do not. Addison may or may not like the fact that one such woman made a political stipulation in her marriage agreement, but he seems to accept fondly a world in which such events happen; he does not side with those who refuse to see any genuine political motive in women's "patches." Given his urbanity, it is

Answer Key

hard to believe he would prefer a world with fewer intelligent women. However, when it comes to arguments for women's rights, he sits on the sidelines.

Comparing and Contrasting Tone

13. Students' responses will vary. A sample response follows:

Addison's satire more closely resembles Pope's than Swift's, both in its style and substance. Addison and Pope are both affectionately mocking the foibles of the upper crust. Swift, on the other hand, is savagely indicting that class, among others, for serious injustices. Stylistically, Addison and Swift are comparable in that both write graceful prose, but Swift's prose takes on the mask, or voice, of that which it parodies. Addison writes in his own natural voice, not a parodic one. Addison's style is probably easier to read today than Swift's, at least as written in *A Modest Proposal*: Addison's sentences tend to be shorter and more conversational and his tone less formal.

Analyzing Satire

14. Students' responses will vary. A sample response follows:

Example of Irony—Addison says that many women patch "out of principle and with an eye to the interest of their country"; *Type of Irony*—verbal; *Implied Meaning*—Patching is a trivial way of working for the interests of one's country.

Example of Irony—Rosalinda, a Whig, has a mole on the Tory side of her forehead; *Type of Irony*—situational; *Implied Meaning*—Using physical appearance to indicate political beliefs is nonsensical.

Collection 5

Collection 5 Diagnostic Test
Literature, Vocabulary, *page 177*

1. B	6. H
2. H	7. A
3. D	8. J
4. H	9. C
5. D	10. G

Literary Period Introduction Test,
page 179

1. D	6. F
2. H	7. B
3. C	8. H
4. G	9. A
5. C	10. G

The Tyger
by William Blake

"Blake Is a Real Name ..."
by Charles Lamb

The Lamb
by William Blake

Selection Test, *page 181*

Comprehension

1. B	6. H
2. G	7. D
3. B	8. F
4. J	9. A
5. C	10. H

Literary Focus

11. B	13. B
12. H	14. F

Constructed Response

15. Students' responses will vary. A sample response follows:

The tiger symbolizes evil and the lamb symbolizes innocence, or good. The tiger is described in figurative terms such as "burning"; in other words, it is a destructive force

Answer Key

related to hell itself. Words such as "dread" and "deadly terrors" are used to describe the tiger's qualities. The image of the stars throwing down their spears and watering heaven with their tears implies that the tiger's creation was a catastrophe. The lamb, on the other hand, stands for all that is innocent and good. The lamb is associated with mildness, with meadows and streams, and with bright woolly clothing. The parallels drawn between the lamb and Jesus in the second stanza clarify the symbol of the lamb.

The Chimney Sweeper
from **Songs of Innocence**
by William Blake

The Chimney Sweeper
from **Songs of Experience**
by William Blake

from **Evidence Given Before the Sadler Committee**

Selection Test, *page 184*

Comprehension

1. C	**6.** J
2. F	**7.** B
3. B	**8.** F
4. J	**9.** A
5. A	**10.** J

Literary Focus

11. A	**13.** B
12. H	**14.** G

Constructed Response

15. Students' responses will vary. Sample response follow:

a. The political purpose is evident in the fact that both poems present a horrific view of child labor in the England of Blake's day. The poem from *Songs of Innocence* does not blunt this reality; innocence can be found in the boys' hopes and dreams, but not in the actual conditions of their day-to-day lives. The first line, "When my mother died I was

very young," establishes this mood, and it continues through the repetitions of the word *weep* and other *eep* words. The reassuring ending is obviously ironic. In the poem from *Songs of Experience* the anti-authoritarian stance is overt: the child's parents, having sold him, tell themselves he's happy, and comfort themselves with prayer.

b. The religious purpose is evident in the fact that both poems, while depicting the abuses of child labor, deal with the possibility of redemption—not only in the hereafter but in this life as well. In light of the harsh circumstances of the speakers' lives, descriptions of goodness, purity, and innocence are meant to be heavily ironic; however, one can't help feeling that the poet sees the first ill-treated chimney sweeper as possessing a kind of innocence, while the second sweep may be redeemed by his clear view of reality.

c. It becomes especially clear at the end of the poem from *Songs of Experience* that for Blake, political protest is a form of religious exercise and vice versa. The speaker's parents go to church hoping for redemption for their sin of selling their child. The child, however, is truly holy, which can be found in the imagery of innocence; in the lilting, rhythmic, rhyming patterns; and in the parallelism which mirrors the childlike simplicity of the truly innocent. In the poem from *Songs of Innocence* the religious sense is more overt; the outrage cloaked behind the speaker's ironic acceptance of his lot. In the poem from *Songs of Innocence* the chimney sweeper is suffering from abuse, but because of his essential innocence, he is able to forgive his abusers.

Answer Key

A Poison Tree
by William Blake
Selection Test, *page 187*
Comprehension

1. D	**6.** F
2. H	**7.** C
3. D	**8.** F
4. F	**9.** A
5. C	**10.** H

Literary Focus

11. A	**13.** D
12. G	**14.** G

Constructed Response

15. Students' responses will vary. A sample response follows:

Blake sees anger as a natural force that can be either quelled or encouraged by human intervention. Confessing one's anger is a way to resolve it; keeping anger suppressed only makes it grow and become poisonous. Blake uses the metaphor of the growth of a plant to describe the growth of anger in the soul. Appropriately, the fruit, or result, of anger is poison. It is interesting that the speaker does not suffer for his own anger; the foe is killed and that's that.

Lines Composed a Few Miles Above Tintern Abbey
by William Wordsworth
Selection Test, *page 190*
Comprehension

1. A	**4.** G
2. J	**5.** C
3. B	**6.** G

Literary Focus

7. B	**9.** A
8. H	

Reading Skills

10. F	**11.** B

Constructed Response

12. Students' responses will vary. A sample response follows:

The easily flowing, rambling, conversational blank verse of the poem is perfectly suited to Wordsworth's subject of a long, rambling walk through nature, as well as to the back-and-forth movement of the speaker's thoughts in time. This style of verse allows the speaker to delve into any thought that comes to him and to examine its shape, muse upon its past and future, and then move on, like a stream curving around a rock. The rhythm of blank verse maintains unity, but the flexibility makes for a meditative tone. Long abstract words alternating with ordinary descriptive language establish a flow in lines such as "These beauteous forms, / Through a long absence, have not been to me / As is a landscape to a blind man's eye." The thoughts spill over from line to line like the endless current of the Wye. The tone is quietly confidential, as in, "And I have felt / A presence that disturbs me with the joy / Of elevated thoughts; a sense sublime / Of something far more deeply interfused. . . ." This sounds exactly like a poet talking to himself as he picks his way over rocks and streams.

Composed upon Westminster Bridge
by William Wordsworth
Selection Test, *page 193*
Comprehension

1. B	**5.** A
2. J	**6.** J
3. D	**7.** B
4. F	**8.** H

Literary Focus

9. B	**11.** A
10. J	**12.** F

Holt Assessment: Literature, Reading, and Vocabulary

Answer Key

Constructed Response

13. Students' responses will vary. A sample response follows:

The emotions Wordsworth evokes are awe at the grandeur and mystery of the city; admiration for its beauty; and perhaps a certain amount of bewilderment at finding the city in such an atypical mood. The personifications add greatly to this mood because, first, picturing the morning as garments for a city adds a mystical touch, enhancing the feeling of awe; and second, saying that the river moves "at his own sweet will" enhances the atypical feeling of tranquillity. It is as if the speaker has captured a very loud, rambunctious person in a rare moment of meditative solitude, or glimpsed a very active child while he or she is sleeping. And the mere fact of confronting an immense city as if it were a single human being adds a fairy tale quality, as if a giant were lying asleep at the speaker's feet.

The World Is Too Much with Us
by William Wordsworth
Selection Test, *page 196*
Comprehension

1. D	**4.** F
2. F	**5.** C
3. D	**6.** H

Literary Focus

7. C	**10.** H
8. G	**11.** B
9. A	

Constructed Response

12. Students' responses will vary. A sample response follows:

The sea baring its bosom to the moon in line 5 gives the poem an ecstatic, romantic feeling and contributes to a tone of lyrical rapture. This figure of speech expresses what the speaker longs for, what he feels modern life has given up. He says that peo-

ple see little that is theirs in nature, but evidently he sees nature and sees it beautifully as in the comparison of the wind to sleeping flowers in lines 6–7. This figure of speech builds on previous ones and creates a mental picture of a seascape at night, with the speaker viewing it "on this pleasant lea." The speaker both admires the scene and wishes he could be more completely swept up by it. Soon after these wonderful images, the poet adds, "It moves us not," which seems contradictory and turns the tone bitter. This underscores the complexity of his response.

Tanka Poetry
Haiku Poetry
Selection Test, *page 199*
Comprehension

1. C	**6.** H
2. F	**7.** C
3. B	**8.** H
4. H	**9.** B
5. A	**10.** G

Literary Focus

11. D	**13.** A
12. J	**14.** H

Constructed Response

15. Students' responses will vary. Sample responses follow:

The tanka convey a feeling of longing and loneliness, in addition to an awareness of the beauty and impermanence of all things. Whether the subject is love, travel, or the moon, tanka poets focus on a single image and isolate it so that we can see the object in its solitary nature. The images are often things that are inherently short-lived, such as reeds, a breeze, or a plum blossom. In Saigyo's poem the speaker says that despite all change, moonlight remains the same. But does it? I think the speaker is deliberately trying to get the reader to disagree with that assertion so the reader will

Answer Key

feel more forcefully the impermanence of all things.

The haiku in this selection contain the imagery of spring, yet spring is imagined differently and evokes different moods in each poem. The only haiku in which spring is clearly *not* the subject matter is Bashō's "On a withered branch," which describes autumn and presents a beautifully stark and bleak image of nightfall. In the other poems flowers and vines herald spring or possibly, in some cases, summer. The mood is joyous, even ecstatic, in Onitsura's poem, in which the very stones of the stream sing in celebration of the wild cherries. In Issa's poem the glory of a flowering vine offsets and celebrates the humility of a simple hut. Through all these various moods, however, what remains constant from poem to poem is the idea of natural beauty as a comfort but also as a rebuke to worldly materialism.

Kubla Khan
by Samuel Taylor Coleridge
Selection Test, *page 202*

Comprehension

1. C	6. F
2. G	7. B
3. B	8. H
4. J	9. D
5. A	10. F

Literary Focus

11. D	13. C
12. J	14. H

Constructed Response

15. Students' responses will vary. A sample response follows:

   a. Xanadu is it! A sacred river, caves of ice, fertile gardens, cedar groves in mysterious haunted caverns—and all of it described in the most musical, alliterative and assonant language. I want to go there immediately, at least every few months. To be sure, there are images of dread and savagery in the

poem, but these are what Coleridge calls "holy dread": the awe and mystery that come with sacred magic, with moonlit women wailing for their demon lovers, and damsels playing on dulcimers. Hey, it doesn't get any better than this!

   b. Xanadu sounds like a really awful place. It is icy and sunless, as the speaker makes all too clear in his description of the underground river, the caves of ice, and the sunless sea. It must be quite cold if these details are reliable. On moonlit nights the locale is downright dangerous—one wouldn't be surprised if, in response to that deranged woman wailing for her demon lover in lines 15–16, nothing less than a werewolf should show up. In the midst of it all, ancestral voices are heard prophesying war—a grim prospect of future ruin if there ever was one.

   c. (Accept any response adequately supported by details from the poem and having a bearing on the selection standards, for example, imagery, figures of speech, sounds, and mood.)

The Rime of the Ancient Mariner
by Samuel Taylor Coleridge

Coleridge Describes His Addiction
by Samuel Taylor Coleridge

from In Patagonia
by Bruce Chatwin
Selection Test, *page 205*

Comprehension

1. B	5. B
2. H	6. H
3. D	7. B
4. G	8. H

Literary Focus

9. A	11. A
10. F	

Holt Assessment: Literature, Reading, and Vocabulary

Answer Key

Reading Skills
12. G

Vocabulary Development
13. b   **16.** c
14. a   **17.** d
15. e

Constructed Response
18. Students' responses will vary. A sample response follows:

    If I were the Wedding Guest and had just finished listening to the Mariner's tale, I would be feeling awe and an almost superstitious dread, combined with religious feelings at the prospect of mankind being forgiven of its sin. Aside from the sheer impact of the events in the poem, the sound of Coleridge's language throughout is solemn, sonorous, and has an archaic ring that makes its events seem mystical and its mood laden with doom. Images of the dead, the rotting ship, the blazing sun, and the gazing eyes of the dying sailors are nightmarishly suited to enter the mind of a listener, such as the Wedding Guest, and making him hope to escape the same fate. The episode with the hermit introduces the subject of forgiveness, as does the image of the Mariner wandering the world in search of listeners. If I were the Wedding Guest, I'd be wondering why the Mariner picked me, and what I'd better do now in my own life to avoid a similar fate.

She Walks in Beauty
by George Gordon, Lord Byron
Selection Test, *page 208*

Comprehension
1. D   **6.** G
2. H   **7.** C
3. A   **8.** J
4. F   **9.** C
5. B   **10.** J

Literary Focus
11. B   **13.** A
12. F   **14.** G

Constructed Response
15. Students' responses will vary. A sample response follows:

    The speaker imagines that the woman possesses inner as well as outer beauty. Her particular type of inner beauty is implied in words such as "grace," "calm," "eloquent," "peace," "innocent," and "serenely sweet." In other words, the speaker imagines that because the woman is a beautiful brunette, she also exemplifies the most beautiful qualities of traditional femininity. This conclusion may or may not actually be true of the woman, but the poet gives the reader no basis for judgment. Thus, the emotions evoked are really those of mystery and allure rather than of adoration of the woman's qualities. In a strange way this mood fits in with the simile of the night, because, although night is not necessarily innocent, calm, and serene, night is mysterious and alluring and often deceptive. The simile supports the portrait of the woman in that sense, though not in the sense the speaker overtly declares.

from Childe Harold's Pilgrimage, Canto IV
by George Gordon, Lord Byron
Selection Test, *page 211*

Comprehension
1. B   **5.** D
2. G   **6.** J
3. B   **7.** D
4. F   **8.** F

Literary Focus
9. C   **11.** B
10. H

Reading Skills
12. F

Answer Key

Constructed Response

13. Students' responses will vary. A sample response follows:

In addition to pleasure, regret is also found in this selection from *Childe Harold's Pilgrimage*. Pleasure can be found in many of the poem's phrases, word choices, and sounds, and even in the brilliant use of the Spenserian stanza with its unexpected rhymes (woods/intrudes; plain/remain; groan/unknown) and in the sweeping rhythm of the long lines, such as lines 10–11. Regret can be found in some of the figures of speech, such as the comparison of the drowning man to a drop of water, and in the overall tone of the fourth and fifth stanzas, where the exclamatory phrase "Farewell!" is repeated and the frequent use of dashes creates the impression of nostalgic or thoughtful pauses. The figure of speech comparing the speaker's spirit to a fluttering glow, and images such as "a sound which makes us linger," enhance this feeling of nostalgic regret.

Ozymandias
by Percy Bysshe Shelley
Selection Test, *page 214*

Comprehension

1. B	**6.** H
2. J	**7.** D
3. C	**8.** F
4. H	**9.** C
5. D	**10.** F

Literary Focus

11. C	**13.** C
12. G	**14.** F

Constructed Response

15. Students' responses will vary. A sample response follows:

The poet's message is: All is vanity. One reason for the various speakers in the poem—the speaker, the traveler, and the words on the pedestal—is that each perceives the ones before him to have been vain. The initial speaker may feel superior to the traveler and the king, since it is his narration that frames the whole poem, but Shelley would probably agree that this speaker is just as ephemeral as the other two. The sequence of speakers heightens the irony of the poem's whole situation—each one sees the others as participating in an endless chain of human vanity. The king's epitaph introduces the sort of irony that can evoke, perhaps, a bitter laugh of understanding.

Ode to the West Wind
by Percy Bysshe Shelley
Selection Test, *page 217*

Comprehension

1. C	**5.** B
2. H	**6.** J
3. A	**7.** B
4. F	**8.** G

Literary Focus

9. D	**12.** H
10. J	**13.** C
11. A	**14.** G

Constructed Response

15. Students' responses will vary. A sample response follows:

Shelley uses the heightened effects consistent with the ode form to evoke the readers' sense of the awesomeness of nature. In phrases such as "Be thou me" and "I fall upon the thorns of life! I bleed!" he shouts to the wind, challenging it to fuse with his soul. The poem expresses the poet's fascination with the power of nature to create and destroy, and with those same forces within himself. Through this kind of exaggerated self-dramatization, the poet elicits a similar emotion in the reader. The use of the ode form, with its elevated language and grand scale, impels readers to confront the mys-

Answer Key

tery, scope, and grandeur of nature, and reinforces the idea that we are powerless in the face of it.

Jade Flower Palace
by Tu Fu

Night Thoughts Afloat
by Tu Fu

Selection Test, *page 220*

Comprehension

1. B	**6.** H
2. J	**7.** B
3. C	**8.** J
4. F	**9.** A
5. A	**10.** G

Literary Focus

11. A	**13.** B
12. G	**14.** H

Constructed Response

15. Students' responses will vary. A sample response follows:

I find "Night Thoughts Afloat" sadder because it presents the sadness of an individual rather than the universal sadness of life. Of course, others might find "Jade Flower Palace" sadder for the very same reason, but for me, the individual focus creates a stronger emotional pang. In "Jade Flower Palace" the mood is philosophical melancholy; the poet details things he observes, rather than experiences in his own life. Aside from noting the impermanence of all things, the poet might be doing just fine in his present life. But "Night Thoughts Afloat" is a contemplation of private failure. The fact that others—the official poets—are doing well only makes the speaker feel worse. The whole world may be rejoicing while he paddles quietly in his little boat amid the grasses of a stream. That's a very self-pitying image.

Quiet Night Thoughts
by Li Po

Question and Answer Among the Mountains
by Li Po

Letter to His Two Small Children
by Li Po

Selection Test, *page 223*

Comprehension

1. B	**6.** J
2. F	**7.** D
3. C	**8.** J
4. G	**9.** A
5. A	**10.** J

Literary Focus

11. D	**13.** B
12. H	**14.** F

Constructed Response

15. Students' responses will vary. A sample response follows:

My favorite image in the three poems is "breaking blossom," used twice in lines 16 and 17 of "Letter to His Two Small Children" and apparently used in line 15 in the original Chinese as well (if it is indeed "P'ing-yang," the speaker's daughter's name). Presumably the speaker gave his daughter this name expressing sadness and separation. Whether the breaking blossom is the daughter, the father, the family, or all of them, it is equally evocative. In translation the alliteration of *B* sounds deepens the mood of sorrow (perhaps coincidentally it is a consonant associated with crying, as in "boo-hoo"). The speaker planted a tree when he left his family, and his daughter's name is a tree image; clearly, tree imagery is central to the expression of deep feelings.

Answer Key

On First Looking into Chapman's Homer
by John Keats

When I Have Fears
by John Keats

Selection Test, *page 226*

Comprehension

1. C	**6.** F
2. F	**7.** D
3. C	**8.** H
4. G	**9.** C
5. A	**10.** H

Literary Focus

11. D	**13.** D
12. F	

Reading Skills

14. H

Constructed Response

15. Students' responses will vary. A sample response follows:

Even though Keats tries to reason love and fame into "nothingness," it seems to me he still places them very high among his values. For one thing, I don't believe he can successfully think them into nothingness, at least not for very long. My evidence for this is my own knowledge of life, plus the fact that "When I Have Fears" is full of references to Keats's desire for poetic fame and is in itself a beautiful poem. Additionally, I infer that he chooses to mention those two values—love and fame—precisely because they are the ones he finds hardest to think away. In fact the images of the teeming brain and the granary high-piled with metaphorical works of literature show that he has not succeeded in putting those thoughts away for even the time needed to write the poem! Supporting this view are the images in "On First Looking into Chapman's Homer," where it is clear that poetic beauty is his highest value. So love of poetry and of a beloved, plus the fame that comes with the highest achievement of poetic beauty, are his supreme values.

Ode to a Nightingale
by John Keats

Selection Test, *page 230*

Comprehension

1. D	**6.** F
2. G	**7.** C
3. B	**8.** G
4. J	**9.** B
5. A	**10.** H

Literary Focus

11. C	**13.** A
12. J	**14.** H

Constructed Response

15. Students' responses will vary.

I think the speaker is obsessed with death, and the mood of the poem is essentially morbid. His obsession pervades the entire poem. In the very first two lines the images are of heartache, anesthesia, and drugs—including hemlock, a deadly poison. In the second stanza, the speaker imagines drinking for the purpose of leaving the world (line 19), and in the fourth stanza he wants to fly away with the bird to a realm that sounds suspiciously like an afterlife. He makes his point openly in the sixth stanza, where he admits being "half in love with easeful Death," and dwells on his inevitable bodily decomposition (lines 59–60).

Holt Assessment: Literature, Reading, and Vocabulary

Answer Key

Ode on a Grecian Urn
by John Keats
Selection Test, *page 233*

Comprehension

1. C   **5.** C

2. H   **6.** J

3. B   **7.** B

4. F   **8.** G

Literary Focus

9. D   **11.** B

10. F

Reading Skills

12. F

Constructed Response

13. Students' responses will vary. A sample response follows:

The poem's primary theme is the lasting power of art. The speaker celebrates the permanence of art, which, when it achieves true beauty, transcends anything else in life. The couple on the urn, the group in pursuit from the first stanza, the priest, heifer, and crowd at the sacrifice, even the absent, empty town from which the religious celebrants have come—all these are metaphors that symbolize one of the great triumphs of art: the capture of an ephemeral moment in an eternal form. The superiority of immortal art to mortal life is perhaps most clearly expressed in the paradoxical statement, "Heard melodies are sweet, but those unheard / Are sweeter." In real life a tune played on a flute will vanish into the air, but the unidentified tune captured for the imagination on the urn has become immortal.

Collection 5 Summative Test,
page 236
Vocabulary Skills

1. B   **4.** J

2. H   **5.** A

3. A

Comprehension

6. F   **9.** D

7. C   **10.** H

8. G

Reading Skills and Strategies:
Constructed Response

Reading Rhyme and Rhythm

11. Students' responses will vary. A sample response follows:

Literary Element—rhythm; *Definition*—alternation of stressed and unstressed syllables; *Example*—"Sweet Highland Girl, a very shower / of beauty is thy earthly dower!"
Literary Element—rhyme; *Definition*—repetition of accented vowel sounds and all sounds following them in words that are close together; *Example*—"Sweet Highland Girl, a very shower / of beauty is thy earthly dower! Twice seven consenting years have shed / Their utmost bounty on thy head."

These elements add to the "sound" of the poem by providing a flowing rhythm that is both meditative in the style of the early Romantics, and songlike in more traditional English poetic style. The simple aabb rhyme scheme contributes greatly to this songlike quality, as does the fact that the lines are in iambic tetrameter rather than the more conversational, ruminative pentameter. Combined with the pastoral subject, these sounds and rhythms evoke an emotion of joy in nature.

Answer Key

Literary Focus: Constructed Response

Identifying Theme

12. J

Understanding Symbolism

13. Students' responses will vary. A sample response follows:

The Highland Girl symbolizes beauty and all that is worthy of love. The speaker refers to the woman's beauty throughout the poem, saying things such as "Sweet Highland Girl, a very shower / Of beauty is thy earthly dower!" The speaker refers to the girl's "perfect innocence," saying he will pray for her even when he is far away.

Evaluating Imagery

14. Students' responses will vary. A sample response follows:

The Highland Girl is described as being "something fashioned in a dream." The speaker says she is the "spirit" of the many beautiful things around her, such as the lake, the bay, and the waterfall. He also describes her as being like a wave in the wild sea, powerful and majestic and not to be claimed. I believe the latter is the stronger image, because it captures both the woman's power and her beauty.

Analyzing Alliteration and Simile

15. Students' responses will vary. A sample response follows:

In the simile in lines 55–56, the speaker compares the Highland Girl to "a wave / Of the wild sea." This is a good comparison because the ocean, like the girl, has an almost mystical power over the speaker. Like the ocean, the girl is beautiful, strong, and majestic—but she is also aloof. The speaker is content to watch her from afar. She belongs to the realm of dream and memory rather than to the real world.

Collection 6

Collection 6 Diagnostic Test

Literature, Vocabulary, *page 241*

1. B	**6.** H
2. H	**7.** B
3. D	**8.** G
4. F	**9.** A
5. D	**10.** J

Literary Period Introduction Test, *page 243*

1. C	**6.** F
2. F	**7.** D
3. C	**8.** G
4. J	**9.** C
5. B	**10.** J

The Lady of Shalott
by Alfred, Lord Tennyson

Selection Test, *page 245*

Comprehension

1. A	**6.** H
2. G	**7.** A
3. D	**8.** G
4. J	**9.** A
5. C	**10.** H

Literary Focus

11. C	**13.** C
12. F	

Reading Skills

14. H

Constructed Response

15. Students' responses will vary. Both stances are supportable. A sample response follows:

I believe Tennyson feels that artists need isolation. Once the Lady of Shalott abandons her weaving and interacts with the outside world, she is doomed. If she had stayed in the tower and not forsaken her art, she would still be creating at the end of

Answer Key

the poem. Actually, she seems contented with her seclusion until she sees the two young newlyweds. Later, she is distressed by the sight of Sir Lancelot. Only love can make her leave her art and her tower. But once in the outside world, separated from her art, she is helpless to the point of death.

Ulysses
by Alfred, Lord Tennyson
Selection Test, *page 248*
Comprehension

1. A	**6.** G
2. H	**7.** D
3. C	**8.** G
4. G	**9.** B
5. C	**10.** F

Literary Focus

11. D	**13.** D
12. H	**14.** G

Constructed Response

15. Students' responses will vary. A sample response follows:

I think Tennyson feels that an old person should live life to its fullest. To this extent I think the poet agrees with his character Ulysses. Whether or not Tennyson thinks Ulysses is making the right choice by leaving home again after surviving the many near-death experiences of the *Iliad* and *Odyssey* is another question. Both Tennyson and Ulysses himself realize that Ulysses's choice is not for most people—certainly not for Telemachus ("He works his work, I mine," line 43). But the encouraging words that Ulysses utters about meeting old age adventurously are inspiring for many people, not just old sailors yearning for the sea. In this sense Tennyson, through his character, is giving sound advice—whether or not he believes Ulysses is going to be happier for taking it is another question.

My Last Duchess
by Robert Browning

Scenes from a Modern Marriage
by Julia Markus
Selection Test, *page 251*
Comprehension

1. A	**6.** J
2. G	**7.** A
3. A	**8.** F
4. H	**9.** C
5. D	**10.** J

Literary Focus

11. D	**12.** H

Reading Skills

13. A	**14.** F

Constructed Response

15. Students' responses will vary. A sample response follows:

The Duke reveals himself to be an arrogant nobleman corrupted by the power of his position, heedlessly willing to use and destroy other people in order to enrich himself and bolster his ego. His arrogance is such that, through his boasting, he unwittingly reveals more about himself than is prudent. The fact that the poem is a dramatic monologue is crucial to this characterization, because it not only allows us to overhear the Duke's self-characterization but shows us that he is so conceited that he can portray himself negatively without even realizing it. While the Duke's tone as a speaker is proud and commanding, the poet's attitude toward him—the implicit tone of the whole poem—is derisive, disgusted, appalled, and perhaps pitying.

Answer Key

Sonnet 43
by Elizabeth Barrett Browning
Selection Test, *page 254*

Comprehension

1. C	5. B
2. H	6. G
3. D	7. C
4. G	8. F

Literary Focus

9. A	12. G
10. G	13. B
11. D	14. F

Constructed Response

15. Students' responses will vary. A sample response follows:

The poem is an expression of deep, happy, lasting love, and Barrett Browning uses a number of sound devices to emphasize and express those emotions. The Petrarchan sonnet form, with its *abbaabba cdcdcd* rhyme scheme, is particularly well suited to expressions of love, because in English, this sonnet form tends to rely on simple words in order to complete all the rhymes, and love is well expressed simply. The musicality of the lines, written in iambic pentameter, is enhanced by the repetition of the simple phrase "I love thee" throughout the poem, building a sense of conviction through reiteration and parallelism. Alliteration and assonance help to shape the poem and give the assertions of love a feeling of intense sincerity.

Pied Beauty
by Gerard Manley Hopkins
Selection Test, *page 257*

Comprehension

1. C	5. A
2. J	6. H
3. C	7. D
4. G	8. G

Literary Focus

9. B	12. F
10. J	13. B
11. A	14. H

Constructed Response

15. Students' responses will vary. A sample response follows:

Hopkins wants the reader to feel a religious or at least aesthetic exaltation similar to Hopkins's own: a feeling of one's soul charged with the spirit of beauty and with praise of the divine force within all things. Hopkins's use of sound conveys the feeling of these bursting emotions rushing forth from his soul. The sprung rhythms of the lines make for a headlong, dizzying movement, without any singsong effect or any plodding. Rhyme is used for songlike purposes, but again the effect is the opposite of repetitious or monotonous; the rhymes work together with the many instances of assonance and alliteration to create a short poem which is almost a web of linked sounds, rather than sounds chiming at the ends of lines. The rapid-fire series of similar word types (adjectives, action verbs, concrete nouns) and compound descriptive words, especially throughout lines 4–9, hasten the lines' pace. Hopkins undoubtedly achieves his purpose: sharing his exaltation of life's beauty.

Dover Beach
by Matthew Arnold
Selection Test, *page 260*

Comprehension

1. A	6. G
2. G	7. A
3. D	8. G
4. G	9. D
5. A	10. J

Literary Focus

11. D	13. C
12. H	14. F

Holt Assessment: Literature, Reading, and Vocabulary

Answer Key

Constructed Response

15. Students' responses will vary. Sample responses follow:

Pessimistic: The speaker sees little hope that the "Sea of Faith" will return; he says we are on a "darkling plain" where nothing will bring us closer to hope. In the last stanza he lists the positive qualities people find in the world—joy, peace, certitude, relief from pain, etc.—only to deny the reality of any of them.

Optimistic: The poem is framed as an intimate talk between two people who love each other; the speaker calls his listener "love" and he puts real hope in their fidelity and in the power of shared love to overcome worldly wrongs. Love is more important to the speaker, and in turn to his world, than it ever was. While the presence of suffering has not changed since ancient times, the remedy for it has.

To an Athlete Dying Young
by A. E. Housman

Death and Other Grave Matters
from **What Jane Austen Ate and Charles Dickens Knew**
by Daniel Pool

Selection Test, *page 263*

Comprehension

1. A	**6.** G
2. G	**7.** A
3. C	**8.** J
4. H	**9.** B
5. C	**10.** F

Literary Focus

11. A	**13.** D
12. J	**14.** H

Constructed Response

15. Students' responses will vary. A sample response follows:

The first two stanzas are indicative of the outstanding quality of the poem. They establish the rhythm and rhyme scheme of the couplets, and show that despite the simplicity of the latter, Housman is up to the task of keeping the sounds interesting by finding unusual rhyming words (*marketplace* and *shoulder-high*). Yet overall the sound of the lines is simple and tenderly sad, thus suited for the subject matter and for the elegiac tone of the poem. Housman, an extremely learned scholar, adopts a remarkably simple (for Victorian England) vocabulary and sentence structure to suit the dead athlete and to suit the gravity of the occasion.

The Mark of the Beast
by Rudyard Kipling

Selection Test, *page 266*

Comprehension

1. A	**6.** G
2. J	**7.** B
3. C	**8.** J
4. G	**9.** A
5. A	**10.** H

Literary Focus

11. C	**12.** G

Reading Skills

13. C	**14.** F

Vocabulary Development

15. c	**18.** d
16. a	**19.** e
17. b	

Constructed Response

20. Students' responses will vary. A sample response follows:

The lessons of the story can be summed up by the Indian proverb at the beginning and by the allusion to Hamlet: "There are more things in heaven and earth . . ." Put the two quotations together, and the reader seriously doubts the alleged superiority of British civilization. The story is about the need for respect between cultures.

Answer Key

Disrespect for Indian beliefs causes catastrophe and near-death for Fleete and could have quite possibly ruined Strickland and the narrator as well. The sacrilege committed by Fleete against the monkey god has serious consequences, whether or not they are supernatural in origin. As for the conflict between British and Indian traditions, both are represented as valid, and yet the practitioners of both are shown to be extremely flawed. The lesson is one of humility, although it could be debated whether the British characters, and Kipling himself, have thoroughly learned it.

How Much Land Does a Man Need?
by Leo Tolstoy
Selection Test, *page 269*

Comprehension

1. D	**6.** G
2. F	**7.** D
3. A	**8.** G
4. F	**9.** C
5. D	**10.** H

Literary Focus

11. D	**12.** G

Reading Skills

13. A	**14.** H

Vocabulary Development

15. C	**18.** F
16. F	**19.** D
17. C	

Constructed Response

20. Students' responses will vary. A sample response follows:

Realism and allegory are both used to establish the theme of "How Much Land Does a Man Need?" The story is firmly grounded in a realistic view of not only Russian peasant life, but of Bashkir (a non-Russian, nomadic people) ways as well. The portrayal of land sales between declin-

ing Russian aristocrats and rising peasants is convincing, as is Pahom's familial relationship. Whether or not Bashkirs actually sold their land by the walk-it-in-a-day method, other details show Tolstoy's familiarity with the customs of his country. Tolstoy found allegory a useful tool to wield alongside realism. The Devil appears as a trickster and is apparently at work behind the scenes throughout the story; Pahom's dreams, although not strictly necessary to the plot, add another element of fantasy. As a result, what might have been a simple story about the rise and fall of one peasant businessman becomes a universally recognizable morality tale on greed.

The Bet
by Anton Chekhov
Selection Test, *page 273*

Comprehension

1. A	**6.** H
2. J	**7.** B
3. A	**8.** G
4. H	**9.** C
5. C	**10.** F

Literary Focus

11. B	**13.** C
12. J	

Reading Skills

14. F

Vocabulary Development

15. indiscriminately

16. renounce

17. frivolous

18. zealously

19. illusory

Constructed Response

20. Students' responses will vary. A sample response follows:

The story seems in some respect to take the form of a parable about questions of

Answer Key

how to live. The bet is a kind of experiment to determine whether a life of solitary study is more fulfilling than a worldly life of commerce. And to some extent it can be assumed that Chekhov had more sympathy with the lawyer who retreats from the world than with the banker who takes advantage of his opponent. But too many questions are left unanswered at the end of the story for that assessment to be final. The banker's failings are portrayed sympathetically; he weeps when his fortune is spared, and at several points he feels sympathy for the lawyer. Meanwhile, although the lawyer's philosophy rings true, it's not clear whether he has become wiser than before: he was given to rash, self-defeating gestures when he undertook the bet, and he makes exactly the same kind of gesture in renouncing the money at the end. Who is going to be happier afterward, the lawyer or the banker? The fact that Chekhov doesn't say is perhaps the most interesting aspect of the story.

The Jewels
by Guy de Maupassant
Selection Test, *page 277*

Comprehension

1. B	**6.** J
2. H	**7.** C
3. A	**8.** F
4. F	**9.** B
5. B	**10.** J

Literary Focus

11. C	**13.** C
12. G	

Reading Skills

14. G

Vocabulary Development

15. e	**18.** b
16. c	**19.** d
17. a	

Constructed Response

20. Students' responses will vary. A sample response follows:

Maupassant depicts a society in which certain proprieties are deemed very important to observe, but in which departures from the conventions are often made surreptitiously and understood by sophisticated social players. Thus, it is important to marry well and to maintain a veneer of conjugal decorum, but infidelity is widespread, and when revealed, it is upsetting for the cheated partner not so much because of its inherent wrong but because of social embarrassment. Lantin's wife has in effect prostituted herself for his benefit; he is mortified to learn of it, but having absorbed the blow he is delighted by the benefit, and in fact part of the gain is that he can now afford to visit prostitutes—a crucial irony. Falling into a virtuous marriage afterward, he is unhappy, raising questions for the reader on whether or not the outward virtues of Maupassant's society had any bearing on good and evil in real life.

Collection 6 Summative Test,
page 280

Vocabulary Skills

1. B	**3.** A
2. G	**4.** J

Comprehension

5. C	**8.** J
6. F	**9.** C
7. B	

Reading Skills and Strategies

10. F	**11.** C

Literary Focus: Constructed Response

12. Students' responses will vary. Sample responses follow:

a. In the first stanza the speaker compares people to islands, conveying loneliness. Later, he says that the islands feel certain they were once part of a single continent. In

Answer Key

line 19 this belief is referred to explicitly as a longing.

b. The final stanza attributes human loneliness and longing to "a God, a god," who decreed the "severance" of human beings from one another. The sea separating human beings is "unplumbed," implying that God's reasons are unfathomable.

c. The second half of the poem expresses longing, but the same passages make clear that longing is not as a general rule fulfilled among humans who desire communion with each other. In fact, the cosmic plan is that "their longing's fire / Should be, as soon as kindled, cooled." Love in this poem is reduced to longing without fulfillment.

d. The tragic nature of life in this poem can be seen in the central image of humanity as a group of islands, hopelessly separated from each other and the fact that they once belonged to the same continent. The tragedy is not so much in the situation itself—is it tragic to be an island, literally, instead of a continent?—but in the fact that, unlike land masses, human beings think and feel about their situations. Part of their thinking and feeling is expressed in works of beauty, comparable to the nightingales' songs in the poem. But the songs, while expressing and arousing emotion, do not solve the situation; in fact they only make it more painful.

13. Students' responses will vary. A sample response follows:

The speaker's purpose in creating this mood was probably to express a personal feeling and, perhaps, a feeling that was central to educated people of the Victorian era. This mood can be seen as part of the disillusionment that was a side effect of scientific and technological progress in the nineteenth century. The dominant figurative image of the sea in which human islands are scattered, unable to touch each other, is a striking expression of this mood and the ideas behind it. Word choices such as

enisled, shoreless watery wild, mortal millions, alone, longing, despair, farthest caverns, vain, deep desire, severance, and *unplumbed, salt, estranging sea* convey this mood in virtually every line of the poem. Details such as the nightingales' song entering the caverns and the figure of speech of the fire cooled as soon as it is kindled contribute as well.

14. Students' responses will vary. A sample response follows:

Image—islands separated by salt water; *Emotion Evoked by the Image*—feelings of isolation, distance between two people as between islands; *Image*—nightingales singing; *Emotion Evoked by the Image*—a pang of yearning for something beautiful that is far away; *Image*—sounds reaching the caverns of the other islands; *Emotion Evoked by the Image*—poignant connection between one individual and another at a distance.

15. Students' responses will vary. A sample response follows:

As in Arnold's "Dover Beach," the themes of isolation and disillusionment in faith are typically Victorian. Arnold was writing at a time when traditional English folkways, such as the communal life of the rural village, were fading, along with unquestioning trust in Anglican theology. (This disaffection can be seen in the ambiguous comment, "A God, a god their severance ruled!") As a result, educated English people felt increasingly unconnected to any unified social organism. Yet, the longing to belong was evident, even if the belonging only consisted—in this poem and even more obviously in "Dover Beach"—of a loving union with one other individual. The Victorian origins of the poem can also be seen in a host of small touches, such as the phrase "we mortal millions," which evokes the image of a rapidly expanding population, and the metaphor of continental drifting, a concept of nineteenth-century geology that influenced evolutionary theory. The mention

Answer Key

of nightingales might be a look back to Keats's nightingale—a rebuttal to Keats from a later, less Romantic era.

Collection 7

Collection 7 Diagnostic Test
Literature, Informational Text, Vocabulary, *page 284*

1. B	**11.** A
2. H	**12.** F
3. C	**13.** B
4. H	**14.** F
5. A	**15.** B
6. G	**16.** G
7. D	**17.** C
8. F	**18.** J
9. D	**19.** A
10. H	**20.** F

Literary Period Introduction Test, *page 288*

1. B	**6.** F
2. H	**7.** A
3. B	**8.** J
4. F	**9.** C
5. D	**10.** J

Dulce et Decorum Est
by Wilfred Owen

The Rear-Guard
by Siegfried Sassoon

Selection Test, *page 290*

Comprehension

1. D	**6.** J
2. G	**7.** C
3. A	**8.** J
4. G	**9.** B
5. D	**10.** H

Literary Focus

11. D	**13.** C
12. F	**14.** G

Constructed Response

15. Students' responses will vary. A sample response follows:

The passage, "And watch the white eyes writhing in his face, / His hanging face, like a devil's sick of sin . . ." conveys Owen's hatred of war by directly describing a detail that is extremely gruesome. The tone of outrage and disgust with war (and with those who support it) is sustained by the speaker's invitation to the reader to watch—something the reader clearly is not naturally inclined to do. It's as if the poet is holding the horror of war up to our faces and making us look. The word "writhing" to describe the eyes, and the emphasis on their whiteness (a color that often conveys terror), call attention to the victim's panic and pain. So does the adjective "hanging" modifying "face." The simile is a stunning one: the face is not just like a devil's, but "like a devil's sick of sin." Just as a demon might realize his errors and wish to escape hell, this soldier, who has probably sinned as soldiers usually must, wishes to escape the battlefield. But the simile implies that there is no escape. These stylistic touches contribute to a vivid picture of war as hell.

Answer Key

The Hollow Men
by T. S. Eliot
Selection Test, *page 293*

Comprehension

1. C	**6.** J
2. F	**7.** D
3. C	**8.** G
4. G	**9.** A
5. A	**10.** H

Literary Focus

11. B	**13.** B
12. F	

Reading Skill

14. F

Constructed Response

15. Students' responses will vary. A sample response follows:

   The view conveyed in the poem's final four lines is that the modern world is spiritually dying or, to put it another way, suffering from despair. The world's ending in a whimper implies that while there may be no physical apocalypse in modern times—no war to end civilization—civilization may come to ruin through its lack of faith. One figurative image that supports this view is the comparison of the hollow men to rats in lines 9 and 33. The rats move quietly, scurrying over broken glass (perhaps the ruins of a modern civilization). If the world were to end in a whimper, rats might well be a remaining species left to scavenge in the ruins. Symbolically, rats connote amoral opportunism and filth rather than noble human aspirations. Another supporting image is that of hollow men, heads stuffed with straw, whispering together in voices as quiet as the wind. This image connotes the meaninglessness of the thoughts found inside the heads of modern people—including, perhaps, the very quotations from literature to which the speaker alludes. The whisper of the hollow men and the whimper of the world's end are, of course, relat-

ed and perhaps refer to a world without the strength to even shout.

On the Bottom
from Survival in Auschwitz
by Primo Levi
Selection Test, *page 296*

Comprehension

1. C	**6.** J
2. F	**7.** B
3. D	**8.** H
4. G	**9.** C
5. A	**10.** F

Literary Focus

11. C	**13.** B
12. F	

Reading Skills

14. G

Vocabulary Development

15. demolition

16. sordid

17. tepid

18. affinity

19. taciturn

Constructed Response

20. Students' responses will vary. A sample response follows:

   The historical context in which Levi lived—the Holocaust—seems to have made him into a pessimistic, even despairing person. This attitude is proved by looking at the record of his work, which shows that the Holocaust has haunted him throughout his life—no matter if he died by accident or suicide more than forty years after his liberation. The final three paragraphs of the selection clearly express Levi's view that a human being can be stripped of all dignity by the inhumanity of others. It is doubtful whether his pessimism would have gone to that length if he had remained a chemistry student in Turin rather than being forced to endure one of the great evils of history.

Answer Key

from The War
by Marguerite Duras

Never Shall I Forget
by Elie Wiesel

Kristallnacht
The United States Holocaust Memorial Museum

Selection Test, *page 299*

Comprehension

1. D	**6.** G
2. H	**7.** A
3. A	**8.** F
4. H	**9.** A
5. D	**10.** J

Blood, Sweat, and Tears
by Winston Churchill

Selection Test, *page 301*

Comprehension

1. C	**4.** F
2. J	**5.** C
3. A	

Vocabulary Development

6. e	**9.** b
7. d	**10.** a
8. c	

The Silver Fifty-Sen Pieces
by Yasunari Kawabata
Selection Test, *page 303*

Comprehension

1. B	**6.** J
2. J	**7.** A
3. B	**8.** H
4. F	**9.** A
5. C	**10.** J

Literary Focus

11. B	**13.** C
12. J	

Reading Skills

14. H

Vocabulary Development

15. B	**18.** F
16. G	**19.** D
17. A	

Constructed Response

20. Students' responses will vary. Sample responses follow:

a. Beauty and happiness, qualities of peace-time life, are symbolized in this story by a glass paperweight, a flimsy umbrella, and some small coins, as well as by the comfortable devotion between a daughter and mother. These things mostly vanish with the war, but they do not vanish from Yoshiko's memory. Ultimately the bygone umbrella is no less important than the paperweight since both are preserved in Yoshiko's mind. Even in war beautiful memories of peace remain. This author views life with hope.

b. The author sets up the most innocuous possible series of events early in the story—an unworldly young woman shopping alone and with her mother—only to shatter them in the end. The young woman knows that neighborhood girls can make a thousand yen a night; the time has long gone when a few fifty-sen pieces were important to her. This change in the economic scale of values is a particularly telling symbol of the author's bitterness toward war. War can make what was once valuable worthless.

Answer Key

The Destructors
by Graham Greene
Selection Test, *page 307*

Comprehension

1. B
2. G
3. D
4. F
5. C
6. F
7. A
8. G
9. A
10. G

Literary Focus

11. D
12. H
13. C

Reading Skill

14. J

Vocabulary Development

15. stealthy
16. exhilaration
17. daunted
18. exploit
19. impromptu

Constructed Response

20. Students' responses will vary. A sample response follows:

   If the story were to take place in an affluent American suburb today, the background setting of a city damaged by war would be absent. Therefore, much of the psychological justification for the boys' behavior would be absent. They would be responding not to the trauma of a deprived childhood and of physical destruction in their environment but to the less obvious stresses of peacetime luxury and complacency. The story would no longer be a comment on World War II and its aftermath. Rather than commenting on the decay of a once-proud city, the story would be commenting on the inherent emptiness of lives in affluence.

In the Shadow of War
by Ben Okri
The End and the Beginning
by Wisława Szymborska
Selection Test, *page 311*

Comprehension

1. C
2. H
3. C
4. H
5. D
6. F
7. A
8. J
9. A
10. G

Literary Focus

11. D
12. F
13. C

Reading Skill

14. J

Vocabulary Development

15. d
16. a
17. e
18. b
19. c

Constructed Response

20. Students' responses will vary. A sample response follows:

   In "In the Shadow of War" Ben Okri uses a third-person-limited point of view to focus on a child and create an atmosphere of confusion during wartime. Political issues do not enter into the story; neither do military reports or mass movements. The war is seen through its effects on the village life of a small boy. Consequently, events are seen as almost supernatural intrusions of violence, terror, and bewilderment. The narrative reduces events to simple details, simple descriptions, and achieves a sobering impact. Yet even these simple details are not always reliable as is seen when the boy's young mind struggles to consciously grasp what his eyes see—canoes, dead animals, and finally, the bloated bodies of men.
   In "The End and the Beginning" Wisława Szymborska's strategy is differ-

Answer Key

ent—she uses the omniscient point of view and an adult voice that is casual, at times almost whimsical—but to a similar effect as Okri. For her, too, war is not a matter of specific ideologies or armies; it is a universal disaster conveyed through the details of a disrupted daily life. The main difference is that Szymborska ends on a note of hope for rebuilding during peacetime, whereas the prospect of peace is absent from Okri's fictional world.

Shakespeare's Sister
from A Room of One's Own
by Virginia Woolf
Selection Test, *page 314*

Comprehension

1. D	**6.** F
2. H	**7.** D
3. A	**8.** F
4. G	**9.** B
5. C	**10.** J

Literary Focus

11. D	**13.** D
12. J	

Reading Skills

14. F

Vocabulary Development

15. propitious

16. suppressed

17. notorious

18. formidable

19. servile

Constructed Response

20. Students' responses will vary. A sample response follows:

An implicit assumption or belief of Woolf's essay is that education, culture, and learning are necessary in order to produce works of genius. The paucity of works of genius produced in the past by people lacking those advantages supports this assump-

tion. Exceptions, such as Robert Burns, are used to prove the rule. Woolf's belief is natural for someone from her background and era since she herself was a member of the privileged class and a writer of great cultivation and sophistication. She was not acquainted with artistic forms that, both before and since her time, have been made by unlearned people: folk art, folk music, spirituals, blues, rock, country, and hip-hop. As one of the British gentry, Woolf's own life was limited in ways which may have blinded her to the achievements of people from other social strata and other cultures.

Shooting an Elephant
by George Orwell
Selection Test, *page 318*

Comprehension

1. D	**6.** F
2. H	**7.** D
3. C	**8.** H
4. G	**9.** B
5. D	**10.** J

Literary Focus

11. A	**13.** D
12. G	

Reading Skills

14. F

Vocabulary Development

15. A	**18.** J
16. H	**19.** B
17. B	

Constructed Response

20. Students' responses will vary. A sample response follows:

Orwell joined the colonial service in 1922 after graduating from Eton College, a prep school. This step was not an unusual one for a youth in Britain at that time, especially one whose father was in the Indian civil service. Orwell was born in India and lived

Answer Key

there in early childhood, so he may well have had a fond longing to return and see the beauty of that country and to get to know its culture. He was also a supporter of British colonialism at the time, as were most people in his society. His disillusionment with colonialism occurred when he became a colonial officer. By the time he wrote this essay, he had experienced poverty in Europe and had become a journalist, accustomed to reflecting on experiences and to viewing official doctrines with skepticism. He was gradually becoming a democratic socialist, as were many British intellectuals in the 1930s. The stage was set for a former colonial official to write a criticism of colonialism.

No Witchcraft for Sale
by Doris Lessing

Selection Test, *page 322*

Comprehension

1. A	**6.** F
2. J	**7.** D
3. C	**8.** H
4. F	**9.** D
5. C	**10.** G

Literary Focus

11. D	**13.** A
12. G	

Reading Skills

14. H

Vocabulary Development

15. e	**18.** b
16. a	**19.** c
17. d	

Constructed Response

20. Students' responses will vary. A sample response follows:

Lessing is saying that colonialism brings people of different cultures together in ways that are almost inevitably corrupting even when the individuals involved are well intentioned. The Farquars and Gideon live in close proximity and entrust large aspects of their lives to each other—the Farquars depend on Gideon not only to do important chores but to save their child's life. Gideon, in return, depends on the Farquars for his living. There is a certain amount of affection back and forth. However, their social roles on both sides, especially the assumption of superiority on the part of the colonists, prevent them from interacting as equals. Despite the evidence of their experience, the Farquars cannot understand that Gideon deserves serious respect. Even Teddy, a white child, whose own life was saved by Gideon, cannot move beyond condescending jocularity when he speaks to Gideon. And Gideon plays along to protect himself. The price of their artificial interaction is heavy and symbolic—such as in the loss of medicine to the Western world, a medicine that would have prevented a loss of vision.

"I Believe in a British Empire"
by Joseph Chamberlain

"The Noble Mansion of Free India"
by Jawaharlal Nehru

Selection Test, *page 325*

Comprehension

1. C	**6.** G
2. J	**7.** C
3. A	**8.** F
4. F	**9.** B
5. C	**10.** H

Reading Skills

11. D	**13.** A
12. H	**14.** J

Constructed Response

15. Students' responses will vary. A sample response follows:

Answer Key

Chamberlain. What happened to my British Empire? It's gone!

Nehru. I'm delighted to see that. Since India gained its independence just about every other British colony has, too. There are no remaining British colonies in Africa, and even Hong Kong has passed out of British hands.

Chamberlain. Yet what has been gained by independence for these countries? In most cases they have remained poor and have struggled for decades to establish secure governments and prosperous societies, and they have little hope of doing so in the near future.

Nehru. On the contrary, there is great hope. Don't forget that India has been a civilization for some five thousand years. It has always had both poverty and wealth. Its few decades as a British colony were hardly its most crucial period of development, only its most recent. India as a democracy in the postindustrial world is well positioned to catch up economically to Western nations in the coming decades, and it is already a more stable democracy than many had predicted. It even has nuclear weapons, though of course it is our hope not to use them.

Chamberlain. But South Africa has terrible problems of crime and disease. I will agree, however, that from the standpoint of black South Africans, majority rule is probably a blessing overall (something I did not agree with in my lifetime). Certainly the apartheid, minority-rule state which preceded was not part of the vision of a sound British Empire.

Nehru. Whether you like to think so or not, Chamberlain, even you must recognize that we are now one world in which all nations are linked together for better or worse.

Once upon a Time
by Nadine Gordimer
Selection Test, *page 329*

Comprehension

1. C	**6.** H
2. G	**7.** D
3. D	**8.** H
4. F	**9.** A
5. C	**10.** J

Literary Focus

11. C	**13.** D
12. G	

Reading Skills

14. G

Vocabulary Development

15. A	**18.** J
16. H	**19.** C
17. B	

Constructed Response

20. Students' responses will vary. A sample response follows:

Gordimer's purpose was to criticize apartheid and especially to highlight the fears of white citizens under apartheid and the potential harm that such a condition of life brings about. Her use of the fairy tale genre is ironic because the story is really about the grim political realities of the specific time and place in which Gordimer wrote, rather than of the fantasized dangers of an unreal world. Fairy tale language such as the title itself and "happily ever after" deepen the ironic contrast between the story's "light" form and its "heavy" content. The use of several different tones— one for the beginning frame of the story, one for the main fairy tale, and one, still darker, for the concluding paragraph— helps to signal the author's intentions and to draw the reader deeper into the final sobering conclusion.

Answer Key

Marriage Is a Private Affair
by Chinua Achebe
Selection Test, *page 333*

Comprehension

1. B   5. D
2. H   6. F
3. B   7. D
4. F   8. H

Literary Focus

9. A   11. B
10. F   12. F

Vocabulary Development

13. cosmopolitan
14. persevered
15. commiserate
16. rash
17. cosmopolitan

Constructed Response

18. Students' responses will vary. A sample response follows:

For Chinua Achebe, race seems to be cultural reality that should be explored, analyzed, celebrated, but not used as a barrier among people. Race is more often viewed as ethnicity—the difference between Ibo and Ibibio, for example. Though this difference may be hard to discern for most American readers unacquainted with Nigerian tribal groups, for the characters it is at least as important as the difference is between black and white for the average American. The ethnic difference between Ibo and Ibibio is a bar to marriage and a cause of gossip by old-fashioned people. But the modern married couple rise above it. They live their lives in a new, unfettered way in which culture, while adding flavor to the relationship and creating difficulties between themselves and the old-fashioned people, is no longer a hindrance within the marriage itself. Achebe clearly shares and speaks for the young couple's view, since the antagonist who opposes it, Okeke, is won over in the end. It can be inferred that racial differences between black and white, black and yellow, etc., would be approached similarly by this author.

Telephone Conversation
by Wole Soyinka
Selection Test, *page 336*

Comprehension

1. C   6. H
2. J   7. D
3. D   8. F
4. G   9. C
5. A   10. J

Literary Focus

11. D   13. A
12. H   14. G

Constructed Response

15. Students' responses will vary. A sample response follows:

Soyinka is commenting on the absurdity of racism. At the beginning of their conversation, the landlady and the young man seem to find each other acceptable. But when the landlady learns that he is African, she seems immediately to forget her good opinion and to base everything on skin color. The fact that over the phone she can't see his skin color makes the situation even more ludicrous. The absurdity is highlighted when the conversation deteriorates into details of precisely how dark the young man is. The young man's sarcastic tone invites the reader to join with him and the author in laughing at the landlady.

Answer Key

The Second Coming
by William Butler Yeats
Selection Test, *page 339*

Comprehension

1. D	**6.** F
2. J	**7.** B
3. B	**8.** J
4. H	**9.** A
5. B	**10.** G

Literary Focus

11. C	**13.** A
12. F	**14.** H

Constructed Response

15. Students' responses will vary. A sample response follows:

"The best lack all conviction, while the worst / Are full of passionate intensity" is an ironic statement, since it reverses the expected situation: One would expect that the worst would lack conviction and the best would be full of passionate intensity. This irony expresses Yeats's view of a world turned morally upside down, controlled by the wrong forces, the wrong people. The next line (line 9), "Surely some revelation is at hand," and the parallel observation in line 10, "Surely the Second Coming is at hand," are verbal ironies in that the speaker does not mean what he says; he means the opposite—a chaotic era is at hand. Here, Yeats is chiding the Western tendency to hold out false hopes for progress. The third mention of the Second Coming, in line 11, is so ironic that it is little more than a bitter, sarcastic outburst. The irony turns situational in the later lines of the poem, where, instead of the expected Second Coming of Christ, or of a renewal of the ideals born in Bethlehem two thousand years ago, a monstrous pagan beast is born to slouch in our time.

The Lake Isle of Innisfree
by William Butler Yeats
Selection Test, *page 342*

Comprehension

1. D	**6.** G
2. F	**7.** C
3. C	**8.** J
4. G	**9.** B
5. B	**10.** H

Literary Focus

11. A	**13.** D
12. F	**14.** G

Constructed Response

15. Students' responses will vary. A sample response follows:

Yeats's style in the poem could be described as gently lyrical, romantic, or serene. Alliteration and assonance are among the techniques he uses to achieve this style, but in particular, the assonance of soothing vowels is very important: long *o*, *ow*, long and short *i*, among them. These vowels seem to stretch out the lines and, thus, stretch out the speaker's vision of Innisfree. Line length and rhythm are part of the style as well. Although the rhythm is lilting and musical, it is quiet and dream-like rather than singsong. The pattern of varying line lengths, repeated in each stanza, creates an effect very similar to that of quietly lapping waves, each of them essentially the same, yet one louder or softer than the other. The purpose of this mimicry is to create a mood of yearning for serenity and, thus, to share the speaker's mood with the reader.

Answer Key

The Wild Swans at Coole
by William Butler Yeats
The Swan
by Rainer Maria Rilke
Selection Test, *page 345*

Comprehension

1. C	**6.** J
2. F	**7.** D
3. C	**8.** H
4. G	**9.** A
5. C	**10.** J

Literary Focus

11. B	**13.** A
12. J	**14.** F

Constructed Response

15. Students' responses will vary. A sample response follows:

In both poems swans symbolize timeless beauty in comparison to the relatively imperfect, fumbling motions of human life. However, swans are used differently in the poems. Rilke's "The Swan" contrasts the swan walking on land with it gliding through water, and compares both to human beings: On land, the swan is as clumsy as a person, while on water, the swan is graceful. The poem equates the swan's transition from land into water with a human's transition from life into death— from an awkward, clumsy element into an element where all is smooth, beautiful, and sensible. Yeats focuses on the contrasts between man and swan. Swans are lifelong lovers, while he has lost his old love. Swans retain energy into advanced age while he seems to feel weary. Swans remain unchanged through time while he, returning after nineteen years, is very different. Both poets use swans as symbols: Rilke uses a swan as a symbol for human immortality while Yeats uses swans as symbols of the unchanging, mysterious state of the natural world.

Araby
by James Joyce
Selection Test, *page 348*

Comprehension

1. B	**6.** F
2. G	**7.** B
3. A	**8.** G
4. J	**9.** D
5. D	**10.** G

Literary Focus

11. C	**13.** D
12. H	**14.** J

Reading Skills

15. A	**16.** J

Vocabulary Development

17. monotonous

18. somber

19. pervades

20. garrulous

21. imperturbable

Constructed Response

22. Students' responses will vary. A sample response follows:

Joyce's story deals with an action that has been thwarted. Both in its form and in many of its details, "Araby" is ironic. The main character fails to reach the goal he has been struggling to attain and, in the end, becomes a completely different person than who he thought he was. This realization is an example of situational irony, but it also forms the basis of the story's epiphany. Another example of irony from the story is the discrepancy between the narrator's romantic view and reality. For instance, the magical Araby turns out to be just a tawdry bazaar.

Answer Key

The Rocking-Horse Winner
by D. H. Lawrence

Selection Test, *page 352*

Comprehension

1. B	**6.** H
2. J	**7.** A
3. D	**8.** F
4. H	**9.** A
5. B	**10.** G

Literary Focus

11. C	**13.** B
12. J	**14.** F

Vocabulary Development

15. C	**18.** H
16. G	**19.** A
17. D	

Constructed Response

20. Students' responses will vary. A sample response follows:

I think Lawrence is making a comment on the corruption and depravity of modern life, specifically but not limited to the corruption represented by materialism and greed. The rocking horse is a symbol of Paul's greed because he rides it fanatically in a crazed effort to get money by harnessing a kind of supernatural power. Translated to the adult level, his actions are equivalent to those who will do anything, no matter how irrational or demeaning, to make money. This attitude contrasts with the statement about money in Lawrence's letter, in which he places the values of life and personal fulfillment above wealth. But the rocking horse can represent more than mere materialism, too. For Paul it can represent a kind of depraved innocence, deluding him into overvaluing money and luck and the pleasing of his mother. Thus it can represent very similar impulses in adults. So perhaps in a wider sense, Lawrence is commenting on a culture in which, just as Paul misuses his rocking horse, natural impulses run amok and are misused; the human need for love becomes an almost demonic need for money.

Lot's Wife
by Anna Akhmatova

All the unburied ones
by Anna Akhmatova

I am not one of those who left the land
by Anna Akhmatova

Selection Test, *page 356*

Comprehension

1. D	**6.** J
2. G	**7.** B
3. B	**8.** H
4. F	**9.** C
5. C	**10.** F

Literary Focus

11. A	**13.** C
12. F	**14.** G

Constructed Response

15. Students' responses will vary. A sample response follows:

Clearly Akhmatova's historical circumstances had a profound effect on the subject matter of her poetry and on her specific ideas about her subjects. All three poems in this selection deal implicitly with the dilemma of whether to leave Russia during the grip of the revolution to save her own life or to stay behind as a witness to the pain of a country she loves. "Lot's Wife," written early in her career, shows a certain ambivalence, a willingness to leave combined with a self-destructive nostalgia to remain. The two later poems, however, are filled with bitterness, directed toward those who chose differently from her and left Russia. It seems very doubtful that Akhmatova's poetry would have been so laced with bitterness and rage had she lived in a better

Answer Key

time and place, or if she had chosen to emigrate from Russia.

The Demon Lover
by Elizabeth Bowen
Selection Test, *page 359*

Comprehension

1. B	**6.** F
2. J	**7.** D
3. A	**8.** G
4. J	**9.** C
5. A	**10.** G

Literary Focus

11. A	**13.** C
12. H	

Reading Skills

14. G

Vocabulary Development

15. b	**18.** a
16. c	**19.** d
17. e	

Constructed Response

20. Students' responses will vary. A sample response follows:

The abrupt shift to Mrs. Drover's past is effective, given her disorientation and anxious frame of mind. However, this technique might be confusing to the reader because the reader doesn't see the connection between the young girl and the older woman until well into the flashback. Bowen may be using this device not only to give us insight into Mrs. Drover's character but to mirror the disorientation and sense of dislocation that she experiences during wartime. Therefore, the setting of the story is critical—wartime London, when German bombing raids were terrifying ordinary citizens. The setting also hearkens back to the previous war when she met the mysterious man who swept her out of an ordinary life.

Axolotl
by Julio Cortázar
Selection Test, *page 362*

Comprehension

1. D	**6.** J
2. H	**7.** A
3. B	**8.** J
4. G	**9.** B
5. A	**10.** G

Literary Focus

11. C	**13.** B
12. H	

Reading Skills

14. G

Vocabulary Development

15. B	**18.** J
16. F	**19.** D
17. B	

Constructed Response

20. Students' responses will vary. A sample response follows:

Cortázar views the world as a magical, mysterious, wonderful place in which strange and often beautiful (though sometimes frightening) metamorphoses occur. If his fictional world is one in which a man changes into a salamander, this transformation may lead the reader to see that the real world is one of marvels which are only slightly less bizarre—such as the metamorphosis of a caterpillar into a butterfly or a tadpole into a frog. Alternatively, the marvel may be the human mind itself, which is capable of observing real axolotls and of dreaming up stories like this one. In another interpretation the parallel between man and axolotl shows the loneliness and stasis of human life, qualities which are so extreme in the narrator that his only recourse, while spending his days obsessively gazing at an aquarium, is to imagine himself changing into a salamander.

Holt Assessment: Literature, Reading, and Vocabulary

Answer Key

The Book of Sand
by Jorge Luis Borges
Selection Test, *page 366*

Comprehension

1. A	**6.** H
2. F	**7.** D
3. C	**8.** F
4. J	**9.** D
5. B	**10.** F

Literary Focus

11. B	**13.** A
12. H	

Reading Skills

14. G

Vocabulary Development

15. pedantic

16. bibliophile

17. misanthropy

18. diabolic

19. defiled

Constructed Response

20. Students' responses will vary. A sample response follows:

The main paradox in the story is derived from the extended comparison the author makes between the book and sand. It is a chilling paradox because we think of sand as insignificant, powerless, valueless, fleeting—the opposite of what we think a book should be. There are other paradoxes in the story, too, such as the author's love and hate for the book, the fact that the book is finite but an infinite number of pages, the book is both important and insignificant—as insignificant as a leaf in a forest. Perhaps Borges is saying that knowledge is infinite but, just maybe, infinite knowledge is maddeningly, paradoxically incomprehensible.

B. Wordsworth
by V. S. Naipaul
Selection Test, *page 370*

Comprehension

1. C	**6.** H
2. J	**7.** C
3. B	**8.** F
4. F	**9.** A
5. D	**10.** H

Literary Focus

11. D	**13.** B
12. F	**14.** G

Vocabulary Development

15. A	**18.** H
16. G	**19.** C
17. D	

Constructed Response

20. Students' responses will vary. A sample response follows:

The theme of the story is that an appreciation of the world's beauty can help a person transcend the difficulties of his or her life. Paradoxically, I think this theme in the story benefits greatly from and relies heavily upon the specific setting, and yet the theme could also be transferred to a great variety of other settings. There is no doubt that the details of setting—the Trinidad vernacular, the island geography, the mangoes and coconuts, the calypso poetry, the social class distinctions—burn the story into the reader's mind and make its lessons especially clear. However, the distilled essence of the story is that a bright, sensitive boy is befriended by an outwardly poor, but inwardly rich, old man who teaches him a poetic worldview. One can imagine a similar relationship with very similar results almost anywhere.

Answer Key

Half a Day
by Naguib Mahfouz
Selection Test, *page 374*

Comprehension

1. C	6. F
2. F	7. A
3. C	8. J
4. G	9. B
5. D	10. H

Literary Focus

11. A	13. C
12. J	14. G

Vocabulary Development

15. b	18. c
16. a	19. e
17. d	

Constructed Response

20. Students' responses will vary. A sample response follows:

The two parallel time sequences are that of a school day and that of a lifetime. The two time tracks are superimposed on each other by having the narrator age from childhood to late maturity and by having the city around him grow enormously while only one school day has passed in the narrator's consciousness. In retrospect the reader sees that the single day has symbolized life and that the passing of a lifetime has been foreshadowed in the description of the school day's activities. One theme this sequence may convey is that life is about teaching and learning. The use of school to symbolize living makes this connection self-evident. Other subjects may include the subjectivity of time, the brevity of a supposedly full life, and the persistent feeling of youthfulness among old people.

Digging
by Seamus Heaney
Selection Test, *page 377*

Comprehension

1. D	6. G
2. F	7. A
3. C	8. J
4. F	9. D
5. D	10. H

Literary Focus

11. C	13. C
12. G	14. H

Constructed Response

15. Students' responses will vary. A sample response follows:

The extended metaphor of "digging" continues throughout the poem: The act of digging done by this father and grandfather is compared to the speaker's metaphorical "digging" up of the past. What the speaker unearths is a vision not only of his own life, but of his father's, grandfather's, and fore-bears'. The poem ends with the speaker's desire to continue digging up the past and writing about it, a task that, in the case of this particular poet, goes all the way back to Beowulf.

The Doll's House
by Katherine Mansfield
Selection Test, *page 380*

Comprehension

1. D	6. F
2. G	7. B
3. C	8. J
4. F	9. C
5. B	10. G

Literary Focus

11. C	13. D
12. F	14. J

Answer Key

Vocabulary Development

15. flagged

16. congealed

17. conspicuous

18. clambered

19. flagged

Constructed Response

20. Students' responses will vary. A sample response follows:

The main symbol in the story is the doll's house. For the rich girls and the poor girls, this toy house seems to symbolize wealth, comfort, propriety, privilege—the good things in domestic life that they all want and that some of them have. For Mansfield, however, it may also symbolize the pettiness of social class differences and of snobbery. The doll's house is probably not as grand a thing as the girls think it is, and by extension their own houses are not as grand either. The houses they live in are oversized doll's houses in which the important thing is that everything and everyone look just right. The doll's house may also symbolize childhood and how children's play can either be turned to innocent constructive uses, or can become a reflection of adult prejudices. A symbol within the symbol is the lamp in the doll's house. It could symbolize everything the doll's house does, and more—perhaps the light of true beauty or innocence in comparison with the falseness of so much of society. So when Else proudly says that she has seen the lamp at the end of the story, she is saying more than she knows.

Musée des Beaux Arts
by W. H. Auden

Selection Test, *page 384*

Comprehension

1. C	**6.** F
2. G	**7.** C
3. B	**8.** H
4. H	**9.** B
5. A	**10.** G

Literary Focus

11. D	**13.** D
12. J	**14.** J

Constructed Response

15. Students' responses will vary. A sample response follows:

Just as Bruegel used ancient subject matter to depict his own Renaissance era, Auden uses Bruegel's Renaissance as a topic upon which to comment on the modern era. Outwardly the poem has nothing to do with such twentieth-century agonies as world wars, concentration camps, or atom bombs. Like great art, the poem provides relief from what is outside the museum. However, it is surely the outside world that prompts Auden to think about Bruegel's painting in terms of suffering and indifference as well as to choose it as a subject for a poem. Examples of this orientation may be found in many of the details and Auden's way of describing them. They are Renaissance details, but Auden's diction turns them into familiar everyday objects: a horse scratching its behind, a dog going on with its "doggy life." The realism of the figures' indifference to Icarus makes them seem modern. Perhaps even the small size of the painted details makes them seem modern: They inhabit an impersonal, panoramic world that does not pay much attention to individual identity. It would be hard to imagine a description of a Renaissance painting that has more to say about modern times.

Answer Key

Fear
by Gabriela Mistral
Selection Test, *page 387*

Comprehension

1. A
2. J
3. A
4. G
5. D
6. J
7. C
8. H
9. B
10. F

Literary Focus

11. A
12. H
13. B
14. F

Constructed Response

15. Students' responses will vary. A sample response follows:

The dominant emotion of the speaker in "Fear" is the emotion named in the title. Perhaps it could be called anxiety instead, because it seems to be a fear of a far-off development rather than of something imminent, and it seems to be chronic rather than temporary. The images that trigger the fear—a swallow, a princess's golden slippers, a queen's throne—show how neurotic the speaker's feelings are, because these are things that almost everyone would consider innocuous and quite desirable in many cases. My own emotions are of sympathy for the speaker, because she obviously loves her daughter and her vision of a simple, outdoor happiness is attractive. Yet my emotions also include impatience with this character who seems to care only about whether her daughter is going to meet her needs in the future and not about whether the daughter will make a better life for herself. The images of the mother wishing to rock her daughter, comb her daughter's hair, and sleep beside her daughter, sweet as they are, make it sound as if the mother views her daughter as a pet.

Fern Hill
by Dylan Thomas
Selection Test, *page 390*

Comprehension

1. B
2. G
3. A
4. H
5. B
6. F
7. D
8. F
9. D
10. J

Literary Focus

11. B
12. H
13. C
14. H

Constructed Response

15. Students' responses will vary. A sample response follows:

In the last stanza the beauty, innocence, and power of childhood are darkened by the passing of time. The speaker has learned that as time passes so pass the idylls of childhood. Even a child is slowly succumbing to death, a captive of onrushing time. With time comes an awareness of mortality that was not present in childhood (line 46). The child's perceptions have not changed in this poem, but the adult speaker's perceptions have, as have the reader's. The last stanza casts a sobering shadow over the rest of the poem, making Thomas's vision one not just of a paradise but of a paradise lost.

Do Not Go Gentle into That Good Night
by Dylan Thomas
Selection Test, *page 393*

Comprehension

1. B
2. J
3. C
4. J
5. D
6. G
7. B
8. F
9. A
10. H

Answer Key

Literary Focus

11. B   **13.** A

12. H   **14.** J

Constructed Response

15. Students' responses will vary. A sample response follows:

The feeling of the poem is an almost ecstatic grief which, while urgently and emphatically mourning, insists on the ability and even the duty of the dying person to reach new heights of life in the very instant before death. This possibility is implied in the line, "Grave men, near death, who see with blinding sight" (line 13). The oxymoron of "blinding sight" implies a final overwhelming vision that may be granted to some only right before death, making that moment supremely worthwhile. Other oxymorons or near-oxymorons in the poem—such as "that good night" meaning death or "the sad height," meaning the moment of imminent death—also imply possible mystic or insight-laden benefits to the near-death experience, as does the simile of the meteors in line 14. Meteors blaze and burn out in virtually the same instant; they cannot blaze without burning. Yet, acknowledging all these possibilities, Thomas is not satisfied. No mystic moment makes life less valuable. There is only one true, known absolute that Thomas champions: life itself.

Sonnet 79 / Soneto 79
by Pablo Neruda
Selection Test, *page 396*

Comprehension

1. D   **6.** J

2. G   **7.** B

3. B   **8.** G

4. F   **9.** A

5. A   **10.** H

Literary Focus

11. C   **13.** D

12. F   **14.** G

Constructed Response

15. Students' responses will vary. A sample response follows:

The figure of speech of the double drum in the first stanza is compelling because it is original and apt. Two people in love are united like two separate drums tied together. They have separate origins and make individual sounds, but they have been joined into one instrument playing for a united purpose. On the other hand, what is tied can be untied; even lovers can separate. The double drum seems a convincing comparison for one interdependent kind of love bond.

Like the Sun
by R. K. Narayan
Selection Test, *page 399*

Comprehension

1. C   **6.** G

2. G   **7.** C

3. D   **8.** J

4. J   **9.** C

5. A   **10.** H

Literary Focus

11. B   **13.** B

12. F   **14.** J

Vocabulary Development

15. a   **18.** c

16. d   **19.** b

17. e

Constructed Response

20. Students' responses will vary. A sample response follows:

The prevailing tone in the story is one of affectionate mockery, and the prevailing kind of irony is situational irony in which the main character, expecting one kind of

Answer Key

outcome, experiences another. Unlike much modern fiction, however, the outcome is often better than expected: He does not seriously suffer for criticizing the dead colleague, and his devastating criticism of his boss ends with Sekhar being thanked. The extra work to grade papers truly is, as the narrator comments, a small price to pay compared to what Sekhar had expected. These positive outcomes contribute to the story's light tone: No one really gets hurt, and all the characters' weaknesses are treated with a certain fond indulgence. Narayan's view of truth, then, would seem to be similarly lighthearted. One does not leave the story feeling that people have a moral obligation to tell the truth, or that telling the truth can be dangerous or fatal—in contrast to the story of Hindu king Harischandra (mentioned in the text). Truth ends up seeming almost as if it can be done on a whim: One can tell the truth and take a risk or tell a flattering lie. One does not imagine Narayan being terribly concerned about either course.

Games at Twilight
by Anita Desai
Selection Test, *page 402*
Comprehension

1. D	**6.** F
2. G	**7.** B
3. C	**8.** J
4. F	**9.** C
5. A	**10.** H

Literary Focus

11. D	**12.** H

Reading Skills

13. A	**14.** H

Vocabulary Development

15. C	**18.** J
16. F	**19.** A
17. B	

Constructed Response

20. Students' responses will vary. A sample response follows:

   At the end of the story, Ravi is lying on the grass, alone, feeling abandoned, insignificant, like an outsider in his own siblings' games and even feeling past the point of crying about it. Clearly the emotions evoked are very sorrowful and tender ones, and the reader is intended to empathize with them. The meaning, perhaps, is that childhood games are not just fun and innocent; they are initiations into a grownup world in which rejection, loneliness, and disillusionment are common. It is this, perhaps, which the older siblings know and which Ravi is only first learning. The story is a comment on the cruelty of human nature, even within an outwardly privileged, protective, loving setting.

Next Term, We'll Mash You
by Penelope Lively
Selection Test, *page 406*
Comprehension

1. D	**6.** J
2. G	**7.** C
3. A	**8.** H
4. G	**9.** B
5. C	**10.** F

Literary Focus

11. B	**13.** C
12. F	**14.** J

Vocabulary Development

15. subdued

16. geniality

17. untainted

18. indulgent

19. inaccessible

Constructed Response

20. Students' responses will vary. A sample response follows:

Holt Assessment: Literature, Reading, and Vocabulary

Answer Key

The story is essentially about people and institutions that are not what they pretend to be. It is a story about pretense, so irony is appropriate as a means of unveiling the pretenses of the characters. The very first sentence, a physical description of a neat, well-kept automobile, actually shows us the shallowness of the characters' values—for they are the kind of people who place excessive value on the kind of car being described.

Although the polite, meaningless chatter among the parents and the headmaster and his wife may mark them as irreproachable people of high standing, for the reader it marks them as phony. The very atmosphere of the school itself can be interpreted ironically, for underneath its picture-perfect veneer is an experience of terror awaiting a child. Crucial small ironies include the repeated comments that everything is "very nice," and Mrs. Spokes's comment about how little prospectuses tell about a school. In the end the parents learn no more about the inner workings of the school than they would have learned from a prospectus.

Saboteur
by Ha Jin
Selection Test, *page 410*
Comprehension

1. A	**6.** J
2. H	**7.** C
3. C	**8.** G
4. F	**9.** C
5. A	**10.** F

Literary Focus

11. C	**12.** G

Reading Skills

13. C	**14.** J

Vocabulary Development

15. b	**18.** d
16. c	**19.** e
17. a	

Constructed Response

20. Students' responses will vary. A sample response follows:

The implicit comment in the story is that people who would otherwise be peaceable, decent citizens are turned into criminals when they are subjected to the cruelties of a criminal state. Mr. Chiu, at the beginning of the story, seems the epitome of a harmless intellectual, and has no apparent gripe with the regime that rules China. By the end of the story, however, he has become what he was wrongly accused of being: a saboteur (and in fact a terrorist). Furthermore, he is not a particularly rational saboteur because his revenge is taken against equally ordinary citizens rather than directly against his oppressors. (If any police officer came down with hepatitis, it would be a coincidence.) So not only does violence beget violence, but irrationality begets irrationality. This story presents a grim view of the world even if parts of the story are intended to be comically ironic. Vengeance in the form of an epidemic does not make for a politically hopeful outcome. The protagonist, whom the reader probably expected to be justified in the end, turns out to be morally monstrous. Obviously this ugly view of life was affected by having experienced the frustrations of living in and dealing with a political situation such as Ha Jin describes in the story. Jin leaves readers to consider whether the pressure that an oppressive regime puts on people actually forces people to act cruelly or merely elicits barbarous behaviors that are already inherent in everyone.

Answer Key

from the Universal Declaration of Human Rights
by the United Nations Commission on Human Rights

from The Question of South Africa
by Desmond Tutu

from Towards a True Refuge
by Aung San Suu Kyi

Selection Test, *page 413*

Comprehension

1. A	**6.** F
2. G	**7.** D
3. A	**8.** F
4. J	**9.** C
5. A	**10.** F

Reading Skills

11. B	**13.** B
12. H	**14.** H

Constructed Response

15. Students' responses will vary. A sample response follows:

In my opinion the Universal Declaration of Human Rights presents a picture of a just world which all the authors here would support. The crucial question is whether Tutu and Aung San Suu Kyi would view the Declaration's aspirations as leading to a just world. That they would becomes apparent in reading the preamble to the Declaration, which recognizes in its first paragraph the "inherent dignity and the equal and inalienable rights of all members of the human family" and warns against "barbarous" contempt for human rights in its second paragraph. Obviously the South African and Burmese orators would share those sentiments. Both of those authors show a concern not only for a righting of wrongs but for a positive establishment of an inclusive, tolerant society, a vision which is inherent in the Declaration.

Collection 7 Summative Test,
page 416

Vocabulary Skills

1. A	**4.** J
2. H	**5.** B
3. C	

Comprehension

6. F	**9.** B
7. D	**10.** F
8. H	

Reading Skills and Strategies: Constructed Response

Making Inferences

11. Students' responses will vary. A sample response follows:

Character traits: observant, sensitive, well-educated, skilled, brave, stoical, paranoid

Evidence: He is alert because he sees the many details of his surroundings. He is sensitive because he is profoundly affected by them. His education is indicated by his vocabulary and syntax; his skill as a navigator or captain is shown by his knowledge of the invisible dangers under the water's surface and his ability to avoid them. His bravery and stoicism are shown by the fact that he "claps his teeth" in the face of deadly dangers. He seems paranoid because he interprets the forest as a brooding personality, a menace that is watching him.

Analyzing Details

12. Students' responses will vary. A sample response follows:

Detail: abundant vegetation and tall trees

Description: ". . . vegetation rioted on the earth and the big trees were kings."

Feeling: A feeling of an intimidating primordial forest where danger lurks and humans are trespassers; a lush gloomy, desolate feeling

Answer Key

Analyzing Setting

13. Students' responses will vary. A sample response follows:

Marlow finds the African setting alien. He is an Englishman whose most positive feelings in Africa are related to his memories of his homeland. He perceives Africa as an unfriendly, foreboding place that is at once "mobbed" by growth while eerily silent and threateningly still. Details of the setting, such as lush vegetation, sluggish air, and joyless sun, are not familiar to this European. He even likens the waterway to a desert, an unmarked expanse with no clear throughway. Clearly Marlow's negative feelings are a reflection of the unfamiliarity of the setting to him, a product of his British culture.

Identifying Aesthetic Devices

14. H

Literary Focus: Constructed Response

15. Students' responses will vary. A sample response follows:

An African native to the Congo waterway would see it as familiar and probably in a more positive light than Marlow. Although there might be realistic threats, such as wild animals, which an African would be aware of, an African would also be aware of positive aspects that Marlow ignores, such as the river as a source of food and the forest as a source of medicine. Whether Conrad should be blamed for the reality of different cultural perspectives is a matter of opinion; it is easy to see that Marlow's (and by extension Conrad's) narrowness of vision in this matter is a result of education rather than of personal wickedness. And surely if Conrad *had* written from the point of view of an African, the author would be criticized for it today. While Marlow's view is not up-to-date by today's standards, there is no reason it should be, since it was written a century ago. *Heart of Darkness* remains a superb piece of prose and an edifying document of the colonialist mentality.

End-of-Year Test, *page 421*

Reading and Literary Analysis

Sample A B

Sample B J

1. A	**16.** G
2. G	**17.** A
3. D	**18.** J
4. F	**19.** C
5. C	**20.** H
6. F	**21.** B
7. B	**22.** G
8. J	**23.** A
9. A	**24.** J
10. G	**25.** C
11. D	**26.** F
12. H	**27.** A
13. C	**28.** F
14. F	**29.** A
15. B	**30.** G

Vocabulary

Sample A B

31. A	**36.** J
32. H	**37.** A
33. B	**38.** J
34. F	**39.** B
35. C	**40.** H

Skills Profile

Skills Profile

Student's Name _____ Grade _____

Teacher's Name _____ Date _____

For each skill, write the date the observation is made and any comments that explain the student's development toward skills mastery.

SKILL	▶ NOT OBSERVED	▶ EMERGING	▶ PROFICIENT
▶ **Literature**			
Analyze characteristics of subgenres of novels, short stories, poetry, plays, and other basic genres.			
Analyze the way the theme of a selection represents a comment on life.			
Analyze the way an author's style achieves specific rhetorical or aesthetic purposes.			
Analyze ways poets use imagery, figures of speech, and sounds.			
Analyze works of American literature:			
a. Trace the development of American literature from the Colonial period forward.			
b. Contrast the major periods and works by members of different cultures in each period.			
c. Evaluate the political, social, and philosophical influences of the historical period that shaped characters, plots, and settings.			
Analyze archetypes drawn from myth and tradition.			
Analyze works of world literature from a variety of authors:			
a. Compare literary works of different historical periods.			

SKILL	▶ NOT OBSERVED	▶ EMERGING	▶ PROFICIENT
b. Relate literary works and authors to the major themes and issues of their eras.			
c. Evaluate the philosophical, political, religious, ethical, and social influences of the historical period.			
Analyze political points of view in a selection of literary works on a topic.			
Analyze the philosophical arguments in literary works and their impact on the quality of each work.			
Informational Text			
Analyze the way authors use the features and rhetorical devices of public documents.			
Analyze the way patterns of organization, repetition of main ideas, and word choice affect the meaning of a text.			
Verify and clarify facts in expository text by using consumer, workplace, and public documents.			
Make reasonable assertions about an author's arguments by using elements of the text to defend interpretations.			
Analyze an author's philosophical assumptions and beliefs about a subject.			
Critique the validity, appeal, and truthfulness of arguments in public documents.			
Vocabulary			
Trace the etymology of historical and political terms.			
Use knowledge of Greek, Latin, and Anglo-Saxon roots and affixes to determine the meaning of scientific and mathematical terms.			

▶ SKILL	▶ NOT OBSERVED	▶ EMERGING	▶ PROFICIENT
Within analogies, analyze specific comparisons as well as relationships and inferences.			